ANNETTE FLAVEL

SPEAK YOUR MIND

TEACHER'S EDITION
+ access to Teacher's App

2

macmillan education

Macmillan Education
4 Crinan Street
London N1 9XW
A division of Macmillan Education Limited

Companies and representatives throughout the world

Speak Your Mind Level 2 Teacher's Edition
ISBN 978-1-380-03128-0
Speak Your Mind Level 2 Teacher's Edition + access to Teacher's App ISBN 978-1-380-03119-8

Written by Annette Flavel
Additional material by Mickey Rogers and Jason Skeet

The authors have asserted their right to be identified as the authors of this work in accordance with the Copyright, Designs, and Patents Act 1988.

First published 2020

Teacher's Edition credits:
Designed by QBS Learning
Original cover design by therestless.co.uk
Cover adaptation by Roberto Martinez
Cover background by Getty Images/Chatuporn Sornlampoo/EyeEm.

The publishers would like to thank all the teachers that piloted and reviewed the series, and a special thanks to Dr. Jason Skeet of the Norwich Institute for Language Education (NILE) for sharing his expertise in the article included in the Introduction.

The authors and publishers would like to thank the following for permission to reproduce their photographs:
NILE p. xxviii; **Macmillan Education** Limited/Getty Images/iStockphoto/zentilia p. xxv, Macmillan Education Limited/iStockphoto/alexsl pp. xxvi–xxvii.

Student's Book credits:

Written by Mickey Rogers, Joanne Taylore-Knowles and Steve Taylore-Knowles

The authors have asserted their right to be identified as the authors of this work in accordance with the Copyright, Designs and Patents Act 1988.

Designed by QBS Learning
Illustrated by Daniel Deamo (Lemonade) pp. 10, 50; Martina Farrow p. 21; Keith Favazza (Wendy Lynn & Co.) pp. 88, 102; QBS Learning pp. 60, 92, 109.
Picture research by Fernanda Rocha/Ikonia LLC

Full acknowledgements for photographs in the facsimile pages can be found in the Student's Book ISBN 978-1-380-03124-2.
Additional sources:

p. 36 – Nigel Lindemann, "What's the average survey response rate? [2018 benchmark]," *Survey Anyplace*, 2018. p. 66 – Data from Bureau of Labor Statistics, "Psychologists," *Occupational Outlook Handbook*, 2018. p. 76 – Adobe, *State of Create Study*, 2012; IBM, CEO Study, 2010; Scott Barry Kaufman, 2014 (cited by John Paul Titlow, "7 Surprising Facts About Creativity, According to Science," *Fast Company*, 2016). p. 82 – Oliver Burkeman, "Five Reasons Why We Should All Learn How to Do Nothing," *The Guardian*, 2015. p. 98 – Bryan Roche, "10 Ways to Improve Your Brain Health," *Psychology Today*, 2014; Hannah Nichols, "How to Boost Your Brain," *Medical News Today*, 2018; Joseph Mercola, "Nine Ways to Make Yourself Smarter," Mercola.com, 2012; Michael Grothaus, "This Is the Only Type of Brain Training that Works, According to Science," *Fast Company*, 2017. p. 108 – mcc_northcutt, "55 Things You Probably Didn't Know About T-Shirts," *The BlueCotton Blog*, 2016. p. 126 – "Entrepreneurship Rankings," *U.S. News & World Report*, 2018.

Printed and bound in Brazil
2025
31

Table of Contents

Speak Your Mind Philosophy

In the 21st century, it is no longer enough just to teach subject matter. Teachers need to help their students develop important skills that can lead to success in whatever they choose to do.

The core objective of ***Speak Your Mind*** is to help students become confident communicators. The focus is on using English to communicate in both local and global contexts. Most students may not live in an English-speaking country, but it is probable they will need to use English in the course of their academic and professional lives. Being a confident and competent communicator involves going beyond language skills. Students need to analyze ideas, work effectively in teams, and solve problems.

Job readiness consists of more than just a strong academic performance. The ability to communicate effectively in English and to use 21st-century skills is essential in order for young adults to enter successfully into or advance within the complex, global world in which they live. ***Speak Your Mind*** is designed to help students achieve their goals.

UNIT 6 Changes

WHAT DO YOU ALREADY KNOW?

1 List five changes in your life in the last year. Include positive and negative changes.
2 IN PAIRS Share and compare your changes. Add more words to your lists.

Changes

DISCUSS & SHARE

VIDEO

3 IN GROUPS Watch the video and answer the question.
SYM Do you view change as a positive or negative thing in your life?

In this unit, you will ...

- talk about risk and change, experiences you want to have, and changes in a city over time.
- use thinking skills: analyze, create, and understand.
- read about how people view change in their lives.
- use strategies to start and keep talking by reacting to information or expressing a point of view.
- use collaboration skills to create a list of recommendations for visitors discovering your town.
- follow an interior designer to learn about this job and the skills needed for the field of architecture.

Unit 6 Changes 57

Speak Your Mind has a number of features that help students in their academic, professional, and everyday lives:

- Every lesson in ***Speak Your Mind*** ends with a specific communicative outcome. Students do a collaborative task in which they use target language from the lesson to communicate their ideas and express their opinions on a topic related to the subject of the lesson.
- Students learn skills that transfer from the classroom to real life. The lessons contain thinking questions that help improve their thinking skills as they learn English. The last lesson in every unit (Language and Life) develops problem-solving and teamwork skills by taking students through a step-by-step process in which they work together to solve a problem or produce a proposal in a real-life scenario.
- Young-adult students already have a great deal of knowledge about the world, and they are encouraged to transfer their real-life knowledge to the classroom. The topics in ***Speak Your Mind*** allow students to express their opinions on real-world events and issues and to learn more about those topics. Students are often asked to give opinions or to say what they already know about a topic before listening to or reading a text on the subject.
- Most young adults will have at least some previous knowledge of English. They are encouraged to share that knowledge and to build on it according to their personal needs and interests. Unit Openers help them be aware of how many words they already know in English and to share their knowledge with their classmates. *Make It Yours* boxes allow them to build their own personal vocabulary lists.
- Videos further help students connect their language learning to real life. For each unit, there is a video that focuses on the Unit Opener topic and acts as a prompt for discussion. For even-numbered units, there are documentary-style Follow A Pro videos that follow a day in the life of a person in a particular profession.

Unit Structure

***Speak Your Mind* Student's Books 1–3** consist of 12 units of 10 pages each. Every unit begins with a one-page Unit Opener designed to introduce the unit topic and to elicit vocabulary and other language that students are already familiar with. Each Unit Opener features a *Video* that can be used to prompt a discussion.

The Unit Opener is followed by four double-page lessons. Lessons 1–3 contain the core GRAMMAR, VOCABULARY, READING, SPEAKING, LISTENING, PRONUNCIATION, and WRITING sections for the unit. Lesson 4 is called Language and Life. It also includes a reading, but its purpose is to provide students with a task that will help them develop key 21st-century skills.

At the end of each unit, there is a REVIEW page with additional practice of the target grammar and vocabulary. This page also contains a section to introduce a study skill (in odd-numbered units) or a profession related to the topic of the unit (in even-numbered units).

At the end of each **Student's Book**, there are lessons connected to the study skills and the professions introduced on the *Review* pages. There is also a list of common irregular verbs, as well as further practice of the target grammar in the book.

Apart from the **Student's Book**, there is a **Workbook** available in print or digital form. The **Student's Resource Center** contains *Reading Worksheets* for extra reading practice, as well as lesson plans adapted from Macmillan's *OneStopEnglish* website. The **Teacher's Resource Center** contains printable tests for unit, mid-course, and end-of-course assessment.

For more information on each feature mentioned in this Introduction, please see the relevant sections that follow.

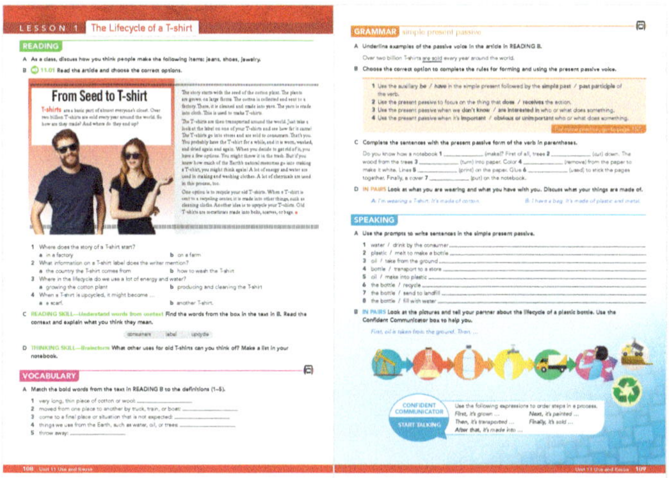

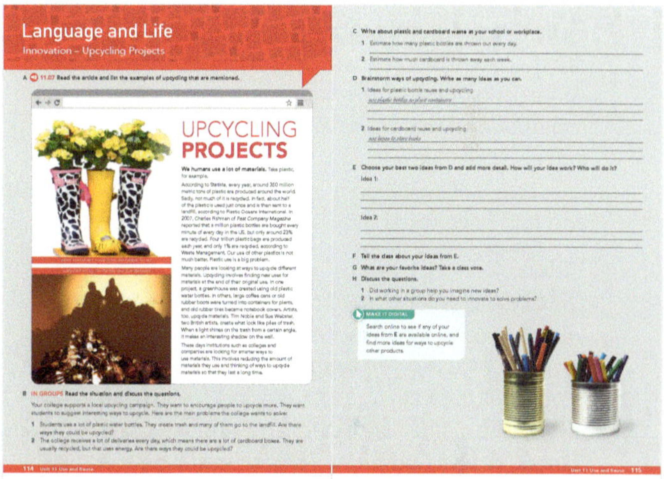

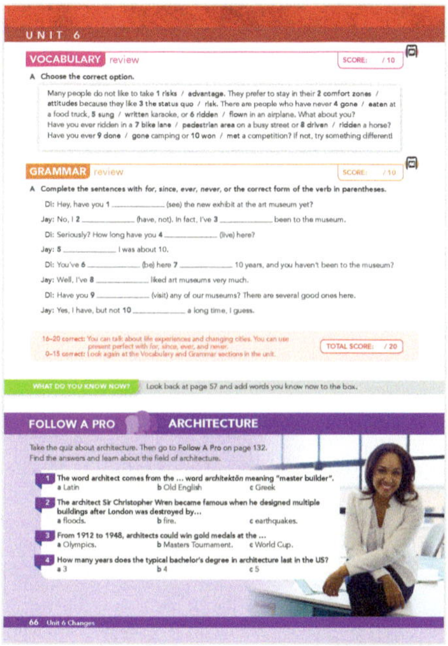

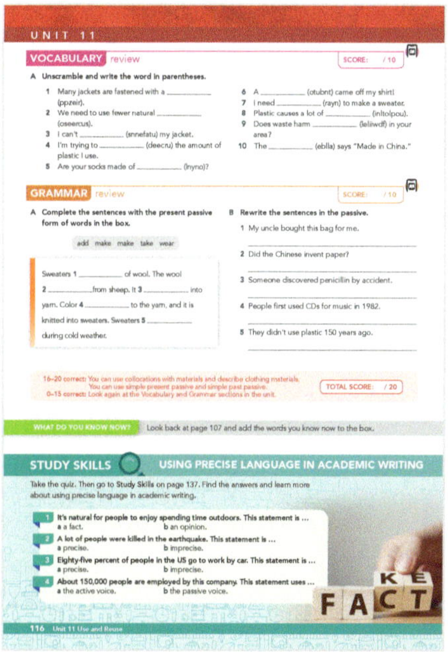

Unit Opener

Each Unit Opener introduces the general topic of the unit in a way that will stimulate the interest and curiosity of young adults. The Unit Openers give students the opportunity to think about topic-related words and phrases they already know and to discuss a question they can think about as they work through the unit. Each Unit Opener features a video to support this discussion.

The ability to use prior knowledge to support the acquisition of new knowledge is an important learning strategy. Having students think about language they already know or knowledge they already have helps them approach new material with greater confidence.

Another important concept in today's classrooms is cooperative learning. Students begin by thinking about something or doing a task individually, then work in pairs to share and build on their individual work. Finally, they work in groups to apply what they have learned individually and in pairs.

PROCEDURE: Teaching the **Unit Opener** in *Speak Your Mind*

① **Individual work.** Have students work individually to list familiar words and phrases related to the unit topic. This helps build their confidence by highlighting the fact that they already know a lot of English. This section also gives them the chance to think about how the unit topic relates to their own lives.

② **Peer teaching and learning.** Put students in pairs and ask them to share the words and phrases they wrote. At the beginning of the course, explain that working together and sharing what they know allows them to increase their knowledge. Note that at the end of the unit, they will be asked to come back to the Unit Opener and add new words they have learned in the unit.

③ **Video.** A short, optional video accompanies each DISCUSS & SHARE section. The purpose of these videos is to provide input that can support students in their discussion of the ***Speak Your Mind*** *Question*. Note that the videos are intended to provide information and context for the discussion, but the ***Speak Your Mind*** *Question* can easily be discussed without viewing them. Teachers are strongly encouraged to use them, as they provide fun and interesting contexts for the discussion, as well as input from both sides of the issue to help students form opinions.

④ ***Speak Your Mind* Question.** Ask students to work in groups to discuss the ***Speak Your Mind*** *Question*. Explain that the questions do not have specific right or wrong answers because the purpose is to make students think and allow them to express their opinions. Note that these questions are part of the critical-thinking thread in ***Speak Your Mind***. Students should think in terms of a continuum. For example, in Unit 10 Wellbeing, some students may think that it's best to focus on nutrition for good health, some students may think that it's best to focus on exercise, while other students may think the best focus is a combination of the two.

⑤ **Unit Summary.** At the bottom of the Unit Opener page, there is a summary of what students will learn in the unit. You may want to go over this so students know what they will learn in the unit.

Vocabulary

Vocabulary plays a very prominent role in ***Speak Your Mind***. Every unit begins with a focus on vocabulary through Unit Opener activities that elicit familiar vocabulary related to the unit topic. Students build on that knowledge through peer sharing. In Lessons 1–3, there is a VOCABULARY section to present and practice new vocabulary related to the specific lesson topic. In Lesson 4, there are opportunities for students to use vocabulary from the unit in the context of the tasks in the lesson.

In ***Speak Your Mind***, vocabulary is presented within the context of the reading or listening text in the lesson. Sometimes the vocabulary is pre-taught in order to help students understand it when they encounter it as they read or listen. Other times, the VOCABULARY section follows the READING or LISTENING section, and students are encouraged to use the context of the text to help them figure out the meaning of the words.

PROCEDURE: Teaching **Vocabulary** in *Speak Your Mind*

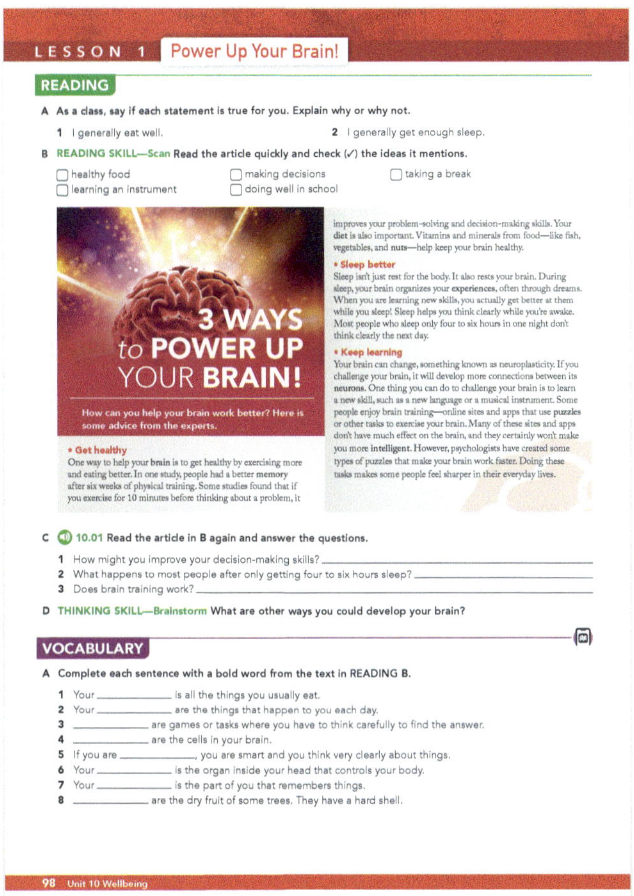
LESSON 1 Power Up Your Brain!

READING

A As a class, say if each statement is true for you. Explain why or why not.

1 I generally eat well.
2 I generally get enough sleep.

B READING SKILL—Scan Read the article quickly and check (✓) the ideas it mentions.

☐ healthy food ☐ making decisions ☐ taking a break
☐ learning an instrument ☐ doing well in school

3 WAYS to POWER UP YOUR BRAIN!

How can you help your brain work better? Here is some advice from the experts.

• Get healthy
One way to help your **brain** is to get healthy by exercising more and eating better. In one study, people had a better **memory** after six weeks of physical training. Some studies found that if you exercise for 10 minutes before thinking about a problem, it improves your problem-solving and decision-making skills. Your **diet** is also important. Vitamins and minerals from food—like fish, vegetables, and **nuts**—help keep your brain healthy.

• Sleep better
Sleep isn't just rest for the body. It also rests your brain. During sleep, your brain organizes your **experiences**, often through dreams. When you are learning new skills, you actually get better at them while you sleep! Sleep helps you think clearly while you're awake. Most people who sleep only four to six hours in one night don't think clearly the next day.

• Keep learning
Your brain can change, something known as neuroplasticity. If you challenge your brain, it will develop more connections between its **neurons**. One thing you can do to challenge your brain is to learn a new skill, such as a new language or a musical instrument. Some people enjoy brain training—online sites and apps that use **puzzles** or other tasks to exercise your brain. Many of these sites and apps don't have much effect on the brain, and they certainly won't make you more **intelligent**. However, psychologists have created some types of puzzles that make your brain work faster. Doing these tasks makes some people feel sharper in their everyday lives.

C 10.01 Read the article in B again and answer the questions.

1 How might you improve your decision-making skills? ______
2 What happens to most people after only getting four to six hours sleep? ______
3 Does brain training work? ______

D THINKING SKILL—Brainstorm What are other ways you could develop your brain?

VOCABULARY

A Complete each sentence with a bold word from the text in READING B.

1 Your ______ is all the things you usually eat.
2 Your ______ are the things that happen to you each day.
3 ______ are games or tasks where you have to think carefully to find the answer.
4 ______ are the cells in your brain.
5 If you are ______, you are smart and you think very clearly about things.
6 Your ______ is the organ inside your head that controls your body.
7 Your ______ is the part of you that remembers things.
8 ______ are the dry fruit of some trees. They have a hard shell.

98 Unit 10 Wellbeing

Topic-related vocabulary. Words or phrases that are related to the topic of the reading or listening are frequently presented by asking students to look at sentences from the text and match the target words to their definitions, or use them to complete sentences or a short text.

When the VOCABULARY section comes after a reading text, encourage students to go back to the text and look at the words in context to help them confirm their answers to the vocabulary activity.

When the vocabulary is presented before a LISTENING section, encourage students to listen for the words during the listening activity. Either before or after students listen, you may want to write the sentences with the vocabulary words on the board and check that they understand how each word is used.

Word formation. Students learn to use prefixes and suffixes to change the meaning or the part of speech of a word.

It is a good idea to have students make a word-formation chart in their notebooks that they can add to as they learn different prefixes and suffixes. Organize the chart into columns by parts of speech: noun, verb, adjective, and adverb. If there are equivalents to the affixes in their own language, you may want to include those in the chart to help students relate the English forms to elements in their own language.

Lexical sets. These are particularly relevant at lower levels, when students need a great deal of basic vocabulary related to topics such as food or sports. The lexical sets are often presented through visuals, and students are asked to match the words to the pictures.

When a lexical set is presented, ask students if they know or want to know any other words related to the set. This is a good way to utilize peer teaching, to make students feel that they are participating in the learning process, and to expand the target vocabulary to include words that students are interested in knowing.

Remember to have students practice saying vocabulary words that are intended for active use. It is also important for them to learn how to spell the words.

Synonyms and antonyms. Learning synonyms and antonyms helps students expand the range and variety of their vocabulary.

There are vocabulary lessons on synonyms and antonyms in ***Speak Your Mind***, but you can teach synonyms or antonyms appropriate to the level as an extension to any vocabulary lesson. For example, if students learn *delicious*, also teach *tasty* or the slang word *yummy*. If they see *shiny* in a text, you can teach them that the opposite is *dull*.

Grammar

Grammar in ***Speak Your Mind*** is taught through an inductive approach in which students are encouraged to observe grammatical structures in context and to go through an analytical process that allows them to figure out rules of structure and function. At the beginning of the course, explain to students that they will be asked to actively participate in their own learning by using observation and thinking skills to figure out grammar rules about form and function. Point out that we tend to learn more effectively when we figure something out for ourselves rather than just being told. Each unit has two GRAMMAR sections: one in Lesson 1 and one in Lesson 2. In Lessons 3 and 4, students have opportunities to use the grammar they have just learned.

PROCEDURE: Teaching Grammar in *Speak Your Mind*

① **Notice the grammar in context.** Students are exposed to the new grammar structure in the context of a reading or listening text before they are asked to study and work with the grammar itself. You may want to point out one or two examples of the new structure in a reading text or explain that students will hear examples of new grammar in a listening text. It is not necessary to pre-teach the grammar in order for them to understand the text. Part of learning a new language is learning to use context to understand the meaning of new grammar or vocabulary.

② **Complete the rule.** Ask students to look at examples of the grammar from the reading or listening text. The examples are usually included in the GRAMMAR section, but sometimes students are asked to look for examples in the text. Explain that they should notice the form of the grammar and also think about the meaning, or the function, of the grammatical structure. Then ask them to do the activity that follows the examples. The activity asks them to complete grammar rules or answer questions about the grammar in order to show that they have understood it. When going over the rules, have students point out the grammar structures in the example sentences that confirm the rules.

③ **Practice.** The analysis of the grammar rules is followed by one or more written activities to practice the new structure. You may want to let students compare their answers in pairs before checking answers as a class. This will provide an opportunity for cooperative learning.

If students have had trouble with an activity, refer back to the grammar rules as you go over each answer to make sure that students understand why the answer is what it is.

④ **Oral practice.** The GRAMMAR sections often include a short pair or group communicative activity to practice the new grammar. Make sure that everyone has an opportunity to use several examples of all forms of the new grammar. For example, if they are learning questions and answers with a verb tense, make sure that students are practicing both the question forms and the answer forms.

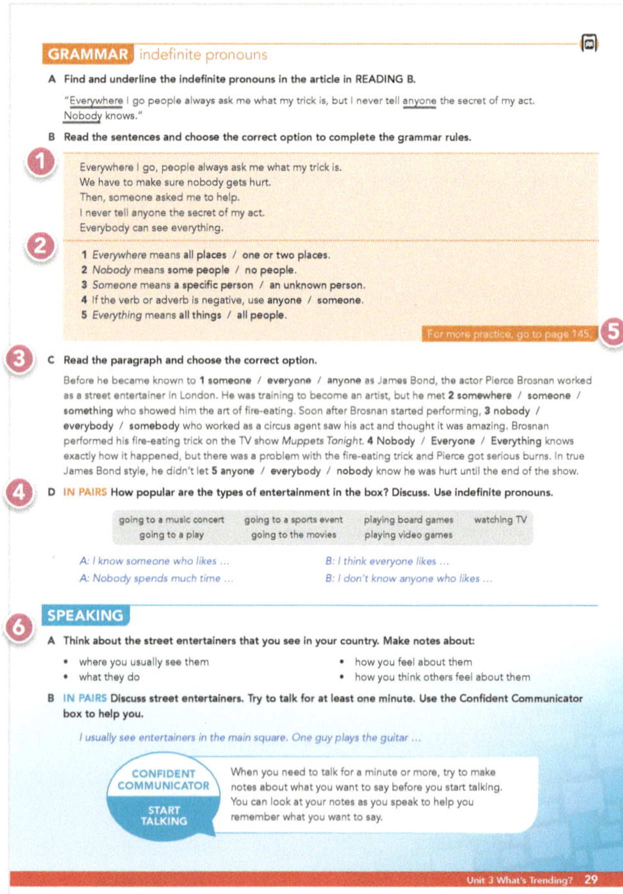
GRAMMAR indefinite pronouns

A Find and underline the indefinite pronouns in the article in READING B.

"Everywhere I go people always ask me what my trick is, but I never tell anyone the secret of my act. Nobody knows."

B Read the sentences and choose the correct option to complete the grammar rules.

1 Everywhere I go, people always ask me what my trick is.
We have to make sure nobody gets hurt.
Then, someone asked me to help.
I never tell anyone the secret of my act.
Everybody can see everything.

2
1 *Everywhere* means **all places** / **one or two places.**
2 *Nobody* means **some people** / **no people.**
3 *Someone* means **a specific person** / **an unknown person.**
4 If the verb or adverb is negative, use **anyone** / **someone.**
5 *Everything* means **all things** / **all people.**

For more practice, go to page 145. 5

3 C Read the paragraph and choose the correct option.

Before he became known to **1 someone** / **everyone** / **anyone** as James Bond, the actor Pierce Brosnan worked as a street entertainer in London. He was training to become an artist, but he met **2 somewhere** / **someone** / **something** who showed him the art of fire-eating. Soon after Brosnan started performing, **3 nobody** / **everybody** / **somebody** who worked as a circus agent saw his act and thought it was amazing. Brosnan performed his fire-eating trick on the TV show *Muppets Tonight*. **4 Nobody** / **Everyone** / **Everything** knows exactly how it happened, but there was a problem with the fire-eating trick and Pierce got serious burns. In true James Bond style, he didn't let **5 anyone** / **everybody** / **nobody** know he was hurt until the end of the show.

4 D IN PAIRS How popular are the types of entertainment in the box? Discuss. Use indefinite pronouns.

going to a music concert | going to a sports event | playing board games | watching TV | going to a play | going to the movies | playing video games

A: I know someone who likes …
B: I think everyone likes …
A: Nobody spends much time …
B: I don't know anyone who likes …

6 **SPEAKING**

A Think about the street entertainers that you see in your country. Make notes about:

- where you usually see them
- what they do
- how you feel about them
- how you think others feel about them

B IN PAIRS Discuss street entertainers. Try to talk for at least one minute. Use the Confident Communicator box to help you.

I usually see entertainers in the main square. One guy plays the guitar …

CONFIDENT COMMUNICATOR
START TALKING
When you need to talk for a minute or more, try to make notes about what you want to say before you start talking. You can look at your notes as you speak to help you remember what you want to say.

Unit 3 What's Trending? 29

⑤ **Further practice.** In the highlighted boxes, there is a reference to further practice in the *Grammar Reference* section at the back of the book. These activities could be done in class if you feel that students need more practice right away to help them understand the grammar, or they could be done as homework or as review before an exam. At the end of this section, there is a list of suggestions for further grammar practice.

⑥ **Further oral practice.** The grammar is also used in the SPEAKING section at the end of each lesson, which gives students communicative practice with the target structure. Remind them that they should use the grammar as much as possible in the speaking activities in order to become comfortable with it. You may want to elicit some examples of how they can use the grammar before they start the speaking activity.

Speak Your Mind provides a number of opportunities for further practice of the grammar:

- The *Grammar Quiz* before Unit 1 is a quick test of what students should have learned before beginning the course.
- The *Grammar Review* after Unit 12 is a review of what students should have learned in prior levels. The *Grammar Review* of Level 2 (A2) reviews language at the A1 level.
- The **Student's App** contains grammar practice. An [app icon] indicates where there is practice in the app.
- A *Grammar Reference* section at the end of the **Student's Book** gives further explanations and practice activities for the grammar points in each unit.
- Grammar practice activities in the **Workbook** reinforce the GRAMMAR sections in the lessons.

Pronunciation

In ***Speak Your Mind***, pronunciation is taught through a combination of observation and practice. There is a PRONUNCIATION section in each unit, and four main areas are emphasized: specific sounds, specific words, stress and intonation, and juncture and reduction.

Students are first asked to listen to examples and to notice a pattern or confirm a rule. It is important to allow them to listen and understand the pronunciation point before asking them to try to produce it.

The noticing activity is followed by practice of the pronunciation point, sometimes as a whole class and other times in pairs.

PROCEDURE: Teaching **Pronunciation** in *Speak Your Mind*

1

PRONUNCIATION /tʃ/ and /ʃ/

A 2.05 **Listen. Notice the difference between the /tʃ/ sound and the /ʃ/ sound.**

1 shop chop 2 ships chips 3 sheep cheap

B 2.05 **Listen again and repeat. Exaggerate the /tʃ/ *and* /ʃ/ sounds as you say the words.**

C IN PAIRS **Practice saying the pairs of words. Can your partner hear the difference between the /tʃ/ *and* /ʃ/ sounds when you say the words?**

2

PRONUNCIATION *–ould* words

A 8.03 **Listen to the conversation and answer the questions.**

Omar: Would you like to go to the new museum tomorrow?
Jamal: That sounds great. We should go early, when there are fewer people.
Omar: Actually, I would rather go in the afternoon. Is that OK?
Jamal: That's fine. Could you pick me up?
Omar: Sure.

1 Do *would*, *should*, and *could* have the same vowel sound or different sounds?
2 Do you hear the *l* in *would*, *should*, and *could*?

B IN PAIRS **Practice the conversation. Pay special attention to the pronunciation of *would*, *should*, and *could*.**

MAKE IT REAL

Although the meaning of *hate*, *like*, *love*, and *prefer* is the same when used with an infinitive or with a gerund, the infinitive form is more commonly used in American English than the gerund form.

3

PRONUNCIATION word stress with modal auxiliaries

A 5.03 **Listen to the sentences. Underline the modal auxiliary if it is stressed. Then practice reading the sentences aloud using the correct word stress.**

1 I can make a cake.
2 May I invite my boyfriend?
3 Could you help me, please?
4 I can design an invitation.
5 I won't have coffee.
6 We can't invite friends.

4

PRONUNCIATION reduced form of *used to*

A 3.03 **Listen to the sentences. Notice how the speakers reduce *used to* as /justə/.**

B IN PAIRS **Practice saying the questions and answers. Use the reduced form of *used to*.**

1 A: Did you use to work in marketing? B: No, I used to work in information technology.
2 A: Did you use to walk to the office? B: No, I used to take the bus.
3 A: Did your parents use to own a restaurant? B: No, they used to own a bakery.

① **Specific sounds:** Make sure students understand the rule and can distinguish the sound. Model the sound for them, first with the sound only and then using the sound in a word. Allow them to practice the sound a number of times until they feel comfortable with it.

② **Specific words:** When students have to recognize specific words in a sentence, you may want to let them listen to the sentences more than once. If they are asked to notice a sound within a word, make sure they can all distinguish it.

③ **Stress and intonation:** You may want to read the sentences yourself before students practice them. In this way, you can exaggerate the stressed words or the intonation pattern to make sure students can recognize the pattern.

④ **Juncture or reduction:** Many languages do not have juncture or reduction features similar to the ones in English, so this can be a difficult concept for students. It is very important to make sure that they understand the explanations of these features. However, especially at beginning levels, it is more important for students to be able to understand native speakers when they reduce unstressed vowels or combine words (as in this example) than for them to be able to produce them perfectly.

Reading

Good readers unconsciously use a number of different skills when they read in their own language. When people learn a second language, they often need to become aware of those skills and learn how to use them when reading in the second language. Reading is considered a receptive skill, but that does not mean that it is a passive activity. Reading involves interacting with a text by reading it with questions in mind, comparing one's own knowledge or opinions to the information in the text, and applying skills to help one understand and interpret the text.

In the classroom, reading is usually done to develop reading skills or as a vehicle for language study. However, a text will be more effective for academic purposes if students find it interesting. In ***Speak Your Mind***, reading texts on a wide variety of topics in a number of different genres are designed to engage students' interest while providing work on key reading skills and general reading comprehension.

PROCEDURE: Teaching **Reading** in *Speak Your Mind*

1. **Pre-reading.** Every READING section begins with a pre-reading activity to remind students of knowledge they already have about the topic or to raise their interest in the topic. Before students read the text, have them discuss what they know, or would like to know, about the topic, have them predict what information they think will be in the text, or have them give their opinions about the topic.

2. **Reading.** The ***Speak Your Mind*** reading texts introduce vocabulary words in bold to help students focus on them. As students read, they should circle words they don't know and keep reading, then go back to unknown words and guess their meaning. Audio recordings are available for reading texts.

3. **Comprehension.** There are two types of comprehension activities that accompany reading texts: activities for general comprehension and activities to develop specific reading skills. For general comprehension activities, it is a good idea to have students read the questions before reading the text in order to help them quickly identify key information while reading. Good readers usually have an idea of what information they want to get from a text before they begin reading. You may want to ask students to underline key words and information as they read, or to make notes or write questions in the margin next to the text.

4. **Reading Skill.** For READING SKILL activities, check that students understand what the skill is and why it is useful before asking them to do the activity. Each unit of the **Workbook** has an explanation of the skill presented in the **Student's Book**, as well as further practice of the skill. You may want to direct students to the explanation in the **Workbook** before having them do the activity in the **Student's Book**.

5. **Thinking Skill.** Reading should cause us to think. In some cases, we may agree or disagree with a text. A text may raise further questions about a topic, or it may excite and motivate us to share information with others or to take some kind of action. While young adult students of a foreign language, especially at lower levels, do not have great ability with the language, they nevertheless possess adult-level thinking skills. It is more motivating for them to read texts if they know that they will be able to interact with the texts or the topics in a way that takes into account their cognitive abilities. For more on thinking skills, see *Thinking Skills* by Dr. Spencer Kagan on pages xxviii-xxxi of ***Speak Your Mind* Teacher's Edition 1**.

Further Reading. For further practice of reading skills and general reading comprehension, there are *Reading Worksheets* available in the **Student's Resource Center**.

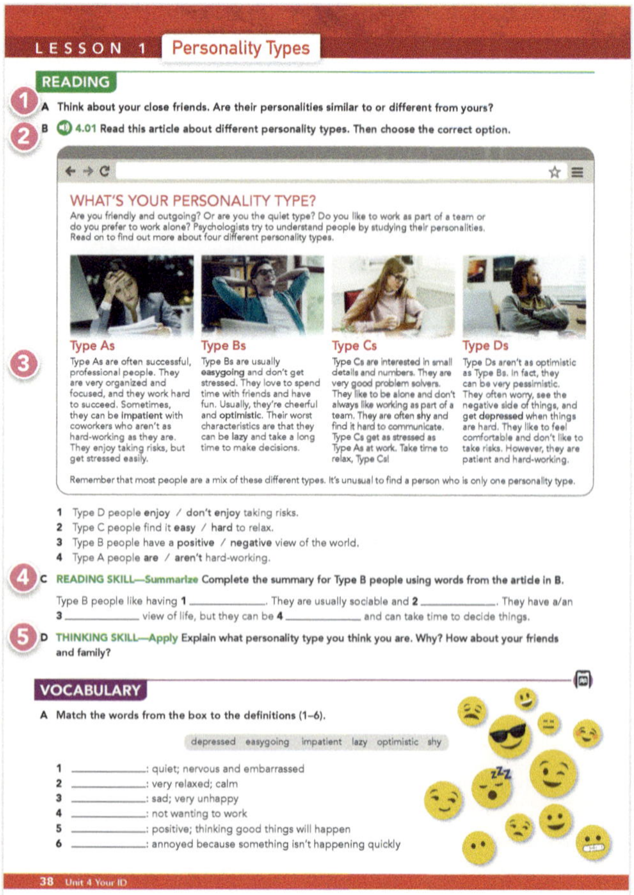
LESSON 1 Personality Types

READING

1 A Think about your close friends. Are their personalities similar to or different from yours?

2 B 4.01 Read this article about different personality types. Then choose the correct option.

WHAT'S YOUR PERSONALITY TYPE?

Are you friendly and outgoing? Or are you the quiet type? Do you like to work as part of a team or do you prefer to work alone? Psychologists try to understand people by studying their personalities. Read on to find out more about four different personality types.

3

Type As
Type As are often successful, professional people. They are very organized and focused, and they work hard to succeed. Sometimes, they can be **impatient** with coworkers who aren't as hard-working as they are. They enjoy taking risks, but get stressed easily.

Type Bs
Type Bs are usually **easygoing** and don't get stressed. They love to spend time with friends and have fun. Usually, they're cheerful and **optimistic**. Their worst characteristics are that they can be **lazy** and take a long time to make decisions.

Type Cs
Type Cs are interested in small details and numbers. They are very good problem solvers. They like to be alone and don't always like working as part of a team. They are often **shy** and find it hard to communicate. Type Cs get as stressed as Type As at work. Take time to relax, Type Cs!

Type Ds
Type Ds aren't as optimistic as Type Bs. In fact, they can be very pessimistic. They often worry, see the negative side of things, and get **depressed** when things are hard. They like to feel comfortable and don't like to take risks. However, they are patient and hard-working.

Remember that most people are a mix of these different types. It's unusual to find a person who is only one personality type.

1 Type D people **enjoy** / **don't enjoy** taking risks.
2 Type C people find it **easy** / **hard** to relax.
3 Type B people have a **positive** / **negative** view of the world.
4 Type A people **are** / **aren't** hard-working.

4 C READING SKILL—Summarize Complete the summary for Type B people using words from the article in B.

Type B people like having **1** ________. They are usually sociable and **2** ________. They have a/an **3** ________ view of life, but they can be **4** ________ and can take time to decide things.

5 D THINKING SKILL—Apply Explain what personality type you think you are. Why? How about your friends and family?

VOCABULARY

A Match the words from the box to the definitions (1–6).

depressed easygoing impatient lazy optimistic shy

1 ________: quiet; nervous and embarrassed
2 ________: very relaxed; calm
3 ________: sad; very unhappy
4 ________: not wanting to work
5 ________: positive; thinking good things will happen
6 ________: annoyed because something isn't happening quickly

38 Unit 4 Your ID

Listening

The importance of good listening skills cannot be over-emphasized, as listening represents 45% of adult communication. In ***Speak Your Mind***, there are listening comprehension sections in two of the four lessons in each unit. These sections are designed to help students develop key listening skills as well as general comprehension skills. The listening texts represent a variety of genres, including conversations, lectures, radio broadcasts, and podcasts, to give students exposure to as many different listening situations as possible.

Like reading, listening is a receptive skill, but it is not a passive activity. Listeners rely on their own prior knowledge of a topic, their expectations about what a speaker will say, as well as contextual clues like body language to help them predict what will be said. Listeners also employ a variety of skills while listening, such as identifying key words to help them understand the gist of a conversation as well as important details.

There are a number of things that teachers can do to help students improve their listening comprehension:

- Do not speak too slowly or enunciate too perfectly. This will make it easier for students to understand in the classroom, but much more difficult when they encounter English outside the classroom. You may want to slow down a word or a sentence occasionally, but in general you should use normal speech.
- Remind students not to worry if they do not understand every word in a listening text. Point out that we often miss words even when listening in our own language. Encourage them to identify key words to help them understand the gist of a listening text as well as important details.
- As students develop specific listening skills, remind them to use those skills when they are listening to the teacher or to their classmates. Point out that they get listening practice not only in the listening sections of their textbook, but also during speaking activities and classroom interactions.

PROCEDURE: Teaching **Listening** in *Speak Your Mind*

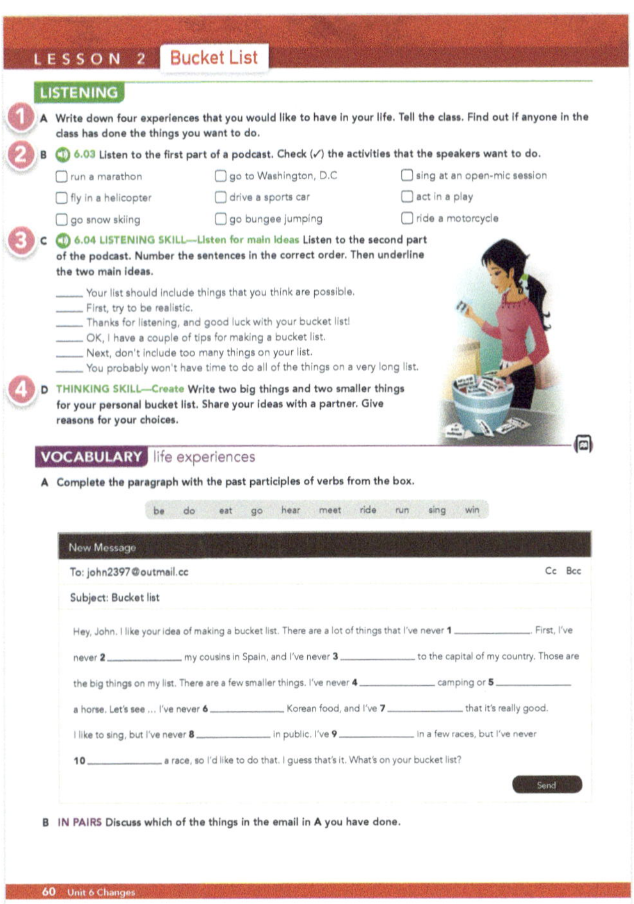
LESSON 2 Bucket List

LISTENING

1 A Write down four experiences that you would like to have in your life. Tell the class. Find out if anyone in the class has done the things you want to do.

2 B 6.03 Listen to the first part of a podcast. Check (✓) the activities that the speakers want to do.

- ☐ run a marathon
- ☐ go to Washington, D.C
- ☐ sing at an open-mic session
- ☐ fly in a helicopter
- ☐ drive a sports car
- ☐ act in a play
- ☐ go snow skiing
- ☐ go bungee jumping
- ☐ ride a motorcycle

3 C 6.04 LISTENING SKILL—Listen for main ideas Listen to the second part of the podcast. Number the sentences in the correct order. Then underline the two main ideas.

_____ Your list should include things that you think are possible.
_____ First, try to be realistic.
_____ Thanks for listening, and good luck with your bucket list!
_____ OK, I have a couple of tips for making a bucket list.
_____ Next, don't include too many things on your list.
_____ You probably won't have time to do all of the things on a very long list.

4 D THINKING SKILL—Create Write two big things and two smaller things for your personal bucket list. Share your ideas with a partner. Give reasons for your choices.

VOCABULARY life experiences

A Complete the paragraph with the past participles of verbs from the box.

be do eat go hear meet ride run sing win

New Message
To: john2397@outmail.cc Cc Bcc
Subject: Bucket list

Hey, John. I like your idea of making a bucket list. There are a lot of things that I've never 1 __________. First, I've never 2 __________ my cousins in Spain, and I've never 3 __________ to the capital of my country. Those are the big things on my list. There are a few smaller things. I've never 4 __________ camping or 5 __________ a horse. Let's see ... I've never 6 __________ Korean food, and I've 7 __________ that it's really good. I like to sing, but I've never 8 __________ in public. I've 9 __________ in a few races, but I've never 10 __________ a race, so I'd like to do that. I guess that's it. What's on your bucket list?

Send

B IN PAIRS Discuss which of the things in the email in A you have done.

60 Unit 6 Changes

1. **Pre-Listening**. Pre-listening activities help students prepare for listening by asking them to predict what speakers will say or talk about what they already know about a topic.
2. **Listening comprehension**. Especially at beginning levels, students often need a lot of support for listening comprehension. It is a good idea to allow them to read through a comprehension activity before listening in order to give them an idea of what to listen for. You may want to ask students to listen to the recording once before attempting to do the activity. After they listen, give them a few minutes to do the activity and then play the recording again for them to check their work.
3. **Listening Skill**. As with reading, every LISTENING section of ***Speak Your Mind*** includes the development of a listening skill. Check that students understand what the skill is and why it is useful. You may want to refer students to the explanation of the listening skill in the relevant unit of the **Workbook**.
4. **Thinking Skill.** In each LISTENING section of ***Speak Your Mind***, there is a thinking activity which encourages students to further analyze what they've heard and to express their opinions or to extend and apply the ideas in the listening text to their own context. For more on thinking skills, see *Thinking Skills* by Dr. Spencer Kagan on pages xxviii-xxxi of ***Speak Your Mind* Teacher's Edition 1**.

Speaking

Foreign-language teachers often comment that students just don't want to speak. There are a number of reasons for this. Sometimes they are afraid of making mistakes. This is especially true of young-adult and adult students who are used to thinking of themselves as competent. Other times students are just not prepared when asked to speak. It can be very difficult for them to think of what to say and how to say it if they are not able to prepare beforehand, especially at lower levels. It is important to create a classroom environment in which students feel confident and motivated to communicate in English.

It is important to provide frequent opportunities for students to speak. In ***Speak Your Mind***, there is a strong emphasis on speaking, and students are given many opportunities throughout the lessons to voice their ideas and to practice the language that they are learning:

- Unit Openers have cooperative learning opportunities and group discussion questions.
- Pre-reading and pre-listening activities often involve class discussions.
- Thinking skills sections have questions for group or class discussions.
- GRAMMAR and VOCABULARY sections frequently include group or pair speaking activities.
- Lessons 1–3 end with a SPEAKING section, which allows students to use the grammar and vocabulary of the lesson to talk about a related topic.
- Language and Life lessons (Lesson 4 in every unit) are designed as collaborative tasks that involve a variety of interactive pair, group, and class activities.

PROCEDURE: Teaching **Speaking** in *Speak Your Mind*

① **Preparation.** SPEAKING sections are scaffolded in order to give students the support they need when they speak. They first think about the topic and make notes, fill in a form, or in some other way prepare for what they are going to say. It is important to give them enough time to do this so that they feel confident when they start speaking. You may want to add a class preparation stage before asking students to work on their own—have a class brainstorming session to help them come up with ideas, or you could elicit vocabulary and grammar structures that they may need for the speaking activity.

② **Practice.** Once students have had a chance to prepare, they work in pairs or groups to share their ideas. Make sure that students understand what they are going to do and exactly what their roles are before you put them in their groups or pairs. You may want to model the activity with a student or ask two students to model it.

③ **Present.** Be sure to allow plenty of time for the speaking activities, as this is the communicative outcome of the lesson. The SPEAKING section frequently takes up less space on the page than other sections in the lesson, so it is easy to make the mistake of thinking that the activity is very short. In fact, it may require the most time. It is important to allow enough time for preparation and for each student to have the chance to speak.

When students are working in groups or pairs, listen for common errors, especially in the target language of the lesson. Have a short review session after the speaking activity. This generally works better than interrupting students while they are speaking. If you have a large class, you may not be able to listen to every pair or group, but you can get a good idea of things they may need more practice with by listening to as many of them as possible.

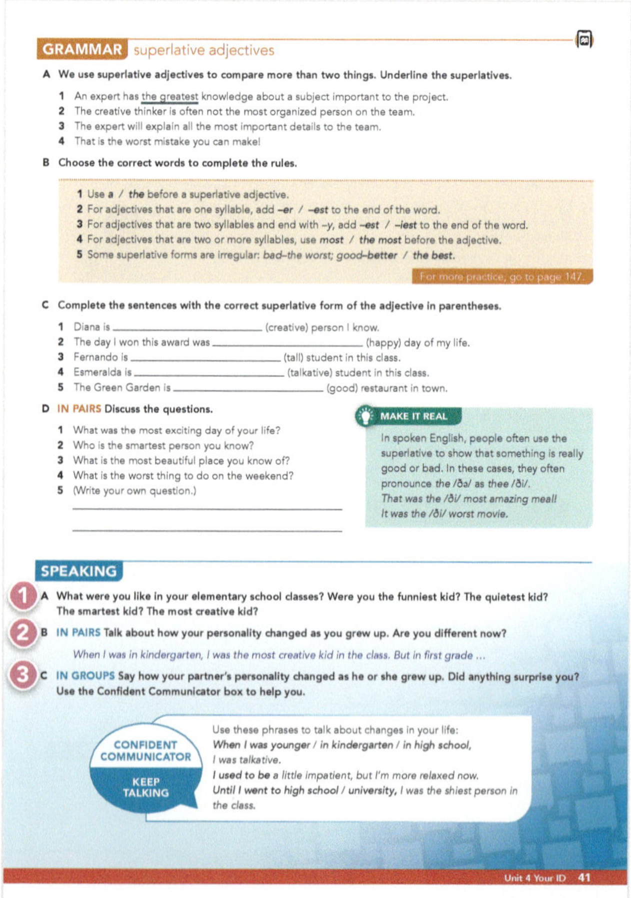

GRAMMAR superlative adjectives

A We use superlative adjectives to compare more than two things. Underline the superlatives.

1 An expert has the greatest knowledge about a subject important to the project.
2 The creative thinker is often not the most organized person on the team.
3 The expert will explain all the most important details to the team.
4 That is the worst mistake you can make!

B Choose the correct words to complete the rules.

1 Use ***a*** / ***the*** before a superlative adjective.
2 For adjectives that are one syllable, add ***–er*** / ***–est*** to the end of the word.
3 For adjectives that are two syllables and end with *–y*, add ***–est*** / ***–iest*** to the end of the word.
4 For adjectives that are two or more syllables, use ***most*** / ***the most*** before the adjective.
5 Some superlative forms are irregular: *bad–the worst; good–better* / ***the best***.

For more practice, go to page 147.

C Complete the sentences with the correct superlative form of the adjective in parentheses.

1 Diana is ________ (creative) person I know.
2 The day I won this award was ________ (happy) day of my life.
3 Fernando is ________ (tall) student in this class.
4 Esmeralda is ________ (talkative) student in this class.
5 The Green Garden is ________ (good) restaurant in town.

D IN PAIRS Discuss the questions.

1 What was the most exciting day of your life?
2 Who is the smartest person you know?
3 What is the most beautiful place you know of?
4 What is the worst thing to do on the weekend?
5 (Write your own question.)

____

____

MAKE IT REAL

In spoken English, people often use the superlative to show that something is really good or bad. In these cases, they often pronounce *the* /ðə/ as *thee* /ði/.
That was the /ði/ most amazing meal!
It was the /ði/ worst movie.

SPEAKING

① **A What were you like in your elementary school classes? Were you the funniest kid? The quietest kid? The smartest kid? The most creative kid?**

② **B IN PAIRS Talk about how your personality changed as you grew up. Are you different now?**

When I was in kindergarten, I was the most creative kid in the class. But in first grade ...

③ **C IN GROUPS Say how your partner's personality changed as he or she grew up. Did anything surprise you? Use the Confident Communicator box to help you.**

CONFIDENT COMMUNICATOR — KEEP TALKING

Use these phrases to talk about changes in your life:
When I was younger / in kindergarten / in high school, *I was talkative.*
I used to be *a little impatient, but I'm more relaxed now.*
Until I went to high school / university, *I was the shiest person in the class.*

Unit 4 Your ID 41

Confident Communicator

One of the core objectives of ***Speak Your Mind*** is that students should become confident users of English—that is, Confident Communicators. Every SPEAKING section in ***Speak Your Mind*** includes a *Confident Communicator* box that gives students tips on what to say and how to say it. Some of the tips focus on functional language, which includes words and phrases used in specific situations, such as greeting someone or asking directions. Others focus on speaking strategies, such as taking time to think or explaining what you mean. The subheadings *Start Talking*, *Keep Talking*, and *Repair It* indicate how the language in the *Confident Communicator* box functions in a conversation.

Before students get into pairs or groups to do the interactive part of the SPEAKING section, go over the language in the *Confident Communicator* box to make sure they understand how to use it. You may want to practice a few short interactions with some or all of the phrases before they start working together.

When applied to language learning, the old saying "Practice makes perfect" should probably be changed to "Practice makes perfectly adequate." Wanting students to be confident communicators does not mean that everything they say should be perfectly constructed. In our own languages, we often communicate with incomplete sentences or even just facial expressions or gestures. The goal is to give students the confidence to express their ideas in English, and the best way to do that is through a combination of frequent opportunities to speak and support with the language.

Confident Communicator feature in *Speak Your Mind*

Start Talking. With the *Start Talking* boxes, students learn phrases for initiating a conversation or topic.

CONFIDENT COMMUNICATOR — START TALKING

To ask another person his or her opinion or experience about the same topic, use one of these questions:
And you?
What about you?
How about you?

Keep Talking. With the *Keep Talking* boxes, students learn strategies and phrases to keep a conversation going even when they are not yet very proficient in the language.

CONFIDENT COMMUNICATOR — KEEP TALKING

To add a further point, say:
Also …
In addition to that, …
Not only that, but … also …
You can express your personality in a subculture. Not only that, but you can also meet people.

Repair It. With the *Repair It* boxes, students learn phrases to use when there is a problem in communication.

CONFIDENT COMMUNICATOR — REPAIR IT

If you don't know a word in English, here are some things you can do:
Use a word that means something similar (e.g., *very worried* for *scared*).
Give a short description of the event (e.g., *a lot of rain* for *storm*).

Writing

The ability to communicate effectively in writing is more important than ever for professional success. In the past, a great deal of business communication was conducted on the phone, but now most business communication is done via email. Email is no longer considered just an informal mode of written communication. Emails, like letters in the past, can have varying degrees of informality or formality, and young adults who are about to enter a very competitive professional world will have to be able to communicate competently in writing.

Teaching students to communicate in written English is complicated by the fact that many students do not have good writing skills, even in their own language. In ***Speak Your Mind***, students are taught basic writing skills like planning before starting to write, reviewing and editing their work after they write, and how to construct different genres of written communication. Learning to write short texts in different genres gives students practice in skills such as describing a situation or event, persuading the reader to agree with a point of view, giving instructions, or presenting a proposal. While the topics they write about may not be directly related to a profession, the skills they learn can be applied later on in business communications, both in English and in their own language. There is a WRITING section in Lesson 3 of every unit in ***Speak Your Mind***.

Remember that the purpose of writing is to communicate ideas, so it is always a good idea to have students share their finished work. You could have them read their texts aloud in small groups and then have a discussion, or you could have them work with a partner and read each other's texts. They can then get together to discuss their ideas or report on each other's texts to different partners.

There is further practice in writing mechanics and editing skills in the **Workbook**. In ***Speak Your Mind***, students are given the support and the practice they need in order for them to become competent writers in English.

PROCEDURE: Teaching **Writing** in *Speak Your Mind*

1. **Read the model.** A model text is provided, either in the WRITING section or in another section in the lesson. Students read the text and do an activity that asks them to notice elements of content, organization, or language commonly used in a specific genre. You may want to have students read the text and then ask some general comprehension questions before having them do the activity.
2. **Organize [Pre-writing].** After students have worked with the model text, they are given a framework to provide them with cues and help them organize their ideas for their own text. You may want to start with a class brainstorming session to help generate ideas. As they work, give individual help with ideas and vocabulary as needed.
3. **Write and share.** Once students have written their texts, give them time to review and correct their work. This may be done individually or in pairs. If it is done in pairs, it is a good opportunity for cooperative learning. You may want to go over some common grammar or spelling errors before they start editing their work in order to help them spot their own errors.

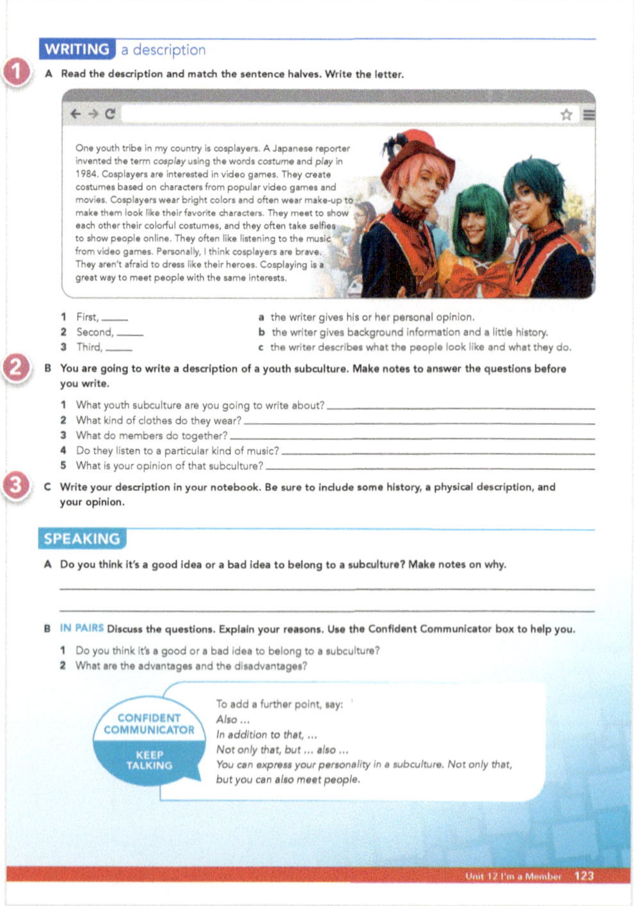
WRITING a description

1 A Read the description and match the sentence halves. Write the letter.

One youth tribe in my country is cosplayers. A Japanese reporter invented the term *cosplay* using the words *costume* and *play* in 1984. Cosplayers are interested in video games. They create costumes based on characters from popular video games and movies. Cosplayers wear bright colors and often wear make-up to make them look like their favorite characters. They meet to show each other their colorful costumes, and they often take selfies to show people online. They often like listening to the music from video games. Personally, I think cosplayers are brave. They aren't afraid to dress like their heroes. Cosplaying is a great way to meet people with the same interests.

1 First, _____
2 Second, _____
3 Third, _____

a the writer gives his or her personal opinion.
b the writer gives background information and a little history.
c the writer describes what the people look like and what they do.

2 B You are going to write a description of a youth subculture. Make notes to answer the questions before you write.

1 What youth subculture are you going to write about? _____
2 What kind of clothes do they wear? _____
3 What do members do together? _____
4 Do they listen to a particular kind of music? _____
5 What is your opinion of that subculture? _____

3 C Write your description in your notebook. Be sure to include some history, a physical description, and your opinion.

SPEAKING

A Do you think it's a good idea or a bad idea to belong to a subculture? Make notes on why.

B IN PAIRS Discuss the questions. Explain your reasons. Use the Confident Communicator box to help you.

1 Do you think it's a good or a bad idea to belong to a subculture?
2 What are the advantages and the disadvantages?

CONFIDENT COMMUNICATOR
KEEP TALKING

To add a further point, say:
Also ...
In addition to that, ...
Not only that, but ... also ...
You can express your personality in a subculture. Not only that, but you can also meet people.

Unit 12 I'm a Member 123

Language and Life

In the 21st century, the teaching of academic subjects is accompanied by the development of the types of skills that are necessary for success in academics, work, and life. These skills for success include communication, collaboration, problem-solving, creativity, self-direction, critical thinking, and media literacy.

In ***Speak Your Mind***, these skills are developed throughout each unit through collaborative activities, training in effective communication, and tasks that require critical thinking and problem-solving. The last lesson in each unit is specifically designed to focus on the development of 21st-century skills while recycling key grammar and vocabulary from the unit.

Every unit in ***Speak Your Mind*** includes a suggestion for online work outside of class. *Make It Digital* often occurs in Lesson 4 because the Language and Life tasks tend to lend themselves to further investigations or to a product that can be posted on a school website. You could have students do the research for homework and then report back to the class.

The lesson ends with questions that encourage students to reflect on the process they followed to achieve the outcome of the lesson and to think about what they might do better in a similar situation in the future. It is a good idea to discuss these questions as a class.

PROCEDURE: Teaching **Language and Life** in *Speak Your Mind*

1. **Present the life skill.** The heading is in two parts. The first part indicates the target 21st-century skill. The second part indicates the outcome of the task sequence in the lesson. Check that students understand both the skill that they will be using and the objective of the task.
2. **Read the text.** The lesson begins with a text that introduces students to the topic of the lesson. The topic is directly related to the overall unit topic. After students have read the text and done the activity, you may want to ask some further questions to check comprehension.
3. **Read the task.** Students are then given a problem or a task, and they have to work through a series of steps in order to achieve an outcome. They work individually to decide how they would solve the problem or carry out the task. Make sure they understand exactly what to do at this stage because everyone's input will be needed for the subsequent activities.
4. **Collaborate.** In the next stage, students work in pairs or in groups, to share the ideas from the previous stage. Depending on the topic and task type, you may want to organize students in different ways. Pair more confident with less confident students, or group students by academic major or interest areas.

   The pairs or groups discuss and combine their ideas and then produce a proposal or set of recommendations in the form of a concrete outcome such as a guide, a presentation, a poster, or an online post. If the final product is a written document, have students write it in the correct format in their notebooks. If it is a presentation, have them write notes on notecards for use during their presentation.
5. **Present.** Students share their proposals or recommendations. They frequently finish the task sequence by discussing their ideas as a whole class and reaching a consensus on the best ideas. Have them work in pairs or small groups so that everyone will have plenty of time to talk, as this is the communicative outcome of the lesson.
6. **Reflect.** Students are asked to reflect on the process of working together through discussion questions.

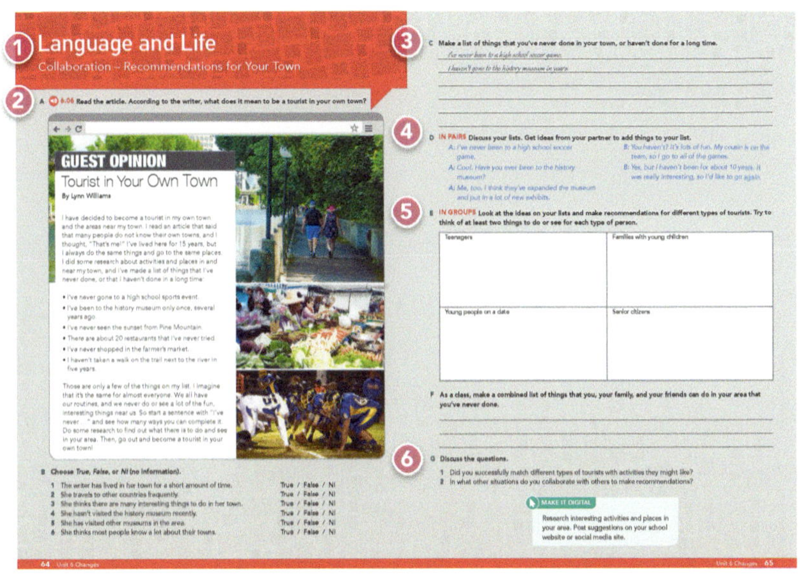

1 Language and Life

Collaboration – Recommendations for Your Town

2 A 6.06 **Read the article. According to the writer, what does it mean to be a tourist in your own town?**

GUEST OPINION

Tourist in Your Own Town

By Lynn Williams

I have decided to become a tourist in my own town and the areas near my town. I read an article that said that many people do not know their own towns, and I thought, "That's me!" I've lived here for 15 years, but I always do the same things and go to the same places. I did some research about activities and places in and near my town, and I've made a list of things that I've never done, or that I haven't done in a long time:

- I've never gone to a high school sports event.
- I've been to the history museum only once, several years ago.
- I've never seen the sunset from Pine Mountain.
- There are about 20 restaurants that I've never tried.
- I've never shopped in the farmer's market.
- I haven't taken a walk on the trail next to the river in five years.

Those are only a few of the things on my list. I imagine that it's the same for almost everyone. We all have our routines, and we never do or see a lot of the fun, interesting things near us. So start a sentence with "I've never . . ." and see how many ways you can complete it. Do some research to find out what there is to do and see in your area. Then, go out and become a tourist in your own town!

B **Choose *True*, *False*, or *NI* (no information).**

1	The writer has lived in her town for a short amount of time.	True / False / NI
2	She travels to other countries frequently.	True / False / NI
3	She thinks there are many interesting things to do in her town.	True / False / NI
4	She hasn't visited the history museum recently.	True / False / NI
5	She has visited other museums in the area.	True / False / NI
6	She thinks most people know a lot about their towns.	True / False / NI

64 Unit 6 Changes

3 C **Make a list of things that you've never done in your town, or haven't done for a long time.**

I've never been to a high school soccer game.

I haven't gone to the history museum in years.

4 D IN PAIRS **Discuss your lists. Get ideas from your partner to add things to your list.**

A: I've never been to a high school soccer game.

B: You haven't? It's lots of fun. My cousin is on the team, so I go to all of the games.

A: Cool. Have you ever been to the history museum?

B: Yes, but I haven't been for about 10 years. It was really interesting, so I'd like to go again.

A: Me, too. I think they've expanded the museum and put in a lot of new exhibits.

5 E IN GROUPS **Look at the ideas on your lists and make recommendations for different types of tourists. Try to think of at least two things to do or see for each type of person.**

Teenagers	Families with young children
Young people on a date	Senior citizens

F **As a class, make a combined list of things that you, your family, and your friends can do in your area that you've never done.**

6 G **Discuss the questions.**

1 Did you successfully match different types of tourists with activities they might like?
2 In what other situations do you collaborate with others to make recommendations?

MAKE IT DIGITAL

Research interesting activities and places in your area. Post suggestions on your school website or social media site.

Unit 6 Changes 65

Make It …

Personalization is an important part of building vocabulary for English language learners. The *Make It …* features in ***Speak Your Mind*** show students where they should add the words and phrases they need to use for work or study. Students should be encouraged to build a list of words, phrases, or expressions that are meaningful to them.

PROCEDURE: Using the **Make It …** features in *Speak Your Mind*

Make It Yours. *Make It Yours* boxes encourage students to expand their vocabulary by making a list of words that are useful for them personally or by using target vocabulary in a personalized way. Go over the information in the boxes and elicit words from the class, or ask them to do the task suggested in the box for homework.

> **MAKE IT YOURS**
>
> Do you live in an apartment, a house, or a townhouse? Search online or use a dictionary to find the right words and phrases.

Make It Happen. The Study Skills page ends with a *Make It Happen* box that has a suggestion for an activity in which students would use the skill they have just learned. These could work well as homework assignments or even short projects.

> **MAKE IT HAPPEN**
>
> Apply some of the problem-solving techniques you have learned to your own studies or work. Keep a journal about the process you used to solve a problem and decide what helped you reach a solution.

Make It Real. GRAMMAR and VOCABULARY sections are often accompanied by a *Make It Real* box. The purpose of this feature is to provide students with examples of language that they may not be formally taught but which is commonly used by native speakers. This helps them understand more easily when they listen to a native speaker, and it can help them sound more natural when they speak English.

> **MAKE IT REAL**
>
> To talk about something you like or enjoy doing, use the phrase *to be into*.
> *I'm really into police dramas. I love them!*

Make It Digital. Every unit in ***Speak Your Mind*** includes a suggestion for online work outside of class. The *Make It Digital* box always appears in Lesson 4 because the Language and Life tasks lend themselves to further investigations or to a product that can be posted on a school website. You could have students do the research for homework and then report back to the class.

> **MAKE IT DIGITAL**
>
> Go online to find a quiz about personality types. Take the quiz and share your results with the class.

Unit Review

Every unit in ***Speak Your Mind*** includes an end-of-unit review of the target grammar and vocabulary from the unit. The activities are designed as a general review to help students and teachers identify areas of strength and weakness so that students know what to focus on when studying for their exams.

PROCEDURE: Teaching the **Unit Review** in *Speak Your Mind*

① **Review.** The VOCABULARY and GRAMMAR *Review* sections each have one or two activities for a total of 10 items per section. The activities are written in a variety of formats that reflect the different activity types that students may encounter on an exam.

For Unit Tests, Mid-Course Tests, and End-of-Course Tests, use the Ready to Go tests or make customized tests with the ***Speak Your Mind* Test Generator**. If possible, it is a good idea to have students do the *Review* section a couple of days before a unit exam so that they have plenty of time to study their weak areas before the exam. The *Review* may be assigned as homework or done in class as a practice test.

② **Score.** There are 10 points per section for a combined total of 20 points for the two sections. Students should write the number of correct answers in the blank in each section and the total number of correct answers in the *Total Score* box. Point out the score interpretations under the *Total Score* box. Remind students that they will be tested on the grammar and vocabulary of the unit, and if they have a low score on the *Review*, they need to go back to the relevant sections in the unit and study the material.

When you go over the answers to the *Review* section, make sure that students understand their errors and that they know which section of their **Student's Book** to study for each incorrect item. Remind them that they need to study all of the vocabulary items in the three VOCABULARY sections in the unit, not just the items that were included in the *Review* activities.

③ **Further review.** Every *Review* section ends with the question WHAT DO YOU KNOW NOW? Students are asked to go back to the vocabulary activity in the Unit Opener and add words that they have learned in the unit. This is useful both as a reflection activity and as a review tool. It raises students' awareness that they are increasing their vocabulary in English. Also, by looking back at the words they listed in the Unit Opener, they are reviewing vocabulary related to the unit topic.

④ **Study Skill / Follow A Pro.** Please see the following pages for explanations of the Study Skills and Follow A Pro sections on the *Review* page.

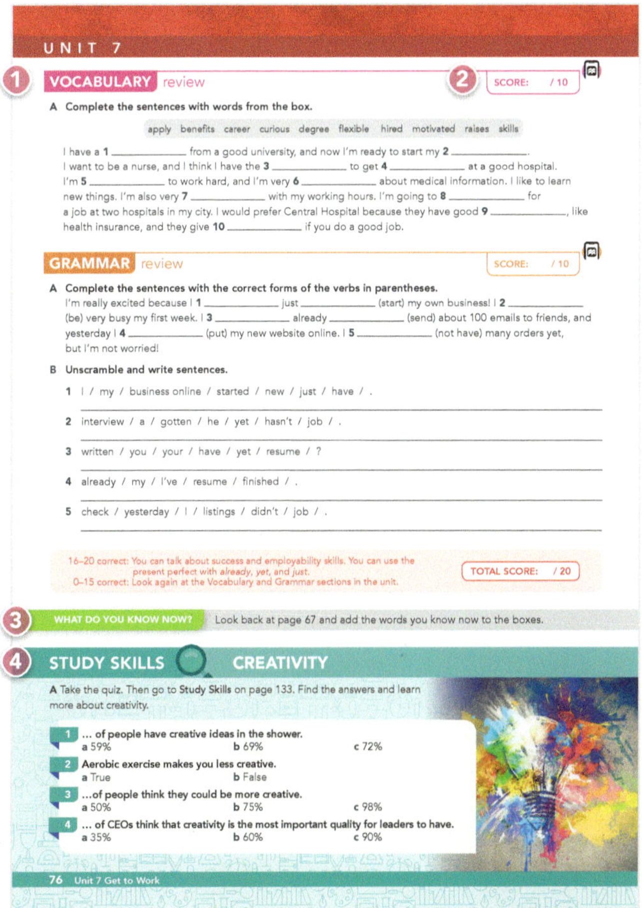

UNIT 7

① VOCABULARY review ② SCORE: / 10

A Complete the sentences with words from the box.

apply benefits career curious degree flexible hired motivated raises skills

I have a **1** ______ from a good university, and now I'm ready to start my **2** ______. I want to be a nurse, and I think I have the **3** ______ to get **4** ______ at a good hospital. I'm **5** ______ to work hard, and I'm very **6** ______ about medical information. I like to learn new things. I'm also very **7** ______ with my working hours. I'm going to **8** ______ for a job at two hospitals in my city. I would prefer Central Hospital because they have good **9** ______, like health insurance, and they give **10** ______ if you do a good job.

GRAMMAR review SCORE: / 10

A Complete the sentences with the correct forms of the verbs in parentheses.

I'm really excited because I **1** ______ just ______ (start) my own business! I **2** ______ (be) very busy my first week. I **3** ______ already ______ (send) about 100 emails to friends, and yesterday I **4** ______ (put) my new website online. I **5** ______ (not have) many orders yet, but I'm not worried!

B Unscramble and write sentences.

1 I / my / business online / started / new / just / have / .

2 interview / a / gotten / he / yet / hasn't / job / .

3 written / you / your / have / yet / resume / ?

4 already / my / I've / resume / finished / .

5 check / yesterday / I / listings / didn't / job / .

16–20 correct: You can talk about success and employability skills. You can use the present perfect with *already*, *yet*, and *just*.
0–15 correct: Look again at the Vocabulary and Grammar sections in the unit.

TOTAL SCORE: / 20

③ WHAT DO YOU KNOW NOW? Look back at page 67 and add the words you know now to the boxes.

④ STUDY SKILLS CREATIVITY

A Take the quiz. Then go to **Study Skills** on page 133. Find the answers and learn more about creativity.

1 **... of people have creative ideas in the shower.**
a 59% **b** 69% **c** 72%

2 **Aerobic exercise makes you less creative.**
a True **b** False

3 **...of people think they could be more creative.**
a 50% **b** 75% **c** 98%

4 **... of CEOs think that creativity is the most important quality for leaders to have.**
a 35% **b** 60% **c** 90%

76 Unit 7 Get to Work

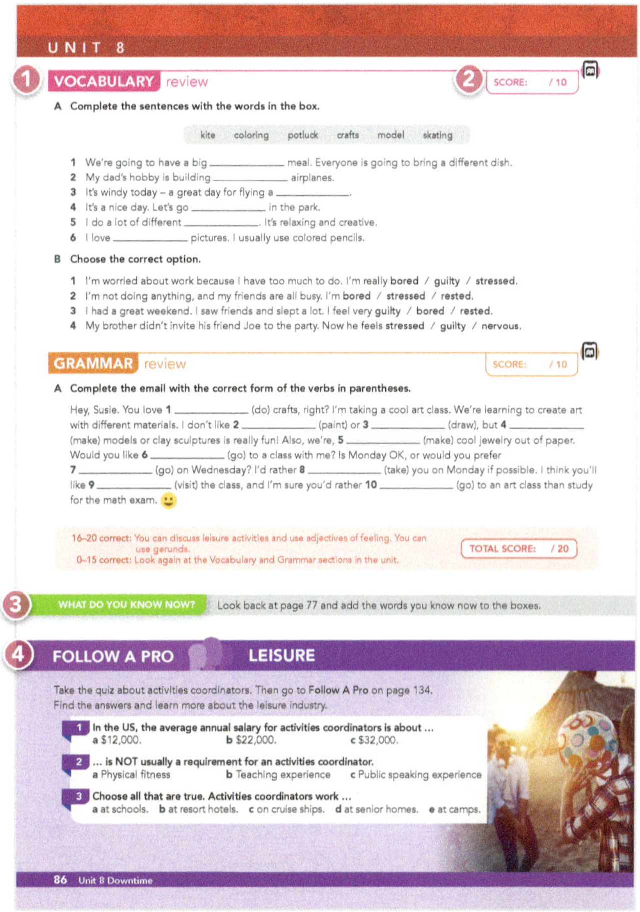

UNIT 8

① VOCABULARY review ② SCORE: / 10

A Complete the sentences with the words in the box.

kite coloring potluck crafts model skating

1 We're going to have a big ______ meal. Everyone is going to bring a different dish.
2 My dad's hobby is building ______ airplanes.
3 It's windy today – a great day for flying a ______.
4 It's a nice day. Let's go ______ in the park.
5 I do a lot of different ______. It's relaxing and creative.
6 I love ______ pictures. I usually use colored pencils.

B Choose the correct option.

1 I'm worried about work because I have too much to do. I'm really **bored** / **guilty** / **stressed**.
2 I'm not doing anything, and my friends are all busy. I'm **bored** / **stressed** / **rested**.
3 I had a great weekend. I saw friends and slept a lot. I feel very **guilty** / **bored** / **rested**.
4 My brother didn't invite his friend Joe to the party. Now he feels **stressed** / **guilty** / **nervous**.

GRAMMAR review SCORE: / 10

A Complete the email with the correct form of the verbs in parentheses.

Hey, Susie. You love **1** ______ (do) crafts, right? I'm taking a cool art class. We're learning to create art with different materials. I don't like **2** ______ (paint) or **3** ______ (draw), but **4** ______ (make) models or clay sculptures is really fun! Also, we're, **5** ______ (make) cool jewelry out of paper. Would you like **6** ______ (go) to a class with me? Is Monday OK, or would you prefer **7** ______ (go) on Wednesday? I'd rather **8** ______ (take) you on Monday if possible. I think you'll like **9** ______ (visit) the class, and I'm sure you'd rather **10** ______ (go) to an art class than study for the math exam. 🙂

16–20 correct: You can discuss leisure activities and use adjectives of feeling. You can use gerunds.
0–15 correct: Look again at the Vocabulary and Grammar sections in the unit.

TOTAL SCORE: / 20

③ WHAT DO YOU KNOW NOW? Look back at page 77 and add the words you know now to the boxes.

④ FOLLOW A PRO LEISURE

Take the quiz about activities coordinators. Then go to **Follow A Pro** on page 134. Find the answers and learn more about the leisure industry.

1 **In the US, the average annual salary for activities coordinators is about ...**
a $12,000. **b** $22,000. **c** $32,000.

2 **... is NOT usually a requirement for an activities coordinator.**
a Physical fitness **b** Teaching experience **c** Public speaking experience

3 **Choose all that are true. Activities coordinators work ...**
a at schools. **b** at resort hotels. **c** on cruise ships. **d** at senior homes. **e** at camps.

86 Unit 8 Downtime

Study Skills

In order to be successful, not only in learning English but also in academics in general, students must develop good study skills, such as how to do efficient research, how to give presentations, and how to improve their memory. In ***Speak Your Mind***, there is a study skills syllabus that is based on universal needs regardless of the subject but modified when appropriate to focus on skills specific to learning a new language.

In each level of ***Speak Your Mind***, study skills are presented and practiced in every other unit. To raise students' interest in the study skill and to give them an idea of what they already know about the skill, there is a short quiz at the end of the *Review* page in odd-numbered units.

PROCEDURE: Teaching **Study Skills** in *Speak Your Mind*

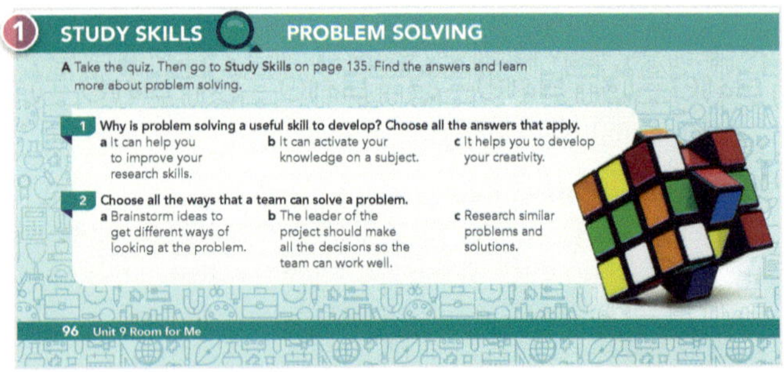

(1) STUDY SKILLS — PROBLEM SOLVING

A Take the quiz. Then go to **Study Skills** on page 135. Find the answers and learn more about problem solving.

1 Why is problem solving a useful skill to develop? Choose all the answers that apply.
a It can help you to improve your research skills.
b It can activate your knowledge on a subject.
c It helps you to develop your creativity.

2 Choose all the ways that a team can solve a problem.
a Brainstorm ideas to get different ways of looking at the problem.
b The leader of the project should make all the decisions so the team can work well.
c Research similar problems and solutions.

96 Unit 9 Room for Me

(2) UNIT 9 STUDY SKILLS

A Read the conversation about a group of students working on a research project. Are the students using good problem-solving skills? Why or why not?

PROBLEM SOLVING

Carla: For our group assignment, we have to offer solutions to the lack of safe, affordable, and quick transportation to the college. It says here that we need to present three ideas for transportation, outlining the advantages and disadvantages of each idea.
Bobby: Right. Well, that's easy. Let's present an idea for a college taxi service. That's all we need!
Maggie: Yeah, it's safe, affordable, and it would be quick, too! Nice job. We're done!
Carla: Hold on! We're not finished yet. We need three different ideas, not just one.
Bobby: Oh, I forgot about that. So, we've already got a taxi service. How about self-driving taxis, too?
Carla: Yeah, OK. And maybe ride sharing, too?
Maggie: Yes. And why don't we find out how most students get to college in a typical week?
Bobby: Good idea. I'll ask my friends, OK? That'll be quick. That can be my part, and you can do all the other stuff.
Carla: No, we need to do more research than that! And we probably need to write a report. What do you think?
Maggie: Is that necessary? Can't we all just say what we want in a presentation?
Bobby: Yeah, that's probably the best plan.
Carla: Hmm ... I'm not sure that's enough.
Maggie: Well, if you think we need a report, you can write it.

(3) **B Choose all the correct answers about the conversation in A.**

The students aren't using good problem-solving skills because ...
1 They haven't divided the work equally.
2 They aren't thinking about how to effectively research the problem.
3 They haven't considered several different solutions before deciding on three.
4 They haven't decided on a good way to research their topic.
5 They aren't sure if they have to write a report or just give the presentation.

(4) **C Number the steps in the problem-solving process in the correct order (1–4).**

_____ Write down how you managed to solve the problem.
_____ Read the task carefully and make sure you understand it.
_____ Look at the problem in a few different ways. Think about many possible solutions.
_____ Decide what information you need to help you solve the problem.

(5) **D In your notebook, rewrite the conversation in A using your ideas and the problem-solving tips in C. Show good problem-solving skills.**

(7) **E** THINKING SKILL—Evaluate **Employers look for employees who can help solve problems. What qualities does a good problem-solver have? Make a list.**

Listens to everyone's opinion, ...

(6) MAKE IT HAPPEN

Apply some of the problem-solving techniques you have learned to your own studies or work. Keep a journal about the process you used to solve a problem and decide what helped you reach a solution.

Answers to the quiz on page 96
1 a, b, c 2 a and c

135

1. **Take the quiz.** Direct students' attention to the skill in the heading and make sure they understand what the skill is. Have them take the quiz. You may want to let them do the quiz in pairs or check their answers with a partner before going to the Study Skills page at the back of the **Student's Book** to check their answers. The answers are at the bottom of the Study Skills page.

2. **Present the study skill.** The quiz on the Unit Review page leads students to the Study Skills page at the back of the book. In the first activity, students are asked to apply critical-thinking skills to do a broad analysis of a text in relation to the target study skill. The topic of the text is often related to the topic of the unit. Have students read the text and then answer the question or do the task as a whole-class activity.

3. **Do the task.** The second activity goes into more detail about the study skill. After students have done the activity, go over it as a class to make sure they have understood the skill.

4. **Read the tips or rules.** The third activity is usually focused on tips and rules for carrying out the study skill effectively. Encourage students to refer back to these from time to time to help them remember the skill.

5. **Apply the skill.** In the fourth activity, students apply what they have learned and use the study skill to do an academic task or discuss how they can use the skill in their own studies. This is the productive outcome of the lesson, so be sure to allow enough time for the activity.

6. **Transfer the skill.** The *Make It Happen* box suggests a task that allows students to apply the skill they have just learned. These could work well as homework assignments or even short projects.

7. **Reflect.** The last activity develops a thinking skill. Students are asked to discuss how the study skill can be applied in real-life academic or professional situations. These often work well as class discussions.

Follow A Pro

Speak Your Mind has a strong emphasis on professional readiness, and in every other unit, a job is highlighted in a section called Follow A Pro. As with the Study Skills section, there is a short quiz at the end of the *Review* page in even-numbered units to generate interest in and highlight previous knowledge of a particular job or professional field.

PROCEDURE: Teaching **Follow A Pro** in *Speak Your Mind*

1. **Take the quiz.** Ask students to take the quiz about a specific job or a general professional area, and then go to the corresponding page at the back of the **Student's Book** to check their answers. Answers are at the bottom of the page.
2. **Read about a professional.** Ask students to read the text about a person who does a particular job or about a job in general. The topic of the text is related to an aspect of the topic of the unit. When students have finished reading, have them answer the comprehension questions individually. Check the answers as a class.
3. **Discuss the job.** Have students discuss different aspects of the job in the text and whether they would be good at or enjoy doing that job themselves. If you have a large class, you may prefer to do the discussion in small groups so that all students will have an opportunity to talk.
4. **Watch the video.** A video follows a professional in a job that is related to or in the same general field as the job in the text. There is an option to view the video script, if desired. Have students answer comprehension questions about the video. For this activity, students work in small groups. It is a good idea to have students read the questions before they watch the video so that they can more easily pick out the information that they need to remember. You may want to play the video once without the video script and ask students to answer the questions as well as they can, and then play it again with the video script in view to reinforce their comprehension. They can then go back and complete or revise their answers to the questions.
5. **Talk about the industry or field.** The final set of discussion questions asks students to think about the job and industry in general. Have students work in pairs or small groups to explain what they know about the job and the skills it requires. Because these questions do not refer specifically to the video, the discussion can be done even if the video is not used.

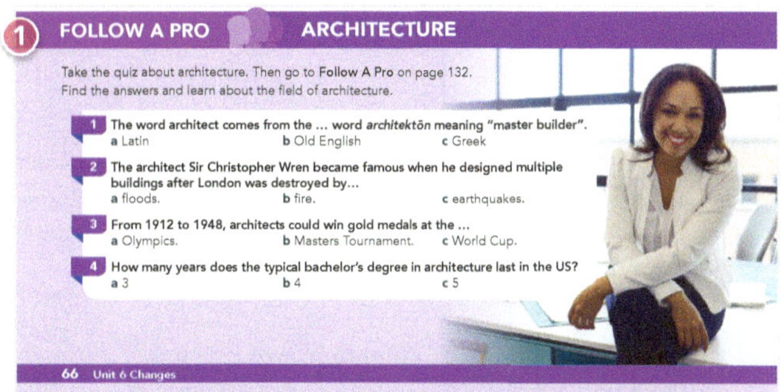

1 FOLLOW A PRO ARCHITECTURE

Take the quiz about architecture. Then go to **Follow A Pro** on page 132. Find the answers and learn about the field of architecture.

1. **The word architect comes from the ... word *architektōn* meaning "master builder".**
   a Latin **b** Old English **c** Greek
2. **The architect Sir Christopher Wren became famous when he designed multiple buildings after London was destroyed by...**
   a floods. **b** fire. **c** earthquakes.
3. **From 1912 to 1948, architects could win gold medals at the ...**
   a Olympics. **b** Masters Tournament. **c** World Cup.
4. **How many years does the typical bachelor's degree in architecture last in the US?**
   a 3 **b** 4 **c** 5

66 Unit 6 Changes

2 UNIT 6 FOLLOW A PRO

A Read about the job of an ecological architect. Choose the option that is NOT correct.

AN ARCHITECT

Emilia Johnson is an architect in a company that specializes in ecological architecture. She completed her bachelor's degree in architecture and environmental design and then got a paid internship with the company. Four years later, she passed the Architect Registration Examination. She has worked at the company for eight years, and she plans to stay there for several more years.

Ecological architects design buildings that are a natural part of the world. They design buildings that use natural resources, such as solar energy. They also design buildings with natural materials, such as a green roof (plants growing on top of a building). Emilia works with civil engineers and interior designers to make sure that her designs have a positive impact on the environment. She explains her designs to urban planners so that her buildings can become part of a larger plan for a city.

Emilia needs good technical skills and creativity. She has to make beautiful buildings that are also water and energy-efficient. She visualizes the design of the project and then creates drawings using CAD (Computer Aided Design) software. She checks that construction workers are following her design.

Emilia loves being an ecological architect. The best part of her job is seeing her clients living and working happily in a building that fits in the world naturally.

1. For four years, Emilia worked **as an intern / as a volunteer / before passing an exam / on ecological buildings.**
2. Ecological architects create buildings with **natural materials / solar panels / plants / plastic roofs.**
3. Emilia's designs are **used by engineers and designers / created on computers / made by clients / explained to urban planners.**
4. Ecological architects need good **marketing / communication / technical / creative** skills.

3 **B Discuss the questions as a class.**

1. Do you think it is important to create ecological architecture? Why or why not?
2. How can architects help make buildings more ecological?
3. Have you been in any buildings that are "green"? How do those buildings save water or energy?

VIDEO WATCH THE VIDEO AND FOLLOW AN URBAN PLANNER.

4 **C IN GROUPS Answer the questions.**

1. What job is the video about? ______
2. What are the person's working hours? ______
3. What are some of the good and bad things about the job? ______
4. Is the person's job hard? Why or why not? ______
5. What skills does the person use at this job? ______

5 **D IN GROUPS Check your answers to the quiz on page 66 and discuss the questions.**

1. What other jobs in architecture do you know?
2. Do you need English to be an architect?
3. What personal qualities do you need for this job?
4. Are there opportunities in the field of architecture in your country?

Answers to the quiz on page 66
1c 2b 3a 4c

132

Unit Opener Videos

The Discuss & Share section of the Unit Opener features an optional ***Speak Your Mind*** video. The video provides information and context for the discussion of the question. In each video, two vloggers answer the ***Speak Your Mind*** SYM **question**. One vlogger expresses one point of view, while the other one answers with the opposite point of view. The video ends with the vloggers posing the question to the students. The two opposing answers provide a model for the students' own responses. In most cases, the students' opinions will fall somewhere between the two opposing points of view. You should encourage students to state their opinion and explain where they are on the continuum of the two opposite points of view.

PROCEDURE: Using the **Unit Opener Videos** in *Speak Your Mind*

① ***Speak Your Mind*** **question.** Make sure students understand the two points of view. You may want to draw a line with the opposing views at either end to show the continuum.

home ———————————— public entertainment

② **Before viewing.** The teacher's page provides a question or questions to ask students before they watch the video. Use the question(s) to focus the students' attention on the differing points of view.

③ **Mark the continuum.** After viewing the video, have students mark where they are on the continuum by placing an X on the line between the points of view. Alternatively, ask students to form a line in the classroom, placing themselves between the two ends of the line, according to their opinion.

④ **Discuss & Share**. Ask students to explain why they have placed themselves at their selected point on the continuum. Encourage them to use the words they wrote in the What Do You Already Know? word list.

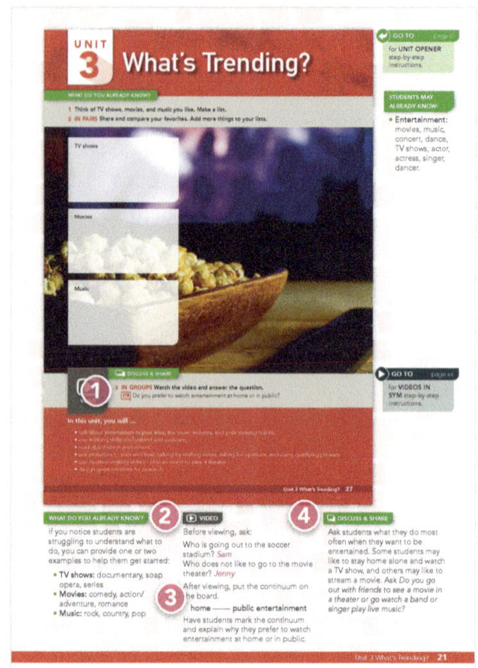

Follow A Pro Videos

The Follow A Pro videos follow professionals through their daily work lives. The job in the video is in the same industry or field as the job on the Follow A Pro page. Students should be able to recycle some of the vocabulary from the text and discussion in activities **A** and **B** as they answer the questions about the video in **C**. There are many ways to maximize learning when using videos. These suggestions support vocabulary acquisition and listening comprehension.

PROCEDURE: Using the **Follow A Pro Videos** in *Speak Your Mind*

① **Look for images.** Tell students they are going to watch the video with the sound off. Give them the list of words to look for, provided on the **Teacher's Edition** page. If they see any of the things on the list, they should circle the words. For further challenge, ask students to predict what the professional will say about his or her life based on the images in the video.

② **Listen for words.** Play the video with the sound on. Provide the list of words or phrases from the Teacher's Edition page. Ask students to circle any words or phrases they hear. Have students answer the questions in activity **C**. A challenge question is provided on the **Teacher's Edition** page to check students' comprehension of the video.

③ **Watch again.** Play the video again with or without the video script visible. Students can check or correct their answers to the questions in activity **C** and the challenge question.

Grammar Quiz

Before students begin their course, have them take the Grammar Quiz on page 6. This quiz is a quick review of language from the Starter level of ***Speak Your Mind***. For a longer review, go to the Grammar Review on page 140.

Grammar Review

At the back of the ***Speak Your Mind*** **Student's Book**, there is a *Grammar Review* section. The section starts with a page containing a list of common irregular verbs.

The *Grammar Review* pages review language that was taught in the previous level of ***Speak Your Mind***. You can use the *Grammar Review* when students begin their level to test what they have retained from previous classes.

Grammar Reference

Following the *Grammar Review* are the *Grammar Reference* pages. They provide an expanded explanation of the function of the grammar points. The form of the grammar is shown in a table. Practice activities follow the explanation. Note that the *Reference* section is in the **Student's Book** only, but the *Answer Key* for the practice activities in this section is at the back of this **Teacher's Edition**. Grammar points are labeled clearly with a heading.

The *Grammar Reference* pages can be used in several ways:

- **Further practice.** When a new grammar point is introduced in a unit, you may want to refer students to the relevant section in the *Grammar Reference* and go over the explanations of form and function with them, pointing out the examples in the table(s). You could do this before or after doing the grammar presentation in the unit.
- **Homework.** You may want to do the grammar practice activity in the unit in class and assign the activities in the *Grammar Reference* section for homework, along with or instead of the activities in the **Workbook**.
- **Review.** The *Grammar Reference* activities can be used for review before an exam.

Grammar Reference

UNIT 1 — past progressive

Function

We use the past progressive to talk about an action that began in the past and continued for some time.

Form

Affirmative		Negative	
I was	watching TV.	I wasn't	watching TV.
You were	studying English.	You weren't	studying English.
He was She was It was	playing video games. learning the guitar. raining.	He wasn't She wasn't It wasn't	playing video games. learning the guitar. raining.
We were	listening to music.	We weren't	listening to music.
They were	dancing together.	They weren't	dancing together.

Yes/No questions		Affirmative short answer	Negative short answer
Was I	sleeping?	Yes, I was.	No, I wasn't.
Were you	listening?	Yes, you were.	No, you weren't.
Was he Was she Was it	cooking? singing? snowing?	Yes, he was. Yes, she was. Yes, it was.	No, he wasn't. No, she wasn't. No, it wasn't.
Were we	working?	Yes, we were.	No, we weren't.
Were they	running?	Yes, they were.	No, they weren't.

UNIT 1 — past progressive vs. simple past

Function

We use the past progressive to describe an action in progress, and the simple past to introduce an interrupting action.

Form

Action in progress	Interrupting action
I was eating a sandwich	when my phone rang.
We were running a marathon	when it started raining.
She was out shopping	when she met a friend.
Were you watching TV	when you heard the news?

Interrupting action	Action in progress
The fire broke out	while they were sleeping.
The accident happened	while my brother was driving.
When I woke up,	it was raining.
Where were you	while this was happening?

A Read the conversation and choose the correct option.

Marta: What **1 were / was** you doing last night? Did you see the match on TV?
Sam: No, I didn't. I **2 was reading / read** a book. It was so good I forgot about the match!
Marta: What was the book about?
Sam: It's a biography about an artist in New York. When he was a child, he was always drawing and **3 painted / painting**. Then one day, when he was playing in the street, a car **4 hit / was hitting** him. He was badly hurt. While he was in the hospital, a nurse **5 gave / was giving** him a book about art. This book made him want to become an artist. Then years later, he **6 was drawing / drew** in the park when he **7 was seeing / saw** the nurse who gave him the book. While they **8 talked / were talking**, he drew her a picture to say thank you.
Marta: Wow! I bet that picture's worth millions of dollars now!

B Complete the sentences with the present progressive or the past tense form of the words in parentheses.

1 Anna ____________ (watch) the sunset when she decided to start her own business. The first thing she needed was some money.
2 When she ____________ (call) her bank, the bank manager was speaking to another customer.
3 Anna ____________ (write) her business plan when the bank manager returned her call.
4 While they ____________ (discuss) Anna's idea, her friend Greta came into the room.
5 Greta ____________ (ask) who Anna was talking to.
6 Anna was explaining her business plan to her friend when she ____________ (get) an email from the bank manager saying the bank could lend her the money.

UNIT 2 — quantifiers: *some, any, too much/many, a lot of, a little, a few*

Function

We use quantifiers to talk about amounts. Some quantifiers go with countable nouns, some go with uncountable nouns, and some go with both.

Form

Countable	Uncountable	Both
a few too many	a little too much	some any a lot of

A Identify the mistakes and rewrite the sentences correctly.

1 There's only a few milk in the refrigerator.
____
2 I think there's too many salt in this meal.
____
3 You need a lot tomatoes to make tomato soup.
____
4 Can you please buy me a little apples when you're at the store?
____
5 Don't eat too many candy! It's not good for you.
____
6 Can I have some grape, please?
____

The following features are accessible via the ***Speak Your Mind*** Resource Centers.

Student's Resource Center

- **Reading Worksheets**
- **Student's Book** and **Workbook** audio files
- **Student's Book** videos
- **Word Lists**

Teacher's Resource Center

- **Reading Worksheets**
- ***OneStopEnglish*** **Worksheets**
- **Student's Book** and **Workbook** audio files
- **Student's Book** videos
- **Printable Ready-to-Go Tests**
- **CEFR Correlations**
- **Word Lists**

Reading Worksheets

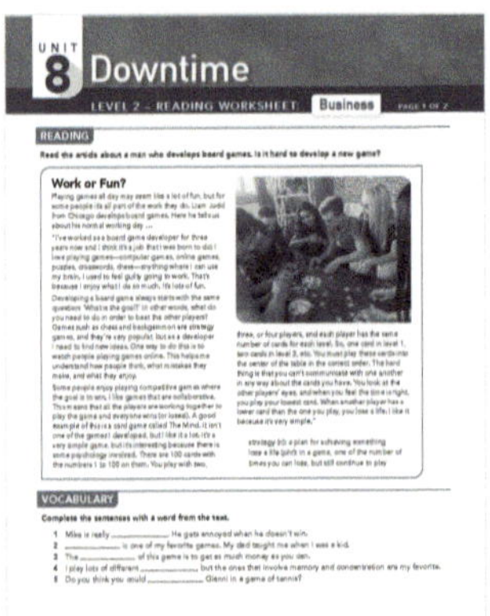
UNIT 8 Downtime

LEVEL 2 – READING WORKSHEET Business

READING

Work or Fun?

VOCABULARY

Each unit of ***Speak Your Mind*** has three extensive **Reading Worksheets**, for a total of 36. The topics of the worksheets extend the themes and vocabulary sets of the units in the areas of General English, Business, Science, and Services. They are designed to appeal to students who are studying academic subjects and young adults who are already working in their careers.

The **Reading Worksheets** have a text with a VOCABULARY activity and COMPREHENSION questions. A THINKING question at the end of the worksheet can be used as a departure for discussion in the classroom or a writing assignment for homework.

OneStopEnglish Worksheets

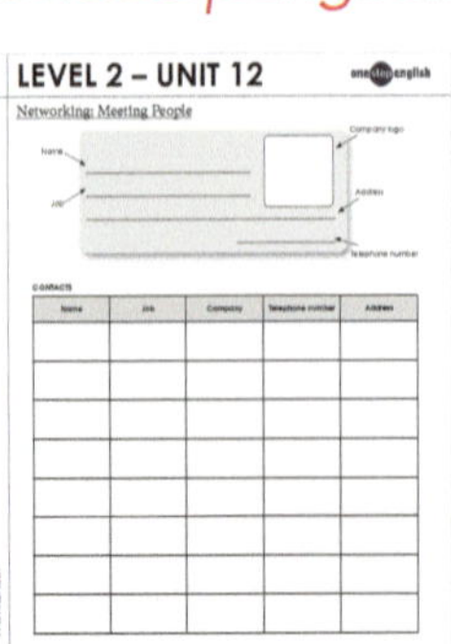
LEVEL 2 – UNIT 12

The ***OneStopEnglish*** **Worksheets** give students further speaking practice in a fun and engaging way. Speak Your Mind has chosen select worksheets from the OneStopEnglish website, the world's number one teacher resource site for English Language teachers. The ***OneStopEnglish*** **Worksheets** have been adapted for the course, with one worksheet for each unit. The worksheets consist of one page of teacher's notes, which includes the aim, procedure, and estimated activity time, and one page with the student's activity.

Printable Ready-to-Go Tests

All the tests for ***Speak Your Mind*** can be found in the **Teacher's Resource Center**. This includes a Placement Test, Unit Tests, a Mid-Course Test, and an End-of-Course Test. All tests are available as ready-to-print PDFs. Tests can be customized using the **Test Generator** (see the **How to Use the Digital Components** section, page xxvii).

- The Placement Test places students in a ***Speak Your Mind*** level.
- The Unit Tests include vocabulary, grammar, listening, reading, writing, and speaking items for each unit.
- The Mid-Course Test include vocabulary, grammar, listening, reading, writing, and speaking items for units 1–6.
- The End-of-Course Test includes vocabulary, grammar, listening, reading, writing, and speaking items for units 7–12.

CEFR Correlations

The Common European Framework of Reference for Languages (CEFR) is an international standard that aims to provide a transparent, coherent, and comprehensive means of describing language ability. It describes what language learners can do in different skills across six broad levels, from A1 to C2, and consists of a set of scales containing descriptors indicating what a learner can do in that context. The **CEFR Correlations** document is a map is organized unit by unit, which allows you to browse the course learning outcomes chronologically. These are mapped to the relevant CEFR descriptors, levels, and scales.

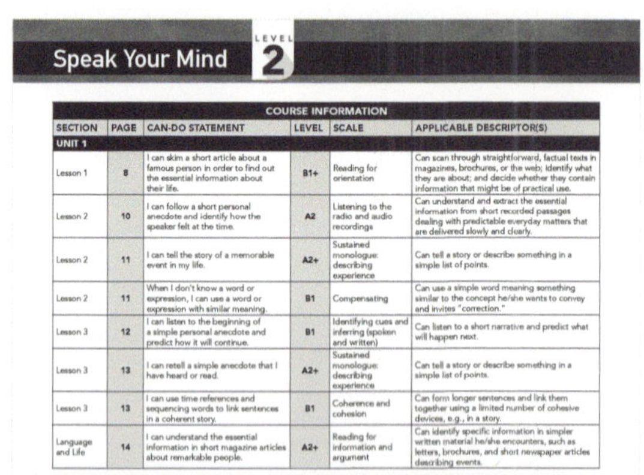
Speak Your Mind LEVEL 2

COURSE INFORMATION					
SECTION	PAGE	CAN-DO STATEMENT	LEVEL	SCALE	APPLICABLE DESCRIPTOR(S)
UNIT 1					
Lesson 1	8	I can skim a short article about a famous person in order to find out the essential information about their life.	B1+	Reading for orientation	Can scan through straightforward, factual texts in magazines, brochures, or the web; identify what they are about; and decide whether they contain information that might be of practical use.
Lesson 2	10	I can follow a short personal anecdote and identify how the speaker felt at the time.	A2	Listening to the radio and audio recordings	Can understand and extract the essential information from short recorded passages dealing with predictable everyday matters that are delivered slowly and clearly.
Lesson 2	11	I can tell the story of a memorable event in my life.	A2+	Sustained monologue: describing experience	Can tell a story or describe something in a simple list of points.
Lesson 2	11	When I don't know a word or expression, I can use a word or expression with similar meaning.	B1	Compensating	Can use a simple word meaning something similar to the concept he/she wants to convey and invites "correction."
Lesson 3	12	I can listen to the beginning of a simple personal anecdote and predict how it will continue.	B1	Identifying cues and inferring (spoken and written)	Can listen to a short narrative and predict what will happen next.
Lesson 3	13	I can retell a simple anecdote that I have heard or read.	A2+	Sustained monologue: describing experience	Can tell a story or describe something in a simple list of points.
Lesson 3	13	I can use time references and sequencing words to link sentences in a coherent story.	B1	Coherence and cohesion	Can form longer sentences and link them together using a limited number of cohesive devices, e.g., in a story.
Language and Life	14	I can understand the essential information in short magazine articles about remarkable people.	A2+	Reading for information and argument	Can identify specific information in simpler written material he/she encounters, such as letters, brochures, and short newspaper articles describing events.

1

Word Lists

The **Word Lists** are a list of the main vocabulary that appears in ***Speak Your Mind***. These include words that appear in the **Student's Book** and **Student's App** VOCABULARY sections, as well as the glossaries of the **Student's Book** READING sections. The word lists include the word, part of speech, IPA pronunciation, definition, and frequency, as well as an example sentence using the word.

How to Use the Teacher's Edition

The up-to-date, innovative approach to the ***Speak Your Mind*** **Teacher's Edition** takes into account that teachers have very busy lives and want the class-planning process to be as streamlined as possible. The introductory pages of the **Teacher's Edition** are designed to provide general explanations and instructions that are needed to teach each section of the unit and use the special features.

The introductory pages also include information on how to use the special features, the **Workbook**, the *Videos*, and the digital material included in the ***Speak Your Mind*** series. The *Answer Keys* for the **Workbook** activities and the **Student's Book** *Grammar Reference* activities are at the back of this book, as are the *Audio Scripts* for the listening activities in the **Student's Book** and **Workbook**.

The core pages of the **Teacher's Edition** include:

① ***GO TO***. Teachers can read the introductory information once for guidelines on how to teach these sections throughout the book. *GO TO* pointers help teachers find the procedure pages they need quickly.

② **Answer Key.** The core pages have the detailed information a teacher needs to teach specific activities. The **Teacher's Edition** has reduced **Student's Book** pages with answers in place or in the margin next to the Student's Book pages.

③ **Specific notes.** Notes below the **Student's Book** reduced page include relevant background information for texts, tips for dealing with specific language issues, common errors to watch out for, cultural information, classroom management ideas, and suggestions for extra or alternative activities.

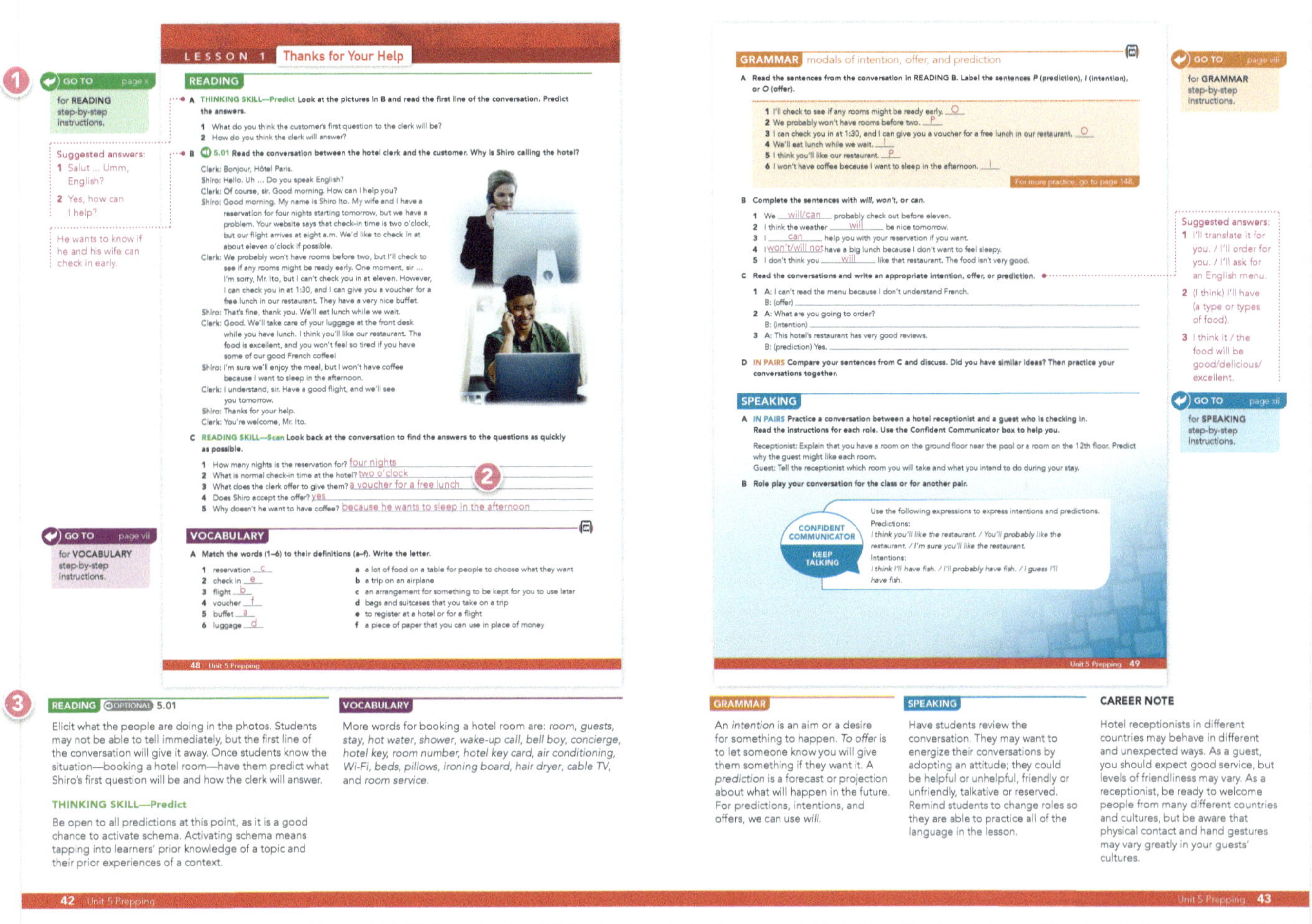

LESSON 1 Thanks for Your Help

① GO TO page x — for READING step-by-step instructions.

READING

A THINKING SKILL—Predict Look at the pictures in B and read the first line of the conversation. Predict the answers.

1 What do you think the customer's first question to the clerk will be?
2 How do you think the clerk will answer?

Suggested answers:
1 Salut ... Umm, English?
2 Yes, how can I help?

B 5.01 Read the conversation between the hotel clerk and the customer. Why is Shiro calling the hotel?

He wants to know if he and his wife can check in early.

Clerk: Bonjour, Hôtel Paris.
Shiro: Hello. Uh ... Do you speak English?
Clerk: Of course, sir. Good morning. How can I help you?
Shiro: Good morning. My name is Shiro Ito. My wife and I have a reservation for four nights starting tomorrow, but we have a problem. Your website says that check-in time is two o'clock, but our flight arrives at eight a.m. We'd like to check in at about eleven o'clock if possible.
Clerk: We probably won't have rooms before two, but I'll check to see if any rooms might be ready early. One moment, sir ... I'm sorry, Mr. Ito, but I can't check you in at eleven. However, I can check you in at 1:30, and I can give you a voucher for a free lunch in our restaurant. They have a very nice buffet.
Shiro: That's fine, thank you. We'll eat lunch while we wait.
Clerk: Good. We'll take care of your luggage at the front desk while you have lunch. I think you'll like our restaurant. The food is excellent, and you won't feel so tired if you have some of our good French coffee!
Shiro: I'm sure we'll enjoy the meal, but I won't have coffee because I want to sleep in the afternoon.
Clerk: I understand, sir. Have a good flight, and we'll see you tomorrow.
Shiro: Thanks for your help.
Clerk: You're welcome, Mr. Ito.

C READING SKILL—Scan Look back at the conversation to find the answers to the questions as quickly as possible.

1 How many nights is the reservation for? four nights
2 What is normal check-in time at the hotel? two o'clock
3 What does the clerk offer to give them? a voucher for a free lunch ②
4 Does Shiro accept the offer? yes
5 Why doesn't he want to have coffee? because he wants to sleep in the afternoon

GO TO page vii — for VOCABULARY step-by-step instructions.

VOCABULARY

A Match the words (1–6) to their definitions (a–f). Write the letter.

1 reservation c
2 check in e
3 flight b
4 voucher f
5 buffet a
6 luggage d

a a lot of food on a table for people to choose what they want
b a trip on an airplane
c an arrangement for something to be kept for you to use later
d bags and suitcases that you take on a trip
e to register at a hotel or for a flight
f a piece of paper that you can use in place of money

48 Unit 5 Prepping

GRAMMAR modals of intention, offer, and prediction

GO TO page viii — for GRAMMAR step-by-step instructions.

A Read the sentences from the conversation in READING B. Label the sentences *P* (prediction), *I* (intention), or *O* (offer).

1 I'll check to see if any rooms might be ready early. O
2 We probably won't have rooms before two. P
3 I can check you in at 1:30, and I can give you a voucher for a free lunch in our restaurant. O
4 We'll eat lunch while we wait. I
5 I think you'll like our restaurant. P
6 I won't have coffee because I want to sleep in the afternoon. I

For more practice, go to page 148.

B Complete the sentences with *will*, *won't*, or *can*.

1 We will/can probably check out before eleven.
2 I think the weather will be nice tomorrow.
3 I can help you with your reservation if you want.
4 I won't/will not have a big lunch because I don't want to feel sleepy.
5 I don't think you will like that restaurant. The food isn't very good.

C Read the conversations and write an appropriate intention, offer, or prediction.

1 A: I can't read the menu because I don't understand French.
B: (offer)
2 A: What are you going to order?
B: (intention)
3 A: This hotel's restaurant has very good reviews.
B: (prediction) Yes.

Suggested answers:
1 I'll translate it for you. / I'll order for you. / I'll ask for an English menu.
2 (I think) I'll have (a type or types of food).
3 I think it / the food will be good/delicious/excellent.

D IN PAIRS Compare your sentences from C and discuss. Did you have similar ideas? Then practice your conversations together.

GO TO page xii — for SPEAKING step-by-step instructions.

SPEAKING

A IN PAIRS Practice a conversation between a hotel receptionist and a guest who is checking in. Read the instructions for each role. Use the Confident Communicator box to help you.

Receptionist: Explain that you have a room on the ground floor near the pool or a room on the 12th floor. Predict why the guest might like each room.
Guest: Tell the receptionist which room you will take and what you intend to do during your stay.

B Role play your conversation for the class or for another pair.

CONFIDENT COMMUNICATOR — KEEP TALKING
Use the following expressions to express intentions and predictions.
Predictions:
I think you'll like the restaurant. / You'll probably like the restaurant. / I'm sure you'll like the restaurant.
Intentions:
I think I'll have fish. / I'll probably have fish. / I guess I'll have fish.

Unit 5 Prepping 49

③ READING OPTIONAL 5.01

Elicit what the people are doing in the photos. Students may not be able to tell immediately, but the first line of the conversation will give it away. Once students know the situation—booking a hotel room—have them predict what Shiro's first question will be and how the clerk will answer.

THINKING SKILL—Predict

Be open to all predictions at this point, as it is a good chance to activate schema. Activating schema means tapping into learners' prior knowledge of a topic and their prior experiences of a context.

VOCABULARY

More words for booking a hotel room are: *room, guests, stay, hot water, shower, wake-up call, bell boy, concierge, hotel key, room number, hotel key card, air conditioning, Wi-Fi, beds, pillows, ironing board, hair dryer, cable TV,* and *room service.*

GRAMMAR

An *intention* is an aim or a desire for something to happen. *To offer* is to let someone know you will give them something if they want it. A *prediction* is a forecast or projection about what will happen in the future. For predictions, intentions, and offers, we can use *will*.

SPEAKING

Have students review the conversation. They may want to energize their conversations by adopting an attitude; they could be helpful or unhelpful, friendly or unfriendly, talkative or reserved. Remind students to change roles so they are able to practice all of the language in the lesson.

CAREER NOTE

Hotel receptionists in different countries may behave in different and unexpected ways. As a guest, you should expect good service, but levels of friendliness may vary. As a receptionist, be ready to welcome people from many different countries and cultures, but be aware that physical contact and hand gestures may vary greatly in your guests' cultures.

42 Unit 5 Prepping — Unit 5 Prepping 43

How to Use the Workbook

The ***Speak Your Mind* Workbook** is designed to give students further practice in grammar and vocabulary, as well as the listening, reading, and writing skills taught in the **Student's Book**. The **Workbook** is available in both print and digital form. The **Digital Workbook** can be accessed through the **Student's App**. At the end of the **Workbook**, there are five pages of activities designed to familiarize students with the most common exam formats (Cambridge suite, TOEFL, and IELTS).

The **Workbook** activities can be used in several ways:

- As homework or further classroom practice after teaching a section in the **Student's Book**.
- As a review of a whole lesson after finishing the lesson.
- As a review session before a unit exam.

① **Reading and listening skills expansion.** Skills boxes give explanations of the reading and listening skills taught in the **Student's Book**. You may want to refer students to the explanation in the **Workbook** before asking them to do the skill activity in the **Student's Book**. Following each skill box, there is an activity to practice the skill.

② **Vocabulary practice.** There is additional practice of the target vocabulary of the lesson.

③ **Grammar practice.** The grammar of the lesson is practiced in a variety of ways.

④ **Writing skills.** In the WRITING section, there is practice in the mechanics of writing.

⑤ **Progress check.** Students check the areas they feel competent in. If they feel that they need to review a particular point, they are directed to the relevant section in the **Student's Book**.

Teacher's App

The ***Speak Your Mind* Teacher's Edition** comes with an innovative **Teacher's App**, which gives access to the **Classroom Presentation Kit**, **Homework Manager**, **Progress Tracker**, **Test Generator**, and **Teacher's Resource Center**.

Classroom Presentation Kit

The **Classroom Presentation Kit** is a page-faithful view of the **Student's Book** and **Workbook**. It is designed to be displayed on an interactive whiteboard (IWB) or using a projector. It is user-friendly for teachers and students, with activities clearly visible for the whole class.

The **Classroom Presentation Kit** allows teachers to play the audio tracks, show the course videos, and present the interactive versions of the book activities from the page. Teachers can zoom in on each activity with one click, then move smoothly through the activities or zoom out to see the whole page. Answer reveal enables teachers to elicit students' responses and check answers one by one or all together.

Embedded tools make it possible to highlight and annotate texts to prompt noticing or self-correction. Teachers also have the option to show scripts when listening to audio or watching video for easy clarification. There is also the option to create a whiteboard area for additional notes.

Homework Manager

Using the practice activities available in the **Student's App**, teachers can assign homework by selecting and publishing content directly to their students' devices. Students will then be alerted by a push notification telling them they have activities to complete. This enables teachers to personalize the amount and kind of practice students have each week and to track their progress using the **Progress Tracker**.

Progress Tracker

The **Progress Tracker** gives teachers an overview of students' progress, allowing teachers to monitor scores and see at a glance that students are performing well or that they may need additional support. Student data is presented in a way that is clear and easy to understand.

Test Generator

Ready-to-Go print tests are available in the **Teacher's Resource Center** for teachers who want to give a test on every skill. If you prefer to customize tests for your students, you can do so through the **Test Generator** in the **Teacher's App**. The **Test Generator** allows you to create tests by selecting only the activities you want from a menu. You can save and print out the tests from the **Test Generator**. You may also use a randomized function to create different tests for the same unit.

Student's App

Each **Student's Book** includes a code for the **Student's App**, which gives access to new **On-the-Go Practice** activities, **Progress Tracker**, **eBook**, **Digital Workbook**, and the **Student's Resource Center**.

On-the-Go Practice

Through the **Student's App**, students will have access to new grammar, vocabulary, and pronunciation activities that have been mapped to the course scope and sequence. These bite-sized activities have been specifically designed for use on smartphones. They include game-like elements to encourage repetition and deeper retention of key language. Questions are shown in random order to increase interest and ensure a thorough understanding of each language point. Students are able to complete activities in a standard practice mode or in a more difficult challenge mode, where they can earn medals based on their performance.

Each **Student's App** unit also contains a new speaking activity that recycles the Unit Opener video, providing an opportunity to review the Unit Opener topic and the language encountered throughout the unit. These activities have been designed to increase students' confidence as they see how their language competence has developed over the course of each unit, while reinforcing what they have learned.

Progress Tracker

The **Student's App** gives a clear overview of students' progress, clearly highlighting areas of strength and areas for improvement. Students have the opportunity to review their weakest activities and repeat them to improve their scores.

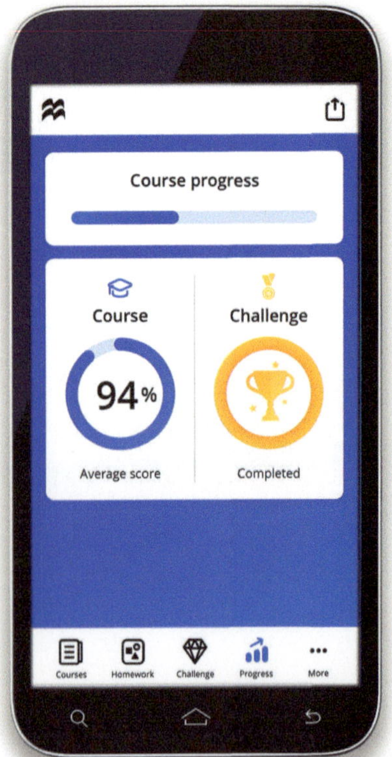

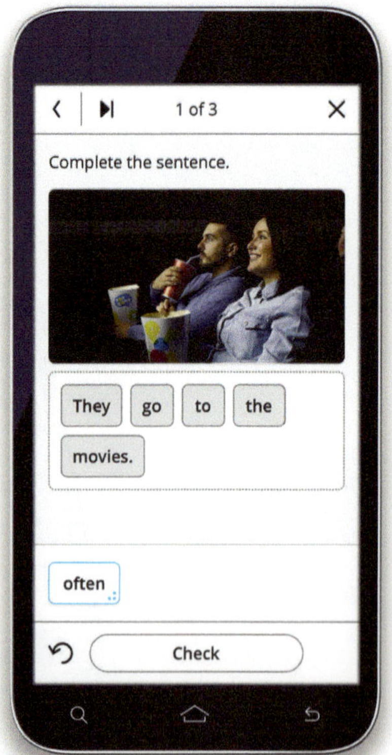

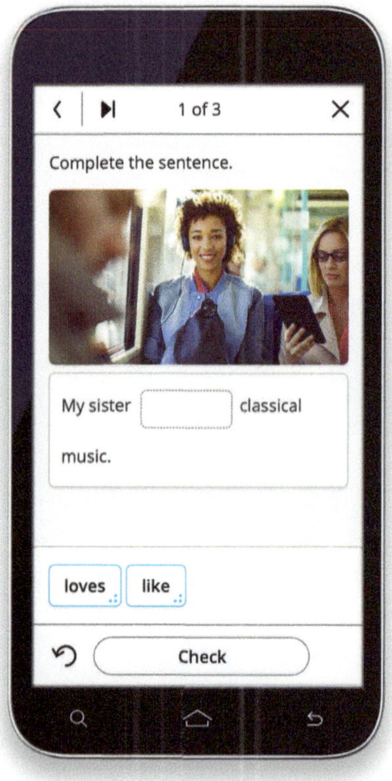

eBook

The **eBook** is a digital version of the **Student's Book** with embedded audio and video files, so students can access the book and its media on their desktop, in their classroom, or at home.

Digital Workbook

The **Digital Workbook** is a new, digital version of the students' **Workbook** designed to be accessible on students' devices. The **Digital Workbook** contains digital versions of the **Workbook** activities designed to work across mobile, tablet, and desktop to provide a rich interactive experience. The **Workbook** audio and video files can be accessed from the page so students have everything they need in one place. Built-in answer keys give instant feedback, while students' scores feed to the **Progress Tracker** for easy monitoring.

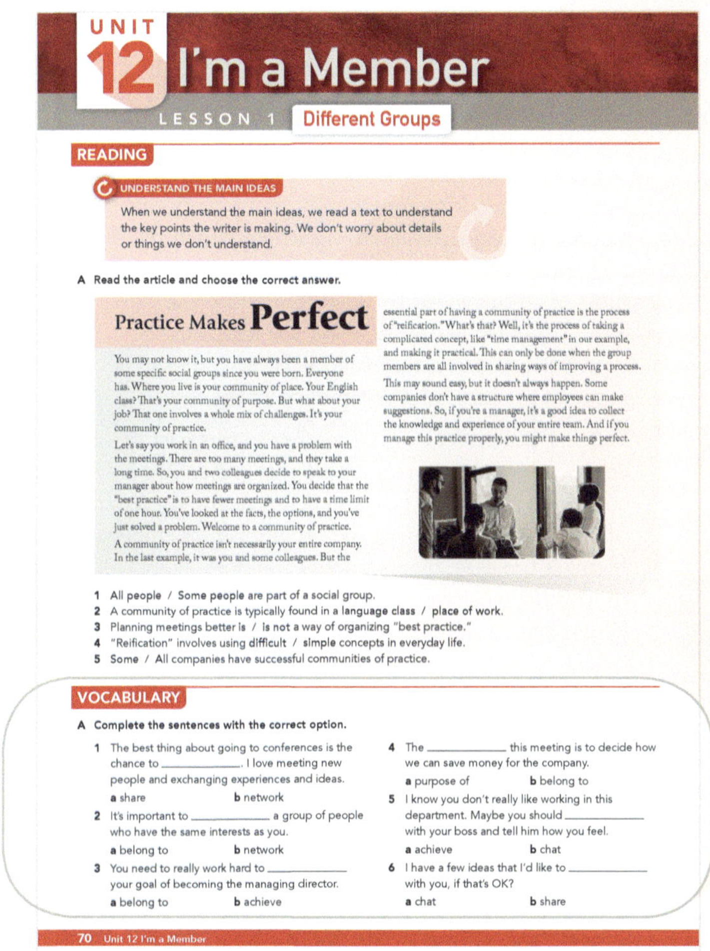

UNIT 12 I'm a Member

LESSON 1 Different Groups

READING

UNDERSTAND THE MAIN IDEAS

When we understand the main ideas, we read a text to understand the key points the writer is making. We don't worry about details or things we don't understand.

A Read the article and choose the correct answer.

Practice Makes Perfect

You may not know it, but you have always been a member of some specific social groups since you were born. Everyone has. Where you live is your community of place. Your English class? That's your community of purpose. But what about your job? That one involves a whole mix of challenges. It's your community of practice.

Let's say you work in an office, and you have a problem with the meetings. There are too many meetings, and they take a long time. So, you and two colleagues decide to speak to your manager about how meetings are organized. You decide that the "best practice" is to have fewer meetings and to have a time limit of one hour. You've looked at the facts, the options, and you've just solved a problem. Welcome to a community of practice.

A community of practice isn't necessarily your entire company. In the last example, it was you and some colleagues. But the essential part of having a community of practice is the process of "reification." What's that? Well, it's the process of taking a complicated concept, like "time management" in our example, and making it practical. This can only be done when the group members are all involved in sharing ways of improving a process.

This may sound easy, but it doesn't always happen. Some companies don't have a structure where employees can make suggestions. So, if you're a manager, it's a good idea to collect the knowledge and experience of your entire team. And if you manage this practice properly, you might make things perfect.

1 **All people** / **Some people** are part of a social group.
2 A community of practice is typically found in a **language class** / **place of work**.
3 Planning meetings better **is** / **is not** a way of organizing "best practice."
4 "Reification" involves using **difficult** / **simple** concepts in everyday life.
5 **Some** / **All** companies have successful communities of practice.

VOCABULARY

A Complete the sentences with the correct option.

1 The best thing about going to conferences is the chance to ___________. I love meeting new people and exchanging experiences and ideas.
a share **b** network
2 It's important to ___________ a group of people who have the same interests as you.
a belong to **b** network
3 You need to really work hard to ___________ your goal of becoming the managing director.
a belong to **b** achieve
4 The ___________ this meeting is to decide how we can save money for the company.
a purpose of **b** belong to
5 I know you don't really like working in this department. Maybe you should ___________ with your boss and tell him how you feel.
a achieve **b** chat
6 I have a few ideas that I'd like to ___________ with you, if that's OK?
a chat **b** share

70 Unit 12 I'm a Member

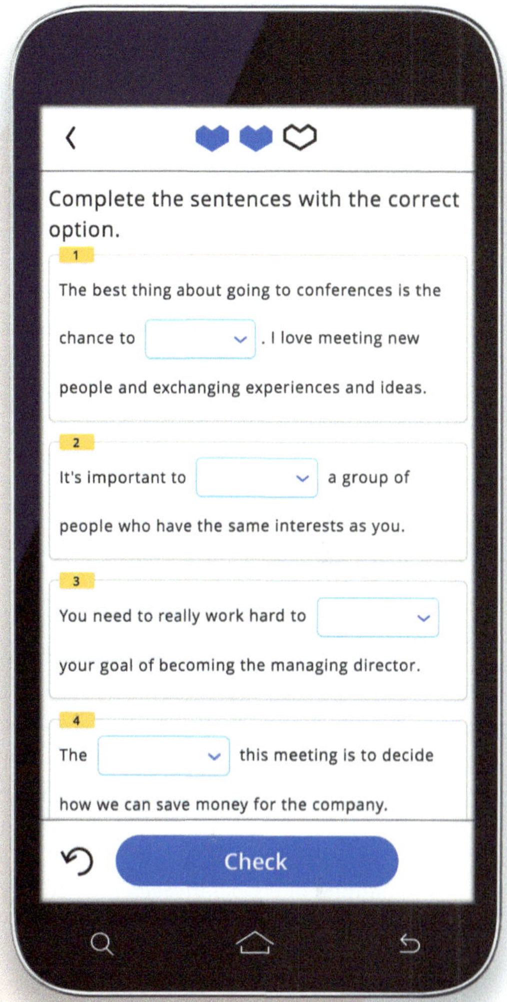

Cooperative Learning

Dr. Jason Skeet

Programme Leader for the MA in Professional Development for Language Education, Norwich Institute for Language Education (NILE), University of Chichester

NILE

PART OF THE **INTO** GROUP

Many of the Unit Openers in ***Speak Your Mind*** use a simple but highly effective structure: students are asked to work on their own, taking a few minutes to think, and write down their answers or ideas. Then, they can talk to a partner to check their answers or combine their ideas. Finally, they share in a small group or with the whole class. This structure is an example of cooperative learning. This particular format is often referred to as *Think, Pair, Share*. The task structure helps students share and combine their ideas in a relaxed and fun way.

There is extensive research evidence about the advantages of using cooperative learning structures like *Think, Pair, Share*. This research has found that the impact of cooperative learning on student achievement is significantly higher than that of competitive, individualistic focused learning. In addition, the research shows there are benefits for students' interpersonal relationships and their psychological well-being.

This research evidence, therefore, confirms how important it is for teachers to understand what cooperative learning is (and what it is not), to have examples of cooperative learning structures or formats to use in their lessons, and to understand the benefits of cooperative learning for their students. Teachers need to know how cooperative learning can contribute to a classroom culture in which all students are able to succeed.

What Is Cooperative Learning?

A simple definition of cooperative learning is *learning that involves students working on a task that can only be completed when they work together.* However, this is just a starting point for understanding what cooperative learning involves. Some digging into this definition is needed to identify what constitutes effective cooperative learning.

Before doing so, it has to be emphasized that *cooperative learning* is not a fancy term for group work, even though it involves students working together in pairs or groups. Teachers can ask students to work together, but this does not automatically mean students are learning cooperatively. Students might be asked to collaborate with each other, but again, collaboration does not equal cooperation until certain conditions for how students are working together have been met.

For a task to be considered cooperative learning, it must foster five essential features of the learning process: *positive interdependence*, *individual accountability*, *group processing*, *small-group and interpersonal skills*, and *face-to-face interaction*. These components of cooperative learning are known by the acronym PIGS-F. Each part of this model provides a particular perspective on what is needed for cooperative learning to take place. Let's look at each element in turn.

Positive Interdependence

Positive interdependence means cooperative learning promotes peer support. For this to happen, a task needs to be set up so that it can only be completed by students working together. In group work that is not based on a cooperative learning structure, it is possible that one or two students could do most or all the work. To avoid this, and make sure all students really do cooperate, the task must be structured so that a contribution by each person is required for successful completion of the task.

Getting students to work together in this way encourages students to support each other. A cooperative learning task should allow the success of one student to benefit the other group members. If this is the case, then students are more likely to work for positive outcomes for each other. This helps create a supportive classroom culture, rather than a culture of competition in which students do not want their peers to do well. In a competitive setting, they may even secretly hope others do poorly so they look good by comparison.

Individual Accountability

Individual accountability means making sure every member of a group has to make a public contribution during the group work and students have to communicate with each other as part of the task. Without this communication between students, the task cannot be accomplished. Therefore, the peer communication has a purpose. Students are more likely to want to communicate with each other in lessons if they have a reason to communicate.

Without an individual public contribution as a required aspect of the learning, some students might prefer to play it safe and be invisible within the group, or without a reason to communicate, they might become disengaged from the task. Cooperative learning helps increase engagement in lessons by giving students a reason to communicate with each other and by making this peer communication a necessary part of the process of learning together.

Group Processing

Group processing means helping students recognize and develop the skills they need to work with each other. It is therefore important to include in lesson time opportunities for students to reflect on their cooperative learning, identifying their individual and group strengths, as well as goals for improving how well their group functions and the quality of their own contributions to the process of learning together.

Another aspect of group processing is to ensure that students have the time and structure to work together effectively, and this must include the equalization of the roles and status of all the members in the group. Each individual's contribution must be of equal importance.

Small Group and Interpersonal Skills

Developing the social and communication skills students need for working together is a key element of using cooperative learning structures in lessons. Teachers can explicitly teach and support students' conflict management, decision-making, and team building. One way to develop the skills students need for working together is to give students roles within the group and rotate these roles regularly so that all students have the opportunity to develop their skills. These roles can include participation checker, noise controller, scribe or recorder, questioner (to get others to explain and justify their ideas), organizer and time manager, materials manager, checker (to check for understanding and agreement), and envoy (to visit other groups to collect new ideas, if this is part of a particular cooperative learning task).

Face-to-Face Interaction

Cooperative learning aims to increase the engagement from all students within lessons. For this to happen, students must be communicating with each other face-to-face and working together simultaneously. This is what face-to-face interaction refers to: students' engagement in the lesson involves their interaction with each other and their individual actions as part of the task happening at the same time and in the same space.

This feature of cooperative learning explains why getting students to work together in groups does not necessarily result in cooperative learning: if group work is set up so it takes place at a distance or collaboration happens on the basis of different students making contributions to a task at different times, then this will not result in cooperative learning.

Examples of Cooperative Learning

There are many different cooperative learning structures and task formats. The following seven examples—in addition to the *Think, Pair, Share* structure outlined previously—are good ways to incorporate cooperative learning into the delivery of a ***Speak Your Mind*** unit, and an indication is given of how a structure might be used alongside the **Student's Book**.

Find Someone Who is a fun and effective way to activate prior knowledge or to consolidate learning. Create a list of questions related to a new unit or to review a unit that has been completed. Students then need to roam around the room talking to each other, trying to find someone who can provide an answer to a question, which they then write down. Requiring students to find a different person to answer each question helps enhance peer communication.

Use *Showdown* to turn grammar or vocabulary activities into cooperative learning tasks. Each student does an exercise on his or her own before receiving help. When "Showdown!" is called, students show teammates their work, and they begin the process of checking and coaching each other. In this cooperative learning format, students are encouraged to help and support each other. They have the common goal of obtaining the correct answers; they know the gain of one is also a gain for the other.

In *Numbered Heads Together*, students are placed in groups and each member has a number (from one to the maximum number in the group; however, keep in mind that groups should ideally never be larger than four). After the teacher asks a question, each student writes his or her best answer, and then students compare answers and put their heads together to improve them. Finally, the teacher calls a number and students with that number share their best answer with the class. This structure requires every student to make a contribution in every round (write their own answer and show it to their teammates), and in some rounds, students are called on to share with the whole class. Teacher questioning is more effective this way because student engagement is increased.

Team writing structures can be used for writing tasks. For example, students work together to complete *graphic organizers* (e.g., an atomistic mind map, T-chart, Venn diagram, or fishbone diagram) as the planning and preparation for their writing. The graphic organizer is a way to organize ideas and information generated and discussed by the group. Peer assessment can then help improve written work: ask students to trade their writing and to review their partner's work, giving each other feedback using success criteria such as "Use paragraphing to show the structure of your writing" or "Give evidence and examples for the points of view you express."

Provide a structure for any group work indicated in ***Speak Your Mind*** units by using a communication regulator to equalize participation and to ensure that the more articulate or confident students don't dominate group discussions. For example, in *Hot Seating*, students take turns in the "hot seat" for a given time (e.g., 30 seconds to 1 minute) and are interviewed by their fellow group members using the questions given in a group activity. This structure enables equal participation, so students who otherwise would not participate become actively engaged.

Pairs Rehearsal is a great way to prepare students for a test. Divide the students into pairs. Supply the students with the content they are to discuss: this could be a review sheet of important information or even specific pages from the **Student's Book**. Students take turns explaining a piece of information or answering a question, with the opportunity to ask each other questions for clarification. Each round of explaining is timed, and each time, the listener must think carefully and correct any error he or she hears.

Students can be asked to reflect on their cooperative learning at the end of lessons or at the end of a unit, identifying both their group strengths and goals for improving how well their group works together. This reflection can use the *Three Stars and a Wish* format: three things that were good (stars) and one area for improvement (wish). Teachers can develop the quality of feedback like this: the teacher collects the feedback (e.g., if feedback is written on sticky notes) and shares the feedback (anonymously) with the class. Students then vote on which comments are most useful and discuss why.

Benefits of Cooperative Learning for Teachers

Cooperative learning has significant benefits for teachers. Let's take a look at three areas in which teachers are likely to see a positive impact on their teaching: behavior management, their teaching role, and the use of formative assessment in lessons.

Helping with Behavior Management

One benefit of cooperative learning for teachers is how it can help with the management of student behavior in lessons. Students tend to become more engaged in lessons that use cooperative- learning structures and more motivated to learn when they have the opportunity to learn together. This means that teachers are able to spend less time getting students back on task and more time moving around the classroom, observing and monitoring the learning, and providing individualized feedback when it is needed. Teachers' stress levels are lowered, since responsibility for staying on task becomes the students' responsibility as part of their cooperative learning.

However, some teachers may experience a feeling of apprehension or worry about a loss of control when they start using cooperative learning structures, so it is important to discuss and establish with students ground rules for how to get the teacher's attention when the classroom is noisy and for acceptable levels of noise when students are working together, to make students aware of the communication and social skills they need for working together effectively.

A Change in Role

A teacher's role in the classroom changes in a cooperative learning classroom. Instead of the "chalk and talk" approach of the traditional classroom, with the teacher leading the learning from the front of the room, in a cooperative learning environment, a teacher has the opportunity to move around, monitoring, observing, and intervening when appropriate. It helps to consider the classroom layout with this in mind: for example, by using a café-style seating arrangement, with tables placed together for four students, no student has to turn his or her head more than 90 degrees to see the front of the classroom.

In a cooperative learning classroom, teachers are able to build personal relationships with the students because this approach allows for opportunities to talk to individual students, giving them personalized feedback on their learning. This change in the teacher's role can be exciting; exploring the use of cooperative learning structures may even refresh and strengthen a teacher's enthusiasm and passion for teaching.

Supporting Formative Assessment

The increase in student engagement that cooperative learning brings leads to another benefit for teachers: cooperative learning provides opportunities for them to undertake formative assessment within the flow of a lesson. Formative assessment within the lesson involves ensuring the students know where they are going with their learning (e.g., by setting clear learning objectives or providing exemplars of work to show what the students are aiming to achieve), making a judgment about where each student is in their learning and the progress they are making (e.g., by using starter activities to activate prior knowledge and using reflection activities at the end of a lesson to check on and consolidate the learning), and providing individualized feedback about a student's next step in their learning, including a "medal" that recognizes what the student has done well and a "mission" in the form of goal they are to work on next.

Cooperative learning can help build classroom practice in which formative assessment is the bridge between the teaching and the learning. By monitoring and observing students as they work on a cooperative learning task together, teachers can see and hear the progress with the learning. A teacher then has opportunities in the flow of the lesson to provide medals and missions feedback, to groups and to individuals. Cooperative learning also helps with involving students in the process of formative assessment through dialogue with the teacher, through discussions with each other so that they are able to share and combine their ideas, and through self-assessment and peer-assessment activities that can be built into the structure of a cooperative learning task. Getting students involved in helping each other with their learning through cooperative learning tasks is an important way to involve students in making judgments about their progress and identifying the next steps in their learning.

Benefits of Cooperative Learning for Students

There are many potential benefits for students learning cooperatively, and it is worth examining these benefits in detail to consider how they can be of relevance to students using ***Speak Your Mind***. Let's look at four areas of learning in which benefits can be expected: language development, critical thinking, and the impact on students' soft skills and self-esteem.

Language Development

Cooperative learning encourages students' spoken language production through an emphasis on peer communication. For students to learn a language, they need opportunities to use the language in meaningful and motivating situations. Cooperative learning structures are an excellent way to create such opportunities.

In language lessons, students need to develop both the "language of learning" and the "language for learning": the former consists of the vocabulary or grammar structures that are focused on in a lesson, while the latter consists of the language needed to engage in group work and discussion. Cooperative learning is a good way to ensure students develop both these aspects of their language learning.

Higher-Order Thinking

Cooperative learning helps students develop their higher-level thinking skills. In a cooperative learning structure, students need to communicate with their peers to explain and justify their ideas, to verbalize their reasoning behind a choice they have made, or, through sharing and combining ideas, to generate new ideas and solutions. All this involves higher-order thinking. The process of working cooperatively with others—and through this cooperation, having to explain and justify one's thinking—results in deeper learning for students.

Soft Skills

Interpersonal and small-group skills, so-called soft skills, are developed with cooperative learning; these include skills such as active listening, expressing ideas clearly, giving and receiving feedback, and noticing and responding to feelings. Teachers therefore need to plan ways to make students aware of these skills and to help them develop the elements of a skill, enabling a student to build up their competence in stages.

Cooperative learning provides opportunities for this development by getting students to practice the skills in small groups, enabling personalized feedback from each other or the teacher, then asking students to reflect on their learning with goal setting that identifies specific actions for improving a specific soft skill. It is also a good idea to regularly "stir up" the class by changing the seating arrangement; getting students to work with new teammates varies group dynamics and helps build their interpersonal skills.

Self-Esteem

Cooperative learning can also have a positive impact on students' self-esteem. The opportunity to work with others enables all students to experience success. The inclusion of reflecting on their learning as part of a cooperative learning process also helps students recognize the thoughts that may stop them from succeeding. Using cooperative learning in lessons can build a classroom culture in which students understand how negative thoughts are barriers to success, and find ways of thinking that enable them to achieve. A key element to fostering positive attitudes toward learning is giving students a sense of ownership over their learning, and cooperative learning encourages this ownership.

Research on how students feel about learning has shown the difference between "fixed" and "growth" mindsets (where *mindset* here refers to attitude, effort, and approach). With a *fixed mindset*, intelligence is perceived as static: either you are smart or you are not, and education cannot change this. With this mindset, challenge and risk-taking is avoided because of the fear of failure. A *growth mindset*, however, views intelligence as something that is not fixed. When students have this mindset, they are not afraid of a challenge. They welcome feedback on their progress, and they react to failure positively and are more likely to try harder. Cooperative learning can be an important way to promote and support a growth mindset in all students.

Student's Book Scope and Sequence

	Outcomes	Vocabulary	Grammar	Speaking
Unit 1 Extraordinary pp. 7–15	• Discuss role models • Talk about a memorable event • Write and talk about an anecdote	• Role models • Reactions • Family situations	• Past progressive • Past progressive vs. simple past Grammar Reference pp. 142–143	• Discuss events in a timeline • Describe personal events • Share anecdotes
	Language and Life—Communication: Present a Citizen Award			
Unit 2 Party! pp. 17–25	• Talk about an idea for a holiday • Talk about money and spending habits • Write about a celebration	• Unique holidays • Money and shopping • Food and drink packaging	• Quantifiers • *enough / not enough* Grammar Reference pp. 143–144	• Talk about new holidays • Discuss opinions about celebrations • Share ideas about special foods
	Language and Life—Creativity: Create a Graduation Ceremony			
Unit 3 What's Trending? pp. 27–35	• Talk about street entertainers in your area • Discuss activities of the past • Write and talk about viewing habits	• Street entertainers • The music industry • TV viewing	• Indefinite pronouns • *used to* Grammar Reference pp. 145–146	• Discuss street entertainers • Compare generations • Talk about TV viewing habits
	Language and Life—Decision-making: Design an Event to Save a Theater			
Unit 4 Your ID pp. 37–45	• Talk about personality types • Describe people with superlatives • Talk about who you are like	• Personality types • Different personalities • Characteristics	• *(not) as … as* • Superlative adjectives Grammar Reference pp. 146–147	• Describe a person's personality • Talk about your personality • Compare family members
	Language and Life—Interpersonal Communication: Understand and Interact with Different Personalities			
Unit 5 Prepping pp. 47–55	• Make predictions and express intentions • Make requests and ask permission • Talk about a social event	• Checking in • Making suggestions • Wedding customs	• Modals of intention, offer, and prediction • Modals of request and permission Grammar Reference pp. 148–149	• Role-play a conversation • Describe plans for a class party • Talk about a social event
	Language and Life—Global Competence: Understand and Appreciate Social Customs			
Unit 6 Changes pp. 57–65	• Talk about risk and change • Discuss life experiences • Discuss positive and negative effects of changes	• Status quo • Life experiences • Changing cities	• Present perfect with *for* and *since* • Present perfect with *ever* and *never* Grammar Reference pp. 149–150	• Discuss changes in your life • Talk about life experiences • Debate changes in your town
	Language and Life—Collaboration: List Recommendations for Visitors Discovering Your Town			

Confident Communicator	Pronunciation	Listening/Reading	Thinking Skills	Writing
Start Talking • Language for speculation *Repair It* • Replacement words *Start Talking* • Sequencing words	• Vowel + consonant + *e*	Read a biography • Skill—Skim a text Listen to people recall memorable events • Skill—Listen for specific information Listen to a story about look-alikes • Skill—Predict the story	• Evaluate • Analyze • Understand	Write an anecdote
Unit Review p. 16 **Study Skills** p. 127—Using Personal Experience				
Keep Talking • Give reasons *Start Talking* • Give opinions *Keep Talking* • Ask follow-up questions	• /tʃ/ and /ʃ/	Read about unofficial celebrations • Skill—Predict the topic Listen to a conversation about the business of holidays • Skill—Identify opinions Listen to a Chinese dumpling recipe • Skill—Listen for specific information	• Analyze • Evaluate	Write about a celebration
Unit Review p. 26 **Follow A Pro** p. 128—A Hotel Manager ▶ An Event Planner				
Start Talking • Make notes *Keep Talking* • Ask for opinions *Keep Talking* • Qualifying phrases	• Reduced form of *used to*	Read a magazine article about street entertainers • Skill—Identify main ideas Listen to an interview with a music producer • Skill—Listen for numbers Listen to a recording about TV viewing habits • Skill—Identify opinions	• Understand • Evaluate	Write about your viewing habits
Unit Review p. 36 **Study Skills** p. 129—Designing a Questionnaire				
Keep Talking • Show disagreement *Keep Talking* • Talk about life events *Keep Talking* • Make comparisons	• Stress on the adjective in *as … as* / *not as … as*	Read an article about personality types • Skill—Summarize Listen to a lecture about personalities of a team • Skill—Identify tone Listen to a recording about family personalities • Skill—Listen for detail	• Apply • Predict	Write about a movie character
Unit Review p. 46 **Follow A Pro** p. 130—A School Psychologist ▶ A Teacher				
Keep Talking • Useful phrases *Keep Talking* • Make requests *Start Talking* • Practice giving a talk	• Word stress with modal auxiliaries	Read a dialogue about a hotel reservation • Skill—Scan Listen to a conversation about a class party • Skill—Listen for gist Listen to a conversation about wedding etiquette • Skill—Listen for main ideas	• Predict • Remember • Analyze	Write about weddings
Unit Review p. 56 **Study Skills** p. 131—Organizing to Help Memorization				
Keep Talking • Useful phrases *Keep Talking* • Reacting to information *Keep Talking* • Point of view	• Present perfect contractions	Read an article about status quo bias • Skill—Identify examples Listen to a recording about bucket lists • Skill—Listen for main ideas Listen to a radio show about changing cities • Skill—Listen for specific information	• Analyze • Create • Understand	Write about your city
Unit Review p. 66 **Follow A Pro** p. 132—An Architect ▶ An Urban Planner				

	Outcomes	Vocabulary	Grammar	Speaking
Unit 7 Get to Work pp. 67–75	• Talk about being career-ready • Discuss a successful person • Talk about skills and qualifications	• Career readiness • Success • Employability skills	• Present perfect with *already, yet,* and *just* • Present perfect and simple past Grammar Reference pp. 151–152	• Discuss how career-ready you are • Talk about someone with a nontraditional career • Discuss your creativity
	Language and Life—Problem-solving: Create a Business Plan for an Entrepreneur			
Unit 8 Downtime pp. 77–85	• Talk about kids' activities that adults like doing • Make plans and talk about preferences • Express your opinion	• Kidult activities • Leisure activities • Adjectives of feeling	• Gerund phrases as subject and object • Verb + gerund or infinitive Grammar Reference pp. 152–153	• Explain enjoyable kids' activities • Discuss weekend activities • Talk about doing nothing
	Language and Life—Mindfulness: Select Calming Activities to Relax Your Mind			
Unit 9 Room for Me pp. 87–95	• Talk about types of housing • Talk about living preferences • Discuss future changes in the home	• Housing solutions • Living together • Appliances	• Future forms • Future possibility and certainty Grammar Reference pp. 154–155	• Discuss housing • Talk about future possibilities • Talk about homes of the future
	Language and Life—Decision-making: Use a Decision Matrix to Plan and Develop a Neighborhood			
Unit 10 Wellbeing pp. 97–105	• Talk about study habits • Talk about hypothetical conditions • Write about small life changes	• Brain power • Accidents and illnesses • Collocations with *get*	• Zero and first conditional • Second conditional Grammar Reference pp. 155–156	• Express opinions about study habits • Role-play a conversation about illnesses • Discuss getting in shape and healthy
	Language and Life—Critical Thinking: Create Campaigns to Improve Public Health			
Unit 11 Use and Reuse pp. 107–115	• Talk about what things are made of • Talk about inventions and gifts • Discuss uses of plastic	• Product lifecycles • Clothing materials • Collocations connected to materials	• Simple present passive • Simple past passive Grammar Reference pp. 157–158	• Discuss the lifecycle of a plastic bottle • Talk about a gift you received • Compare how you use plastic
	Language and Life—Innovation: Suggest Upcycling Projects			
Unit 12 I'm a Member pp. 117–125	• Talk about social groups • Discuss networking • Talk about belonging to youth tribes	• Types of community • Networking • Appearance	• Reflexive pronouns • Review of tenses Grammar Reference pp. 158–159	• Discuss social groups • Talk about expanding your network • Discuss subcultures
	Language and Life—Media Literacy: Design an Ad Campaign to Reach a Target Group			

Confident Communicator	Pronunciation	Listening/Reading	Thinking Skills	Writing
Keep Talking • Give negative answers *Keep Talking* • Express doubt *Start Talking* • Describe images	• /j/ and /dʒ/	Read an informative article about career readiness • Skill—Understand vocabulary in context Listen to an interview with an entrepreneur • Skill—Understand attitude Listen to a lecture about employability skills • Skill—Identify key words	• Summarize • Analyze	Write a personal statement
Unit Review p. 76 **Study Skills** p. 133—Creativity				
Start Talking • Describe an activity *Keep Talking* • Agree with a proposal *Start Talking* • Explain a concept	• *–ould* words	Read an article about kidult activities • Skill—Read for main ideas Listen to people plan weekend activities • Skill—Listen for details Listen to a class discussion about the psychology of doing nothing • Skill—Listen for reasons	• Apply • Analyze • Understand	Write a blog entry
Unit Review p. 86 **Follow A Pro** p. 134—A Resort Activities Coordinator ▶ A Recreation Coordinator				
Keep Talking • Ask for opinions *Keep Talking* • Ask for reasons for opinions *Keep Talking* • Give reasons for opinions	• /aʊ/ and /oʊ/	Read an article about housing solutions • Skill—Predict Listen to a conversation about where to live • Skill—Listen for attitude Listen to a talk about solar panels • Skill—Take notes	• Understand • Evaluate	Write an opinion paragraph
Unit Review p. 96 **Study Skills** p. 135—Problem Solving				
Start Talking • State agreement or disagreement *Keep Talking* • Ask about an illness *Start Talking* • Make a statement stronger	• Intonation in conditional sentences	Read an article on ways to improve your memory • Skill—Scan Listen to an interview with a health expert • Skill—Listen for cause and effect Listen to a dialogue about a fitness program • Skill—Listen for gist	• Brainstorm • Evaluate • Understand	Write a website comment
Unit Review p. 106 **Follow A Pro** p. 136—A Family Physician ▶ A Physical Therapist				
Start Talking • Order steps in a process *Keep Talking* • State who made something *Start Talking* • State alternatives	• Silent *t*	Read an article about the lifecycle of a T-shirt • Skill—Understand words from context Listen to an interview about accidental discoveries • Skill—Listen for key words Listen to a lecture on upcycling items • Skill—Listen for gist	• Brainstorm • Understand • Analyze	Write an email
Unit Review p. 116 **Study Skills** p. 137—Using Precise Language in Academic Writing				
Start Talking • Make a guess *Start Talking* • Show certainty *Keep Talking* • Further a point	• /s/ vs. /ʃ/	Read an article on types of community • Skill—Understand the main ideas Listen to a podcast about networking • Skill—Listen for the main ideas Listen to an interview about different social groups • Skill—Listen for gist	• Analyze • Understand	Write a description
Unit Review p. 126 **Follow A Pro** p. 138—An Entrepreneur ▶ An Entrepreneur				

GO TO page xxi

for **GRAMMAR REVIEW** step-by-step instructions.

Grammar Quiz: What Do You Already Know?

A Complete the conversation with words from the box.

are is 'm not 's 's what's

Esme: Hi, my name's Esme. **1** What's your name?

Monique: My name **2** 's Monique.

Esme: Nice to meet you, Monique. Where **3** are you from?

Monique: I **4** 'm from France. I work here. I'm an interpreter.

Esme: Really? That **5** 's interesting.

Monique: It **6** is. I love my job! What about you? Are you American?

Esme: No, I'm **7** not. I'm British.

B Complete the paragraph with the simple present form of the verbs in parentheses.

My sister, Emily, really **1** loves (love) her phone. She **2** checks (check) her phone when she **3** wakes (wake) up. I think she **4** sends (send) about a hundred text messages a day! She **5** uses (use) about five different social media sites, too. I **6** have (have) a smartphone, too, but I can live without it. I **7** don't need (not need) to post pictures of my food every time I have a nice meal! What about you? How much time **8** do you spend (spend) on your phone?

C Choose the correct option.

Leo: What **1** do you have / **are you having** for lunch today, Jill?
Jill: Today **2** **I'm having** / I have noodle salad with shrimp and chili sauce.
Leo: It looks delicious! **3** **Did you buy** / Do you bought it from the café?
Jill: No, **4** **I made it** / I'm making it at home. It's cheap, and it's healthy, too.
Leo: I think I **5** **should** / could start to bring food from home. The cafeteria always **6** **serves** / serving the same things. I **7** **want to** / want eat a more balanced diet.

D Find one error in each line of the conversation. Write the corrected sentence.

Rob: Is you almost ready, Julie? **1** Are you almost ready, Julie?

Julie: Yes! I'm so excited about going to ~~the~~ Amsterdam! **2** I'm so excited about going to Amsterdam!

Rob: Where do you want to do when we're there? **3** What do you want to do when we're there?

Julie: I want to go sightseeing around a city. **4** I want to go sightseeing around the city.

Rob: Yeah, I like to do that, too. Can we go by bicycle? **5** Yeah, I'd / I would like to do that, too.

Julie: I'd like to, but I can ride a bike! **6** I'd like to, but I can't/cannot ride a bike!

E Complete the email with words from the box.

a a her 's the the X (no article) your

Hi Malu,

Thanks for your email! I'm really excited about **1** the school trip to France next summer. **2** Your hometown looks beautiful. It's great that there is **3** a waterfall just three kilometers away. Is there **4** a forest, too? I love **5** X trees! Can we climb **6** the mountain you told me about? I know the weather is sometimes rainy in France, so I've borrowed my friend **7** 's waterproof jacket and I've also borrowed **8** her walking boots.

See you soon!

Reba

Go to the Grammar Review on pages 140–141

GRAMMAR QUIZ

This quiz tests students' knowledge of language presented in **Student's Book** Starter level. For further review of the Starter level, have students do the Grammar Review on pages 140–141.

GO TO page vi
for **UNIT OPENER** step-by-step instructions.

UNIT 1 Extraordinary

WHAT DO YOU ALREADY KNOW?

1 What extraordinary people do you know? Write their names, countries, and careers in the box.

2 IN PAIRS Share and compare your words. If possible, add more words to the box.

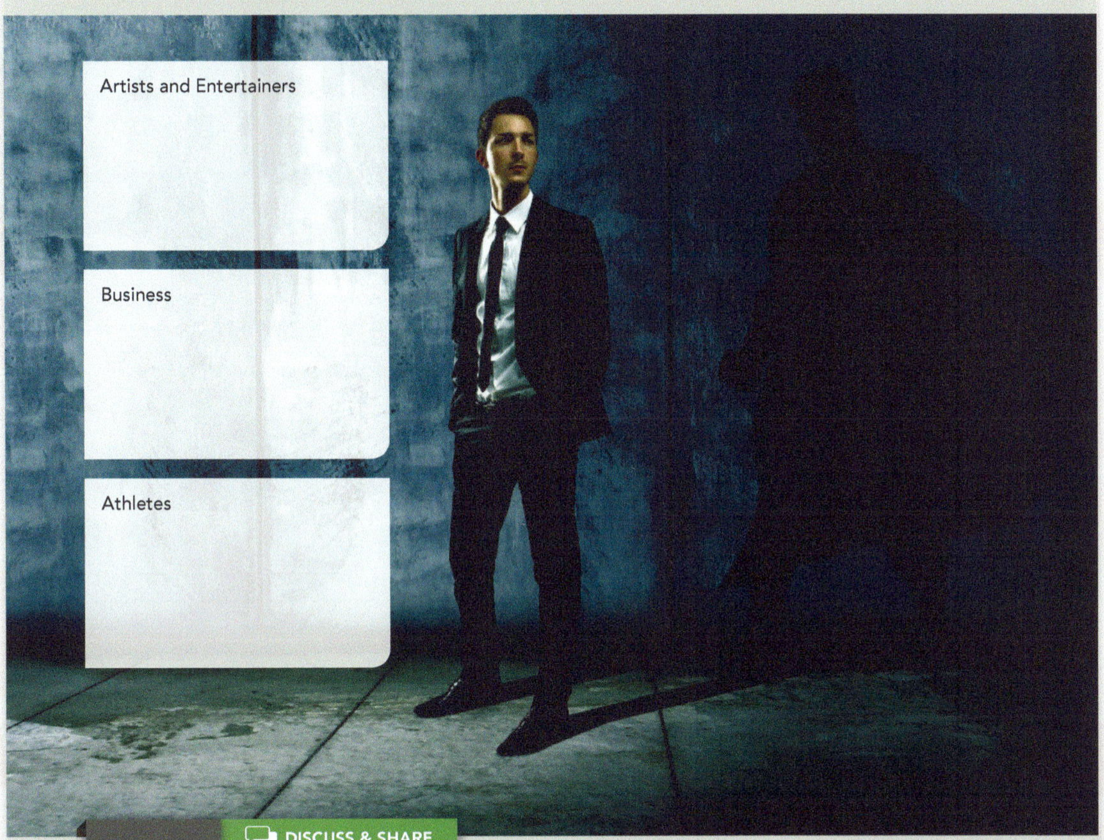

STUDENTS MAY ALREADY KNOW:

- **Artists and Entertainers:** Penélope Cruz, Spain, actress; Justin Bieber, Canada, musician.
- **Business:** Bill Gates, United States, technology expert.
- **Athletes:** Roger Federer, Switzerland, tennis player.

VIDEO

DISCUSS & SHARE

3 IN GROUPS Watch the video and answer the question.
SYM Is being famous the same as being extraordinary?

GO TO page xx
for **VIDEOS IN SYM** step-by-step instructions.

In this unit, you will ...

- talk about a role model, describe a memorable event, and tell an anecdote.
- use thinking skills: evaluate, analyze, and understand.
- read a biography.
- use strategies to speculate about reasons, sequence events, use words you know when you don't know an exact word.
- use communication skills to give a short speech for a citizen award.
- learn strategies for using personal experience in writing.

WHAT DO YOU ALREADY KNOW?

If you notice students are struggling to understand what to do, you can provide one or two examples to help them get started:

- **Artists and Entertainers:** Frida Kahlo, Mexico, painter; Mozart, Austria, musician
- **Business:** Mark Zuckerberg, the US, technology expert
- **Athletes:** Maria Sharapova, Russia, tennis player

VIDEO

Before viewing, ask:
What does Sam consider to be extraordinary? *Famous people with fans, everybody kowns their names.*
What does Jenny consider to be extraordinary? *People who aren't celebrities, with no fans, who do amazing things.*
After viewing, put the continuum on the board.

famous —— extraordinary

Have students mark the continuum and explain their preferences.

DISCUSS & SHARE

Have students consider what the differences are between being famous and being extraordinary. Are the differences in a person's personality or actions? Have students discuss if a person can be famous but not extraordinary. Ask *Should extraordinary people be famous?* Tell students to give reasons to support their answer.

GO TO page x

for **READING** step-by-step instructions.

LESSON 1 **Role Models**

READING

A **Do you have any role models? Why do you admire them?**

B **1.01 READING SKILL—Skim a text** **Look at the text quickly for one minute. Don't try to read every word. Then close your book and note down any information you remember.**

LILA DOWNS

My role model is Lila Downs. She was born in Oaxaca, Mexico, in 1968. She is a Mexican-American singer-songwriter and actress. At the age of eight, she started singing mariachi songs. She became a professional singer when she was at school. Her family **emigrated** from Mexico to the US when she was 14. While they were living there, her father died. After that, Lila and her mother moved back to Mexico.

While she was working in her mother's store, she met her future husband, the musician Paul Cohen. He had a business in the US, so Lila moved from Oaxaca to Minnesota. She went to the University of Minnesota. While she was studying there, she started a music group called La Trova Serrana. It was very **successful**, and Lila decided to leave school to **focus on** music. Lila had a small **role** in the movie *Frida* and worked on the music for the movie *Like Water for Chocolate*. Here are three things you probably don't know about Lila:

- In 2010, while she was traveling the world on her Black Magic Woman Tour, she **revealed** that she had an adopted son named Benito Dxuladi.
- In 2014, scientists named an **insect** after her. The Liladownsia fraile is a very colorful grasshopper. They named it after her because Lila often wears colorful, traditional clothes.
- She sings in Spanish, English, and her native language of Mixtec.

I really **look up to** Lila Downs because she looks for ways to **improve** people's lives through music. I'd love to meet her and ask her this question: "What were you singing about in the song 'Shake Away'?"

C **Scan the article in B and answer the questions.**

1 Where is Lila from? Oaxaca, Mexico
2 How old was Lila when she moved to the US? 14 years old
3 When did Lila reveal that she had adopted her son? 2010
4 What type of animal did scientists name after Lila? an insect / a grasshopper
5 What languages does Lila sing in? Spanish, English, and Mixtec

D **Read the article in B in detail to check your answers.**

E **THINKING SKILL—Evaluate** **Is it important to have role models? Are most famous people good role models? Discuss and give examples.**

GO TO page vii

for **VOCABULARY** step-by-step instructions.

VOCABULARY

A **Match the bold words from the text in READING B to the definitions.**

1 emigrated: left your country to move to a different country (verb)
2 look up to: admire; think someone is a good role model (phrasal verb)
3 improve: make something better (verb)
4 revealed: told a secret (verb)
5 insect: a small animal with six legs and wings (noun)
6 successful: achieving wealth, admiration, or popularity (adjective)
7 focus on: pay attention to; concentrate on (phrasal verb)
8 role: a part in a movie or a play (noun)

MAKE IT YOURS

Choose a famous role model that you look up to. Find an article about his or her life. Write down any interesting facts that you find in the article.

READING OPTIONAL 1.01

READING SKILL—Skim a text

A role model is a person who is considered a good example for other people, and should be a person whose values are to be admired. He or she should be a positive influence. A role model can be a famous person or someone close, such as a family member or a friend.

THINKING SKILL—Evaluate

In order to give examples, have students discuss the qualities and positive values of famous people they consider to be good role models. Have them consider that a poor role model is someone with negative qualities—for example, someone who is greedy and self-interested, disloyal, or dishonest.

VOCABULARY **Extra Practice**

You may want to extend the practice of the VOCABULARY section by asking students to write the words in sentences of their own. Then have them share their sentences in pairs. This will demonstrate a deeper understanding of the words.

GRAMMAR past progressive

GO TO page viii for GRAMMAR step-by-step instructions.

A Underline the past progressive verb forms in READING B.

While they were living there, her father died.

B Complete the rules with words from the box.

–ing were continued was

1 The past progressive describes actions that began in the past and continued for some time.
2 The past progressive always includes the form was / were or were / was.
3 In the past progressive, add -ing to the base form of the verb.

For more practice, go to page 142.

C Complete the conversation with the past progressive form of the verb in parentheses.

Ben: I called you last night, but you didn't answer. What 1 were you doing (you do)?
Ashley: We 2 were celebrating (celebrate) my great-grandfather's 100th birthday.
Ben: Really? One hundred! That's amazing. Was he your role model while you 3 were growing (grow) up?
Ashley: Yes, definitely. He was my hero! He 4 was opening (open) presents when you called. Everyone 5 was clapping (clap).
Ben: I'm sure he had a great time yesterday.
Ashley: I think so. We 6 weren't planning (not plan) for the party to end at midnight!

D IN PAIRS Ask and answer the questions.

1 What were you doing …
a in the summer? **b** in 2016? **c** last Thursday? **d** last night?

A: What were you doing last night? *B: I was visiting my grandparents.*

SPEAKING

GO TO page xii for SPEAKING step-by-step instructions.

A Read about Ann Makosinski, a young inventor and role model. Why is she famous?

She invented a flashlight that uses body heat.

Ann Makosinski
1997—born October 3, Canada
2011—in Philippines, her friend fails exam because there's no electricity at night
2011—Ann gets idea for flashlight
2012—develops flashlight powered by body heat

B IN PAIRS Discuss the events in Ann's life using information from the notes.

C IN GROUPS Discuss how you think Ann's flashlight works. Use the Confident Communicator box to help you.

CONFIDENT COMMUNICATOR
START TALKING

Use the following expressions to talk about something you are not 100% sure about:
I'm not sure, but I think it may/could be …
Maybe it works without …
Perhaps/Maybe you can use it …

GRAMMAR Additional Activity

Play *What Were You Doing At …?* Students work in groups of four, designated as A, B, C, and D. Give each group two dice. A rolls the dice. B asks *What were you doing at [X] o'clock yesterday?* (depending on the number rolled). A answers the question—for example, *I was watching TV*. Then, C asks a follow-up question—for example, *What were you watching?* and A answers. Then, D adds a comment to show they were listening—for example, *I was watching TV, too.* Students take turns: B now rolls, C asks the question, D asks the follow-up question, and A gives a reaction. Make sure students refer to activities between noon and midnight.

SPEAKING

Have students read the information about Ann Makosinski's life. Ask them to try to imagine what she was doing when she reached the milestones mentioned. She was 14 in 2011 and probably in junior high school.

CONFIDENT COMMUNICATOR

Direct students to the Confident Communicator box to help them talk about how they think Ann's flashlight works. If necessary, ask a student to read the box aloud.

LESSON 2 Memorable Events

VOCABULARY reactions

A Match the sentences (1–6) to the pictures (a–f). Write the letter.

1 Were you **disappointed** that you didn't get a good grade? e
2 Walt's phone rang in the middle of the night. He was **worried**. c
3 There was a snake crossing the path. I was so **scared**. I'm afraid of snakes! b
4 I won a free trip around the world. I'm **thrilled**! d
5 I was **glad** the bus came. It was raining very heavily. f
6 I'm **confused**! Which way do I go? a

GO TO page xi for **LISTENING** step-by-step instructions.

LISTENING

A 1.02 **LISTENING SKILL—Listen for specific information** **Listen to four people talk about memorable events. Match the speakers (1–4) to how they felt (a–d).**

1	Katrin: c	a	thrilled
2	Giovanni: a	b	glad
3	Kyle: d	c	worried
4	Gemma: b	d	confused

GO TO page 136 for **AUDIO SCRIPT**.

B THINKING SKILL—Analyze **Why do you think the speakers felt the way they did? Evaluate if you would feel the same way.**

I think Katrin was worried because she loves animals. I would feel …

GO TO page ix for **PRONUNCIATION** step-by-step instructions.

PRONUNCIATION vowel + consonant + e

A 1.03 **Listen and notice the change in the vowel sounds. The e changes the vowel to a long sound.**

Suddenly, a police officer shouted, "**Hide**!"
We **hid** in a café.

B 1.04 **Practice saying the words. Listen and check your pronunciation.**

1	hid	hide	2	at	ate	3	mad	made	4	rid	ride

VOCABULARY

Have students practice the vocabulary by suggesting other scenarios in which they feel these emotions. Tell students that body language is important when we speak. Have them represent the emotions with gestures. They should be aware that gestures differ from country to country. Have them research differences in how they represent them in their country and in different English-speaking countries.

LISTENING Additional Activity

You may want to have your students investigate Vanessa Van Edwards's seven universal micro expressions.

Tell them the emotions are named and should be changed to the *I am/I feel* form. So, happiness becomes *I am happy*, surprise becomes *I am surprised*, and disgust becomes *I feel disgusted*.

PRONUNCIATION Extra Practice

Extend the activity by asking students to brainstorm more words that follow the same pattern (e.g., *bit–bite*, *kit–kite*, *sit–site*, *cap–cape*, *hat–hate*).

GRAMMAR past progressive vs. simple past

A Underline the action in progress and circle the action that interrupts it.

1 I was watching the game at my friend's house when the phone rang.
2 I was working for NASA on the Mars mission when it happened.
3 My boss called me in the middle of the night while I was sleeping.
4 When the plane came down, we were staying in a hotel.

B Choose the correct option to complete the grammar rules.

1 The past progressive describes an interrupting action / action in progress.
2 The simple past describes the interrupting action / action in progress.
3 We use *when* / *while* to introduce the action in progress.
4 We use *when* / *while* to introduce the interrupting action.
5 We use a comma after *when* and *while* clauses at the beginning / end of a sentence.

For more practice, go to page 142.

C Complete the text with the correct form of the verb in parentheses. Use the past progressive or the past simple.

Kiera: Did you hear that news story about the animal rescue?
Asha: No. What **1** ___happened___ (happen)?
Kiera: I **2** ___was reading___ (read) about it on the way to work yesterday. Well, you know there was that hurricane in Texas? Hurricane Harvey, I think it was.
Asha: Yes, I remember it.
Kiera: Well, after the hurricane, when people **3** ___left___ (leave) their homes, there were lots of pets that **4** ___were living___ (live) on the streets. The animal rescue centers had no room for them. So, an airline organized a flight to take about 60 of the animals from Houston to San Diego to find new forever homes! I **5** ___was crying___ (cry) when I read the story. There was a photo of the pilot and he **6** ___was holding___ (hold) some of the puppies. They were so cute!
Asha: The perfect happy ending, huh?

D IN PAIRS What happened on your way to class today? Describe the actions in progress and interrupting actions.

A: While I was walking to class today, I saw my friend Gabriel.

B: My phone rang while I was getting on the bus.

SPEAKING

A Think about a memorable event in your life. Make notes about:

- what happened
- where you were
- when it happened
- what you were doing
- how you felt

B IN GROUPS Take turns describing the events. Ask questions about the details. Use the Confident Communicator box to help you.

A: I remember the storm in 2016. I was living in Monterrey at the time. It started raining while I was walking to work.

B: Were you scared?

CONFIDENT COMMUNICATOR
REPAIR IT

If you don't know a word in English, here are some things you can do:
Use a word that means something similar (e.g., *very worried* for *scared*).
Give a short description of the event (e.g., *a lot of rain* for *storm*).

GRAMMAR

To practice the past progressive interrupted by the simple past, ask students to talk about the last time they got injured. For example, *I was peeling a potato, when I stabbed myself with a knife.*

Additional Activity

Play *I Was, When* ... This is a mingling activity. Have half of the class think of phrases in the past progressive starting with *I was* … and memorize them. Have the other half of the class think of phrases in the simple past starting with *when I* … and memorize them. The two halves should then mingle with each other to make sentences. There may be many hilarious, nonsensical combinations!

SPEAKING

Tell students to use facial expressions when they are telling their stories about a memorable event. Gestures and expressions are good tools for storytelling. The grammar from this lesson is perfect for setting the scene and then moving the anecdote along. Tell them to use the tips in the Confident Communicator box to keep the story moving.

LESSON 3 **Coincidences**

VOCABULARY family situations

A Match the words and phrases from the box to the pictures (1–8).

adopted | divorced | engaged | large family | only child | single | single parent | twins

1 
twins

2 
single parent

3 
large family

4 
single

5 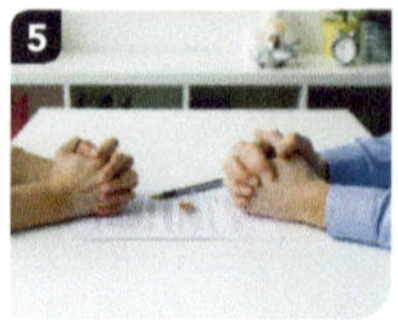
divorced

6 
only child

7 
adopted

8 
engaged

B Complete the sentences with the words and phrases from A.

1 My sister and I are __twins__. She was born 10 minutes before I was. We look the same, but we are different.
2 Jack comes from a __large family__. He has eight brothers and sisters.
3 I am __single__, but I want to get married in the future.
4 I am an __only child__. When I was growing up, I wanted a brother or sister.
5 My parents are __divorced__. My mom got married again last year.
6 Dan is a/an __single parent__. His wife died about five years ago, so he takes care of his kids on his own.
7 We got __engaged__ last year. We're getting married this summer.
8 Lois's parents __adopted__ her when she was six weeks old.

C IN PAIRS Discuss your family. Ask questions to find out more information.

LISTENING

A Look at the picture. What do you notice about the people?

B 1.05 LISTENING SKILL—Predict the story
Listen to the first half of an anecdote about an amazing coincidence. What do you think will happen next?

C 1.06 Listen to the second half of the anecdote to check. Were you correct?

GO TO page 136 for AUDIO SCRIPT.

GO TO page 136 for AUDIO SCRIPT.

VOCABULARY

Have students identify the stressed syllables in the vocabulary words and practice saying them with the correct stress.

Some questions for VOCABULARY **C** students can ask each other to keep the conversation about families going are: *Where did you go on family vacations when you were a child? What makes your family special? Who are you closest to in your family?*

LISTENING

LISTENING SKILL—Predict the story

Have students look at the picture and predict what they will hear. They may predict it is a listening about twins.

When predicting what will happen in the second half of the anecdote, tell students they should use clues from what they have heard in the first half. Accept all answers at this stage.

D 1.07 Now listen to the whole anecdote. Circle the sequencing phrases you hear.

about two years ago	about a month after that	the next day
about six months ago	about three months later	a few days later
a week later	later that day	finally
a month later	later on	in the end

E **THINKING SKILL—Understand** What was the coincidence in this anecdote? Summarize.

MAKE IT REAL

To show you are surprised about something in an anecdote or story, you can say:

You're kidding! *That's unbelievable!* *No way!*

GO TO page 136 for AUDIO SCRIPT.

WRITING

GO TO page xiv for WRITING step-by-step instructions.

A Read this anecdote about an amazing coincidence. What do you think is interesting about it?

This is an anecdote a friend told me. It's about a woman who was adopted at six months old. One day, she was in the hair salon in the new neighborhood she was living in, when she saw a woman who looked similar to her. They talked a little bit about their lives. The young woman said she was adopted as a baby.

"When's your birthday?" asked the older woman.

"January 25, 1998," said the young woman. The older woman was shocked.

"I gave a daughter up for adoption. She was born on January 25, 1998," she said.

After that, they both took a DNA test and discovered they were mother and daughter. They were so glad to find one another. I think this story is interesting because it is an amazing coincidence.

B Think of an interesting anecdote that happened to you or someone you know. Make notes about the following:

- who the anecdote involves
- what happened
- where it happened
- what the people were doing
- how they felt
- why you think the anecdote is interesting

C Write the main events of your anecdote.

____

____

____

D Write your anecdote in your notebook. Make sure that the events are in the correct order.

E **IN PAIRS** Share your writing. What was interesting about your partner's anecdote?

SPEAKING

A Think of an interesting anecdote you read in a book, heard on the news, or saw on TV.

B **IN GROUPS** Share your anecdotes. Decide on the anecdote that you all like. Use the Confident Communicator box to help you.

CONFIDENT COMMUNICATOR
START TALKING

Use sequencing words and phrases to connect the events in an anecdote.
About three months ago ... / Two weeks ago ... / Last week ...
After that ... / Then ...
In the end ... / Finally ...

MAKE IT REAL

Have students practice saying these phrases until they are as natural and as spontaneous as possible. Encourage them to use gestures and body language.

WRITING

In WRITING **B**, have students make as many notes as they can. They won't include all of the ideas in their writing. They should be generating ideas.

In WRITING **C**, have students use time phrases to structure their writing and use transitional words and phrases to help the writing and storytelling flow smoothly.

SPEAKING

In the SPEAKING section, students retell a story they have read, heard, or seen. As they are talking about someone else, make sure they use the third person. Give a quick overview of some of the grammar they will use in the past tense. For example, *He/She was [X]ing when he/she won the award.*

GO TO page xv
for LANGUAGE AND LIFE step-by-step instructions.

Language and Life

Communication – Citizen Award

A What is a hero? Do you know of any heroes in your community?

B 1.08 Read the magazine article about heroes. Then choose *True* or *False*.

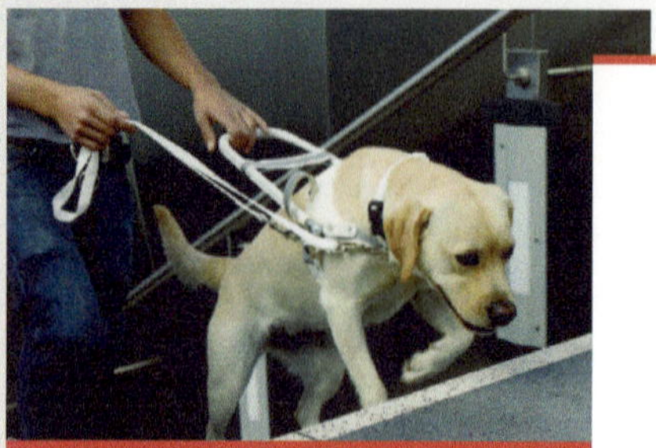

Victor Karlsson

Meet 20-year-old Victor Karlsson from Malmo, Sweden. When Victor was eight years old, he became blind in an accident. With help from his family and friends, Victor is now a local hero in Malmo. Victor and his guide dog Charlie are helping improve the lives of blind children and adults by raising money. In 2018, Victor raised 1,500 euros walking 111 km between Malmo and Copenhagen. In 2020, he is planning to run a half-marathon. "Everyone looks up to Victor," says his friend Katya. "He's a true role model."

Petra Gonzalez

Nineteen-year-old Petra Gonzalez saved her sister from a fire in their home in Mexico. Petra, a university student, woke up one night to the smell of smoke. She woke up her sister. She was carrying her sister out of their apartment when she saw the fire on the other side of the house. Amazingly, firefighters arrived in time to save both girls. Petra got an award from the local mayor. "I was really scared," said Petra, "but I was just doing what any sister would do."

Mimi Kallas

While Mimi Kallas was working in a tourist office in her home town in Greece, she noticed men and women on the streets asking for food. Mimi stopped working at her job and started a food service for homeless people. She collects extra food from stores and cooks up to 100 meals a day in the kitchen of a school. She gives out the food for free to anyone who needs it. "Without Mimi, we couldn't survive," said one man. "She is an amazing woman. I'm so glad she is here to help us."

OBJECTIVE

In this lesson, students learn how to evaluate personal qualities and achievements to decide who should receive an award for being a hero. They use what they have learned about role models to judge the merits of people who have done extraordinary things and propose other people who deserve awards.

PROCESS OPTIONAL 1.08

Students first read three short articles that discuss people who have done extraordinary things, overcome disabilities, raised money for others, saved others from dangerous situations, or helped the community. Then, they analyze why the featured people are heroes. Based on the examples in the articles, students research other people who have done extraordinary things and make a list. From the list, they make proposals for citizens' awards. Using the criteria they have been considering for what makes a hero, students choose people from their list to recognize in an awards ceremony. Finally, students role-play an awards ceremony and discuss questions.

1 Victor was eight when he went blind. True / False
2 Victor ran a half-marathon in 2018. True / False
3 Petra is an only child. True / False
4 The fire was in Petra's school. True / False
5 Mimi works in a tourist office. True / False
6 Mimi cooks food for people at a school. True / False

C IN PAIRS Discuss why each person from B is a hero. Give reasons.

A: Who do you think is the most heroic?
B: I think … is the most heroic because …
A: Oh, really? I think … is the most heroic because …

D IN GROUPS Imagine you work for a local community committee. You want to offer a Citizen Award to a person who did something extraordinary. Research news websites online to find examples of heroic acts and write a list.

This woman in Sao Paulo is a hero. She saved a child's life.

E IN GROUPS Role-play an awards ceremony where the heroes are given their awards and make short thank-you speeches.

A: Please welcome …, who gets a Citizen Award today for helping out every week at the local baseball club …
B: I'd like to say how thrilled I am to get this award. I love helping out at the local baseball club because …

F Discuss the questions.

1 Did you clearly communicate the reasons for giving the award? Why or why not?
2 In what other situations does a group of people decide who wins an award?

MAKE IT DIGITAL

Go online and find examples of heroic acts in your country. Talk about which ones you think are extraordinary and why.

CLASSROOM MANAGEMENT

After activity **C**, have students brainstorm a list of actions and adjectives to describe the people in the articles.

Before activity **E**, remind students that they will use the *–ed* form of the adjectives to describe how they feel about winning the award (e.g., *I'm thrilled …*, *I'm honored*, etc.).

CULTURE NOTE

Remind students that heroes can be people who have done extraordinary things for their own community. They don't have to be recognized by an official group before they can be considered heroes to the students.

MAKE IT DIGITAL

Tell students to look for heroic acts on local news websites. Tell them to navigate to local news and then search for "heroes."

GO TO page xvii
for **UNIT REVIEW** step-by-step instructions.

UNIT 1

VOCABULARY review

SCORE: / 10

A Choose the correct option.

1 Raul was glad / disappointed when he got bad grades in his final exams.
2 Were you scared / thrilled when you heard a hurricane was coming?
3 Please don't talk to me while I'm studying, or I will get glad / confused.
4 I'm a little worried / disappointed about tomorrow's party. What will happen if people don't come?
5 My parents were scared / thrilled when I told them I got an award.
6 Jackson is / isn't an only child. He has a brother named Harrison.
7 Dad comes from a large / small family. He has five brothers and two sisters.
8 Pavlos and Christina got adopted / divorced. Pavlos is getting married again next month.
9 My parents got engaged / adopted when they were in their 30s.
10 I'm an only parent / a single parent, but the kids see their dad on the weekends.

GRAMMAR review

SCORE: / 10

A Correct the errors and rewrite the sentences.

1 What you were doing last New Year's Eve? What were you doing last New Year's Eve?
2 In 2016, I living in Mexico City. In 2016, I was living in Mexico City.
3 At noon, my friends and I were eat lunch. At noon, my friends and I were eating lunch.
4 My brother were making breakfast this morning. My brother was making breakfast this morning.
5 They was watching a movie last night. They were watching a movie last night.

B Unscramble and write.

1 started raining / While / was / for the bus, / it / waiting / I ______
2 while / The movie / our tickets / started / we / buying / were ______
3 rang / was / I / my phone / working / when ______
4 swimming / We / were / when / happened / the accident ______
5 got / watching TV / The kids / when / home / were / their father ______

1 While I was waiting for the bus, it started raining.
2 The movie started while we were buying our tickets.
3 I was working when my phone rang.
4 We were swimming when the accident happened.
5 The kids were watching TV when their father got home.

16–20 correct: You can discuss family situations and reactions. You can use the past progressive.
0–15 correct: Look again at the Vocabulary and Grammar sections in the unit.

TOTAL SCORE: / 20

WHAT DO YOU KNOW NOW? Look back at page 7 and add words you know now to the boxes.

GO TO page xviii
for **STUDY SKILLS** step-by-step instructions.

STUDY SKILLS USING PERSONAL EXPERIENCE

Take the quiz. Then go to Study Skills on page 127.
Find the answers and learn more about using personal experience.

1 Which two of the following things do we usually find in personal narratives?
a evidence **b** feelings **c** descriptions

2 Personal narratives are usually subjective.
a True **b** False

3 Which two of the following things do we usually find in factual accounts?
a chronological events **b** numbers and statistics **c** use of the word *I*

CLASSROOM MANAGEMENT

Give students a few minutes to look over the VOCABULARY and GRAMMAR sections of the lessons in the unit before giving them 15 minutes to complete the VOCABULARY and GRAMMAR review activities.

FURTHER DISCUSSION

Put students in groups of three and ask the following questions for them to discuss:

- What do you think are the main qualities in a role model?
- Can young people be role models?
- What would make you a better storyteller?
- What new words did you learn to talk about families?

UNIT 2

Party!

GO TO page vi
for **UNIT OPENER** step-by-step instructions.

WHAT DO YOU ALREADY KNOW?

1 Think about occasions you celebrate. Write the words.

2 **IN PAIRS** Share and compare your ideas. Think of more words to add to each category.

Celebrations only in my country

International celebrations

STUDENTS MAY ALREADY KNOW:

- Days of the week.
- Months of the year.
- **Celebrations:** holiday, vacation, lunch, dinner, party.

VIDEO

DISCUSS & SHARE

3 **IN GROUPS** Watch the video and answer the question.

SYM Do you prefer to buy gifts or buy experiences for celebrations?

GO TO page xx
for **VIDEOS IN SYM** step-by-step instructions.

In this unit, you will ...

- talk about official and unofficial holidays, spending habits, and celebrations.
- use thinking skills: analyze and evaluate.
- read about unusual holidays.
- use strategies to start and keep talking by giving reasons, giving opinions, and asking follow-up questions.
- use creativity skills to work with others and create your own graduation ceremony.
- follow a hotel manager to learn about the jobs and skills needed in the hospitality industry.

WHAT DO YOU ALREADY KNOW?

If you notice students are struggling to understand what to do, you can provide one or two examples to help them get started:

- **Celebrations only in my country:** Independence Day
- **International celebrations:** New Year's Eve

VIDEO

Before viewing, ask:

Why does Ken like giving gifts? *It's fun to give his friends something they will really love.*

Why does Theresa like giving experiences? *She likes to remember the fun time she had with her friends.*

After viewing, put the continuum on the board.

gifts —— experiences

Have students mark the continuum and explain their preferences.

DISCUSS & SHARE

Students should discuss different ways they like to express themselves on holidays. Do they prefer to buy things as a way to show participation in a holiday? Or do they have special traditions that they participate in? Perhaps they do both, but for different holidays.

GO TO page x

for **READING** step-by-step instructions.

The people in the first picture are taking a selfie.

The person in the second picture is eating a peach.

LESSON 1 **Days of the Year**

READING

A Look at the pictures in B. What are the people doing?

B **READING SKILL—Predict the topic** Read the title and look at the pictures. What do you think you are going to read about? Check (✓) one of the ideas.

- ☐ a story about someone's birthday
- ☑ an article about celebrating unusual days of the year
- ☐ a blog about celebrations around the world

EVERY DAY *is a* HOLIDAY!

Take a look at your **calendar** for the year ahead. Some dates show an **official** event that people **celebrate** somewhere in the world. For example, Americans celebrate Independence Day on July 4. On October 8, the Japanese celebrate Health and Sports Day. A lot of people **get the day off** work, and schools and businesses are closed. People may eat special food on these days or give and **receive** gifts.

Then, there are unofficial holidays. These are days when people sometimes **arrange** a party at school or at work. Unofficial holidays celebrate unimportant and fun things like food, movies, books, and TV shows.

To show you what I mean, last week, a **colleague** said, "It's 'Take a Selfie Day'! Today you can take a lot of selfies." In my opinion, there's too much time spent taking selfies—you don't need a special day for it!

There are a few websites that list all these celebrations. Think of any day of the year, and there is something to celebrate. I learned there are days of the year for everything: Read in the Bathtub Day (February 9), World Yoga Day (February 22), and my favorite, Make Music Day (June 21). A lot of days celebrate food, like Caesar Salad Day on July 4 and Eat a Peach Day on August 22. There are too many dates for me to remember!

I am thinking of asking my **boss** if I can get the day off on the second Friday of March. It's World Sleep Day. And a little advice for you—don't think of asking me to do anything on Lazy Day (August 10)!

C 2.01 Read the text in B to check your answer.

D Read the text again and choose the correct option.

1	When do people in Japan celebrate Health and Sports Day?	**a** July 4	**b** October 8
2	Who told the writer about Take a Selfie Day?	**a** her boss	**b** a colleague
3	What is the writer's favorite Day of the Year?	**a** Make Music Day	**b** World Yoga Day
4	What day of the week is World Sleep Day on?	**a** Monday	**b** Friday

E **THINKING SKILL—Analyze** What holidays are celebrated in your country but not in other countries?

GO TO page vii

for **VOCABULARY** step-by-step instructions.

VOCABULARY

A Match the bold words from the text in READING B to the definitions.

1. agreed upon or arranged by people in power (adjective) official
2. a chart with days of the year showing seasonal information (noun) calendar
3. when you don't have to go to work or school (phrase) get the day off
4. do something to recognize an important or special event (verb) celebrate
5. a person who is in charge at work (noun) boss
6. make plans for an event (verb) arrange
7. get something from someone (verb) receive
8. a person you work with (noun) colleague

MAKE IT YOURS

Search online for "days of the year" and find more fun holidays. Select a day and share it with your classmates.

READING OPTIONAL 2.01

If students are having a hard time making predictions from the photos, tell them to read the statements in READING **B** and then make some more predictions about what they think the article will be about.

THINKING SKILL—Analyze

Have students work in groups of four. Ask each student to research national holidays in different countries, report back to the group, and discuss inferences that can be made about a country based on holidays that are observed. Have students discuss holidays that are celebrated in their country but not in others.

VOCABULARY

Have students broaden their knowledge of the words by encouraging them to look up synonyms in an online or monolingual dictionary.

GRAMMAR quantifiers

GO TO page viii for GRAMMAR step-by-step instructions.

A Look back at the text in READING B. Circle these words: *some, a lot of, a little, too many, any, too much, a few*. Underline the noun that follows. Write the phrases in the correct column.

Countable	Uncountable
some dates	a lot of people
a lot of selfies, too many dates	a little advice
a few websites, any day	too much time

B Choose the correct option to complete the grammar rules.

1 Use *some* with countable nouns / uncountable nouns / both.
2 Use *a lot of* with countable nouns / uncountable nouns / both.
3 Use *a little* with countable nouns / uncountable nouns / both.
4 Use *too many* with countable nouns / uncountable nouns / both.
5 Use *any* with countable nouns / uncountable nouns / both.
6 Use *too much* with countable nouns / uncountable nouns / both.
7 Use *a few* with countable nouns / uncountable nouns / both.

For more practice, go to page 143.

C Choose the correct quantifier.

Pasteles de hoja are a popular dish in Puerto Rico, but they are also made in the Dominican Republic, Colombia, and El Salvador. They are usually made around Christmas and families often spend **1** a little / a few days preparing them. It's common to make **2** a lot of / a few pasteles at the same time (usually between 50 and 200!). Here is the basic recipe: Make a vegetable dough from green banana flour. Fill the dough with **3** some / a few meat. Don't add **4** too many / too much meat because you have to add the chickpeas, raisins, and olives, too. Wrap the pasteles in banana leaves and steam them. People usually freeze some of them to enjoy on Three Kings Day on January 6. Or they take **5** a little / some boxes of pasteles as a gift to family or friends. They are delicious, but very big, so you may not want to eat **6** too much / too many!

D IN PAIRS Think about a celebration that you went to recently that had food and drinks. What did you have? Discuss. Use quantifiers where necessary.

I went to a party for my colleague's birthday. There was a lot of food. I had a few sandwiches and some salad.

SPEAKING

GO TO page xii for SPEAKING step-by-step instructions.

A March 26 is Make Up Your Own Holiday Day. On this day you can choose to celebrate anything you like. Think about what you would like to celebrate on this holiday. Make notes about:

- the name of your holiday
- what you do to celebrate it
- where you want to celebrate
- why you want to celebrate it

B IN GROUPS Share your ideas about your own holiday. Use the Confident Communicator box to help you. Whose ideas do you like best? Why?

CONFIDENT COMMUNICATOR
KEEP TALKING

Use *because* and *because of* to give reasons.
Because + subject + verb
I'd like to make a holiday for pets ***because I think*** *…*
Because of + noun
I probably won't celebrate the day at the beach ***because of the weather****. It's too hot.*

GRAMMAR

Countable nouns are known as unit nouns. They have units and can be plural. Uncountable nouns are known as mass nouns. They have to be divided up or measured to be counted and are not plural.

Remind students that *some* and *any* can be used when the exact number or amount is not known. They can be used with both countable and uncountable nouns. For example, *I need some raisins for the cake. I don't add any sugar in my coffee. Are there any ingredients missing?*

You will hear many native speakers use *a lot of* instead of *much* or *many* for both countable and uncountable nouns.

SPEAKING

Write an example on the board for students to use. For example, *The name of my holiday is International Pamper Your Neighbor Day. To celebrate this holiday, you bake special treats for your neighbor and visit them at home. I want to celebrate this holiday because I think we really should value our neighbors and spend more time with them. It will promote peace in our communities because I think neighbors who know each other look out for each other.*

Tell students that the more convincing reasons they give, the more likely it is their group will choose their holiday.

LESSON 2 The Business of Holidays

VOCABULARY money and shopping

A Match the underlined phrases (1–6) to the definitions (a–f). Write the letter.

1 I love traveling, so I usually spend money on trips abroad. d
2 You can make money by selling handmade gifts online. a
3 I don't like to lend money to friends. e
4 I never waste money on things I don't need. c
5 It's easy to overspend at certain times of the year. I spend too much money at Thanksgiving. f
6 Sometimes I borrow money from my parents, but I always pay it back. b

a get money by working or selling something
b ask someone to give you money because you don't have enough
c buy things you don't need
d buy something
e give someone money because they don't have enough
f spend more money than you have

MAKE IT REAL

There are many informal synonyms for money in English. Here are a few: *cash, bucks, loot, bread, dough, capital.*

B Choose the correct option to complete the text.

Are you looking for extra ways to **1** make / spend money? Instead of **2** borrowing / lending money from a friend or member of your family, here are a few simple ideas to help:

- Don't **3** waste / lend money on expensive gifts when, with a little imagination, you can make your own. How about making cookies and giving them as gifts to family and friends?
- Many stores have sales in January. It's easy to find things at good prices at this time of year. Buy the items you need to make your card and gifts. Decide how much you can afford so you don't **4** waste / overspend.

C IN PAIRS Ask and answer questions using the phrases in A.

A: Do you lend money to friends? *B: Sometimes, if they really need it.*

GO TO page xi for LISTENING step-by-step instructions.

GO TO page 137 for AUDIO SCRIPT.

They agree with one another. They use phrases to show agreement, e.g., *You're right. I know. That's true. Exactly. Yeah!*

LISTENING

A 2.02 LISTENING SKILL—Identify opinions Listen to a conversation in a store. Do you think the man and woman agree or disagree with one another?

B Write the phrases under the correct headings.

Exactly. I disagree. I know. I'm not sure about that. That's true. Yeah! You're right.

Phrases for agreeing

I know. That's true.
You're right. Yeah!
Exactly.

Phrases for disagreeing

I disagree. I'm not sure about that.

C THINKING SKILL—Evaluate Do you agree or disagree that you should never borrow or lend money? Why or why not?

VOCABULARY

Have students practice the money phrases by categorizing them into two columns:

- **Money coming in:** make money, borrow money
- **Money going out:** spend money on, lend money, waste money on, overspend

LISTENING

Possible reasons for lending money include:

- You trust the person very much, and you are sure they will pay you back.
- You have lent them money in the past, and they have always paid it back.
- One day, you might have to borrow money from them.

Possible reasons for not lending money include:

- You don't have any extra.
- You don't trust the person.
- You know they have borrowed money from others and haven't paid it back.

GRAMMAR enough / not enough

A Decide if the nouns that follow *enough* and *not enough* are *Countable* or *Uncountable*.

1 Not enough people shop around these days. countable
2 They don't have enough money. uncountable
3 I have enough decorations. countable

B Choose the correct option to complete the rules.

1 *Enough* shows that the amount is **the right amount** / not the right amount.
2 *Not enough* shows that the amount is the right amount / **not the right amount**.
3 *Enough* and *not enough* are used with countable nouns / uncountable nouns / **both**.

For more practice, go to page 144.

C Look at the pictures and write sentences with *enough* or *not enough*.

1

2
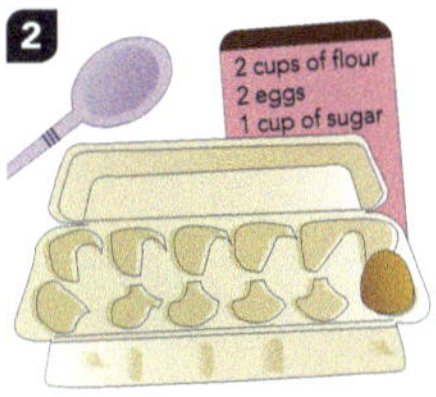

3

4

1 I / have enough / money / buy / this hat.
I don't have enough money to buy this hat.

2 There / be enough / eggs / make / the cake.
There aren't enough eggs to make the cake.

3 She / have enough / food / on her plate.
She has enough food on her plate.

4 He / have enough / casual / shoes.
He has enough casual shoes.

D IN PAIRS Do you think there are enough national celebrations throughout the year in your country? Discuss the days in the year when people get the day off.

SPEAKING

A Do you think some people spend a lot of money on celebrations these days? On which celebrations?

B IN PAIRS Discuss your opinions about what people spend money on for different celebrations. Use the Confident Communicator box to help you.

CONFIDENT COMMUNICATOR — START TALKING

Use informal or formal language depending on your situation.

Informal
I think people waste money on decorations for holidays.
I don't think it's a good idea to borrow money for celebrations.
I bet some people spend lots of money on gifts.
I guess lending money to a friend is OK.

More formal
In my opinion, people shouldn't feel they have to buy gifts.
From my point of view, Independence Day is an important celebration.

GRAMMAR Additional Activity

Play *Why Don't You …?* Tell students to ask each other hypothetical questions starting with *Why don't you …* and answer with *enough* or *not enough*. For example, *Why don't you drive a Ferrari? I don't have enough money*. Have them report back to the class on the best answers.

SPEAKING

Things people spend their money on for celebrations are the venue, food, music, decorations, invitations, equipment rental, presents, transportation, activities, and entertainment.

Have students discuss alternatives to spending so much money on a celebration. Is it possible to celebrate without overspending?

CONFIDENT COMMUNICATOR

If necessary, read the Confident Communicator box aloud using the correct intonation and pronunciation. Have students do the speaking activity in pairs using informal language. Then ask them to present some of their findings to the class using formal language.

LESSON 3 Celebration Food and Drink

VOCABULARY food and drink packaging

A Label the food items in the pictures (1–8) with words from the box.

bag of oranges	box of chocolates	carton of juice	jug of apple cider
bottle of water	can of nuts	jar of olives	package of cookies

1 
bag of oranges

2 
package of cookies

3 
jar of olives

4 
can of nuts

5 
jug of apple cider

6 
box of chocolates

7 

carton of juice

8 
bottle of water

B **IN PAIRS** What do you usually give or receive as a gift on holidays? Discuss.

A: I usually make cookies and give a box to my friends at Christmas.

B: I get a jar of honey from my aunt. She keeps bees.

LISTENING

GO TO page 137 for AUDIO SCRIPT.

A 2.03 You are going to listen to a chef describing food he is making for a special celebration. Listen to the introduction and choose the celebration he is talking about.

1 St. Patrick's Day **2** Thanksgiving **3** Chinese New Year **4** International Women's Day

GO TO page 137 for AUDIO SCRIPT.

B 2.04 **LISTENING SKILL—Listen for specific information** Listen to the recipe and complete each ingredient with one word.

Dumplings (makes about 30)

2 packages *of dumpling wrappers*
1 can of water chestnuts
1 bag *of green onions*
2 boxes of mushrooms
2 teaspoons of Chinese spices
garlic

small bottle *of oil*
For the dipping sauce:
1 jar *of sweet chili sauce*
ginger
sesame seeds
1/2 bottle *of soy sauce*

VOCABULARY Extra Practice

For more practice naming containers, have students name other things that are bought in bags, boxes, cartons, jugs, bottles, cans, jars, and packages. For example, *bag of apples, box of cereal/chocolates, carton of milk/cream, jug of water, bottle of soda, can of tuna, jar of olives,* and *package of toilet paper*.

LISTENING

Allow students to look up ingredients online and use a translator when they are discussing the celebration food they like. Tell them that if there is a food in their country that doesn't have a direct translation, they should describe the food. For example, *Epazote is an herb used to flavor Mexican dishes.*

THINKING SKILL—Evaluate

Have students evaluate a list of possible celebration foods or drinks based on their own criteria. This could be the most popular, the most representative, the easiest to make, or the most delicious. They have to say why they think a particular food is a good representation.

C **IN PAIRS** Think about a celebration food that you like. Make a note of the ingredients you need and discuss.

A: I really love pavlova.
B: What do you need to make it?
A: You need a carton of eggs, a carton of cream, and ...

D **THINKING SKILL—Evaluate** Which celebration food or drink from your country would you recommend to a foreign visitor? Why?

PRONUNCIATION /tʃ/ and /ʃ/

A 2.05 Listen. Notice the difference between the /tʃ/ sound and the /ʃ/ sound.

1 shop chop
2 ships chips
3 sheep cheap

B 2.05 Listen again and repeat. Exaggerate the /tʃ/ *and* /ʃ/ sounds as you say the words.

C **IN PAIRS** Practice saying the pairs of words. Can your partner hear the difference between the /tʃ/ *and* /ʃ/ sounds when you say the words?

GO TO page ix for PRONUNCIATION step-by-step instructions.

WRITING

A Read the paragraph describing a celebration. What does the festival celebrate? Do you have a celebration like this in your country?

the end of the sugar cane season (or harvest)

We celebrate Grand Kadooment Day at the end of the Crop Over festival. A lot of people in the Caribbean celebrate it, too, **but** it's the national celebration of Barbados. In the past, Crop Over was a celebration to mark the end of the sugar cane season. People dress up in costumes or in their best clothes, **and** there are street parades and street food festivals all over the island. We normally eat fried fish **or** fish cakes and sno-cones—ice with flavors such as ginger or coconut. I really like it **because** it's a holiday. We get the day off work, **so** we can have some family time.

GO TO page xiv for WRITING step-by-step instructions.

B Match the bold linking words in A to their use.

1 but: introduces a contrasting idea
2 and: adds extra information
3 because: gives a reason
4 so: gives a result
5 or: gives an alternative

C In your notebook, write a short paragraph about a celebration you like. Use linking words to connect your sentences.

SPEAKING

A Imagine you are ordering a food gift box online for a friend who lives abroad. You want to add some special celebration foods that are typical of your country. Make a list of the items you would include.

B **IN PAIRS** Show your list to your partner. Add any items from your partner's list that you would like to include. Use the Confident Communicator box to help you.

C **IN GROUPS** Share your ideas with the members of your group. Decide whose gift box you would most like to receive. Explain why.

CONFIDENT COMMUNICATOR
KEEP TALKING

You can use *Did you* to ask follow-up questions in a conversation. For example:
Did you include a jar of ...?
No! I forgot. But I should. I included a box of ... Did you?
Yes, I did. You can't celebrate ... without those!

PRONUNCIATION

Tell students to pay particular attention to the position of the tongue and the flow of air when saying /ch/ and /sh/. They should listen for the difference in sound before they attempt to say the sounds.

Write the words *same* and *different* on the board. Put students into pairs. Have the listener point to the word *same* or *different* as she or he listen to the sounds.

WRITING

Tell students to think about the *Wh–* question words *who*, *what*, *where*, *when*, *how*, and *why* when they are thinking about the information to include in their paragraph. They should keep in mind that the reader might be someone who is unfamiliar with the celebration, and so they should be descriptive and informative in their writing.

SPEAKING

Have students reach a group consensus on the items that should go in the food gift box. Tell them to agree on 10 items for the gift box that represent celebration food typical of their country.

GO TO page xv
for LANGUAGE AND LIFE step-by-step instructions.

Language and Life

Creativity – Graduation Celebrations

A 2.06 **Read an article about different graduation celebrations from around the world. Then choose** *Yes* **or** *No.*

Graduation Ceremonies Around the **World**

Sweden
Swedish graduates wear sailor's caps to their graduation ceremony. The ceremony usually starts with singing. Parents arrive and give their children gifts tied with ribbons, and the graduates wear the ribbons around their necks. At the end of the ceremony, there is a parade through the streets of the town, and local people come to congratulate the students.

Japan
In Japan, graduation happens in March, before the new school year. High school students wear their school uniforms for their graduation ceremony. If their school doesn't have a uniform, they wear formal clothes, such as a suit for men and a kimono for women. The principal usually gives a speech. Then, the student president gives a speech.

United States
In the US, it's common for a famous person (sometimes a graduate of the university) or a politician to give a speech to congratulate the graduates. In some large American universities, the ceremony happens in a sports stadium. Students normally wear special caps and gowns in the colors of their university or department.

South Africa
Graduates from the University of Witwatersrand in Johannesburg have an interesting musical tradition. The graduation ceremony there starts with a formal procession by the teachers and workers at the university. After that, they play the song "I Got You (I Feel Good)" by James Brown for the students to dance to.

Argentina
Students in Argentina usually wear old clothes for their graduation ceremony. The reason? Family and friends throw sticky or messy food at the graduates, like flour, eggs, ketchup, and soda. It's supposed to bring them good luck!

1 Graduates in Sweden wear traditional caps and gowns. Yes / **No**
2 Graduation ceremonies in Japan happen at the end of the year. Yes / **No**
3 In Argentina, graduates wear formal clothes. Yes / **No**
4 One university in South Africa plays a particular song at graduation. **Yes** / No
5 In the US, graduation ceremonies often happen in large outdoor spaces. **Yes** / No

OBJECTIVE

In this lesson, students propose ideas for a graduation ceremony and present them to a university president (the teacher). They will make suggestions based on some of the ideas from case studies of graduation ceremonies in other countries. Let students know that as they grow in the educational setting, their opinions will be sought and valued. Some may already be members of student committees. Everyone should seek to be proactive in their academic communities, especially with sports-related events.

PROCESS OPTIONAL 2.06

Students review five graduation ceremonies from around the world and discuss some things people in their countries do to celebrate. Then, they will read an email from a university president calling for the students' suggestions for invited speakers, what students should wear, venue, student speakers, and music. Students make a list of ideas and give a presentation in which they outline their ideas for the subcommittee. Last, students vote on the ideas that people like most. Let students know that they should be gracious if their ideas are not accepted.

B **Which graduation ceremony described in A would you like to go to? Why?**

C **IN PAIRS Discuss some of the things that people do in your country to celebrate high school or university graduation. Use the prompts to help you.**

- have a family meal
- celebrate with a night out with friends
- go on vacation with classmates
- have a party at home
- go to a formal organized event
- other: ______________________________

A: People usually celebrate by going to a formal organized event at a hotel or club.

B: Yes, they do. But sometimes they go on vacation with their classmates. We went to …

D **IN GROUPS Imagine you are on the Student Committee at your university. Read the email from the university president and brainstorm ideas for your ideal graduation ceremony.**

New Message

From: johnwilson@university.uni

To: studentcommittee@university.uni Cc Bcc

Subject: RE: Graduation Speakers

Dear Student Committee members,

As you may know, we are looking for speakers for next year's graduation ceremony. We would like your help in choosing one or two public figures who our graduating students respect and admire. We would also like your thoughts on the following things for the ceremony:

- what students should wear
- where the ceremony should take place
- which students should give a speech
- what music you think should be played

We look forward to your ideas.

Please present your ideas to me at our next meeting on March 15.

Regards,

John Wilson
University President

Send

E **Make a list of one or two suggestions for each of the points in the university president's email.**

____

____

____

____

F **Give a presentation to the class and the university president (your teacher). Which ideas for a graduation ceremony do most people like? Take a vote.**

G **Discuss the questions.**

1. Was it easy or hard to work together to think of creative ideas?
2. In what other situations do you listen to different people offer creative ideas?

MAKE IT DIGITAL

Go online and watch videos of graduation ceremonies from around the world. Which ones do you think you would like to go to?

CLASSROOM MANAGEMENT

When voting for the best proposals for the graduation ceremonies, let students know they can refer to different ideas from different groups' proposals. They should give reasons for their voting preferences.

CULTURE NOTE

Discuss respecting all cultures equally. Differences are to be valued and celebrated. Graduation ceremonies reflect something of the culture of a place. Generally, education is universally valued.

MAKE IT DIGITAL

Graduation ceremonies in the United States usually include a speech by a famous person invited by the university to speak. This is called a commencement speech or address. Have students find and watch online a famous person giving a commencement speech. Some famous people who have given a commencement speech are Steve Jobs (co-founder of Apple Inc.), J. K. Rowling (author), and Jim Carrey (actor).

GO TO page xvii
for **UNIT REVIEW** step-by-step instructions.

UNIT 2

VOCABULARY review

SCORE: / 10

A Complete the sentences with the words from the box.

bag | boxes | can | jar | package

1. How many ___boxes___ of breakfast cereal do you buy a month?
2. I ate nearly a whole ___package___ of chocolate cookies!
3. Dad bought my mom a ___jar___ of marmalade when he went to Spain.
4. I'd rather get a ___bag___ of potato chips than a box of raisins for my snack.
5. Do you want to get a ___can___ of tomato soup or a bag of tomatoes?

B Choose the best option.

It's easy to **1** overspend / waste at holidays. I try to **2** borrow / save some money every week so that I can buy little gifts for everyone in my family. My dad loves chocolate, so I often get him a **3** box / can of Swiss chocolates. My mom loves scarves, so I shop **4** around / about to find her pretty ones. My sister's easy to buy for. I usually get her a **5** jug / bottle of perfume. And then, there's the dog. He always gets a toy!

GRAMMAR review

SCORE: / 10

A Choose the correct option.

1. A few / lot of people came to the office party. There were only about 20 people there.
2. This coffee has too much / many sugar in it. I can't drink it.
3. Some / A little people go to their graduation ceremony in formal clothes!
4. I don't think there are a little / enough public holidays in my country.
5. The party dress was too much / many money for me to buy.

B Complete the text with the words and phrases from the box.

a few | a lot | enough | some | too many

One country with **1** ___a lot___ of public holidays is Argentina. In total, there are 19 public holidays. **2** ___Some / A few___ people say that 19 holidays is **3** ___too many___. Others say that holidays help people relax and that, in general, people don't have **4** ___enough___ time off work. **5** ___Some / A few___ countries have a similar number; Colombia has 18 days and Thailand has 16 days.

16–20 correct: You can discuss money, shopping, and food and drink packaging. You can use quantifiers to talk about *enough* / *not enough*.
0–15 correct: Look again at the Vocabulary and Grammar sections in the unit.

TOTAL SCORE: / 20

WHAT DO YOU KNOW NOW? Look back at page 17 and add the words you know now to the boxes.

GO TO page xix
for **FOLLOW A PRO** step-by-step instructions.

FOLLOW A PRO HOSPITALITY

Take the quiz about hospitality. Then go to Follow A Pro on page 128. Find the answers and learn more about the hospitality industry.

1 When did the world's oldest hotel, located in Japan, open?
a 705 **b** 1205 **c** 1505

2 What country gets the most international tourists per year?
a the US **b** China **c** France

3 How many hotel rooms are there in the world (in millions)?
a 5.1 **b** 8.5 **c** 17.2

26 Unit 2 Party!

CLASSROOM MANAGEMENT

For an added challenge, have the students do the review activities while timed. Give them five minutes to complete each review activity.

FURTHER DISCUSSION

Put students in groups of three and ask the following questions for them to discuss:

- What was the last celebration you attended?
- What kinds of containers and packaging are in your weekly grocery bags?
- How would you like your next graduation ceremony to be?

UNIT 3 What's Trending?

GO TO page vi
for UNIT OPENER step-by-step instructions.

WHAT DO YOU ALREADY KNOW?

1 Think of TV shows, movies, and music you like. Make a list.

2 IN PAIRS Share and compare your favorites. Add more things to your lists.

STUDENTS MAY ALREADY KNOW:

- Entertainment: movies, music, concert, dance, TV shows, actor, actress, singer, dancer.

TV shows

Movies

Music

DISCUSS & SHARE

VIDEO

3 IN GROUPS Watch the video and answer the question.

SYM Do you prefer to watch entertainment at home or in public?

GO TO page xx
for VIDEOS IN SYM step-by-step instructions.

In this unit, you will ...

- talk about entertainers in your area, the music industry, and your viewing habits.
- use thinking skills: understand and evaluate.
- read about street performers.
- use strategies to start and keep talking by making notes, asking for opinions, and using qualifying phrases.
- use decision-making skills to plan an event to save a theater.
- design questionnaires for research.

WHAT DO YOU ALREADY KNOW?

If you notice students are struggling to understand what to do, you can provide one or two examples to help them get started:

- **TV shows:** documentary, soap opera, series
- **Movies:** comedy, action/ adventure, romance
- **Music:** rock, country, pop

VIDEO

Before viewing, ask:

Who is going out to the soccer stadium? *Sam*
Who does not like to go to the movie theater? *Jenny*

After viewing, put the continuum on the board.

home ——— public entertainment

Have students mark the continuum and explain why they prefer to watch entertainment at home or in public.

DISCUSS & SHARE

Ask students what they do most often when they want to be entertained. Some students may like to stay home alone and watch a TV show, and others may like to stream a movie. Ask *Do you go out with friends to see a movie in a theater or go watch a band or singer play live music?*

GO TO page x

for **READING** step-by-step instructions.

Suggested answers:
Juan Eze is a street entertainer who doesn't move. He looks like a statue.

Marcel Debard is a fire-eater. He blows fire from his mouth.

Huang Jun does puppet shows. People watch him control the puppets.

GO TO page vii

for **VOCABULARY** step-by-step instructions.

LESSON 1 Street Entertainers

READING

A Look at the pictures in the article in B. Which street entertainer do you think is the most talented?

B 3.01 READING SKILL—Identify main ideas Read the magazine article about street entertainers around the world. Then write 1–2 sentences for each entertainer. Explain what they do.

Street Entertainers From Around the WORLD

Juan Eze is a street entertainer from Buenos Aires. "Everywhere I go, people always ask me what my **trick** is," he says, "but I never tell anyone the secret of my act. Nobody knows." Juan sits for up to four hours at a time without moving, but he says he doesn't get bored. What's amazing is that he looks like he's **floating**. "Everyone thinks I'm doing nothing, but I'm actually watching everything around me."

Marcel Debard, a fire-eater and acrobat, works on the streets of Casablanca. "I started **performing** about 15 years ago in a circus in Paris. Then someone asked me to help with the fire-eating act and I started to learn how to do it. Is it dangerous? Well, yes, but it's more **dangerous** for the audience. We have to make sure nobody gets hurt. That's why we **blow** the **fire** over the heads of the people."

Huang Jun does a **puppet** show on the streets of Yangzhou, China. "Puppets are popular forms of entertainment in China, for adults and kids," he explains. "In most puppet shows around the world, no one sees the person **controlling** the puppets. In Chinese puppet shows, everybody can see everything. It's part of the entertainment—to see how we make the puppets move."

C Read the article in B again. Match the questions (1–3) to the answers (a–c). Write the letter.

1 Whose act is the most dangerous? b
2 Whose act is popular with people of all ages? c
3 Whose act has the least movement? a

a Juan Eze
b Marcel Debard
c Huang Jun

D THINKING SKILL—Understand "Street entertainers are usually very talented." Do you agree or disagree? Give reasons.

VOCABULARY

A Match the bold words from the article in READING B to the definitions (1–8).

1 performing: doing something entertaining for an audience
2 puppet: a small model character that you move with your hands
3 trick: an entertaining act that looks like magic
4 controlling: making something do what you want
5 floating: moving in the air
6 dangerous: not safe; likely to cause pain or harm
7 blow: to push out air from your mouth
8 fire: flames and heat from something burning

28 Unit 3 What's Trending?

READING

More popular street entertainment includes: mime, acrobatics, juggling, contortion, gymnastics, and comedy routines.

When people play music in the street and ask for donations, it is called *busking*. People can busk alone or with a band. They use almost any instrument you can think of, including violins, accordions, cellos, guitars, and so on.

THINKING SKILL—Understand

To give an opinion about street performers' talent, students must first understand what they have read. Ask them to use examples in the text to support their position.

VOCABULARY

Encourage students to read the sentence around the bold words in READING **B** to help them identify the meaning in VOCABULARY **A**. If necessary, ask students to read the sentences aloud.

GRAMMAR indefinite pronouns

A Find and underline the indefinite pronouns in the article in READING B.

"Everywhere I go people always ask me what my trick is, but I never tell anyone the secret of my act. Nobody knows."

B Read the sentences and choose the correct option to complete the grammar rules.

Everywhere I go, people always ask me what my trick is.
We have to make sure nobody gets hurt.
Then, someone asked me to help.
I never tell anyone the secret of my act.
Everybody can see everything.

1 *Everywhere* means all places / one or two places.
2 *Nobody* means some people / no people.
3 *Someone* means a specific person / an unknown person.
4 If the verb or adverb is negative, use anyone / someone.
5 *Everything* means all things / all people.

For more practice, go to page 145.

C Read the paragraph and choose the correct option.

Before he became known to **1** someone / everyone / anyone as James Bond, the actor Pierce Brosnan worked as a street entertainer in London. He was training to become an artist, but he met **2** somewhere / someone / something who showed him the art of fire-eating. Soon after Brosnan started performing, **3** nobody / everybody / somebody who worked as a circus agent saw his act and thought it was amazing. Brosnan performed his fire-eating trick on the TV show *Muppets Tonight*. **4** Nobody / Everyone / Everything knows exactly how it happened, but there was a problem with the fire-eating trick and Pierce got serious burns. In true James Bond style, he didn't let **5** anyone / everybody / nobody know he was hurt until the end of the show.

D IN PAIRS How popular are the types of entertainment in the box? Discuss. Use indefinite pronouns.

going to a music concert | going to a sports event | playing board games | watching TV | going to a play | going to the movies | playing video games

A: I know someone who likes …
A: Nobody spends much time …
B: I think everyone likes …
B: I don't know anyone who likes …

SPEAKING

A Think about the street entertainers that you see in your country. Make notes about:

- where you usually see them
- what they do
- how you feel about them
- how you think others feel about them

B IN PAIRS Discuss street entertainers. Try to talk for at least one minute. Use the Confident Communicator box to help you.

I usually see entertainers in the main square. One guy plays the guitar …

CONFIDENT COMMUNICATOR
START TALKING

When you need to talk for a minute or more, try to make notes about what you want to say before you start talking. You can look at your notes as you speak to help you remember what you want to say.

GO TO page viii for GRAMMAR step-by-step instructions.

GO TO page xii for SPEAKING step-by-step instructions.

GRAMMAR

Before GRAMMAR **A**, write more examples on the board to get students started. For example, *Everyone in my family likes going to concerts. Nobody I know spends much time playing video games.*

Encourage students to ask follow-up questions to make the interactions into discussions.

SPEAKING

Encourage students to speak for a minute uninterrupted. Tell them to use the strategies they know to give them thinking time. Remind them to use fillers like *umm*, *well*, and *as I was saying*. Tell them to use similar words when they can't bring a word to mind.

CONFIDENT COMMUNICATOR

Tell students to make notes using key words and symbols or images to help remind them of what they wanted to say next. They shouldn't write full sentences.

GO TO page xi
for **LISTENING** step-by-step instructions.

GO TO page 138
for **AUDIO SCRIPT**.

LESSON 2 The Music Industry

LISTENING

A Where can you find good music videos? How often do you watch them? Discuss as a class.

B 3.02 LISTENING SKILL—Listen for numbers Listen to this interview with a music producer. Then complete the statements.

1 Michael Jackson's music video for *Thriller* was ___13___ minutes long.
2 *Gangnam Style*, a music video from Korea, became popular in ___2012___.
3 In 2017, the music video for the song *Despacito* had ___three___ billion views on YouTube.

C 3.02 Listen again. Choose *True* or *False*.

1 Scott Fleming used to be in a band. True / **False**
2 He used to be a DJ. **True** / False
3 Scott Fleming writes songs for bands. True / **False**
4 Most bands still write their own music. True / **False**
5 Music videos started an important change in the music industry. **True** / False
6 Today, anyone can make a music video and post it to YouTube. **True** / False

D THINKING SKILL—Evaluate Can a good music video make a song popular? Give examples.

VOCABULARY the music industry

A Match the job descriptions (1–8) to the jobs (a–h). Write the letter.

This person ...

1 writes songs for a band. ___c___
2 is the main singer in a band. ___b___
3 controls the band's business side. ___g___
4 makes music videos. ___h___
5 sings in the background. ___d___
6 records the songs in a music studio. ___a___
7 checks equipment so the audience can hear the band. ___f___
8 focuses on the band's clothes, hair, and makeup. ___e___

a producer
b lead vocalist
c songwriter
d backup singer
e stylist
f sound technician
g manager
h director

B IN PAIRS Imagine you could have one of the jobs from A. Which one would you like to have and why? Discuss.

A: I would like to be a backup singer. You get to sing with different bands.

B: Yeah, that sounds like fun. I like fashion, so I think I'd like to be a stylist.

GRAMMAR *used to*

A Read sentences from the interview. Then choose the correct option.

Bands **used to** write their own music.
People **used to** listen to music on the radio.
Did you **use to** be in a band?
People **didn't use to** do that.

1 *Used to* is used for a past action that is still happening now / **isn't happening now**.
2 After *used to*, use the *–ing* / **base** form of the verb.
3 In questions and negative statements, use *used to* / ***use to***.

For more practice, go to page 145.

LISTENING

THINKING SKILL—Evaluate

Have students answer the following questions to evaluate what makes a music video good:

- Should the band appear in the video?
- Should the band dance or do something else?
- Should there be some special effects?

CULTURE NOTE

Music videos were widely viewed in the 1980s. That was when Music Television (MTV) came on the air as a cable TV channel dedicated to music. Music videos had already existed as a way for bands to promote themselves anywhere in the world when they were on tour and unable to appear in interviews. These days, we access music videos online.

VOCABULARY Extra Practice

Ask students to brainstorm music genres and discuss the vocabulary words in relation to different genres. Some music genres are: pop, rock, classical, heavy metal, hip-hop, house, electronic, blues, jazz, dance, folk, country, punk, and reggae. You might like to have students find examples of the ones they are not familiar with on their phones.

B Complete the sentences with *used to*, *didn't use to*, or *did* … *use to*.

1 Where ___did___ you ___use to___ take music lessons?

2 I ___didn't use to___ download music, but now I download music every week.

3 ___Did___ Tom ___use to___ work in a music store?

4 Those guys ___used to___ be in a band called Kings and Queens.

5 That restaurant ___used to___ be a movie theater.

6 My brother ___didn't use to___ like hip hop, but he does now.

7 ___Did___ you ___use to___ watch cartoons when you were a kid?

8 Where ___did___ they ___use to___ live?

C IN PAIRS Make questions with *Did* … *use to*. Use the phrases below and your own ideas. Then ask and answer the questions.

- watch music videos on TV
- wear a school uniform
- take music lessons
- hang out with friends at the mall

A: Did you use to watch music videos on TV? *B: Yes, I did. / No, I didn't.*

MAKE IT REAL

You can also use *would* to talk about something that happened in the past.
When I was younger, I used to watch music videos all the time.
When I was younger, I would watch music videos all the time.
Don't use *would* to describe a past state.
I used to live in Mexico City.
~~*I would live in Mexico City.*~~

PRONUNCIATION reduced form of *used to*

A 3.03 Listen to the sentences. Notice how the speakers reduce *used to* as /justə/.

B IN PAIRS Practice saying the questions and answers. Use the reduced form of *used to*.

1 A: Did you use to work in marketing? B: No, I used to work in information technology.
2 A: Did you use to walk to the office? B: No, I used to take the bus.
3 A: Did your parents use to own a restaurant? B: No, they used to own a bakery.

GO TO page ix for PRONUNCIATION step-by-step instructions.

SPEAKING

A How did your parents or grandparents do these activities when they were your age? How do you do them now? Make notes in your notebook.

- watch movies
- contact family or friends
- do math problems
- listen to music
- take pictures

B IN GROUPS Compare your ideas. Use the Confident Communicator box to help you.

A: I think my parents used to listen to CDs when they were my age. I listen to music online.

B: My parents used to watch DVDs. I stream movies online.

CONFIDENT COMMUNICATOR — START TALKING

To ask another person his or her opinion or experience about the same topic, use one of these questions:
And you?
What about you?
How about you?

GRAMMAR

Used to …, *didn't use to …*, and *Did you use to …?* are useful chunks of language for talking about past habits. Let students know that they can contrast their past and present habits by using the word *but*. However, they can use the phrase *used to* for past habits that continue into the present with *and*.

PRONUNCIATION

Explain to students that the schwa is the most common sound in English and it represents weak sounds. Have them practice /justə/ in isolation and then identify it in speech. Tell students not to read the sentences as they try to emulate them in speech, just listen and repeat.

SPEAKING

Have students report back to the class about similarities and differences they discover as they talk to each other. Tell them to find trends in their parents' and grandparents' habits and common elements in their past and present.

LESSON 3 Viewing Habits

VOCABULARY TV viewing

A Complete the definitions (1–7) with words from the box.

binge-watch | channel-surf | commercials | episode | on demand | stream | TV series

1 __on demand__ (*adjective*): ready to watch at any time
2 __channel-surf__ (*verb*): to go quickly from one channel to another looking for something to watch
3 __TV series__ (*noun plural*): a set of TV shows with the same characters
4 __episode__ (*noun*): a TV program that is one part of a set
5 __stream__ (*verb*): to play a video or game using wi-fi without downloading it
6 __binge-watch__ (*verb*): to watch several shows in a TV series at one time
7 __commercials__ (*noun*): advertisements on TV

B Complete the text with words from A.

1 This show is not __on demand__. You can only watch it on Saturday at 6 p.m.
2 When I don't know what to watch on TV, I __channel-surf__ until I find something I like.
3 My favorite TV __series__ is at 8 p.m. every Tuesday night.
4 Did you watch last night's __episode__ of *City Hospital*? It was amazing!
5 On rainy evenings, I like to stay home and __binge-watch__ my favorite show.
6 There is no wi-fi here, so I can't __stream__ that video on my computer.
7 When I watch TV, I often get a snack during the __commercials__.

C IN PAIRS Think about the TV shows you like and don't like. Say why you like them and how you watch them.

A: I like funny TV series. Sometimes I binge-watch … *B: I stream episodes of a TV series called …*

LISTENING

A Look at the pictures. Which one is most similar to the way you watch TV?

a

b

c

d

B 3.04 LISTENING SKILL—Identify opinions Listen to four people talk about their TV viewing habits. Match each speaker to a picture in A.

1 Speaker 1: __b__ 2 Speaker 2: __d__ 3 Speaker 3: __c__ 4 Speaker 4: __a__

GO TO page 138 for AUDIO SCRIPT.

VOCABULARY

As an introduction to VOCABULARY **C**, ask students what they think the most popular TV shows in their country are now, both foreign and domestic. Ask for a quick show of hands to survey the class to determine the most popular TV shows in the class.

LISTENING

Allow students to compare their answers in LISTENING **A** with others before checking LISTENING **B**. Have them share words that helped them identify the right pictures as they listened.

Ask students to circle the phrases in LISTENING **C** that they agree with.

MAKE IT REAL

Saying *I'm really into …* expresses what you like. To refer to the programs someone is watching or binge-watching, ask *What TV shows are you into at the moment?* for *What TV shows are you watching at the moment?*

C 3.04 **Listen again. Write the speaker who expresses each opinion.**

This person…

1 thinks there wasn't so much choice in the past. Speaker 4
2 says he/she doesn't watch very much TV. Speaker 2
3 likes watching foreign-language TV shows. Speaker 1
4 watches TV shows at the same time as doing something else. Speaker 2
5 isn't interested in watching TV commercials. Speaker 3
6 likes watching things that make him/her laugh. Speaker 2

MAKE IT REAL

To talk about something you like or enjoy doing, use the phrase *to be into*.
I'm really into police dramas. I love them!

D THINKING SKILL—Evaluate How much time do you usually spend watching TV in a day? How does your amount compare to your classmates?

WRITING

GO TO page xiv for **WRITING** step-by-step instructions.

A Read the text. Underline the three words the writer uses to make contrasts.

I used to watch TV with my brother, but now that I'm older, I stream videos and TV series on my laptop. I rarely watch TV these days, although there are some shows I like. I still watch them, though I don't usually watch them on TV. I watch them online. The only time I watch TV is when I watch soccer on the weekend with my friends.

B Make notes comparing your viewing habits in the past and your viewing habits now.

In the past	Now
shows I watched:	shows I watch:
how I watched them:	how I watch them:
who I watched them with:	who I watch them with:

C In your notebook, write a paragraph comparing your viewing habits now with your viewing habits in the past. Use *but*, *although*, and *though* to make contrasts.

I used to … but now …

D IN PAIRS Share your paragraphs from C. Suggest other ways to make contrasts between the past and now.

SPEAKING

A Check (✓) all the activities that you like to do.

- ☐ watch TV with my friends and family
- ☐ watch TV alone
- ☐ stream shows on my computer, laptop, or phone
- ☐ watch TV while I'm doing something else
- ☐ watch shows I download on my computer, laptop, or phone
- ☐ watch TV in bed
- ☐ watch only one or two YouTube channels or TV series

B IN GROUPS Ask and answer questions about viewing habits. Use the Confident Communicator box to help you.

A: Do you like to watch TV? B: Yes, sometimes. I like watching …

CONFIDENT COMMUNICATOR

KEEP TALKING

Use the following qualifying phrases with adjectives to make what you're saying more interesting:
sort of / kind of *really/pretty*
My favorite show is a science fiction series. It's kind of / sort of scary and funny.
Did you see the new episode? It was pretty/really good.

WRITING

Before WRITING **D**, review the phrases to compare the past and the present:

- *used to*: I used to … but now I …
- *would*: When I was young, I would always …
- simple past vs. present: *Were, was* and *are, is, am*
- comparatives: TV was better/more boring in the past than now.
- present perfect: There have been many changes …

SPEAKING

For SPEAKING **B**, have students write conversation questions based on the prompts they have just checked. For example, *Do you like to watch TV with friends or alone? Do you stream shows?* You may want to extend the discussion with some more questions. For example, *Do you binge-watch any programs? Do you like commercials?*

CONFIDENT COMMUNICATOR

Tell students that using qualifying phrases with adjectives is a useful tool for sounding natural when speaking but that they shouldn't be used in writing.

GO TO page xv

for **LANGUAGE AND LIFE** step-by-step instructions.

Language and Life

Decision-making – Saving a Theater

A Do you go to the movie theater? If so, which movie theaters do you go to? Do they look like any of the theaters in the article in **B**?

B 3.05 Read the article about movie theaters. Then complete the sentences.

LET'S GO TO THE MOVIES!

Nowadays, large movie theaters (called multiplexes) are everywhere. They have many screens showing different movies. They show 2D and 3D movies. Some show IMAX movies on giant-sized screens. Some also stream live theater shows or music concerts. In addition, some movie theaters that used to sell only popcorn and candy now have restaurants or cafés where you can enjoy a meal before or after the show. Because of competition from TV movies and home entertainment, movie theaters must find new ways to get people back into their seats. Some movie theaters now provide an experience where the audience dresses in costumes or sings along to the music. Outdoor or rooftop movie theaters are popular in some cities in the summer. You can also go to a drive-in movie theater (where you watch the movie in your car). There are about 400 drive-in movie theaters in the US today, although they're not as popular as in the 1950s and '60s.

In the past, almost everyone went to the movies. No one had a TV, so it was an exciting form of entertainment. Many beautiful movie theaters opened in the 1920s and '30s when people of all ages went to see the latest Hollywood movie on the big screen. Some of these theaters, such as the Pathé Tuschinski movie theater in Amsterdam and the Orinda Theater in California, are still open today. However, many of the old buildings that used to be movie theaters now have other uses or are closed.

1 Another word for a large movie theater is multiplex.
2 At an IMAX movie, the screen is giant-sized.
3 In the summer, outdoor, rooftop, and drive-in theaters are popular.
4 In the US, drive-in movies were popular in the 1950s and '60s.

OBJECTIVE

In this lesson, students propose new activities to introduce as part of the renovation of an old movie theater. They respond to a call for ideas by developers of the project. In order for these iconic theaters to survive, creative solutions are needed. Young people have fresh ideas. Involving them in the process gets them involved in their local communities. Using their input will give young people a sense of ownership of the local project.

PROCESS OPTIONAL 3.05

First, students read about different kinds of movie theaters and movie-going experiences. Then, students read an ad from a local newspaper asking for their input in a new project. There are funds available to make a historical movie theater ready for the pubic for its 100th birthday. In pairs, students use a visual organizer to record ideas. Finally, they present their ideas to a group and present the best ideas to the class.

C **IN PAIRS** Read the ad from a local newspaper. Then make notes about your answers to the questions.

DO YOU LOVE WATCHING MOVIES?

Are you between the ages of 16 and 25? Then we'd love to hear from you!

We are looking for young people to help with ideas for our historic movie theater, The Ritzy. Opened in May 1922, it is a fine example of the magical days of Hollywood. Thanks to a large donation of $2 million, we can now make it ready for the 21st century! The Grand Re-opening is planned for the theater's 100th birthday in 2022.

To help with our project, contact us in writing with your answers to these questions:

- What kind of movies should we show?
- What foods and drinks should we sell?
- How much should tickets be?
- What other services should we provide?
- Should we have other events at the theater?
- What popular actors should we invite?
- What other ideas do you have for the Grand Re-opening?

We look forward to hearing from you!
The Ritzy Project Team

What movies to show?

____

____

Other services?

____

____

Eating options?

____

____

Other events at the theater?

____

____

Ticket prices?

____

____

Other ideas for the Grand Re-opening?

____

____

D **IN GROUPS** Share your ideas. Work together to write a clear, creative plan for the Grand Re-opening.

E Discuss the questions.

1 Were you able to make decisions with members of your group effectively? Why or why not?
2 In what other situations do you need to make decisions about a plan of action with others?

MAKE IT DIGITAL

Go online to find out about a historic movie theater that is popular today. How has it changed?

CULTURE NOTE

Discuss the differences students perceive in films made in Hollywood for the international mainstream and films made in their countries. How are they similar and how are they different? What are movies made in their countries about? Discuss other foreign films they have seen and liked. What differences do they see in films made in different English-speaking countries? What are the differences between US and UK films? Have they seen any films made in Australia or Canada? How do films in general reflect the culture of a place?

MAKE IT DIGITAL

Some interesting articles about historical theaters in Mexico and the United States can be found online by searching using phrases such as "historic movie theaters in Mexico" or "best art house movie theaters in Mexico City" (switch out "Mexico" and "Mexico City" for "the US" and any American city).

GO TO page xvii

for **UNIT REVIEW** step-by-step instructions.

1 channel-surf
2 sound technician
3 commercials
4 dangerous
5 on demand
6 stream
7 backup singer
8 binge-watch
9 songwriter
10 blow

UNIT 3

VOCABULARY review

SCORE: / 10

A Complete the sentences with the words from the box.

backup singer	blow	commercials	on demand	sound technician
binge-watch	channel-surf	dangerous	songwriter	stream

1 I usually ____________ until I can find something I want to watch on TV.
2 I'm a ____________ for the band. I check the equipment to make sure everything works right for the concert.
3 I like to watch ____________. Some are funny, but they don't change my ideas about what to buy.
4 Be careful doing that trick. It's ____________!
5 You can watch many shows anytime. Most of my favorite shows are available ____________.
6 I don't really watch much TV, but I like to ____________ music videos online.
7 One day I hope to be a famous singer, but right now I am a ____________ for one.
8 I ____________ my favorite shows on weekends. One Sunday afternoon, I watched eight episodes!
9 I'm not a good singer, but I'm good at creating words with music. I'm a good ____________.
10 Did you see the street performer ____________ fire from her mouth?

GRAMMAR review

SCORE: / 10

A Complete the sentences with the correct form of *used to*.

1 Did you __use to__ work at the music store downtown?
2 I didn't __use to__ like classical music, but I enjoy listening to it now.
3 Emile and Isaac __used to__ own a recording studio.
4 Did Paolo __use to__ be a street performer before he became an actor?
5 My grandmother __used to__ have a small black-and-white TV.

B Choose the correct option.

There was an amazing street entertainer that I saw every day on my way to work. **1** Everyone / Anyone watched him, but **2** no one / anyone understood how he did his trick. He looked like **3** nothing / something from a science fiction film because he wore a black and yellow robot costume. He used to stand very still until **4** something / someone walked past him. Then, he moved his body and changed shape until he looked like a small yellow truck. Then, he drove away. **5** Everybody / Somebody who saw his performance said it was amazing.

16–20 correct: You can discuss the music industry and TV viewing habits. You can use indefinite pronouns and the phrase *used to*.
0–15 correct: Look again at the Vocabulary and Grammar sections in the unit.

TOTAL SCORE: / 20

WHAT DO YOU KNOW NOW? Look back at page 27 and add words you know now to the boxes.

GO TO page xviii

for **STUDY SKILLS** step-by-step instructions.

STUDY SKILLS DESIGNING A QUESTIONNAIRE

Take the quiz about questionnaires. Go to **Study Skills** on page 129 to find the answers. Then learn more about designing a questionnaire.

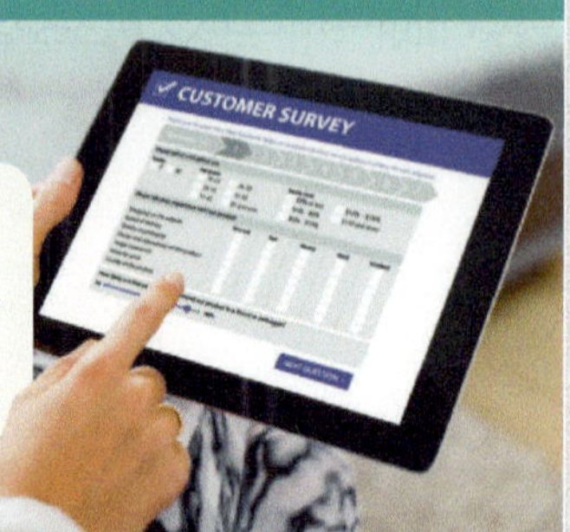

1 **The language in a questionnaire should be as clear and simple as possible.**
a True **b** False

2 **What is the maximum number of questions your questionnaire should have?**
a 5 **b** 10 **c** 20

3 **On average, what percentage of people respond to surveys?**
a 5% **b** 33% **c** 78%

36 Unit 3 What's Trending?

CLASSROOM MANAGEMENT

For added accountability, have students record the results of each unit's review activities. Tell them to record them in the same place to keep a running record and compare their results as they progress through the units. Organizational skills such as these will be widely beneficial to them in their lives.

FURTHER DISCUSSION

Put students in groups of three and ask the following questions for them to discuss:

- How has entertainment changed over the years?
- What do you think about the cost of music concerts?
- Do you watch entertainment award shows?
- What popular movie has everyone seen recently?

UNIT 4

Your ID

GO TO page vi
for UNIT OPENER step-by-step instructions.

WHAT DO YOU ALREADY KNOW?

1 Think of people you know. Write one word to describe each person.

2 IN PAIRS Share and compare your list. Say who the people are and describe them. Add more words to your list, if possible.

Person—Description

STUDENTS MAY ALREADY KNOW:

- **People at home:** family, mother, father, brother, sister, cousins.
- **People at school:** teacher, student, classmate, partner.

VIDEO

DISCUSS & SHARE

3 IN GROUPS Watch the video and answer the question.

SYM Are you an introvert or an extrovert?

GO TO page xx
for VIDEOS IN SYM step-by-step instructions.

In this unit, you will ...

- talk about personality types, describe people using superlatives, and compare appearance to others.
- use thinking skills: apply and predict.
- read about personality types in the workplace.
- use strategies to start and keep talking by showing disagreement, describing yourself in the past, and making comparisons.
- use interpersonal communication skills to understand and interact with different personalities.
- follow a school psychologist to learn about this job and the skills needed for a career in education.

WHAT DO YOU ALREADY KNOW?

If you notice students are struggling to understand what to do, you can provide one or two examples to help them get started:

- **People at home:** parent, sibling, aunt, uncle, neighbor
- **People at work:** boss, co-worker
- **People at school:** administrator, faculty, school principal

VIDEO

Before viewing, ask:

What are some characteristics of introverts? *They are not shy but like to be alone and work independently.* What are some characteristics of extroverts? *They are a lot of fun to be around and very social.*

After viewing, put the continuum on the board.

introvert —— extrovert

Have students mark the continuum and explain their preferences.

DISCUSS & SHARE

Have students place themselves on a continuum that has *introvert* at one end and *extrovert* at the other. Not everyone will land on the ends, and many people might find themselves somewhere in between. Have them revisit the continuum after the unit to see if they change where they placed themselves.

GO TO page x

for **READING** step-by-step instructions.

GO TO page vii

for **VOCABULARY** step-by-step instructions.

LESSON 1 Personality Types

READING

A **Think about your close friends. Are their personalities similar to or different from yours?**

B 4.01 **Read this article about different personality types. Then choose the correct option.**

WHAT'S YOUR PERSONALITY TYPE?

Are you friendly and outgoing? Or are you the quiet type? Do you like to work as part of a team or do you prefer to work alone? Psychologists try to understand people by studying their personalities. Read on to find out more about four different personality types.

Type As

Type As are often successful, professional people. They are very organized and focused, and they work hard to succeed. Sometimes, they can be **impatient** with coworkers who aren't as hard-working as they are. They enjoy taking risks, but get stressed easily.

Type Bs

Type Bs are usually **easygoing** and don't get stressed. They love to spend time with friends and have fun. Usually, they're cheerful and **optimistic**. Their worst characteristics are that they can be **lazy** and take a long time to make decisions.

Type Cs

Type Cs are interested in small details and numbers. They are very good problem solvers. They like to be alone and don't always like working as part of a team. They are often **shy** and find it hard to communicate. Type Cs get as stressed as Type As at work. Take time to relax, Type Cs!

Type Ds

Type Ds aren't as optimistic as Type Bs. In fact, they can be very pessimistic. They often worry, see the negative side of things, and get **depressed** when things are hard. They like to feel comfortable and don't like to take risks. However, they are patient and hard-working.

Remember that most people are a mix of these different types. It's unusual to find a person who is only one personality type.

1 Type D people **enjoy** / **don't enjoy** taking risks.
2 Type C people find it **easy** / **hard** to relax.
3 Type B people have a **positive** / **negative** view of the world.
4 Type A people **are** / **aren't** hard-working.

C **READING SKILL—Summarize** **Complete the summary for Type B people using words from the article in B.**

Type B people like having **1** ____________. They are usually sociable and **2** ____________. They have a/an **3** ____________ view of life, but they can be **4** ____________ and can take time to decide things.

1 fun
2 friendly/cheerful
3 optimistic/positive
4 lazy

D **THINKING SKILL—Apply** **Explain what personality type you think you are. Why? How about your friends and family?**

VOCABULARY

A **Match the words from the box to the definitions (1–6).**

depressed easygoing impatient lazy optimistic shy

1 __shy__: quiet; nervous and embarrassed
2 __easygoing__: very relaxed; calm
3 __depressed__: sad; very unhappy
4 __lazy__: not wanting to work
5 __optimistic__: positive; thinking good things will happen
6 __impatient__: annoyed because something isn't happening quickly

READING OPTIONAL 4.01

Brainstorm adjectives that students may need to talk about their friend's personalities and write them on the board (e.g., *happy, sad, energetic, lazy, clever, friendly, talkative, hardworking, funny,* and *reserved*). Give students an example from your life and use comparatives to talk about how you and a friend are different.

VOCABULARY

Have students practice the vocabulary words and words in the definitions by categorizing them. Students can use categories like negative and positive meanings, long and short words, or words they know and words that are new for them.

GRAMMAR (not) as ... as

A Choose the sentence with the same meaning.

1 Type Ds aren't as optimistic as Type Bs.
- a Types Ds and Type Bs are equally optimistic.
- b Type Ds are more optimistic than Type Bs.
- c Type Bs are more optimistic than Type Ds.

2 Type Cs are as stressed as Type As at work.
- a Type Cs and Type As are equally stressed at work.
- b Type Cs are more stressed than Type As at work.
- c Type As are more stressed than Type Cs at work.

For more practice, go to page 146.

B Choose the correct option.

Because my sister and I are twins, people think we have the same personality, but we are very different. My sister, Danni, is more of a Type A personality. I'm more of a Type B. Danni **1** isn't as patient as / is as patient as I am. She gets mad about small things, but I don't. In general, Type A people **2** aren't as easygoing as / are as easygoing as Type B people. Of course, Type B people aren't always relaxed. For example, I'm **3** as impatient as / not as impatient as Danni when I have to wait in line at the store. We both want to buy our things and leave quickly! Danni and I are different, but we have a good relationship. I think we are both outgoing, and I'm **4** as friendly as / not as friendly as her. For example, we both like going out together to see friends. But I'm **5** as hard-working as / not as hard-working as Danni, so I go out more often! I usually stay out with friends longer, and she comes home and does her homework!

C IN PAIRS Compare people. Use adjectives from the reading and any others you know.

brother/sister classmate/friend Dad/Mom Type A personalities/Type B personalities

My brother isn't as easygoing as my sister.

MAKE IT YOURS

Go online or use a dictionary to find more words for characteristics that you and your friends have.

PRONUNCIATION stress on the adjective

A 4.02 Listen to the opinions. Notice the stress on the adjectives.

B 4.03 IN PAIRS Listen and repeat.

1 I don't think swimming is as difficult as skiing.
2 I'm not as cheerful as my best friend.
3 Learning grammar isn't as easy as learning vocabulary.

SPEAKING

A IN PAIRS Play a game of Guess Who. Think of a well-known character from a movie or TV series. Describe their positive and negative characteristics. Ask your partner to guess who it is. Take turns.

B IN GROUPS Talk about what percent (%) of each personality type you think you are. Give reasons. Use the Confident Communicator box to help you.

CONFIDENT COMMUNICATOR – KEEP TALKING

Use the following expressions to estimate:
I think I'm about/roughly/approximately 25% Type A, because ...
Off the top of my head, I'd say I'm about 50% Type D, because ...
I have a feeling I'm probably mostly a Type B, because ...

GO TO page viii for GRAMMAR step-by-step instructions.

GO TO page ix for PRONUNCIATION step-by-step instructions.

GO TO page 139 for AUDIO SCRIPT.

GO TO page xii for SPEAKING step-by-step instructions.

GRAMMAR Additional Activity

Ask students to say jobs and write them on the board. Tell students to describe the best personality for each job. For example, *I think police officers should be outgoing and hardworking. They should be strong, but they will probably need to be patient when dealing with the public.*

PRONUNCIATION

Have a competition to see who can say the pronunciation sentences from PRONUNCIATION **B** the best. Ask for volunteers. Have three judges from the student body. Play a sentence, and then have the competitors repeat as clearly and fluidly as they can.

SPEAKING Extra Practice

If time allows, play an extra round of *Guess Who*. Ask students to work in pairs. Have them take turns describing people in the room in relation to others and guessing who is being described. For example, *This person is more outgoing than me. This person is not as easygoing as you.*

LESSON 2 Teamwork and Personality

VOCABULARY different personalities

A **Match the types of people (1–6) to their descriptions (a–f). Write the letter.**

1 A leader d
2 An expert e
3 A loner b
4 A workaholic a
5 A creative thinker f
6 A risk taker c

a likes to work a lot.
b likes to be alone.
c likes to try new and sometimes dangerous things.
d is responsible for a group of people.
e has specialized knowledge.
f has new and imaginative ideas.

B **IN PAIRS Which type of person from A do you think you are? Which type(s) of people do you like to work with? Discuss and give reasons.**

I think I am a creative thinker because I like to think of new ideas. I wouldn't like to work with a workaholic because …

GO TO page xi for LISTENING step-by-step instructions.

LISTENING

A **Do you prefer to work in a large group, in a small group, or alone? Discuss.**

GO TO page 139 for AUDIO SCRIPT.

B **4.04 LISTENING SKILL—Identify tone Listen to the talk about teamwork and different personalities. What is the style of the talk? Choose and explain.**

a serious b amusing c critical

C **4.04 Listen again. Choose *True* or *False*.**

1 All the members of a team should have the same personality type. True / False
2 A good leader sometimes lets other members lead the team. True / False
3 Many companies have a technology expert on the team. True / False
4 Creative thinkers are often very organized. True / False
5 The information in the talk is only useful for people at work. True / False

D **THINKING SKILL—Apply Think about groups/teams that you are in at school, at work, or in the community. Which role do you usually take? Which one do you prefer?**

40 Unit 4 Your ID

VOCABULARY

Ask students to write an example sentence for each type of person about a person they know. Tell them the more connections they make to their own lives, the easier it will be to remember the new words. For example, *My uncle Fred is a natural leader. He is the captain of his soccer team.*

LISTENING

For the opening discussion, tell students to share their general preferences for working in groups or alone. They may then want to identify different situations where they are more comfortable working alone or on groups.

THINKING SKILL—Apply

Tell students that people behave differently in different situations. There may be some situations where they show leadership, some situations where they prefer to be a loner, and others where they find themselves taking on the role of creative thinker.

GRAMMAR superlative adjectives

A We use superlative adjectives to compare more than two things. Underline the superlatives.

1 An expert has the greatest knowledge about a subject important to the project.
2 The creative thinker is often not the most organized person on the team.
3 The expert will explain all the most important details to the team.
4 That is the worst mistake you can make!

B Choose the correct words to complete the rules.

1 Use *a* / *the* before a superlative adjective.
2 For adjectives that are one syllable, add *-er* / *-est* to the end of the word.
3 For adjectives that are two syllables and end with *-y*, add *-est* / *-iest* to the end of the word.
4 For adjectives that are two or more syllables, use *most* / *the most* before the adjective.
5 Some superlative forms are irregular: *bad–the worst; good–better* / *the best*.

For more practice, go to page 147.

C Complete the sentences with the correct superlative form of the adjective in parentheses.

1 Diana is the most creative (creative) person I know.
2 The day I won this award was the happiest (happy) day of my life.
3 Fernando is the tallest (tall) student in this class.
4 Esmeralda is the most talkative (talkative) student in this class.
5 The Green Garden is the best (good) restaurant in town.

D IN PAIRS Discuss the questions.

1 What was the most exciting day of your life?
2 Who is the smartest person you know?
3 What is the most beautiful place you know of?
4 What is the worst thing to do on the weekend?
5 (Write your own question.)

____

____

MAKE IT REAL

In spoken English, people often use the superlative to show that something is really good or bad. In these cases, they often pronounce *the* /ðə/ as *thee* /ði/.
That was the /ði/ most amazing meal!
It was the /ði/ worst movie.

SPEAKING

A What were you like in your elementary school classes? Were you the funniest kid? The quietest kid? The smartest kid? The most creative kid?

B IN PAIRS Talk about how your personality changed as you grew up. Are you different now?

When I was in kindergarten, I was the most creative kid in the class. But in first grade ...

C IN GROUPS Say how your partner's personality changed as he or she grew up. Did anything surprise you? Use the Confident Communicator box to help you.

CONFIDENT COMMUNICATOR
KEEP TALKING

Use these phrases to talk about changes in your life:
***When I was younger** / **in kindergarten** / **in high school**, I was talkative.*
***I used to be** a little impatient, but I'm more relaxed now.*
***Until I went to high school** / **university**, I was the shiest person in the class.*

GRAMMAR

As students discuss the questions in pairs in GRAMMAR **D**, monitor and write down mistakes as you listen. Then, at the end of the activity, write the sentences on the board. As a class, analyze the mistakes. Have students identify mistakes and attempt to correct them.

MAKE IT REAL

The emphasis on *the* in phrases used to describe something really good or really bad is an example of hyperbole. Hyperbole is exaggerated language used for dramatic effect. Hyperbole is figurative language, and it should not be taken literally.

SPEAKING

For clarity and fluidity when speaking, have students record themselves speaking using their smartphones. Then tell them to listen to their own recordings. They may be reluctant to listen to themselves speaking English. Advise them that this technique will help them improve their speaking dramatically.

LESSON 3 Who Are You Like?

VOCABULARY characteristics

A Complete the sentences with words from the box.

adventurous bossy generous honest rude selfish smart

Someone who is ...

1. bossy tells people what to do.
2. smart is intelligent.
3. rude isn't polite.
4. generous enjoys giving things to people.
5. adventurous loves new and exciting experiences.
6. selfish thinks only about himself or herself.
7. honest tells the truth.

B Complete the table with the words in A.

Positive characteristics	Negative characteristics
honest	bossy
smart	rude
adventurous	selfish
generous	

C IN PAIRS Compare your answers from B. Can you add any other characteristics?

D IN GROUPS Choose one characteristic from A that describes you and one that does not. Explain.

I think I'm very generous. I love giving gifts. So, I don't think I'm selfish.

LISTENING

A Look at the pictures. Guess how the people are related. Use the words from the box to help you.

A: I think these two are father and son. He's the oldest because ...

B: I don't think they're father and son. I think they're ...

aunt/niece brother/sister brothers cousins father/daughter father/son mother/daughter mother/son sisters twins

Suggested answers:
- **a** brother/sister, father/daughter
- **b** father/son, cousins, uncle/nephew
- **c** mother/daughter, sisters, twins, aunt/niece
- **d** brothers, cousins

a

b

c

d

GO TO page 139 for AUDIO SCRIPT.

B 4.05 Listen to the speakers talk about who they are like. Then match each speaker to his or her picture in A.

1. Speaker 1: photo a
2. Speaker 2: photo d
3. Speaker 3: photo c
4. Speaker 4: photo b

VOCABULARY

For students to become independent learners, encourage them to record vocabulary. Suggest a number of ways for them to choose from, such as writing lists in a notebook, writing words on index cards, or taking notes on a smartphone. Tell students to experiment with memory techniques until they find ways that work best for them (e.g., categorizing, writing words in sentences, or drawing pictures).

LISTENING

Explain the difference between fraternal and identical twins. Fraternal twins don't look the same and can be different genders. Identical twins look the same and are always the same gender.

Write the terms *to look like*, *to like*, and *to be like* on the board and elicit the differences in meanings and examples.

THINKING SKILL—Predict

To predict is to figure out or anticipate what you think will happen in the future. In predicting, past experiences are important to make correct decisions.

In LISTENING **D**, students will predict about whether people become more similar to their parents and grandparents as they get older based on what they have seen in their families and the families around them.

C 4.05 LISTENING SKILL—Listen for detail **Listen again and choose the words the speakers use to describe themselves.**

Speaker 1: tall / bossy / creative / blond hair / blue eyes
Speaker 2: short / tall / slim / brown hair / blond / adventurous / smart
Speaker 3: brown eyes / small / selfish / brown hair
Speaker 4: bald / tall / easygoing / strict

D THINKING SKILL—Predict **As people grow older, do they become more similar to their parents and grandparents in appearance? How about in personality?**

WRITING

A **Read the description of a character from a movie. Can you guess who the character is?**

One of my favorite characters is ▬▬ from the movie ▬▬. The American actor Harrison Ford plays this role. He is a pilot and the leader of the Rebel Alliance. In the early movies, he travels around the galaxy with his copilot, Chewbacca. He's easygoing and very smart, but he is sometimes rude. Princess Leia is in love with him, but she says she is not. They get married in the end and have a son named Ben. I really like him because he's a hero, but he's not perfect.

GO TO page xiv for WRITING step-by-step instructions.

Han Solo, *Star Wars*

B **You are going to write a description of a character from a movie, TV show, or book. Make notes about ...**

the movie, TV show, or book ______
the character's appearance ______
the character's personality ______
what the character does ______
how you feel about the character ______

C **Write your description in your notebook. Try to write about 100 words.**

SPEAKING

A IN PAIRS **Compare yourself to a member of your family. Describe how you are the same or different. Use the Confident Communicator box to help you. Consider the criteria.**

- physical appearance, e.g. hair color, eye color, hair type (e.g. wavy, straight, curly), weight, height
- your personality
- interests and abilities, e.g. artistic ability, sports, music, career

I'm like my dad. We are both adventurous. But I look like my mom and my aunt.

CONFIDENT COMMUNICATOR
KEEP TALKING

Use the following phrases to talk about who you are like:
I look like/don't look like my mom/dad.
I take after/don't take after my mom/dad.

Use the following phrases to talk about characteristics:
I'm like/not like my mom/dad.
My brother/sister and I are alike/not alike.

WRITING

Review ways to talk about people's appearance and personality. Elicit a list of movie, TV, and book characters. Tell students to write as many notes as they can at the planning stage—they don't have to use *all* ideas. Have students share their description with a partner, making sure the name has been omitted. The partner should guess the character.

SPEAKING

Tell students to look for unusual habits that they and their family member might have in common or to use as examples of differences. Tell them to use all of the usual descriptors and personality traits and then end with a twist. This will make their speaking more interesting.

GO TO page xv
for **LANGUAGE AND LIFE** step-by-step instructions.

Language and Life

Interpersonal Communication – Working with Different Personalities

A 4.06 **Read the conversation. Decide which person has each type of personality.**

Lana: Thanks for coming to the meeting. I made notes on the things we need to do. I think we need to focus on this year's fundraiser and organize it.
Ben: A fundraiser? We tried that last year. You know, we spent a lot of money on T-shirts, and we didn't make any money. I think that's a bad idea.
Lana: How much money did we make? And how much did we lose? Alex?
Alex: I have that information right here. We spent $456 on T-shirts, and we made $153. We had a lot of T-shirts that didn't sell. We also spent $120 on food and drink.
Marta: I think fundraisers are fun! I had a great time at the one last year and I think people enjoyed it. OK, so we didn't sell many T-shirts, but maybe we can do something different this year, like have a raffle or a popcorn stand.
Ben: A popcorn stand? I hate popcorn.
Marta: OK, maybe not popcorn. How about we sell cookies? Everyone loves cookies! I can make some.
Alex: Maybe we should find out how much the ingredients cost and how many we need to make. I'm happy to do that.
Lana: Those are all interesting ideas, but I think we need to focus on two things. First, we need to decide on a date for the fundraiser and second, which person can do which job. I think that would be very useful. Alex, take notes, please …

1 Type A Lana **2** Type B Marta **3** Type C Alex **4** Type D Ben

B **Choose the adjective that describes each person.**

1	Lana:	organized	easygoing	lazy
2	Ben:	focused	negative	relaxed
3	Alex:	selfish	bossy	logical
4	Marta:	cheerful	pessimistic	honest

OBJECTIVE

In this lesson, students learn how to work with people with different personality types. This activity gets students to understand that working with others takes patience and understanding. They will figure out how to identify personality types and how to work with them. Furthering your students' understanding of personality types will help them develop patience and professionalism when faced with the prospect of working with others.

PROCESS OPTIONAL 4.06

Before students start the Language and Life lesson, have them reread the article about different personality types from Lesson 1.

Students analyze and identify the personality types of characters in the conversation. They predict what characters would say based on their personality types. Students then prepare a role-play. Each student takes on the role of a different personality type and participates in a conversation to plan an event in that role. Finally, they identify who was playing which personality type.

C **Read lines from the rest of the conversation. Who do you think said each line?**

Alex Ben Lana Marta

1 ____Ben____: "I think we should forget about a fundraiser. I don't think people will come."
2 ____Marta____: "These are great ideas. Having a popcorn stand, having a raffle, selling cookies … I'm sure we can make money!"
3 ____Lana____: "We really need to make a decision by the end of this meeting. We can't wait another week. We have to get started as soon as possible!"
4 ____Alex____: "It's good to know how much money we can make. Popcorn is cheap to make, but we can sell it for a lot more money, I think."

D **IN GROUPS** **Prepare a role-play about planning a class event, such as a party or a celebration. Use the suggested phrases to help you.**

Student A: You have a Type A personality.
Suggested phrases:
I made notes on …
I think we need to focus on …
First, we should decide …

____
____

Student B: You have a Type B personality.
Suggested phrases:
… is / are fun!
I love …!
These are great ideas!

____
____

Student C: You have a Type C personality.
Suggested phrases:
I have that information …
Maybe we should find out how much …
I am happy to …

____
____

Student D: You have a Type D personality.
Suggested phrases:
We tried that …
I think that's a bad idea…
I don't think people …

____
____

E **Role-play your discussion from D for the class. Can your classmates guess who played each personality type?**

F **Discuss the questions.**

1 Did you understand the different personalities better in the role play? Why or why not?
2 In what other situations do you need to interact successfully with people who have different personalities?

MAKE IT DIGITAL

Go online to find a quiz about personality types. Take the quiz and share your results with the class.

CULTURE NOTE

A stereotype is a strong idea that a person may have about someone or something in particular. We often hold stereotypes about personality types of certain cultures. Share stereotyped impressions you have of different cultures' personalities and discuss how these stereotypes are mistaken and sometimes dangerous.

MAKE IT DIGITAL

There is a lot of information online about personality types. (Tell students to be careful when searching for personality tests, as these can lead to websites wanting them to sign up for something.) They will find information about the psychologist Carl Jung and his theories. They may find it easier to just type in "personality types" and then choose a subtopic that interests them and go from there.

GO TO page xvii
for **UNIT REVIEW** step-by-step instructions.

UNIT 4

VOCABULARY review

SCORE: / 10

A Match the personality types (1–5) to their synonyms (a–e). Write the letter.

1 easygoing d
2 depressed e
3 outgoing c
4 stressed b
5 cheerful a

a happy
b worried
c friendly
d relaxed
e unhappy

B Complete the sentences with words from the box.

expert leader loner risk taker workaholic

1 My best friend is a real risk taker. He isn't afraid of anything and loves anything dangerous!
2 I was a loner when I was teenager. I didn't want to make friends with anyone.
3 My eldest daughter is a workaholic. She works very long hours.
4 Dr. Milagros is a psychology expert. She knows a lot about how people think and behave.
5 John is the leader of this project. He tells everyone else on the team what to do.

GRAMMAR review

SCORE: / 10

A Complete the sentences using *as ... as* and the adjectives in parentheses.

1 Jack isn't / is not as tall as as Garth. (not/tall)
2 Emily is as shy as Marty. (shy)
3 Greg and Henry aren't / are not as outgoing as Barbara. (not/outgoing)
4 Uncle Garth as cheerful as Dad. (cheerful)
5 Raul and his sister aren't / are not as hard-working as Patty. (not/hard-working)

B Complete the sentences using the superlative form of the adjectives in parentheses.

1 My brother is the thinnest (smart) person in our family.
2 Auntie Jill is the most creative (creative) person I know.
3 That was the scariest (scary) movie ever! I didn't like it.
4 Martina is the bossiest (best) manager in the office.
5 Fernando is the youngest (young) child in the Perez family.

16–20 correct: You can identify different personalities and characteristics. You can use superlative adjectives.
0–15 correct: Look again at the Vocabulary and Grammar sections in the unit.

TOTAL SCORE: / 20

WHAT DO YOU KNOW NOW? Look back at page 37 and add words you know now to the box.

GO TO page xix
for **FOLLOW A PRO** step-by-step instructions.

FOLLOW A PRO EDUCATION

Take the quiz about education. Then go to Follow A Pro on page 130. Find the answers and learn more about education.

1 How many students does the largest school in the world, in India, have?
a 15,000 b 25,000 c 55,000

2 How much time do elementary school students in China spend on homework each day?
a about one hour b about two hours c about three hours

3 What is the oldest English-speaking university in the world?
a Oxford b Cambridge c Yale

46 Unit 4 Your ID

CLASSROOM MANAGEMENT

Allow students time to review the vocabulary and grammar of the unit before they complete the review activities. Then allow them to compare answers with others before checking. If they identify any weak areas, ask them to review those sections again.

FURTHER DISCUSSION

Put students in groups of three and ask the following questions for them to discuss:

- What three words would you use to describe your personality?
- If you didn't have your personality, what personality would you like to have?
- Who is your favorite celebrity, and what do you like about their personality?

UNIT 5 Prepping

GO TO page vi
for **UNIT OPENER** step-by-step instructions.

WHAT DO YOU ALREADY KNOW?

1 Think about the types of plans or arrangements you often make. Write the words.

2 **IN PAIRS** Share and compare your information. Add more words to your list.

STUDENTS MAY ALREADY KNOW:

- **Family events:** birthday party, wedding.
- **Social events:** dinner party, book club.
- **Professional events:** award presentation, work convention.

VIDEO

DISCUSS & SHARE

3 **IN GROUPS** Watch the video and answer the question.
SYM Do you do one thing at a time, or are you a multi-tasker?

GO TO page xx
for **VIDEOS IN *SYM*** step-by-step instructions.

In this unit, you will ...

- talk about making arrangements for a hotel, a school event, and a wedding.
- use thinking skills: predict, remember, and analyze.
- read a dialogue about checking a hotel reservation.
- use strategies to keep talking by making requests and practicing before giving a talk.
- use global competence skills to understand and appreciate social customs.
- learn research skills for school and work.

WHAT DO YOU ALREADY KNOW?

If you notice students are struggling to understand what to do, you can provide one or two examples to help them get started:

- **Family events:** funeral, family reunion
- **Social events:** barbeque, friend reunion
- **Academic or professional events:** seminar, conference

VIDEO

Before viewing, ask:

What does a multi-tasker do? *He/She does more than one thing at a time.* What professions demend multi-tasking? *doctors, nurses, chefs*

After viewing, put the continuum on the board.

one thing at a time —— multi-tasker

Have students mark the continuum and explain if they do one thing at a time or they are a multi-tasker.

DISCUSS & SHARE

Discuss how busy everyone's lives can be with family, work, school, and friends. Sometimes, it's hard to schedule everything. Is it better to do one thing at a time or to try to take care of everything at the same time? Have students brainstorm a pro/con list and write opinions on the board.

LESSON 1 Thanks for Your Help

READING

GO TO page x for READING step-by-step instructions.

A THINKING SKILL—Predict Look at the pictures in B and read the first line of the conversation. Predict the answers.

1 What do you think the customer's first question to the clerk will be?
2 How do you think the clerk will answer?

Suggested answers:
1 Salut ... Umm, English?
2 Yes, how can I help?

B 5.01 Read the conversation between the hotel clerk and the customer. Why is Shiro calling the hotel?

He wants to know if he and his wife can check in early.

Clerk: Bonjour, Hôtel Paris.
Shiro: Hello. Uh ... Do you speak English?
Clerk: Of course, sir. Good morning. How can I help you?
Shiro: Good morning. My name is Shiro Ito. My wife and I have a **reservation** for four nights starting tomorrow, but we have a problem. Your website says that check-in time is two o'clock, but our **flight** arrives at eight a.m. We'd like to **check in** at about eleven o'clock if possible.
Clerk: We probably won't have rooms before two, but I'll check to see if any rooms might be ready early. One moment, sir ... I'm sorry, Mr. Ito, but I can't check you in at eleven. However, I can check you in at 1:30, and I can give you a **voucher** for a free lunch in our restaurant. They have a very nice **buffet**.
Shiro: That's fine, thank you. We'll eat lunch while we wait.
Clerk: Good. We'll take care of your **luggage** at the front desk while you have lunch. I think you'll like our restaurant. The food is excellent, and you won't feel so tired if you have some of our good French coffee!
Shiro: I'm sure we'll enjoy the meal, but I won't have coffee because I want to sleep in the afternoon.
Clerk: I understand, sir. Have a good flight, and we'll see you tomorrow.
Shiro: Thanks for your help.
Clerk: You're welcome, Mr. Ito.

C READING SKILL—Scan Look back at the conversation to find the answers to the questions as quickly as possible.

1 How many nights is the reservation for? four nights
2 What is normal check-in time at the hotel? two o'clock
3 What does the clerk offer to give them? a voucher for a free lunch
4 Does Shiro accept the offer? yes
5 Why doesn't he want to have coffee? because he wants to sleep in the afternoon

VOCABULARY

GO TO page vii for VOCABULARY step-by-step instructions.

A Match the words (1–6) to their definitions (a–f). Write the letter.

1 reservation c
2 check in e
3 flight b
4 voucher f
5 buffet a
6 luggage d

a a lot of food on a table for people to choose what they want
b a trip on an airplane
c an arrangement for something to be kept for you to use later
d bags and suitcases that you take on a trip
e to register at a hotel or for a flight
f a piece of paper that you can use in place of money

READING OPTIONAL 5.01

Elicit what the people are doing in the photos. Students may not be able to tell immediately, but the first line of the conversation will give it away. Once students know the situation—booking a hotel room—have them predict what Shiro's first question will be and how the clerk will answer.

THINKING SKILL—Predict

Be open to all predictions at this point, as it is a good chance to activate schema. Activating schema means tapping into learners' prior knowledge of a topic and their prior experiences of a context.

VOCABULARY

More words for booking a hotel room are: *room, guests, stay, hot water, shower, wake-up call, bell boy, concierge, hotel key, room number, hotel key card, air conditioning, Wi-Fi, beds, pillows, ironing board, hair dryer, cable TV,* and *room service.*

GRAMMAR modals of intention, offer, and prediction

A Read the sentences from the conversation in READING B. Label the sentences *P* (prediction), *I* (intention), or *O* (offer).

1 I'll check to see if any rooms might be ready early. O
2 We probably won't have rooms before two. P
3 I can check you in at 1:30, and I can give you a voucher for a free lunch in our restaurant. O
4 We'll eat lunch while we wait. I
5 I think you'll like our restaurant. P
6 I won't have coffee because I want to sleep in the afternoon. I

For more practice, go to page 148.

B Complete the sentences with *will, won't,* or *can.*

1 We will/can probably check out before eleven.
2 I think the weather will be nice tomorrow.
3 I can help you with your reservation if you want.
4 I won't/will not have a big lunch because I don't want to feel sleepy.
5 I don't think you will like that restaurant. The food isn't very good.

C Read the conversations and write an appropriate intention, offer, or prediction.

1 A: I can't read the menu because I don't understand French.
B: (offer) ______
2 A: What are you going to order?
B: (intention) ______
3 A: This hotel's restaurant has very good reviews.
B: (prediction) Yes. ______

D IN PAIRS Compare your sentences from C and discuss. Did you have similar ideas? Then practice your conversations together.

SPEAKING

A IN PAIRS Practice a conversation between a hotel receptionist and a guest who is checking in. Read the instructions for each role. Use the Confident Communicator box to help you.

Receptionist: Explain that you have a room on the ground floor near the pool or a room on the 12th floor. Predict why the guest might like each room.
Guest: Tell the receptionist which room you will take and what you intend to do during your stay.

B Role play your conversation for the class or for another pair.

CONFIDENT COMMUNICATOR
KEEP TALKING

Use the following expressions to express intentions and predictions.
Predictions:
*I **think** you'll like the restaurant. / You'll **probably** like the restaurant. / **I'm sure** you'll like the restaurant.*
Intentions:
*I **think** I'll have fish. / I'll **probably** have fish. / I **guess** I'll have fish.*

GO TO page viii
for **GRAMMAR** step-by-step instructions.

Suggested answers:
1 I'll translate it for you. / I'll order for you. / I'll ask for an English menu.
2 (I think) I'll have (a type or types of food).
3 I think it / the food will be good/delicious/ excellent.

GO TO page xii
for **SPEAKING** step-by-step instructions.

GRAMMAR

An *intention* is an aim or a desire for something to happen. *To offer* is to let someone know you will give them something if they want it. A *prediction* is a forecast or projection about what will happen in the future. For predictions, intentions, and offers, we can use *will*.

SPEAKING

Have students review the conversation. They may want to energize their conversations by adopting an attitude; they could be helpful or unhelpful, friendly or unfriendly, talkative or reserved. Remind students to change roles so they are able to practice all of the language in the lesson.

CAREER NOTE

Hotel receptionists in different countries may behave in different and unexpected ways. As a guest, you should expect good service, but levels of friendliness may vary. As a receptionist, be ready to welcome people from many different countries and cultures, but be aware that physical contact and hand gestures may vary greatly in your guests' cultures.

GO TO page xi for **LISTENING** step-by-step instructions.

GO TO page 140 for **AUDIO SCRIPT**.

LESSON 2 Party On!

LISTENING

A Discuss the questions about parties as a class.

1 Why do you and your friends usually have parties?
2 How often do you go to parties?

B 5.02 LISTENING SKILL—Listen for gist Listen to two conversations. Then answer the questions.

1 What are the two conversations about? a party
2 What are the students celebrating? the end of the semester
3 What do they need permission for? to use the auditorium
4 Does Ms. Jenkins give them permission? yes
5 Which conversation is more formal? Why? the second one, because Zara is talking to the director of the school

C 5.02 THINKING SKILL—Remember List the party preparations the students talked about in the first conversation. Listen again to check your list.

1 *the date*
2 the location
3 music
4 food and drinks
5 invitations

VOCABULARY making suggestions

1 Let's
2 Why don't
3 What/How about
4 a suggestion
5 What/How about
6 let … know

A Complete the conversation with the phrases from the box.

a suggestion	let … know	What about
How about	Let's	Why don't

Jen: OK, **1** ________ talk about the party. Where can we have it?
Yao: 2 ________ we have it at Paul's house? He has a swimming pool.
Jen: Awesome! **3** ________ food and drinks?
Ana: Tony and I can bring food. Could you guys bring the drinks?
Yao: Can I make **4** ________?
Ana: Sure.
Yao: 5 ________ asking everyone to bring one thing to eat and one thing to drink?
Jen: Good idea. I'll talk to Paul and **6** ________ you ________ about having the party at his house.
Ana: Cool. Text us, OK?
Jen: I will.

B IN PAIRS Use the cues to write short conversations. Then practice the conversations with your partner.

1 A: How about meeting after class tomorrow?
B: I don't know. How about Wednesday?
A: Maybe. I'll check and let you know.
B: OK, no problem.

2 A: How about having lunch on Saturday?
B: OK, why don't we make a reservation
A: Can I choose?
B: Sure.
A: What about an Italian restaurant
B: Cool.

LISTENING

Note that there can be many reasons for parties: birthdays, graduations, ends of terms, ends of courses, friends visiting from out of town, anniversaries, promotions, or just because.

THINKING SKILL—Remember

Once students have listed the party preparations in the listening text, have them practice the vocabulary by reorganizing the preparations by priority (the most important first) or in chronological order (what should be done first), and so on. This is an excellent exercise for students to remember new vocabulary.

VOCABULARY

Remembering phrases in chunks is an effective way to learn another language. This leads to experimentation with language. Highlight useful phrases from VOCABULARY **A** and tell students to repeat them until they know them well—for example, *How about we … Could you bring …? What about …? I'll let you know.*

GRAMMAR modals of request and permission

A 5.02 **Listen to the conversations and complete the examples with *can*, *can't*, *could*, and *may*. Listen again to check your answers.**

1 Could you talk to the director about that? (formal request)
2 Can you design an invitation? (informal request)
3 Could I talk to you for a minute? (formal permission)
4 May we use the auditorium for it? (formal permission)
5 Can I make a suggestion? (informal permission)
6 You can't/cannot stay after 10 p.m. (refusal of permission)

For more practice, go to page 148.

B Number the sentences from the conversation in order.

1 Zara: Great news, guys! Ms. Jenkins says we can use the auditorium.
4 Lucas: Yes, 10 o'clock is fine. What else do we need to plan?
5 Mika: We need decorations. Lucas, can you design some posters to put on the walls?
3 Zara: Yes, it's fantastic. We can't stay after 10 p.m., but that's OK, I think.
7 Mika: Zara and I will write the text. Mr. Wilson, could you check our English?
6 Lucas: Sure. I can do the design, but my English isn't great, so I can't write the text.
8 Mr. Wilson: Of course. OK, we have to go to class now.
2 Lucas: That's awesome news!

C IN GROUPS Read the conversation in B aloud to check your answers.

D IN PAIRS Find one example each of an offer, permission, a formal request, an informal request, and a refusal of permission in B.

An offer: Zara and I will write the text.
Permission: Ms. Jenkins says we can use the auditorium.
A formal request: Mr. Wilson, could you check our English?
An informal request: Lucas, can you design some posters to put on the walls?
A refusal of permission: We can't stay after 10 p.m.

PRONUNCIATION word stress with modal auxiliaries

A 5.03 **Listen to the sentences. Underline the modal auxiliary if it is stressed. Then practice reading the sentences aloud using the correct word stress.**

1 I can make a cake.
2 May I invite my boyfriend?
3 Could you help me, please?
4 I can design an invitation.
5 I won't have coffee.
6 We can't invite friends.

GO TO page ix for PRONUNCIATION step-by-step instructions.

SPEAKING

A IN GROUPS Plan a class party. Ask questions and make suggestions and offers. Make notes about your decisions in your notebook.

B Describe your plan to your class. You can refer to your notes and the Confident Communicator box to help you. Vote on the best party plan.

A: We can have our party at ..., but we can't ...

B: Paula says she'll bring ... She's also going to ...

CONFIDENT COMMUNICATOR — KEEP TALKING

Remember to use formal or informal language, depending on the situation.

Requests
Formal: *Could you ...? Yes, of course. / Certainly.*
Informal: *Can you ...? Sure. / No problem.*

Permission
Formal: *May I ...? / Could I ...? Yes, you may. / Of course. / Certainly.*
Informal: *Can I ...? Go ahead. / Sure. / Yeah, no problem.*

GRAMMAR

Remind students that after modals, the simple form of the verb is used. With modals of request, there are subtle differences in shades of meaning with *could* and *may*, some being slightly more formal than others.

PRONUNCIATION

Play the recording as many times as necessary for students to clearly hear the stressed words. Then pause the recording briefly between sentences to allow students to repeat them. After much repetition, students will have the confidence to say the sentences naturally.

SPEAKING

Have students review the list of party preparations in LISTENING **C** to help them plan a class party.

After each group presents their plan for a class party, have an impartial judge decide on the winning proposal and say why.

LESSON 3 Wedding Customs

LISTENING

A Look at the picture and answer the questions in your notebook.

1 How is this wedding similar to weddings in your country?
2 How is it different?

GO TO page 141 for AUDIO SCRIPT.

B 5.04 LISTENING SKILL—Listen for main ideas Listen to two friends talking. Then answer the questions.

1 What is the topic of the conversation?
a wedding
2 Are Susana and Jessica both invited to the event?
yes

C 5.04 Listen again. Then choose the correct answer.

1 Susana is **excited** / nervous about going to the wedding.
2 This wedding is in a church / **outside**.
3 The wedding is / **is not** very formal.
4 Jessica tells Susana to buy a wedding gift in a store / **online**.
5 The wedding and the reception are **in the same place** / in different places.
6 Jessica offers to **take Susana to the wedding** / give Susana directions to the wedding.

D THINKING SKILL—Analyze In your opinion, why does Susana have a lot of questions about the wedding?

Suggested answers: She says, "Can you tell me about weddings here," and she has an accent in English, so she is probably from another country and doesn't know about American wedding customs.

VOCABULARY wedding customs

A Match the words and phrases from the box to the definitions (1–8).

accept an invitation	gift registry	send an RSVP	wedding
dress up	pick up	show up	wedding reception

1 wedding: a ceremony for two people to get married
2 accept an invitation: to agree to attend an event or social activity
3 wedding reception: a formal party after a wedding ceremony
4 gift registry: a list of things online or in a store that a person or a couple would like to receive
5 dress up: to wear clothes that are more formal than usual
6 show up: to arrive in a place or at an event
7 pick up: to take a person somewhere in a vehicle
8 send an RSVP: to let someone know if you are going to attend an event

B IN PAIRS Discuss the questions about weddings in your country.

1 Where do people usually have weddings?
2 Is there usually a reception after the wedding? If so, what happens at the reception?
3 Do couples have gift registries online or at stores? What are some typical wedding gifts?

MAKE IT YOURS
Make a list of words that describe wedding customs in your country.

LISTENING

Before answering the questions in LISTENING **A**, ask students to look at the photo and name things they can see or say words to describe the photo. Allow them to use a dictionary. Things in the photo include: *wedding, bride, groom, dress, suit, flowers, bouquet, smile, curls, beard, handkerchief, bow tie, lace,* and *gaze*. Some words to describe the photo are: *colorful, love, happiness,* and *romantic*.

VOCABULARY

Write some prompts for the discussion in VOCABULARY **B** on the board:

- **Places to get married:** church, hall, community center, beach
- **Activities at a reception:** eat, drink, dance, talk, take photos, record videos, make speeches
- **Typical wedding gifts:** toaster, towels, china, silverware, tableware, money

CULTURE NOTE

Wedding customs can vary by place and religion.

- Mexican weddings can include a string of flowers or beads draped around the couple to show their union.
- In Japan, it is customary to give money—an odd amount, as even numbers are thought to be unlucky.
- In the Jewish faith, the couple often stands under a canopy symbolizing the home they will create together.

WRITING

A Read a short essay about American weddings. Then answer the questions.

American Wedding Customs

In the US, some people have very traditional wedding ceremonies, but others prefer nontraditional ceremonies. Many people get married in places like event centers or even at home. Some weddings are in the morning, but most weddings are in the afternoon or the evening. If you receive a wedding invitation, you should send an RSVP. You can do this online if the wedding couple has a wedding website. There is usually an online gift registry so that you can send gifts directly to the bride and groom. Guests at traditional weddings usually wear suits and dresses. People also dress up for nontraditional weddings, but the clothes are usually a little less formal.

On the day of the wedding, the bride and groom do not see each other before the ceremony. In traditional weddings, the bride walks to the groom with her father, but now some brides walk with both parents. After the ceremony, there is a wedding reception, where there's a big meal, and friends and family members give short speeches. There is usually a band or a DJ, and people dance and celebrate through the night with the newly married couple.

1. Where do people get married? ______
2. At what time of day do people get married? ______
3. Where do people usually buy wedding gifts? ______
4. What do guests wear to weddings? ______
5. What happens at the wedding? ______
6. What happens after the wedding ceremony? ______

B Use the questions in A to make notes about typical weddings in your country. Add other information if you want to.

C Use your notes from B to write in your notebook about weddings in your country.

D IN PAIRS Read each other's texts from C. Are your descriptions similar? Compare and discuss.

GO TO page xiv for WRITING step-by-step instructions.

1 event centers or at home
2 sometimes in the morning, but mostly in the afternoon or evenings
3 online gift registry
4 suits and dresses
5 The bride walks to the groom with her father or both parents.
6 There's a wedding reception with a meal, speeches, and dancing.

SPEAKING

A Make notes about another social event you attended.

Type of event ______
Location and time ______
Clothing ______
Ceremony ______
Other activities ______
Other information ______

B IN GROUPS Tell your group about the social event from A. Use the Confident Communicator box to help you.

CONFIDENT COMMUNICATOR — START TALKING

Before you give a talk, practice it. Remember that you can refer to your notes while you are talking to help you remember what to say, but you need to look at your audience, so it's a good idea to practice your talk several times.

WRITING

Before students write about typical weddings in their country, tell them to think about weddings they have been to recently and decide which elements of the weddings were typical of a traditional wedding experience. Let them know that "typical" may change from region to region within their country.

When they have compared and discussed their writing in WRITING **D**, ask for volunteers to share their descriptions with the group.

SPEAKING

Tell students to use signposting when they tell their group about an event they have been to recently. For example, *I'm going to tell you about ..., The next thing was ..., And the last thing that happened was ...*

Tell students to practice their talk a couple of times. They should practice looking at the audience and using open body language. They can refer to their notes, but they shouldn't read from them.

GO TO page xv
for LANGUAGE AND LIFE step-by-step instructions.

Language and Life

Global Competence – Give Advice about Social Customs

A 5.05 **Read the excerpt from a guidebook to the US. Then choose *True* or *False*.**

Social Customs in the US

When you travel to another country, it is important to understand the customs of the country. Here are some useful tips for visitors to the US.

GREETINGS

- When Americans meet someone for the first time, especially in business situations, they usually shake hands. Young people do not usually shake hands in informal situations. Kissing on the cheek is not a common form of greeting.
- At small social events, Americans sometimes greet each person, but normally people say hello to the group in general.
- Use a person's title (Mr., Ms., Dr.) and last name in business situations or when the other person is much older than you. Never use a title with a first name.

SOCIAL EVENTS

- Do not accept an invitation to an event if you don't plan to go. Simply say something like, "I'm sorry, but I have plans that evening. Thanks for the invitation."
- For a dinner party, arrive on time or no more than 5 or 10 minutes late. For an informal party, you can arrive and leave at any time.
- It is typical to take a small gift like flowers or chocolate to a dinner party but not to more informal events.

FOOD AND RESTAURANTS

- In restaurants, Americans often divide the bill so that everyone pays an equal part. If someone says, "My treat," or "I'll get it," that person will pay the bill. Don't argue. Just thank the person.
- If you invite someone to go out to eat, ask if there are foods that they can't eat or don't like before you choose a restaurant.
- Americans often have potluck dinners. This means that everyone brings a large dish to share.

TIPPING

- In the US, the normal amount to tip in a restaurant is about 15%, but 20% is common in a very good restaurant. You don't have to tip in fast-food or self-service restaurants. For groups of six people or more, restaurants sometimes add the tip to the bill.
- It is common to tip taxi drivers about 15%.
- In hotels, tip car valets and bellhops \$2.00 to \$3.00.

1 People often kiss each other on the cheek when they meet. True / **False**
2 You can use a title with a first name, for example, Mr. John. True / **False**
3 You shouldn't accept an invitation if you don't plan to go. **True** / False
4 It isn't important to arrive on time to an informal party. **True** / False
5 It is common for Americans to share a restaurant bill. **True** / False
6 At a potluck dinner, you should only eat the food you bring. True / **False**
7 Most Americans tip about 10% in restaurants. True / **False**
8 Americans usually tip taxi drivers. **True** / False

54 Unit 5 Prepping

OBJECTIVE

In this lesson, students learn how to think critically about their own culture and give advice about social customs in their country. Students have to consider social customs they are familiar with in a new way. They look at themselves from the point of view of an outsider and practice empathy for someone visiting their country.

PROCESS OPTIONAL 5.05

Students first read an excerpt from a guidebook about social customs in the United States. Then, they are presented with a task. An American friend's email outlines his upcoming visit and his questions about social customs in the students' country. Students work in pairs to think of answers to his questions and then consider any other important customs in their country they think visitors should be aware of. Then, in groups, they share their information and add details to it. Finally, they discuss any points of disagreement.

B IN PAIRS **An American friend is coming to study in your country. Read the email and discuss answers to his questions.**

New Message

From: jefftheexplorer@usanett.us

To: abl4519@yourcountry.net   Cc Bcc

Subject: Social Customs

Wow, I'm going to study in your country! Could you give me some information about social customs?
I have a lot of questions!

- Do people usually shake hands when they meet for the first time?
- Do friends kiss on the cheek when they greet each other?
- If I go to someone's house, should I take a gift?
- If I go to someone's house, should I arrive early, on time, or a little late?
- If someone asks me to go to a restaurant, do they pay, or do we share the bill?
- When do people usually leave tips, and how much?

Can you let me know about any other important customs? I don't want to make mistakes!
Thanks for your help!

Jeff

Send

C IN PAIRS **Make notes about any other important customs in your country. Use the ideas below or your own ideas.**

- business meetings
- dating
- gift giving
- holidays

____

____

____

D IN GROUPS **Discuss the customs that you made notes about in C and give more information. Discuss any points of disagreement.**

We made notes about ordering in a restaurant. First, we ask what everyone likes or doesn't like. Then each person orders one dish and we share all the dishes with everyone.

E Discuss the questions.

1 Did members of your group describe the customs and explain what to do clearly? Why or why not?
2 In what other situations do you need to understand differences in customs?

MAKE IT DIGITAL

Find out about a social custom in an English-speaking country. Write about it and post it on your school's website.

CLASSROOM MANAGEMENT

Giving feedback is a great life skill to master. It is a skill that can be practiced and honed with time. Good feedback techniques require good active listening strategies. Tell students to approach feedback in three steps:

1 Listen to their classmate.
2 Say two or three things they liked.
3 Add a suggestion about how it could be improved.

CULTURE NOTE

Remind students to be respectful of other cultures' customs. Remind them that there are different cultures within their own country, and they should be respectful of those, too.

MAKE IT DIGITAL

Ask students to find out about a social custom in an English-speaking country. Have them choose one specific custom (e.g., what to take to a party, punctuality, host/hostess, gifts, greetings, weddings, parties, or how to say *thank you*). They are free to choose any English-speaking country.

GO TO page xvii
for UNIT REVIEW step-by-step instructions.

UNIT 5

VOCABULARY review

SCORE: / 10

A Complete the sentences with the words from the box.

buffet	dressed up	suggestion	reception	show up
checked in	flight	picked up	reservation	wedding

My best friend got married last weekend, and I went to his **1** wedding. My **2** flight to Houston arrived at 3:00 and I went to my hotel. The hotel found my **3** reservation and I **4** checked in to my room. I had to hurry because the wedding was at 5:00, and I didn't want to **5** show up late! I **6** dressed up in my best clothes. My friends from Houston **7** picked me up at the hotel and we arrived a little before the ceremony started. The **8** reception was in the same place as the ceremony, and it was a lot of fun. The food was fantastic, but I'm going to make a **9** suggestion—if you go to a big wedding, arrive for the **10** buffet early, because the best food disappears fast!

GRAMMAR review

SCORE: / 10

A Choose the correct modal auxiliary.

Sara: I think the math test tomorrow **1** will / would be really difficult.
Robert: I'm pretty good at math. **2** I may / I'll help you study if you want.
Sara: Great, thanks! **3** May / Will I look at your class notes?
Robert: Sure. **4** I'll / I may come to your house about 5:00 this evening, OK?
Sara: Great. **5** May / Could you bring your laptop?
Robert: Sure. See you later.

B Decide what Sara and Robert are communicating in A. Then write *R* (request), *PR* (prediction), *I* (intention), *O* (offer), or *PE* (permission).

1 PR **2** O **3** PE **4** I **5** R

16–20 correct: You can make suggestions and talk about wedding ceremonies. You can use modals of intention, offer, prediction, request, and permission.
0–15 correct: Look again at the Vocabulary and Grammar sections in the unit.

TOTAL SCORE: / 20

WHAT DO YOU KNOW NOW? Look back at page 47 and add the words you know now to the box.

GO TO page xviii
for STUDY SKILLS step-by-step instructions.

STUDY SKILLS ORGANIZING TO HELP MEMORIZATION

Take the quiz. Then go to **Study Skills** on page 131 and learn more about organizing to help memorization.

1 Which do you find easiest to memorize? Rank in order of 1 (very easy) to 6 (very hard).

____ one word
____ one word with a picture
____ a two-word phrase
____ an underlined word in a sentence
____ a group of sentences that make a story about a word
____ a word with a translation

2 Check the techniques that help you memorize new information.

☐ make a song about the thing you want to learn
☐ connect ideas using a story
☐ draw a picture / use color

56 Unit 5 Prepping

CLASSROOM MANAGEMENT

Before starting the review activities, give students some time to glance over the unit and review the VOCABULARY and GRAMMAR sections in each lesson. Once they have looked over the material, they will find the review activities more relevant.

FURTHER DISCUSSION

Put students in groups of three and ask the following questions for them to discuss:

- What apps do you use for planning?
- Do you plan your vacations far in advance?
- Do you like planning activities, or do you prefer spontaneity?
- What do you usually contribute to a party?

GO TO page vi
for UNIT OPENER step-by-step instructions.

UNIT 6 Changes

WHAT DO YOU ALREADY KNOW?

1 List five changes in your life in the last year. Include positive and negative changes.
2 IN PAIRS Share and compare your changes. Add more words to your lists.

Changes

STUDENTS MAY ALREADY KNOW:

- Life changes: move (away), get married, change jobs, graduate from school, get sick, find a boyfriend/ girlfriend, lose money, win money.

VIDEO

DISCUSS & SHARE

3 IN GROUPS Watch the video and answer the question.
SYM Do you view change as a positive or negative thing in your life?

GO TO page xx
for VIDEOS IN SYM step-by-step instructions.

In this unit, you will ...

- talk about risk and change, experiences you want to have, and changes in a city over time.
- use thinking skills: analyze, create, and understand.
- read about how people view change in their lives.
- use strategies to start and keep talking by reacting to information or expressing a point of view.
- use collaboration skills to create a list of recommendations for visitors discovering your town.
- follow an interior designer to learn about this job and the skills needed for the field of architecture.

WHAT DO YOU ALREADY KNOW?

If you notice students are struggling to understand what to do, you can provide one or two examples to help them get started:

- **Life changes:** leave home, get divorced, get a job, get fired, fail a class, break up with a boyfriend/girlfriend, go broke, inherit money

VIDEO

Before viewing, ask:

Why doesn't Dan like change? *He lives where he grew up, has the same friends and the same job.*
Why does Emily like change? *Change is exciting. She wants to go to college, meet new people, and find oportunities.*

After viewing, put the continuum on the board.

positive change — negative change

Have students mark the continuum and explain their preferences.

DISCUSS & SHARE

Encourage students to think about a time in their life when a big change occurred. Then have them consider how they felt about it—were they comfortable with the change, or did they struggle with it? If students struggled, have them consider how they got through the situation.

GO TO page x

for **READING** step-by-step instructions.

LESSON 1 Change or Stay the Same?

READING

A Choose the answers that are correct for you.

I usually prefer to …

1 eat at the same / different restaurants.
2 eat the same / different foods.
3 go out to the same / different places.
4 listen to the same / new music.
5 go to the same / different places on vacation.

MAKE IT YOURS

Think of other situations in which you usually prefer to do the same thing or usually prefer to do different things.

B 6.01 Read the article. Do Joe and Elena have the same opinion about changes in their lives?

No, they don't. Joe prefers the status quo, and Elena likes change.

THE STATUS QUO BIAS—

Why People Don't Like Change!

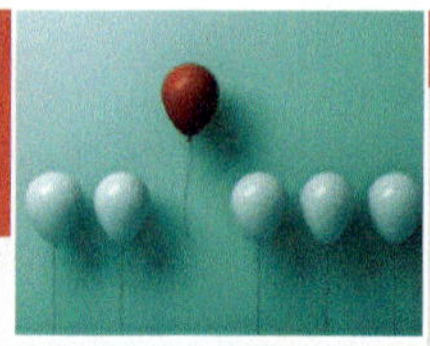

If you prefer the status quo, you don't like change. You prefer things to stay the same. Psychologists call this the **status quo** bias. Many people have a status quo bias, but some people really like change.

Joe and Elena are both 35 years old, but they have very different **attitudes** about change. Joe has lived in the same
1 city, in the same apartment since 2005. He has been with the same company for 12 years. He hasn't bought a new phone for five years, and he has had his car since 2010. Elena has moved three times in the past two years, and she has had four different jobs since 2012. She has worked in her current job
for two years, but she thinks she'll probably look for a new job 2
next year.

There are some **advantages** to the status quo. Life is less
stressful in your **comfort zone**. You feel that you are **in control** 3
because everything is familiar. There are no **risks**!

However, it can be a good idea to leave your comfort zone and take some risks. This can help you in your professional and personal life. How long have you had the same job? Are there other jobs that pay better or are more interesting? Do you sometimes feel bored with your living situation or your social life? How many times have you eaten at the same restaurant, listened to the same music, gone to the same places on the weekend? If the answer is "a lot," try making a few small changes. Go ahead, order something different the next time 4
you go to that restaurant!

C READING SKILL—Identify examples Read the article in B again. Underline examples that show the following things:

1 the fact that Joe prefers the status quo
2 the fact that Elena prefers change
3 advantages to the status quo
4 a suggestion for a small change

D THINKING SKILL—Analyze Do you think the writer is more in favor of change or the status quo? Use your ability to infer and explain why.

The writer is more in favor of change: Getting out of your comfort zone and taking some risks can help you in your professional and personal life. Try making a few small changes.

GO TO page vii

for **VOCABULARY** step-by-step instructions.

VOCABULARY

A Match the words from the box to the definitions.

advantage attitude comfort zone in control risk status quo

1 status quo: the present situation, or the way things usually are
2 comfort zone: a situation or place that you feel good in
3 advantage: a positive characteristic of something
4 risk: the possibility that something bad or dangerous will happen
5 attitude: your opinions or feelings about something
6 in control: the ability to make decisions and decide what will happen

READING OPTIONAL 6.01

After reading, consider advantages to maintaining the status quo and advantages to change. Have students place themselves on a continuum. Ask them to draw a line and write *change* on the left and *status quo* on the right. Tell them to mark the line wherever they consider themselves to be.

THINKING SKILL—Analyze

For students to analyze the article, tell them to use their abilities to infer clues to arrive at a conclusion. Ask which clues in the text helped them infer. Note that the writer writes more about change than the status quo and seems more enthusiastic about change, particularly at the end when encouraging the reader to order something different.

VOCABULARY

Encourage students to go back to the text and read the words in context as they are matching the words to the definitions. Then, to practice and learn the words, tell students to write their own sentences in their notebooks.

GRAMMAR present perfect with *for* and *since*

A Read the sentences and choose the correct answer to complete the rules.

Joe has lived in the same city in the same apartment since 2005.
He has been with the same company for 12 years.
How long have you had the same job?

1 The present perfect with *How long*, *for*, and *since* refers to …
  a actions or situations that began in the past and continue in the present. b finished actions or situations.
2 *For* is used with …
  a a specific point in time. b a period of time.
3 *Since* is used with …
  a a specific point in time. b a period of time.
4 *How long* means the same thing as …
  a *How much time*. b *When*.
5 The present perfect is formed with *have/has* and the … of the main verb.
  a simple past form b past participle form

For more practice, go to page 149.

B Use *How long* and the cues to write questions.

1 your family / live in this area? How long has your family lived in this area?
2 you / live in your house? How long have you lived in your house?
3 you / know your best friend? How long have you known your best friend?
4 you / study English? How long have you studied English?
5 you / have your cell phone? How long have you had your cell phone?

PRONUNCIATION present perfect contractions

A 6.02 Listen and repeat. Pay attention to the pronunciation of the contractions with *have* and *has*.

1 I've studied English for several years.
2 You've been here since four o'clock.
3 She's lived here since November.
4 It's been very hot outside for two weeks.
5 We've been in class for 45 minutes.
6 They've worked here for a long time.

B IN PAIRS Practice reading the sentences from A aloud. Remember to stress the main verb, not the contraction with *have*.

SPEAKING

A Answer the questions from GRAMMAR B in your notebook. Then think of more questions to ask a partner.

B IN GROUPS Ask each other the questions you answered in A and the new questions you and your partner wrote. Use the Confident Communicator box to help you. Who likes change and who doesn't like change?

CONFIDENT COMMUNICATOR — KEEP TALKING

Use the following words to talk about periods of time.
For exact amounts of time, use *for six hours, days, months, years*.
For inexact amounts of time, use *about/almost/around/more or less six hours, days, months, years*.

GO TO page viii for GRAMMAR step-by-step instructions.

GO TO page ix for PRONUNCIATION step-by-step instructions.

GO TO page xii for SPEAKING step-by-step instructions.

GRAMMAR

Although most languages contain the present perfect form, it is used more in some places than in others. The present perfect is used more in the United Kingdom than in the United States, and more in Spain than in Mexico. Elicit examples in students' language and have them reflect on whether they use it much.

PRONUNCIATION

Contractions in the present perfect form and the weak sounds make it difficult to hear the grammar. Tell students to practice speaking naturally by stressing the verb and not the contraction. Often, students will mistakenly stress the *have* or *has* to show they know the grammar, but this sounds unnatural.

SPEAKING

Some more questions for SPEAKING **A** might be: *How long have you lived in this city? How long have you had these jeans? How long have you been studying [English]? How long have you had your pet? How long have you been playing [sport]?*

GO TO page xi
for **LISTENING** step-by-step instructions.

GO TO page 141
for **AUDIO SCRIPT**.

GO TO page 142
for **AUDIO SCRIPT**.

LESSON 2 Bucket List

LISTENING

A **Write down four experiences that you would like to have in your life. Tell the class. Find out if anyone in the class has done the things you want to do.**

B **6.03 Listen to the first part of a podcast. Check (✓) the activities that the speakers want to do.**

☐ run a marathon	☑ go to Washington, D.C	☑ sing at an open-mic session
☑ fly in a helicopter	☑ drive a sports car	☐ act in a play
☐ go snow skiing	☐ go bungee jumping	☐ ride a motorcycle

C **6.04 LISTENING SKILL—Listen for main ideas** **Listen to the second part of the podcast. Number the sentences in the correct order. Then underline the two main ideas.**

3 Your list should include things that you think are possible.
2 First, try to be realistic.
6 Thanks for listening, and good luck with your bucket list!
1 OK, I have a couple of tips for making a bucket list.
4 Next, don't include too many things on your list.
5 You probably won't have time to do all of the things on a very long list.

D **THINKING SKILL—Create** **Write two big things and two smaller things for your personal bucket list. Share your ideas with a partner. Give reasons for your choices.**

VOCABULARY life experiences

A **Complete the paragraph with the past participles of verbs from the box.**

be do eat go hear meet ride run sing win

New Message

To: john2397@outmail.cc Cc Bcc

Subject: Bucket list

Hey, John. I like your idea of making a bucket list. There are a lot of things that I've never **1** done. First, I've never **2** met my cousins in Spain, and I've never **3** been to the capital of my country. Those are the big things on my list. There are a few smaller things. I've never **4** gone camping or **5** ridden a horse. Let's see … I've never **6** eaten Korean food, and I've **7** heard that it's really good. I like to sing, but I've never **8** sung in public. I've **9** run in a few races, but I've never **10** won a race, so I'd like to do that. I guess that's it. What's on your bucket list?

Send

B **IN PAIRS** **Discuss which of the things in the email in A you have done.**

LISTENING

Do LISTENING **A** as an open-class activity or using the list in **B** for ideas if needed. When listening to students share the things they would like to do, tell students to volunteer information if they have done those things. Tell students to write down the names of the people who have done the things they want to do so they can talk to them about it later.

VOCABULARY Alternative Activity

Play *Never Have I Ever*. In groups of three, tell students to make two small signs each, one with *I have* written on it and the other with *Never have I ever*. Students take turns telling their groups an experience they have had, and group members should respond by showing one of their signs to show if they have or haven't done it. If they have, they should share some information about the experience.

GRAMMAR present perfect with *ever* and *never*

A Read the sentences and choose the correct option to complete the grammar rules.

Have you ever flown in a helicopter? Yes, I have. / No, I haven't.
I've never driven a sports car.

1 *Ever* and *never* refer to actions …
- a at a specific time in the past.
- b at an unspecific time in the past.

2 *Ever* is used in …
- a statements.
- b questions.

3 *Never* is used with …
- a an affirmative verb.
- b a negative verb.

4 In short answers to *yes/no* questions, use …
- a the main verb.
- b *have* or *has*.

For more practice, go to page 150.

B Complete the conversations using the present perfect with *ever* and *never*. Then practice the conversations with a partner.

1 A: Have you __ever__ driven a sports car?
B: Yes, I __have__.

2 A: __Has__ your brother ever __been__ to Canada?
B: No, he __hasn't/has not__, but he's __been__ to the US.

3 A: I __'ve/have__ never __eaten__ an exotic food. Have you?
B: Yes, I __have__. I __'ve/have__ eaten snake meat.

4 A: __Have__ you __ever__ gone rock climbing?
B: Yes, I __have__. It's scary!

SPEAKING

A Complete the questionnaire for you.

Have you ever …	You	Student 1	Student 2
1 ridden a motorcycle or a horse?			
2 been to another country?			
3 made a video and posted it online?			
4 won a competition or a prize?			
5 flown in a plane?			

B IN GROUPS Talk to two different classmates. Complete the questionnaire in A for them. Ask more questions if you want to. Use the Confident Communicator box to help you.

CONFIDENT COMMUNICATOR
KEEP TALKING

To react to information in a conversation, use the following phrases:
Wow! / Really? That's interesting / awesome / really cool!
You've never done that? / You've done that?
I can't believe it!

GRAMMAR

Let students know that the only tricky parts of the present perfect form are the change from *have* to *has* in the third-person singular and the use of the past participle. Once they learn the past participles, including the common irregular ones, they'll understand it. Encourage them to review the past participles of the verbs and test each other. Tell students they can use the Irregular Verbs list on page 139 on their Student's Book.

SPEAKING

To heighten interest in the questionnaire, have students guess their group members' answers before asking them. Before they speak in groups, draw students' attention to the Confident Communicator box and practice the responses as a class so that students feel confident of the expressions and respond to their partners during the activity.

LESSON 3 Changing Cities

VOCABULARY changing cities

A Match the words from the box to the pictures.

bike lane	green space	pedestrian area	shopping mall
food truck	high-rise building	playground	walking trail

1 
pedestrian area

2 
high-rise building

3 
bike lane

4 
walking trail

5 
green space

6 
food truck

7 
playground

8 
shopping mall

B **IN PAIRS** Which of the features from A are in your area? Discuss.

There are a lot of green spaces, but there aren't many walking trails.

LISTENING

A Look at old and new pictures of Pittsburgh, Pennsylvania. Then answer the question: In what ways do you think the city has changed since the 1970s?

___

___

VOCABULARY

More words to talk about cities are: *stadium, residential development, skate park, outdoor gym, garden, traffic, overpopulation, high density, overdevelop, litter, air/noise/light pollution*, and *waterway*.

LISTENING

Words that the photos may generate include: *factory, plant, rust, industry, pollution, clean, river, bridge, downtown*, and *tourism*.

THINKING SKILL—Understand

When summarizing, students should look for the general idea that is supported by examples. Ask students leading questions like: *Does she think the city has gotten better or worse? Does she think the changes have been positive or negative?*

CULTURE NOTE

The picture of new Pittsburgh shows the Duquesne Incline funicular. It was completed in 1877 and was used to take cargo up to the coal mines. It was renovated in the 1960s. Today it is a popular tourist attraction.

B 6.05 LISTENING SKILL—Listen for specific information **Listen to the radio show *Changing Cities*. Check (✓) the changes to Pittsburgh that Amy mentions.**

They've …

- [ ] built new factories.
- [x] cleaned up the city.
- [x] created green spaces.
- [ ] built new high-rise buildings.
- [x] made walking trails.
- [x] put in playgrounds.
- [x] put in pedestrian areas.
- [x] created bike lanes.

C 6.05 THINKING SKILL—Understand **Listen again. Then write one or two sentences that summarize Amy's opinion of Pittsburgh in the 1970s and her opinion now.**

____

____

MAKE IT YOURS

Make a list of words to describe other features of your city or town.

GO TO page 142 for **AUDIO SCRIPT**.

WRITING

A **Read the letter to the editor. Decide whether the writer thinks the changes to his city have been positive or negative. Underline examples that support his opinion.**

LETTER TO THE EDITOR

Our city has seen a lot of changes in the past 10 years. Some of the changes have been good. The city government has repaired many streets, and they've built new bridges. They've also built a new school and a new hospital.

However, there have been a lot of negative changes. They've destroyed several parks and have built high-rise buildings there. They've built large apartment buildings and condominiums in several neighborhoods, and now the traffic is terrible in those areas. They've taken out a lot of bike lanes, and now we can't ride our bikes on those streets. Finally, they've banned food trucks in the city center, so now there are fewer places to eat lunch downtown.

He thinks the changes have been generally negative.

GO TO page xiv for **WRITING** step-by-step instructions.

B **Think about the changes in your town. Have the changes been positive or negative?**

C **Write about changes in your town or city in your notebook. Remember to include several examples to support your opinion.**

SPEAKING

A IN PAIRS **Create a combined list of changes to your town and their effects. Use the text you wrote in WRITING C to help you. Decide which changes have been positive and which have been negative.**

B IN GROUPS **Discuss whether the changes to your town or city have been generally positive or negative. If there is disagreement, try to convince your group to agree with you. Use the Confident Communicator box to help you.**

CONFIDENT COMMUNICATOR
KEEP TALKING

Use these phrases to argue your point of view.
It's true that …, but the fact / problem is that …
The city has built / made / created …, and the effect is that …
That's true, but a positive / negative effect is …
Yes, but on the other hand, …

MAKE IT YOURS

Here is a list of words to describe other features of your city or town: *block, city center, downtown, plaza, main square, neighborhood, Chinatown, market, outskirts, pedestrian mall, riverfront, oceanfront, slum, harbor, river, castle, parklands, main street, nightlife, industrial area.*

WRITING

Students should make their own choice and use examples about whether the city has seen positive or negative changes. They can focus on one area of life. They should pick examples that support their main idea. Note that the writer starts out mentioning a few positive changes, but that is only the introduction to convincing the reader that there have been more negative changes and it is therefore more persuasive in that section.

SPEAKING Alternative Activity

Write the name of the town you are in and draw a T-chart with *positive changes* and *negative changes* written in the headers. Elicit ideas and write them in the grid. Have an open-class discussion about positive and negative changes in your town. Have students break up into groups with opposing views and tell them to try to convince the group of their point of view.

GO TO page xv for **LANGUAGE AND LIFE** step-by-step instructions.

Language and Life

Collaboration – Recommendations for Your Town

It means that you find out about and do things in your area that you have never done, or haven't done in a long time.

A 6.06 **Read the article. According to the writer, what does it mean to be a tourist in your own town?**

GUEST OPINION

Tourist in Your Own Town

By Lynn Williams

I have decided to become a tourist in my own town and the areas near my town. I read an article that said that many people do not know their own towns, and I thought, "That's me!" I've lived here for 15 years, but I always do the same things and go to the same places. I did some research about activities and places in and near my town, and I've made a list of things that I've never done, or that I haven't done in a long time:

- I've never gone to a high school sports event.
- I've been to the history museum only once, several years ago.
- I've never seen the sunset from Pine Mountain.
- There are about 20 restaurants that I've never tried.
- I've never shopped in the farmer's market.
- I haven't taken a walk on the trail next to the river in five years.

Those are only a few of the things on my list. I imagine that it's the same for almost everyone. We all have our routines, and we never do or see a lot of the fun, interesting things near us. So start a sentence with "I've never ..." and see how many ways you can complete it. Do some research to find out what there is to do and see in your area. Then, go out and become a tourist in your own town!

B **Choose *True*, *False*, or *NI* (no information).**

1 The writer has lived in her town for a short amount of time. True / **False** / NI
2 She travels to other countries frequently. True / False / **NI**
3 She thinks there are many interesting things to do in her town. **True** / False / NI
4 She hasn't visited the history museum recently. **True** / False / NI
5 She has visited other museums in the area. True / False / **NI**
6 She thinks most people know a lot about their towns. True / **False** / NI

OBJECTIVE

In this lesson, students learn how to reflect on what their town has to offer tourists and how residents can be tourists in their own towns. Sometimes, residents can get stuck in a rut. Point out to students that sometimes we should look at our towns through the eyes of an outsider to appreciate changes that have occurred.

PROCESS OPTIONAL 6.06

Students read an article written about being a tourist in your own town. The author researches activities and places in her area and makes a list of things she's never done in her town but would like to do. Students make their own list of things they haven't done in their own town. Then, students discuss their lists, get more ideas from each other, and use this information to make recommendations for different types of tourists. As a class, they make a combined list of things they have never done. Finally, they reflect on how well they made recommendations for different types of tourists.

C Make a list of things that you've never done in your town, or haven't done for a long time.

I've never been to a high school soccer game.

I haven't gone to the history museum in years.

______

______

______

______

D **IN PAIRS** Discuss your lists. Get ideas from your partner to add things to your list.

A: I've never been to a high school soccer game.

B: You haven't? It's lots of fun. My cousin is on the team, so I go to all of the games.

A: Cool. Have you ever been to the history museum?

B: Yes, but I haven't been for about 10 years. It was really interesting, so I'd like to go again.

A: Me, too. I think they've expanded the museum and put in a lot of new exhibits.

E **IN GROUPS** Look at the ideas on your lists and make recommendations for different types of tourists. Try to think of at least two things to do or see for each type of person.

Teenagers	Families with young children
Young people on a date	Senior citizens

F As a class, make a combined list of things that you, your family, and your friends can do in your area that you've never done.

______

______

______

G Discuss the questions.

1 Did you successfully match different types of tourists with activities they might like?
2 In what other situations do you collaborate with others to make recommendations?

MAKE IT DIGITAL

Research interesting activities and places in your area. Post suggestions on your school website or social media site.

CULTURE NOTE

How we define a village, a town, or a city varies from country to country and region to region depending on the size of the place, the number of inhabitants, and local rules. Additionally, political boundaries may use different terminology; they may be states, counties, provinces, or departments. Ask students if they have been abroad and if they visited a village, a town, or a city. What was the name of the state or province they visited? Is their hometown a village, town, or city? How is the region defined?

MAKE IT DIGITAL

Search popular online travel sites to see what they say about activities and places of interest in your city or town. If you can't find anything on your town, try a larger town or a city near you.

GO TO page xvii
for UNIT REVIEW step-by-step instructions.

UNIT 6

VOCABULARY review

SCORE: / 10

A Choose the correct option.

Many people do not like to take **1** risks / advantage. They prefer to stay in their **2** comfort zones / attitudes because they like **3** the status quo / risk. There are people who have never **4** gone / eaten at a food truck, **5** sung / written karaoke, or **6** ridden / flown in an airplane. What about you? Have you ever ridden in a **7** bike lane / pedestrian area on a busy street or **8** driven / ridden a horse? Have you ever **9** done / gone camping or **10** won / met a competition? If not, try something different!

GRAMMAR review

SCORE: / 10

A Complete the sentences with *for*, *since*, *ever*, *never*, or the correct form of the verb in parentheses.

Di: Hey, have you **1** ___seen___ (see) the new exhibit at the art museum yet?

Jay: No, I **2** ___haven't___ (have, not). In fact, I've **3** ___never___ been to the museum.

Di: Seriously? How long have you **4** ___lived___ (live) here?

Jay: **5** ___Since___ I was about 10.

Di: You've **6** ___been___ (be) here **7** ___for___ 10 years, and you haven't been to the museum?

Jay: Well, I've **8** ___never___ liked art museums very much.

Di: Have you **9** ___visited___ (visit) any of our museums? There are several good ones here.

Jay: Yes, I have, but not **10** ___for___ a long time, I guess.

16–20 correct: You can talk about life experiences and changing cities. You can use present perfect with *for*, *since*, *ever*, and *never*.
0–15 correct: Look again at the Vocabulary and Grammar sections in the unit.

TOTAL SCORE: / 20

WHAT DO YOU KNOW NOW? Look back at page 57 and add words you know now to the box.

GO TO page xix
for FOLLOW A PRO step-by-step instructions.

FOLLOW A PRO ARCHITECTURE

Take the quiz about architecture. Then go to Follow A Pro on page 132. Find the answers and learn about the field of architecture.

1 The word architect comes from the … word *architektōn* meaning "master builder".
a Latin b Old English c Greek

2 The architect Sir Christopher Wren became famous when he designed multiple buildings after London was destroyed by…
a floods. b fire. c earthquakes.

3 From 1912 to 1948, architects could win gold medals at the …
a Olympics. b Masters Tournament. c World Cup.

4 How many years does the typical bachelor's degree in architecture last in the US?
a 3 b 4 c 5

66 Unit 6 Changes

CLASSROOM MANAGEMENT

Once students have completed the VOCABULARY and GRAMMAR review activities, instead of doing open-class feedback to check each answer, post the answers in small print in different places in the classroom. Tell students that, as they finish, they are free to go and check the answers.

FURTHER DISCUSSION

Put students in groups of three and ask the following questions for them to discuss:

- Has someone you know changed a lot recently?
- Are there any ways you would like to change?
- What's the strangest bucket-list activity you have heard of?
- How has your neighborhood changed over the years?

UNIT 7

Get to Work

GO TO page vi
for **UNIT OPENER** step-by-step instructions.

WHAT DO YOU ALREADY KNOW?

1 Think about the career you want and the qualifications and abilities you need to be successful. Write the words.

2 **IN PAIRS** Share and compare your ideas. Add more words to your lists.

STUDENTS MAY ALREADY KNOW

- **Qualifications:** school, degree, course.
- **Abilities:** computer skills, teamwork.

VIDEO

DISCUSS & SHARE

3 **IN GROUPS** Watch the video and answer the question.

SYM Are you born with talent or is it something you learn?

GO TO page xx
for **VIDEOS IN SYM** step-by-step instructions.

In this unit, you will ...

- talk about career readiness, career alternatives, and employability skills.
- use thinking skills: summarize and analyze.
- read about being ready for a career.
- use strategies to start and keep talking by giving negative answers, expressing doubt, and describing images.
- use problem-solving skills to create a business plan for an entrepreneur.
- learn tips for developing creativity.

WHAT DO YOU ALREADY KNOW?

If you notice students are struggling to understand what to do, you can provide one or two examples to help them get started:

- **Qualifications:** postgraduate degree, certificate, diploma
- **Abilities:** public speaking, hardworking, organizational skills, time management

VIDEO

Before viewing, ask:

How does Jenny sing? *It is easy and natural, she sings all the time.*
How does Sam play the guitar? *He practices a lot, but it doesn't feel like work.*

After viewing, put the continuum on the board.

born —— learn

Have students mark the continuum and explain if you are born with talent or it is something you learn.

DISCUSS & SHARE

Take a poll of the class to see who thinks talent is something a person is born with or something a person has learned. Pair students with opposing views so that they can discuss their opinions. Encourage students to understand their partner's point of view.

GO TO page x

for **READING** step-by-step instructions.

A career is an occupation in a professional field that you have over a number of years or during your working life. A job is specific full-time or part-time work that you are employed to do for a short time or a long time.

The three factors are knowledge, skills, and personal characteristics.

LESSON 1 Are You Career-Ready?

READING

A **What is the difference between a career and a job? Discuss as a class.**

B **7.01 IN PAIRS THINKING SKILL—Summarize** **Read the article. Together, describe in your own words the three main factors in being career-ready.**

How Career-Ready Are You?

Have you started your career yet? If you have just started working, you are probably very happy and are learning a lot about your job. However, if you have already worked for a while, you are probably thinking about how to **improve** your career options. If you haven't started working yet, you are probably thinking about what kind of career you want. It is always a good idea to think about the next step in your working life.

First, it is important to understand that being **career-ready** refers to more than training and knowledge about a job or a career. It refers to a combination of **knowledge**, skills, and personal characteristics.

Knowledge includes the academic or technical information that you need for a career area or a specific job, but it also includes other types of knowledge. For example, you may need general math skills or a good level of English.

Skills include specific technical skills, but they also include skills like using your time well, the **ability** to communicate, and working in a team. One of the most important skills today is the ability to **solve** problems.

Finally, you need to understand what personal characteristics and personality types are ideal for different jobs and careers. Some people with excellent academic **qualifications** are unhappy in their careers because their jobs don't really match their personalities.

It doesn't matter if you have just graduated from high school or college, haven't graduated yet, or already have a job; you should take some time to think about your future. How career-ready are you?

C **READING SKILL—Understand vocabulary in context** **Choose the meaning of the words in bold from the article in B.**

1 improve
  a make something better **b** understand **c** know about
2 career-ready
  a prepared to work **b** ready to go to college **c** having skills for a specific job
3 knowledge
  a only academic information **b** the opposite of *opinion* **c** the facts you know about a topic
4 ability
  a a fact **b** a skill **c** a characteristic
5 solve
  a find a solution or an answer **b** understand **c** think about
6 qualifications
  a grades in school **b** skills or experience you need for a job **c** hobbies

GO TO page vii

for **VOCABULARY** step-by-step instructions.

VOCABULARY

A **Complete the sentences with words from the box.**

career degree knowledge qualifications skill training

1 Many companies have ___training___ programs to teach their employees new technology.
2 The ability to work well with other people is an important ___skill___.
3 For many jobs, you have to have a college ___degree___.
4 Primary school teachers have to have a lot of ___knowledge___ about many subjects.
5 Good math and technical skills are ___qualifications___ for engineering jobs.
6 For a successful ___career___, you need a combination of knowledge and skills.

READING OPTIONAL 7.01

A career is an occupation to be undertaken for a long period of time and usually requires formal higher education. There is usually opportunity for promotion to a more senior position within the organization. A job is when you work to make money at an hourly rate. You need skills for a job.

THINKING SKILL—Summarize

Let students know they can use the thesaurus to search for words to use in their summary. A thesaurus is a great tool for expanding vocabulary. Demonstrate how to use a thesaurus to the class.

VOCABULARY

This vocabulary activity extends the reading skill. To write the words in context, tell students to look for clues in the sentences. They should look for related words and collocations (words that usually appear together), and they should consider the situation. Tell students to trust their judgment when understanding vocabulary in context.

GRAMMAR present perfect with *already, yet,* and *just*

A **Read the first paragraph of the article in READING B and underline sentences with *already, just,* and *yet.***

B **Complete the grammar rules with *already, just,* and *yet.***

1 To indicate that an action happened in the very recent past, use ___just___ and the present perfect.
2 To indicate that an action has happened, sometimes sooner than expected, use ___already___ and the present perfect.
3 To indicate that an action is going to happen but hasn't happened, use ___yet___ and the negative present perfect.
4 To ask if an action has happened, use ___yet___ and the present perfect in a question.

For more practice, go to page 151.

C **Complete the conversations with *already, just,* and *yet.***

1 A: Have you studied for your test ___yet___? B: Yes, I've ___already/just___ finished studying.
2 A: I haven't read the story for English class ___yet___. B: I've ___already/just___ read it. It was good.
3 A: Has my package arrived ___yet___? B: I don't know. Oh, here it is. It has ___just___ arrived.
4 A: It's only six o'clock and I've ___already___ finished my homework. B: Really? I haven't started mine ___yet___!

D **In your notebook, write something that you have already done today, something you have just done in the last few minutes, and something you haven't done yet today.**

E **IN PAIRS Ask and answer questions that you wrote in D.**

GO TO page viii
for **GRAMMAR** step-by-step instructions.

PRONUNCIATION /j/ and /dʒ/

A **7.02 Listen and say the words. Pay attention to the sound of the first letter. Then answer: In which sound is your tongue closer to your top teeth?**

yard	year	yellow	yes	yesterday	yet	you	young
jacket	jet	job	John	juice	Julie	jump	just

Your tongue is closer to your top teeth in the /j/ sound.

B **7.03 IN PAIRS Listen and repeat. Then practice reading together. Correct each other's pronunciation when necessary.**

1 Julie bought a yellow jacket yesterday.
2 Yes, you can have some juice.
3 Have you met John yet?
4 James has just started a new job in New York.

GO TO page ix
for **PRONUNCIATION** step-by-step instructions.

SPEAKING

A **IN PAIRS Make a list in your notebook of any skills, abilities, training, and qualifications you have. Do you think you're career-ready?**

B **IN GROUPS Discuss your lists and decide who you think is the most career-ready. Use the Confident Communicator box to help you.**

CONFIDENT COMMUNICATOR
KEEP TALKING

When we give negative answers, we often add reasons or further information.

A: Have you graduated yet? *B: Not yet. / No, I haven't. / No, but I'm going to graduate this year.*

A: What have you done to improve your knowledge in social work? *B: Nothing (yet). / I haven't done anything (yet), but I'm going to do an internship*

GO TO page xii
for **SPEAKING** step-by-step instructions.

GRAMMAR

Just refers to something that has happened a short time ago. Often, there is a result in the present that links the now to the near past. For example, if someone has wet hair, they might explain their current state by using the present perfect with *just*—for example, *I've just taken a shower.*

PRONUNCIATION

Students should be aware of the position of their tongue when making the /j/ and /dʒ/ sounds. With /j/, the sides of the tongue are curled, touching the upper back teeth with air flowing freely over the tongue to the front of the mouth. With /dʒ/, the front of the tongue touches the top palate behind the teeth.

SPEAKING Alternative Activity

As students make notes, they will discover many skills and qualifications that may not have been obvious to them at first. If they have played on a sports team, they may have developed skills of commitment, perseverance, punctuality, flexibility, and leadership. Encourage them to think broadly about their experiences.

GO TO page xi
for **LISTENING** step-by-step instructions.

GO TO page 142
for **AUDIO SCRIPT.**

LESSON 2 **Career Alternatives**

LISTENING

A Discuss the questions as a class.

1 Do you need a business degree to have your own business?
2 In general, do you need a college degree to have a successful career?

B 7.04 Listen to the interview. Choose *True* or *False*.

1	Carmen's business sells food.	**True** / False
2	The business was very small when she started it.	**True** / False
3	Carmen studied business in college.	True / **False**
4	She graduated from college.	True / **False**
5	She started making ice cream as a hobby.	**True** / False
6	Customers like the flavor that Carmen has just created.	**True** / False

C 7.04 LISTENING SKILL—Understand attitude Listen again. Write the words from the box that indicate the speakers' attitudes.

bored excellent fantastic great not interested

1 Carmen's opinion of the ice cream: great
2 The interviewer's opinion of the ice cream: fantastic
3 How Carmen felt one summer: bored
4 Carmen's attitude toward college: not interested
5 Carmen's opinion of her sister's idea: excellent

D THINKING SKILL—Analyze Compare how Carmen felt about learning about ice cream to how she felt about learning about architecture. How does motivation help you succeed?

VOCABULARY success

A Complete the text with words from the box.

apply for a job career path get a promotion hires benefits get a degree get a raise the corporate ladder

The key to success has traditionally been fairly similar for most people. You **1** get a degree and then you **2** apply for a job. If you're lucky, a good company **3** hires you, and you get a good salary and **4** benefits. After working for a while, you **5** get a promotion, and you usually also **6** get a raise in your salary. If you are good at your job, you climb **7** the corporate ladder. However, these days many people do not follow the traditional **8** career path. Many young people are choosing to be entrepreneurs and start their own businesses. Most do this after college, but some don't graduate or don't go to college at all. There are many different ways to have a successful career.

B IN PAIRS Number the list in order of importance to you. Then share your list. Add more things, if possible.

_____ a good salary
_____ the chance to learn new things
_____ the chance to get frequent raises
_____ good benefits like a company car, health insurance, or long vacations
_____ the chance to get promotions and climb the corporate ladder

70 Unit 7 Get to Work

LISTENING

Alternatives to having a business degree might be on-the-job training, an apprenticeship at a local business, a technical course, self-education through reading and doing online courses, and watching seminars online.

Corporate ladder refers to a company's corporate hierarchy, where junior positions are at the bottom and executive positions are at the top.

LISTENING SKILL—Understand attitude

Tell students that once they tune in to the attitude of the speaker, it will tell them a lot about the context and help with their understanding. It may help understanding to listen for the intention, feeling, and tone a speaker portrays in their speech.

VOCABULARY

Get is a very common verb in informal speaking and writing. In *get a job*, *get a promotion*, and *get a degree*, it means *to obtain* or *to achieve*.

GRAMMAR present perfect and simple past

A Match the examples from the interview (1–8) to the descriptions (a–h). Write the letter.

1 We've been in business for five years now. f
2 When school was out in the spring, I opened the ice cream shop. d
3 I made the ice cream and she served the customers. c
4 I made about 20 kinds of ice cream that summer. a
5 How many flavors have you invented so far? h
6 I've just created a new flavor called Orange Chill. g
7 Have you started selling it yet? e
8 We've already sold out! b

a an event that happened at a specific time in the past
b an event that happened sooner than expected
c routines in the past
d an event that happened at the same time or immediately after another event
e a question about whether something has happened
f an action that has been in progress for an amount of time
g an action that happened in the very recent past
h an action that began in the past and will continue in the future

For more practice, go to page 152.

B Complete the text with the present perfect or simple past forms of the verbs in parentheses.

Carmen Vega's ice cream shop **1** has been (be) open for about five years. Carmen **2** took (take) a class to learn how to make ice cream, and since then she **3** has invented (invent) a lot of new ice cream flavors. When her shop **4** opened (open), only Carmen and one other person **5** worked (work) there, but in the past four years, she **6** has hired (hire) 10 more people. She **7** hasn't opened (not open) any more shops yet, but she wants to open two more next year. It **8** has been (be) a great success so far!

MAKE IT REAL

In American English, people often use the simple past instead of the present perfect:
Did you eat yet? = *Have you eaten yet?*
I just bought a car. = *I've just bought a car.*
I already did my homework. = *I've already done my homework.*

SPEAKING

A Make notes about a person you know about who has been successful with a non-traditional career path.

- Who is the person and what did he/she do?
- Did that person go to college?
- How did the person prepare for his/her career?
- What else has the person done?

B IN GROUPS Discuss the career of the person you chose in A. Use the Confident Communicator box to help you.

CONFIDENT COMMUNICATOR
KEEP TALKING

Use these phrases to express doubt or uncertainty when you answer a question:
Yes/No questions: *I (don't) think so. / Maybe. I don't (really) know. / I'm not sure.*
Information questions: *I'm not sure. / I don't (really) know.*

GRAMMAR

Often a question in the present perfect will be followed by a question in the simple past. Naturally, if you ask someone *Have you ever owned your own business?*, the follow-up questions might be *What was it? When did you do that? Was it successful? Did you like it?*

MAKE IT REAL

If students watch American TV, they will often hear the simple past used in place of the present perfect. Challenge them to find an example of this and report back to the class.

SPEAKING

Examples of non-traditional career paths include: *optometrist, inventor, professional sports person, hypnotherapist,* and *cosmetologist.*

Alternative Activity

Have students choose an unusual career. They can find these by searching for "unusual jobs" online. Have them decide which skills and qualifications would be important for the career and present it to their group.

LESSON 3 Employability

VOCABULARY employability skills

A Complete the sentences with words from the box.

creative curious flexible honest independent motivated organized

1. If you can make changes when necessary, you are flexible.
2. Paul is very organized. He always plans and does things in a logical order.
3. Sandra enjoys working alone. She's very independent.
4. If you always tell the truth, you are honest.
5. Martina works hard and is very motivated. She wants to get a promotion.
6. If you have a lot of new, interesting ideas, you are creative.
7. Most children are very curious and like learning about many things.

B Write the words from A in the appropriate categories.

Types of employability skills		
Intrapersonal (personal characteristics)	Interpersonal (how you interact with people)	Cognitive (thinking skills)
Suggested answers: independent, motivated	Suggested answers: flexible, honest	Suggested answers: organized, creative, curious

LISTENING

GO TO page 143 for AUDIO SCRIPT.

A 7.05 **You are going to listen to a talk called *Getting a Job in the 21st Century*. What do you think the main idea of the talk will be? Listen and check your answer.**

Now employers want other skills, not just a university degree or work experience.

B 7.05 **LISTENING SKILL—Identify key words** **Listen again. Choose all of the things the speakers mentioned.**

1. In the past, employers usually focused on … and … .
   a a high school diploma **b a college degree** c personality **d work experience**
2. Someone who is …, …, and … could get a better job than someone with a degree.
   a organized **b creative** c interesting **d motivated**
3. In the example, James got the job because he was …, …, and … .
   a friendly **b flexible** **c curious** **d motivated**
4. The speaker says that it's best to have … and … .
   a a college degree **b excellent skills** c good contacts **d great qualifications**

MAKE IT YOURS

Think of characteristics and skills that are important in your career area. Make a list and share it with classmates in the same career area.

VOCABULARY

More words for employability skills are: *innovative*, *imaginative*, *versatile*, *interested*, *ethical*, and *efficient*.

Extra Practice

Do a spelling bee competition with the employability skills words. Tell students that good spelling is an important part of presenting yourself for a job. You must have a perfectly proofread resume.

LISTENING

Have students write down their ideas for what they think the main idea of the talk will be. Tell them they can write anything that comes to mind. A prediction activity like this is designed to tap into students' current knowledge, so any connections they can make at this point are valid.

MAKE IT YOURS

This activity allows students to explore characteristics and skills that are relevant to their own career areas. Once they have worked on their own, put them into groups with others with the same career interest. Tell them to expand their lists of skills by sharing ideas.

WRITING

A Read the personal statement. Then choose *True* or *False*.

PERSONAL STATEMENT

I am an English teacher, and I have taught at a language school in Sao Paulo for five years. I have a degree in education from the University of Virginia, but I'm Brazilian, so I know that it's very difficult to learn English! I'm very patient, and I'm good at communicating with my students. I enjoy working with my students and my colleagues. I'm very motivated, and I have just taken some extra courses in classroom management and teaching techniques. I think one of my best qualities is curiosity because teachers should always want to learn new things.

1	A personal statement has information about things like family and pets.	True / **False**
2	The statement gives some information about education and work experience.	**True** / False
3	The statement has a complete list of degrees and work experience.	True / **False**
4	The statement has some information about the writer's personality.	**True** / False
5	The statement is a general introduction to the writer.	**True** / False

B Make general notes about your skills and qualifications in your notebook. Then use your notes to write a personal statement.

C IN PAIRS Read each other's personal statements. Circle any incorrect verb forms. Make suggestions for adding information.

MAKE IT DIGITAL

When you get ready to write a resume, look up sample resumes and personal statements online. Find one that is appropriate for you and use it as a model.

GO TO page xiv
for WRITING step-by-step instructions.

SPEAKING

A Many employers say they want employees who are creative. Use basic geometric shapes to create a drawing on a piece of paper. It doesn't matter if you have artistic talent or not. The objective is to think creatively!

square circle rectangle triangle oval

B IN GROUPS Compare your drawings. If necessary, explain your drawing. Use the Confident Communicator box to help you. In your opinion, who has the most creative drawing?

CONFIDENT COMMUNICATOR
START TALKING

Describing geometric images:
I've used five circles to create a …
I've put together eight triangles to represent a …
The oval shape is a …
The rectangle and the square form a …

WRITING Extra Practice

Once students have finished writing and editing their personal statements, have them memorize them. Then have them present their statements to others. Tell students to work in pairs. Give them three minutes each to say their statements. Then tell them to change partners. Next, give them two minutes to say the same statement. Then give them just one minute with yet another partner. Ask students if it got easier or harder. Do they think they have improved their fluency?

MAKE IT DIGITAL

Tell students that they will adapt their resume to suit the job they are applying for. Even though they are the same person with the same skills and qualifications, on their resumes they will emphasize different skills and qualifications depending on the job they are going for.

Students can find examples online of one person's resume for different jobs if they do a search for "one resume for different jobs" or "one resume for different industries."

GO TO page xv

for **LANGUAGE AND LIFE** step-by-step instructions.

1 They are not expensive to start.
2 creativity, photography, cooking, computer skills, speaking, writing, performing
3 selling things online; Students' own answers

Language and Life

Problem-solving – Becoming an Entrepreneur

A 7.06 Read the article. Then discuss the questions as a class.

1 What is the main characteristic of all of the business possibilities in the article?
2 What specific characteristics and skills are mentioned in the article?
3 What is one of the easiest businesses to start and run? Why?

Turn Skills into Sales

Have you ever thought about starting your own business? These days, more and more young people are doing just that. There are many types of businesses that are not very expensive to start. Often you just need a computer, but you also need to be motivated and patient because starting a business takes a lot of time and hard work.

There are several areas that offer good business opportunities for young people.

- If you are creative, make handmade items: clothes, jewelry, soap, hand-painted T-shirts, origami designs, or greeting cards.

- Are you good at photography? Take pictures and sell them to online stock photo companies. Take photos or make videos of events like weddings, family reunions, or community events. Start a pet portrait business.
- Can you cook? Make cookies or cupcakes to sell to friends, at community events, or online.
- Do you love animals? Think about dog walking or pet sitting. You can also make different flavors of dog treats.
- If you have good computer skills, there are many possibilities for making money. Start a device setup service to help people get started with new computers, tablets, phones, or any other device. Become a tech tutor to teach children or older people how to use computers.
- Do you like public speaking, writing, or performing? If you have interesting things to say, you can start a blog or a vlog and get money from advertisers. Maybe you can become a video personality, or create videos to teach people how to do things.
- Finally, one of the easiest ways to make money is to sell things online. Sell items that your family doesn't use anymore, and buy things online or at garage sales and resell them.

OBJECTIVE

In this lesson, students consider different businesses that people have created and come up with options for starting their own. They will consider criteria for each business, match their skills and abilities with the criteria, and make a small-business profile. Point out that having a clear idea of a business profile is a great start for learning how to write a business plan.

PROCESS OPTIONAL 7.06

Students first read an article about starting a business and answer questions about the businesses mentioned in the article. Then, they write three possible small businesses and analyze them against criteria that apply to each. They then further examine the businesses against education, experience, knowledge, skills, and personality characteristics necessary for those businesses. Students then choose one of the businesses they think would be best suited to them and write a small-business profile for it. Finally, they present their business idea to the class, and the class votes on the best idea. They then reflect on the task.

B IN PAIRS Write three possible small business ideas in the table. Check the criteria that apply to each business.

Business idea	We have experience in this work.	We know a lot about this.	It isn't too expensive to start.	It's fun.	We don't need a store or an office.
1	☐	☐	☐	☐	☐
2	☐	☐	☐	☐	☐
3	☐	☐	☐	☐	☐

C IN PAIRS For each business you chose in B, make a list of education, experience, skills, and personality characteristics that you think are necessary for that business.

Business 1
Education: ______
Experience: ______
Knowledge or skills: ______
Personality characteristics: ______

Business 2
Education: ______
Experience: ______
Knowledge or skills: ______
Personality characteristics: ______

Business 3
Education: ______
Experience: ______
Knowledge or skills: ______
Personality characteristics: ______

D IN PAIRS Choose the business that you think would be the best for you and your partner. Consider your experience and personality characteristics. Complete the business profile.

SMALL BUSINESS PROFILE

Type of business: ______
Name of business: ______
Location (online, store, etc.): ______
Products or services: ______
Main customers: ______

E IN GROUPS Present your business idea. Vote on the best business idea.

F Discuss the questions.

1 What was the most important part of your decision?
2 In what other situations do you use problem-solving skills to make decisions?

MAKE IT DIGITAL

Do research online about small business opportunities in your country or your area. Share the ideas with your class

CAREER NOTE

Think about licenses and permits you might need for a small business. Opening your own business requires a lot of patience with bureaucracy.

CULTURE NOTE

In many countries, there are grants available to start a small business. Check with your local government office to see what kind of entrepreneurs they support.

MAKE IT DIGITAL

When starting a small business, one should follow one's passion. Ask your students to think about what they are passionate about and then look online for possible businesses related to their passion. Are they interested in working out? They could open a gym. Are they health nuts? They could start a health blog.

GO TO page xvii for **UNIT REVIEW** step-by-step instructions.

UNIT 7

VOCABULARY review

SCORE: / 10

A Complete the sentences with words from the box.

apply benefits career curious degree flexible hired motivated raises skills

I have a **1** degree from a good university, and now I'm ready to start my **2** career. I want to be a nurse, and I think I have the **3** skills to get **4** hired at a good hospital. I'm **5** motivated to work hard, and I'm very **6** curious about medical information. I like to learn new things. I'm also very **7** flexible with my working hours. I'm going to **8** apply for a job at two hospitals in my city. I would prefer Central Hospital because they have good **9** benefits, like health insurance, and they give **10** raises if you do a good job.

GRAMMAR review

SCORE: / 10

A Complete the sentences with the correct forms of the verbs in parentheses.

I'm really excited because I **1** 've/have just started (start) my own business! I **2** 've/have been (be) very busy my first week. I **3** 've/have already sent (send) about 100 emails to friends, and yesterday I **4** put (put) my new website online. I **5** haven't had (not have) many orders yet, but I'm not worried!

B Unscramble and write sentences.

1. I / my / business online / started / new / just / have / .
   I have just started my new business online.
2. interview / a / gotten / he / yet / hasn't / job / .
   He hasn't gotten a job interview yet.
3. written / you / your / have / yet / resume / ?
   Have you written your resume yet?
4. already / my / I've / resume / finished / .
   I've already finished my resume. / I've finished my resume already.
5. check / yesterday / I / listings / didn't / job / .
   I didn't check job listings yesterday.

16–20 correct: You can talk about success and employability skills. You can use the present perfect with *already, yet,* and *just.*
0–15 correct: Look again at the Vocabulary and Grammar sections in the unit.

TOTAL SCORE: / 20

WHAT DO YOU KNOW NOW? Look back at page 67 and add the words you know now to the boxes.

GO TO page xviii for **STUDY SKILLS** step-by-step instructions.

STUDY SKILLS CREATIVITY

A Take the quiz. Then go to Study Skills on page 133. Find the answers and learn more about creativity.

1 ... of people have creative ideas in the shower.
a 59% b 69% c 72%

2 Aerobic exercise makes you less creative.
a True b False

It makes you more creative.

3 ...of people think they could be more creative.
a 50% b 75% c 98%

4 ... of CEOs think that creativity is the most important quality for leaders to have.
a 35% b 60% c 90%

76 Unit 7 Get to Work

CLASSROOM MANAGEMENT

You can manage the review activities as competitive or collaborative activities. A collaborative way to approach the vocabulary activity might be to have students work in groups of three and assign part of the activity to each student. Tell each student to do their items and then share their answers with the group.

FURTHER DISCUSSION

Put students in groups of three and ask the following questions for them to discuss:

- Do you want a career or a job?
- Are you working your way through college?
- What is the best idea for a small business you've heard in this unit?
- What do you think are the most important qualities for an entrepreneur?
- Do you want to advance in your chosen career?
- Do you think you'll work in the same career or change careers at some point?

UNIT 8 Downtime

GO TO page vi
for UNIT OPENER step-by-step instructions.

WHAT DO YOU ALREADY KNOW?

1 **Read the definition of *downtime*. Then think of different types of activities you do when you have downtime.**

downtime (n.): a time when you are not working or busy

2 **Compare and share your activities. Add more words to your lists.**

Relaxing activities

Energetic activities

STUDENTS MAY ALREADY KNOW

- **Relaxing activities:** read, sleep, watch TV, go to the movies.
- **Energetic activities:** walk, run, dance, go out, work out.

VIDEO

DISCUSS & SHARE

3 **IN GROUPS** **Watch the video and answer the question.**

SYM Do you have a lot of downtime, or are you always busy?

GO TO page xx
for VIDEOS IN SYM step-by-step instructions.

In this unit, you will ...

- talk about creative activities for adults, leisure activities for a weekend, and "do nothing" time.
- use thinking skills: apply, analyze, and understand.
- read about "kidults."
- use strategies to repair talking by describing an activity, agreeing with a proposal, and explaining a concept.
- use mindfulness to manage your life and relax your mind.
- follow a resort activities coordinator to learn about this job and the skills needed for the leisure industry.

WHAT DO YOU ALREADY KNOW?

If you notice students are struggling to understand what to do, you can provide one or two examples to help them get started:

- **Relaxing activities:** meditating, napping, thinking
- **Energetic activities:** jogging, skydiving, bungee jumping

VIDEO

Before viewing, ask:

What is Emily's schedule? *lunch, study, doctor's appointment, dinner, and laundry.*

What is Dan's schedule? *work, take a course, downtime on weekends.*

After viewing, put the continuum on the board.

downtime —— busy

Have students mark the continuum and explain their preferences.

DISCUSS & SHARE

Have students evaluate their normal schedules for weekdays and weekends. Do they have any free time? If so, what do they do with their free time? Is it spent running errands or doing fun activities?

GO TO page vii

for **VOCABULARY** step-by-step instructions.

LESSON 1 Kidults

VOCABULARY

A Label the pictures with the activities from the box.

building a model	coloring	flying a kite	making things with clay

1 
making things with clay

2 
building a model

3 
flying a kite

4 
coloring

MAKE IT YOURS

Find the names of three or more activities that you liked doing when you were a child. Do you still like doing them?

GO TO page x

for **READING** step-by-step instructions.

Suggested answer: an adult doing activities that kids do

READING

A As a class, discuss what you think the term *kidult* refers to.

B 8.01 READING SKILL— Read for main ideas Read the text. Then match the main ideas (1–4) to the paragraphs (a–d). Write the letter.

KIDS + ADULTS = KIDULTS

a Adults like having toys—no, not boats, sports equipment, or expensive audio equipment, but actual children's toys. They are making things with building blocks, coloring in coloring books, making art with 3D pens, and doing difficult puzzles; they are bouncing inside enormous plastic balls and flying kites. There is a new term for adults who love playing like children: *kidults*.

b Why is this happening? Experts think that in part it is because people, especially millennials, want an escape from the complications of the modern world. Acting like a child is a way to return to a simpler time, but there is another reason for this trend. Doing kids' activities is fun! Why shouldn't adults enjoy doing things like flying kites or coloring?

c People over 50 also spend time doing children's activities. Many grandparents are very healthy and active, and they love playing with their grandchildren. Seniors are playing board games, doing arts and crafts, and participating in other activities that kids love.

d Being an adult doesn't mean that you have to be serious all the time or pay a lot of money for entertainment. Are you creative? Try building a model or making a sculpture with clay. Maybe you love being active, but you can't stand playing competitive sports. Try jumping rope or flying a kite. Find your inner child and enjoy being a kidult!

1 There are two main reasons why young people like being kidults. Paragraph b

2 Adults are doing many children's activities. Paragraph a

3 You don't always have to act like an adult. Paragraph d

4 There is a large group of older *kidults*. Paragraph c

VOCABULARY

In the 1960s, the term *kidult* appeared. It refers to an adult who has childish tastes or likes to do activities that are usually for children. There has been a recent increase in the popularity of childish activities for adults, like the boom in adult coloring books.

MAKE IT YOURS

More activities might be: play board games, play video games, draw cartoons, play on the playground, go to amusement parks, ride a roller coaster, or build a sandcastle.

READING OPTIONAL 8.01

Have students underline kidult activities in the text. These include making things with building blocks, coloring in coloring books, making art with 3D pens, doing difficult puzzles, bouncing inside enormous plastic balls, flying kites, doing arts and crafts, and jumping rope. Ask students to circle three that appeal to them and share them with a partner.

C IN PAIRS Discuss the questions. Look back at the text in B for help if necessary.

1 According to the article, what is the definition of *kidults*?
2 What are the two main reasons that adults like being kidults?
3 According to the article, kidult activities are not necessarily expensive. Which ideas in the article are inexpensive? Which are probably a little expensive?

1 Adults who like to do activities usually for children.
2 They want an escape from the complications of the modern world and it is fun.
3 Suggested answers: inexpensive: coloring, jumping rope, having water balloon fights, making a sculpture with clay, painting with a water gun; expensive: making things with building blocks, making art with 3D pens, bouncing inside plastic balls; doing puzzles, flying kites, and building models can be expensive or inexpensive, depending on what products you buy.

D THINKING SKILL—Apply Think about things you like to do in your leisure time. Do you think you are or could be a kidult? Why or why not?

GRAMMAR gerund phrases as subject and object

A Read the sentences and answer the questions.

a Acting like a child is a way to return to a simpler time.
b People over 50 also often prefer doing children's activities.

1 What is the subject in sentence *a*? Acting like a child
2 What is the object in sentence *b*? doing children's activities
3 What is similar between the subject in *a* and the object in *b*? They have an *–ing* verb.
4 What form of the verb is used after *prefer, enjoy, can't stand, like, love,* and *hate*? the *–ing* form

For more practice, go to page 152.

B Look back at READING B. Underline two more examples of gerunds as subjects and two more examples of gerunds as objects. "Doing kids' activities" (para. 2) and "Being an adult" (para. 4) are gerund as subject. The rest are gerund as object.

C Write answers for you using gerunds.

1 Are there any children's toys that you enjoy playing with?
I enjoy making model cars.

2 How can playing with children be good for older people?

3 Do you think being a kidult is a good idea for young adults? Why or why not?

D IN PAIRS Discuss your ideas from C.

SPEAKING

A Make a list of kids' activities that you enjoy or would enjoy doing.

B IN GROUPS Tell your group the activities you chose and explain why. If necessary, explain what an activity is. Use the Confident Communicator box to help you.

A: I love playing Hide-and-Seek. It's great because you play with friends, you get exercise, and you laugh a lot.
B: What's Hide-and-Seek?
A: You play in a group. One person is "It." The others hide and the person has to try to find them ....

CONFIDENT COMMUNICATOR — START TALKING

You can use these phrases to describe an activity or a game:
You play … on teams / in a group / on a field.
There's … a base / a large ball.
One person is … "It" / the leader.
You have to … bounce a ball / run to a base / find the person.

GO TO page viii for GRAMMAR step-by-step instructions.

GO TO page xii for SPEAKING step-by-step instructions.

THINKING SKILL—Apply

This task has students think on things they like to do in their leisure time and consider whether they are, or could be, kidults. Personalizing the issues allows students to apply the concepts to their own world and make connections. When students apply information to their own world it probably means they understand this information. It also helps you get to know your students better.

GRAMMAR

The gerund form allows the phrase to act as a noun, and students should consider the entire noun phrase as one unit.

Reiterate that after the verbs *prefer, enjoy, can't stand,* and *hate,* students should use the gerund form (*I enjoy making things with clay.*) and that with *like* and *love* they can use the gerund or the infinitive form (*I love jumping rope. / I love to jump rope.*).

SPEAKING Alternative Activity

Describe some children's games and have students guess the game. For example, one person is "it." That person has to run and chase the others until they catch someone. The person they catch then becomes "it." (Tag.)

LESSON 2 **Plan for Fun!**

VOCABULARY leisure activities

A Match the words from the box to the verbs (1–4). Use a dictionary if necessary.

a barbecue	aerobics	jewelry	paddle boarding	to a park
a potluck meal	furniture	kayaking	skating	yoga

Leisure activities

1 Have: a picnic, a potluck meal, a barbecue
2 Make: pottery, jewelry, furniture
3 Do: crafts, aerobics, yoga
4 Go: for a drive, to a park, skating, kayaking, paddle boarding

B Complete the online comments with the correct forms of *have*, *make*, *do*, and *go*.

I do all kinds of things that people say help with stress. I **1** do yoga; in fact, I **2** go to my yoga class four days a week. I almost always **3** go swimming or skating on weekends, and I also **4** do aerobics. I exercise a lot, but I'm still really stressed! Molly

@Molly Wow, you need to relax! **5** Doing yoga and lots of exercise is great, but what about relaxing and having fun? **6** Do a craft—**7** make jewelry or candles, or color in a coloring book. I **8** make really bad furniture, but it's fun and relaxing! Jen

@Jen I'm not into arts and crafts, but I agree with Jen. Relax! I like **9** going for a drive in the country or **10** having a picnic with friends. Get together with a group of friends and **11** have a potluck meal or **12** go to a park. Have some fun! Lance

LISTENING

GO TO page xi for LISTENING step-by-step instructions.

A Take a class survey and answer the questions.

1 How many people usually do more or less the same activities every weekend?
2 What are some of the most common weekend activities?
3 How many people usually plan their weekend activities ahead of time?

GO TO page 144 for AUDIO SCRIPT.

B 8.02 LISTENING SKILL—Listen for details Listen to a conversation about weekend activities. Answer the questions. Listen again to check.

1 What activities does Kate describe as "the same stuff"?
2 What does Ken say he does not like doing?
3 What activities do they decide to do on Saturday?
4 What do they decide to do on Sunday?

1 going to a movie, hanging out at somebody's house
2 arts and crafts
3 go out to hear live music, go paddle boarding
4 go for a drive, have a picnic

C THINKING SKILL—Analyze Write the activities from the conversation in B in the categories below. Add other activities to each category.

1 Creative: doing arts and crafts, making candles, making jewelry
2 Cultural: going to a movie, going out to hear live music
3 Physical: going paddle boarding
4 Social: hanging out at somebody's house, going for a drive, having a picnic

Note: Going for a drive might also be a cultural activity if you are driving around to look at landmarks or other cultural sites.

VOCABULARY

Have, *make*, and *do* are tricky in English. They are collocations that learners have to learn as they go. We say *do yoga* but *go to (or take) a yoga class*. The verbs *take*, *make*, and *have* don't carry the meaning of the phrase—this lies with the noun.

LISTENING

Have students work in groups of four, survey their group, and then report their findings back to the class.

THINKING SKILL—Analyze

Some other activities for the categories are:

- **Creative:** learn to knit, go to a sewing class, do sculpture, do pottery.
- **Cultural:** go to a museum, an art gallery, a bookstore, a festival.
- **Physical:** work out, go to the gym, go hiking.
- **Social:** go out with friends, visit a neighbor, go out for coffee.

GRAMMAR verb + gerund or infinitive

A **Read the sentences. Then choose the correct form of the verb to complete the rules. Choose more than one option if possible.**

I love going out to hear live music.
I like to go to dinner and a movie.
I prefer to watch TV at home.
I prefer doing physical activities.

I'd like to do something creative.
I'd rather do a physical activity.
I would prefer to have the picnic first.

1 *love, like, hate, prefer* + base verb / infinitive / *–ing* verb
2 *would like* + base verb / infinitive / *–ing* verb
3 *would prefer* + base verb / infinitive / *–ing* verb
4 *would rather* + base verb / infinitive / *–ing* verb

For more practice, go to page 153.

B **Complete the email with the correct form of the verbs in parentheses.**

Hey, guys. Would you like **1** to see (see) the boat show this weekend? I can get tickets for either Saturday or Sunday. I'd rather **2** go (go) on Sunday, I think, because I prefer **3** doing / to do (do) housework and errands on Saturdays. Also, I'd rather **4** take (take) the bus because I hate **5** driving (drive) in a lot of traffic, and I'd kind of prefer **6** to get (get) there early. What do you think? Does all of that sound OK?

PRONUNCIATION *–ould* words

A **8.03 Listen to the conversation and answer the questions.**

Omar: Would you like to go to the new museum tomorrow?
Jamal: That sounds great. We should go early, when there are fewer people.
Omar: Actually, I would rather go in the afternoon. Is that OK?
Jamal: That's fine. Could you pick me up?
Omar: Sure.

1 Do *would*, *should*, and *could* have the same vowel sound or different sounds?
2 Do you hear the *l* in *would*, *should*, and *could*?

B **IN PAIRS Practice the conversation. Pay special attention to the pronunciation of *would*, *should*, and *could*.**

MAKE IT REAL

Although the meaning of *hate*, *like*, *love*, and *prefer* is the same when used with an infinitive or with a gerund, the infinitive form is more commonly used in American English than the gerund form.

GO TO page ix for **PRONUNCIATION** step-by-step instructions.

1 the same vowel sound
2 no

SPEAKING

A **IN PAIRS In your notebook, make a list of activities that you can do in your area in each category.**

- Creative
- Cultural
- Physical
- Social

B **IN GROUPS Compare your lists from A. Create one list of activities that you all like doing.**

C **IN GROUPS Discuss activities for a group activity weekend. Use the Confident Communicator box to help you.**

A: I love / like / don't really like / can't stand … *B: I would like to / prefer to / rather …*

CONFIDENT COMMUNICATOR
KEEP TALKING

Agreeing with a proposal
Sure. / That's fine with me. / That sounds good.

Objecting to a proposal
The problem is that … / Sorry, but I don't really like … / Unfortunately, I can't …

GRAMMAR

Tell students that after *would*, as in *I'd like …*, *I'd rather …*, or *Would you prefer …?*, they should use the infinitive form.

Alternative Activity

Play *Would You Prefer?* Mark an imaginary line on the floor for students to stand on, then ask *Would you prefer…?* questions. For example, *Would you prefer to go to a movie or a music festival?* If students prefer the first option, they move right. If they prefer the second option, they move left. Nominate a couple of students to answer with *I'd rather …* Ask the questions in quick succession for an upbeat game. Ask for more explanation to slow the game down.

SPEAKING

Depending on your group, you can define *area* as neighborhood, town, or city. You may want students from one area to work together first and then talk to students from another area to compare activities. For SPEAKING **C**, the whole group should decide on one group activity they will all enjoy.

GO TO page 144 for AUDIO SCRIPT.

LESSON 3 Is It OK to Do Nothing?

LISTENING

A Do you enjoy doing nothing? Why or why not? Discuss as a class.

B 8.04 LISTENING SKILL—Listen for reasons Listen to a class discussion and check (✓) the reasons you hear for and against doing nothing.

For	Against
☐ It's fun.	☑ It's boring.
☑ It helps you relax.	☐ It makes you tired.
☑ It helps you be more creative.	☑ It makes you feel guilty.
☑ It helps you solve problems.	☐ It's unhealthy.

C THINKING SKILL—Understand List the examples of activities that are classified as *doing nothing* in the class discussion from **B**. Add several more examples of activities that you consider to be *doing nothing*.

Suggested answers: sitting around, sitting in the park, lying on the sofa; some people also think that things like watching a movie or checking social media are "doing nothing."

VOCABULARY adjectives of feeling

A Match the words from the box to the definitions (1–5).

bored guilty nervous rested stressed

1 nervous: worried or a little scared
2 bored: not interested in the activity or conversation
3 guilty: feeling bad because you are doing something wrong
4 stressed: worried about professional, financial, or personal problems
5 rested: not tired

B IN PAIRS Ask and answer the questions.

1 How do you feel when you do nothing?
2 What situations make you feel nervous?
3 What do you do if you feel stressed?
4 When do you get bored?

A: I feel bored when I do nothing.

B: I eat when I feel stressed.

LISTENING

Set the listening text for homework and have students take notes. Discuss it the following day. Some ideas to encourage students to discuss are: *Do nothing, at least one hour, and I mean absolutely nothing. No social media, TV, reading, or whatever. Just do nothing. After one hour, write down what you were thinking and feeling while you were doing nothing. Was it a positive or a negative experience?*

THINKING SKILL—Understand

Students may disagree about what is meant by *doing nothing*. Some may think doing nothing is disconnecting, as in sitting and thinking, or looking at the sky. They may think reading or doing meditation is doing something. Allow students to debate whether things like using social media are relaxing, distracting, or stimulating.

VOCABULARY

More adjectives of feelings are:

- **Positive feelings:** calm, cheerful, chilled out, contented, enthusiastic, excited, fantastic
- **Negative feelings:** angry, anxious, depressed, tired, tense

WRITING

GO TO page xiv for WRITING step-by-step instructions.

A Read the blog entry. Then answer the questions.

MY PROFILE

Some people say that it's good to do nothing, but I disagree. I think doing nothing is bad for you. First, most people think that doing nothing is not productive, and I agree. It's better to use your time studying, working, or helping other people. Second, some people say that doing nothing helps you think creatively and solve problems. However, when people say they are doing nothing, they are usually doing things like looking at social media or watching TV. Those activities don't help you think creatively or solve problems. Finally, the main problem is that doing nothing can become a habit. If you take a break to relax and do nothing, it is difficult to start working or studying again. It is easier if you finish working or studying before you take a break.

1 How many reasons does the writer give to support his argument? three

2 What words does the writer use to indicate that he is introducing a new point? First, Second, Finally

3 Where does the writer place his most important argument? Last—this gives it more emphasis.

B In your opinion, is it good or bad to do nothing? Think about the question and make notes in your notebook.

C Use your notes from B to write a blog entry in your notebook.

D IN PAIRS Exchange papers with someone who has the opposite opinion from yours. Read each other's blog entries and then discuss the question.

Did your partner's arguments change your opinion?

SPEAKING

A Make notes on the questions.

1 How often do you do nothing?

____

____

2 When you do nothing, what do you do?

____

____

B IN GROUPS Compare your ideas. Say what the perfect do-nothing day would be for you. Use the Confident Communicator box to help you.

A: On a do-nothing day, I'd like to ...   *B: Really? I'd rather ...*

CONFIDENT COMMUNICATOR — START TALKING

Explaining a concept

Doing nothing **means** *sitting around just thinking about things.*

To me, *doing nothing* **is** *reading a good book and not going out.*

For me, *the perfect do-nothing day* **is** *sitting/going/having ...*

I think *doing nothing* **is when you ...**

WRITING

This is an example of persuasive writing. An opinion piece is based on the writer's thoughts about the topic. The writer gives a subjective view of the topic and then needs to give reasons for that perspective and examples to support those reasons.

The questions have the student exploring the profile in WRITING **A** as a model text. You may want to write up a list of opinion phrases (*I think ..., I believe ..., I feel ..., I'm convinced that ..., The best ..., The worst ...*) and more transition words (*Next ..., Besides ..., Obviously ..., Clearly ..., For all these reasons ...*).

SPEAKING

Have students record themselves talking about their ideal "do-nothing" days on their phones. Then have them listen to themselves. Only if they feel ready, have them listen to each other and give kind critiques or feedback.

GO TO page xv

for **LANGUAGE AND LIFE** step-by-step instructions.

Language and Life

Mindfulness – Relaxing Your Mind

A 8.05 **IN PAIRS** Read the article. Then discuss the questions.

1 We are less efficient, less creative, and less happy.

2 It's paying attention to what you are doing at the moment, to your feelings, and to the things that are happening around you. You are not thinking about things that have already happened or worrying about what is going to happen.

3 In a normal activity, we are usually thinking about the finished product, or the result. In a mindful activity, we are thinking about the process.

4 You feel less stressed and more rested. The result is more creativity and better problem solving.

MINDFULNESS FOR MENTAL RELAXATION

Study, work, family, friends, pets, social media … We feel tired and stressed because we can't do everything. The effects of this are that we are less efficient, less creative, and less happy. We all try to do leisure activities like playing sports or watching movies, but what about leisure time for the mind?

In recent years, many people have started to practice *mindfulness*. Being mindful means that you are paying attention to what you are doing at the moment, to your feelings, and to the things that are happening around you. You are not thinking about things that have already happened or worrying about what is going to happen. For example, if you notice how the sun feels on your face, or how your clean clothes smell, you are being mindful.

There are some simple things that you can do to practice mindfulness. Do you like walking? Go for a walk, but don't think about walking fast or going a certain distance. Walk slowly. Think about how your body feels. Stop and look at trees or flowers. Stop and close your eyes. What do you hear, feel, or smell? Would you rather do something creative? Paint something or do a craft. Don't worry if it isn't good. Think about the process. How does the paintbrush feel in your hand? What does each color make you think of? Giving your brain time to relax can help you feel less stressed and more rested. The result is more creativity and better problem solving.

1 What are the effects of being tired and stressed?
2 What is mindfulness?
3 How is a mindful activity different from the normal way we do things?
4 What are the effects of giving your brain time to relax?

OBJECTIVE

In this lesson, students learn how to give advice about mindfulness activities. Students consider the importance and benefits of learning how to relax the mind. Living in a constantly connected environment means our minds are often overloaded. Students learn how to rest their minds and how to encourage others to do the same.

PROCESS OPTIONAL 8.05

First, students read an article defining mindfulness and giving examples of ways to practice it. Then, they learn about positive reflection, observation, and visualization; these are types of mindfulness techniques. They choose and try one of the activities and afterward reflect on them in groups, with questions to guide the reflection. Next, students use the knowledge they have gained from the article and activities, or from mindfulness activities they have created, and recommend mindfulness activities for characters in a case-study situation. Finally, students will reflect on the usefulness of relaxation and other ways they use to calm themselves.

B Choose one of the mindfulness activities and try it.

Positive reflection (5 minutes)

1 Think of three things that you are thankful for and write them down.
2 Think of three good things that you have done or that have happened to you this week and write them down.
3 Close your eyes. Breathe slowly. Take a few minutes to reflect on the things on your lists. How do you feel?

Observation (5 minutes)

1 Go to a window in your classroom. If there are no windows, choose an area of your classroom to focus on.
2 Look at everything you see. Don't think about the names of the things at all. Notice shapes and colors.
3 Notice changes in the light or movement of the objects.
4 If you start thinking about other things, notice a color or a shape again. Focus only on that color or shape.

Visualization (5 minutes)

1 Think of a place that you love. Close your eyes and imagine that you are in that place.
2 Think about what is around you. For example, if you are in the mountains, what do you see? Are there tall trees? Is there snow on the mountains? Is the grass green?
3 Use your other senses. What do you smell? Flowers? What do you hear? Birds singing? A waterfall? What do you feel? The sun? A cool wind on your skin?
4 Breathe slowly and relax. If you start thinking about other things, focus on the details of the place.

C IN GROUPS Discuss your experience. Use the questions as a guide.

1 Which activity did you choose?
2 Was it easy or hard to do the activity?
3 How do you feel after the activity?
4 Did you like doing the activity?
5 Do you think mindfulness activities can help your mind relax when you are feeling stressed?

D IN PAIRS Choose a situation and suggest a mindfulness activity to help the person feel less stressed. You can use an activity from B or invent your own activity.

1 Paul is very nervous about a big exam tomorrow. He's at home, and he's trying to study, but he can't concentrate. He's messaging friends on social media and saying that he thinks the exam will be very hard.
2 Sam is worried about his health. He knows that he doesn't always eat well and he doesn't sleep enough. When he worries, he eats junk food and watches TV very late at night. He says that junk food and action movies make him feel happy!
3 Kathy is on the bus, on her way to her university classes. There is a lot of traffic, and the bus is going very slowly. Kathy is really bored, and she is getting angry because she's probably going to be late for class.

E IN GROUPS Share your mindfulness activity from D with your group. Then discuss the questions.

1 Have you ever been in any of the situations in **D**? How did you feel? What did you do?
2 Of the ideas that you heard, which activities would you prefer to do?

F Discuss the questions.

1 Was it useful to take time to relax? Why or why not?
2 What other ways do you use to calm yourself?

MAKE IT DIGITAL

Do research to find more mindfulness activities. Choose one or two and try them. Use questions 1–5 from **C** to report to your class about the activities you did.

Unit 8 Downtime **85**

CULTURE NOTE

Ask students to research and discuss where in the world meditation comes from. How long has it been around? When did it become popular worldwide? When did it become popular in their country?

MAKE IT DIGITAL

There are many free mindfulness apps available for smartphones. Have students search for a selection and try out two or three. Then have them report back to the class on the kinds of activities the apps offer and whether they found them useful or not.

GO TO page xvii
for UNIT REVIEW step-by-step instructions.

UNIT 8

VOCABULARY review

SCORE: / 10

A Complete the sentences with the words in the box.

kite coloring potluck crafts model skating

1 We're going to have a big potluck meal. Everyone is going to bring a different dish.
2 My dad's hobby is building model airplanes.
3 It's windy today – a great day for flying a kite.
4 It's a nice day. Let's go skating in the park.
5 I do a lot of different crafts. It's relaxing and creative.
6 I love coloring pictures. I usually use colored pencils.

B Choose the correct option.

1 I'm worried about work because I have too much to do. I'm really bored / guilty / **stressed**.
2 I'm not doing anything, and my friends are all busy. I'm **bored** / stressed / rested.
3 I had a great weekend. I saw friends and slept a lot. I feel very guilty / bored / **rested**.
4 My brother didn't invite his friend Joe to the party. Now he feels stressed / **guilty** / nervous.

GRAMMAR review

SCORE: / 10

A Complete the email with the correct form of the verbs in parentheses.

Hey, Susie. You love **1** doing (do) crafts, right? I'm taking a cool art class. We're learning to create art with different materials. I don't like **2** painting (paint) or **3** drawing (draw), but **4** making (make) models or clay sculptures is really fun! Also, we're, **5** making (make) cool jewelry out of paper. Would you like **6** to go (go) to a class with me? Is Monday OK, or would you prefer **7** going (go) on Wednesday? I'd rather **8** take (take) you on Monday if possible. I think you'll like **9** visiting (visit) the class, and I'm sure you'd rather **10** go (go) to an art class than study for the math exam. 🙂

16–20 correct: You can discuss leisure activities and use adjectives of feeling. You can use gerunds.
0–15 correct: Look again at the Vocabulary and Grammar sections in the unit.

TOTAL SCORE: / 20

WHAT DO YOU KNOW NOW? Look back at page 77 and add the words you know now to the boxes.

GO TO page xix
for FOLLOW A PRO step-by-step instructions.

FOLLOW A PRO LEISURE

Take the quiz about activities coordinators. Then go to Follow A Pro on page 134. Find the answers and learn more about the leisure industry.

1 In the US, the average annual salary for activities coordinators is about …
a $12,000. b $22,000. c **$32,000.**

2 … is NOT usually a requirement for an activities coordinator.
a Physical fitness b **Teaching experience** c Public speaking experience

3 Choose all that are true. Activities coordinators work …
a **at schools.** b **at resort hotels.** c **on cruise ships.** d **at senior homes.** e **at camps.**

86 Unit 8 Downtime

CLASSROOM MANAGEMENT

Allow students time to look over the unit and ask questions before giving them time limits to complete the review activities. Tell students a good way to start the review activities is to first read the sentences without answering them and then answer the items. Have student volunteers read the answers aloud.

FURTHER DISCUSSION

Put students in groups of three and ask the following questions for them to discuss:

- Do you do any kidult activities?
- What high-energy activities do you do?
- Have you ever tried mindfulness activities?
- Who is the most relaxed person you know?

UNIT 9

Room for Me

GO TO page vi
for UNIT OPENER step-by-step instructions.

WHAT DO YOU ALREADY KNOW?

1 Think about where you live. Is it a house, an apartment, or something else? Write words that describe your home and what's in it.

2 IN PAIRS Share and compare your information. Add more words to your list.

STUDENTS MAY ALREADY KNOW

- Furniture: bed, TV, sofa, chair, table, desk, lamp.
- Parts of a house/rooms: kitchen, dining room, living room, bedroom, bathroom.

Furniture

Parts of a house/rooms

VIDEO

DISCUSS & SHARE

3 IN GROUPS Watch the video and answer the question.

SYM Would you prefer to live in a house or an apartment?

GO TO page xx
for VIDEOS IN SYM step-by-step instructions.

In this unit, you will ...

- talk about different kinds of housing, where you prefer to live, and what houses will be like in the future.
- use thinking skills: understand and evaluate.
- read about housing solutions.
- use strategies to keep talking by asking for and giving opinions.
- use decision-making skills to plan and develop a neighborhood.
- learn tips for problem solving in group work.

WHAT DO YOU ALREADY KNOW?

If you notice students are struggling to understand what to do, you can provide one or two examples to help them get started:

- Furniture: wardrobe (closet), bedside table, chest of drawers
- Parts of a house/rooms: traditional style, modern style, balcony, basement

VIDEO

Before viewing, ask:

Name advantages of living in an apartment. *organized, few rooms to clean, if there is a problem you can call the management office.*

Name advantages of living in a house. *plenty of room to cook, eat, relax, play*

After viewing, put the continuum on the board.

house —— apartment

Have students mark the continuum and explain their preferences.

DISCUSS & SHARE

Take a poll of students about where they live now—a house or an apartment. Is it how they want to live? If not, what would their ideal home be like? Also, ask the class for ideas about unusual housing.

GO TO page x
for READING step-by-step instructions.

LESSON 1 Housing Solutions

READING

A **READING SKILL—Predict** **Look at the picture and the title of the article in B. What do you think the article is about?**

B 9.01 **Read the article. Then check (✓) the correct options.**

Half-houses in Chile

In many areas, people can't **afford** to buy or **rent** a place to live. It's a problem that will become worse in the future. Some cities have found interesting solutions.

One example is half-houses in Chile. An earthquake hit the town of Constitución in 2010 and destroyed about 80% of the buildings. The local government hired an architecture firm to provide **low-cost** houses. They built houses that are only half-finished. The owners finish the house when they have the money. It means that each family can decide what they need: a garage, another bedroom, a **hall**, a **balcony**. One resident says: "We're going to build another bedroom and bathroom in two years. We can add our personal style."

Another solution is micro-units, like those at Carmel Place in New York City. These are very small apartments, around 28 square meters. They are too small for a family, but perfect for single young professionals. Each one-room apartment has the usual appliances—a stove, a refrigerator, and a microwave—and there's a room in another part of the building for washing clothes. The smart use of special furniture means the room can become a bedroom, kitchen, office, or living room. The desk becomes a dining table and the couch becomes a bed. The coffee table folds down and goes under the bed at night. A young resident says: "I'm having a friend over for dinner tonight. I just turn the bed into a **couch**, the desk into a table, and we're good to go!"

1 What are the advantages of half-houses for the city?

- ☑ They are low-cost.
- ☐ They don't collapse in an earthquake.
- ☐ They are big enough for families.
- ☐ They have a garage.
- ☑ Residents choose what to build.
- ☐ The half-houses are built in a traditional style.

2 What are the apartments like at Carmel Place?

- ☑ People can change the small space in many ways.
- ☐ They are big enough for families.
- ☐ They have a kitchen and an office in two rooms.
- ☑ There are washing machines in the apartment building.

C **THINKING SKILL—Understand** **Compare these examples to your own area. What housing programs does your area offer? Do people use these programs?**

GO TO page vii
for VOCABULARY step-by-step instructions.

VOCABULARY

A **Complete each sentence with a bold word from the text in READING B.**

1 Something that is ___low-cost___ is cheap, not expensive.
2 A ___balcony___ is a place where you can stand outside a window.
3 If you can ___afford___ something, you have enough money for it.
4 A ___couch___ is a seat for two or three people.
5 The long, narrow area in a house that leads to different rooms is the ___hall___.
6 When you ___rent___ a place, you pay money each month to live there.

MAKE IT REAL

When people say they are "good to go," it means they are ready to do something, e.g. *We have popcorn, soda, and tickets for the movie. We're good to go!*

READING OPTIONAL 9.01

The title "Housing Solutions" indicates there is a problem. You may want to have students predict what they think the problems with housing are.

In many Latin American countries, the possibility of earthquakes is very real, and they could have devastating effects. You may want to discuss housing issues they and their community have experienced as a result of earthquakes.

THINKING SKILL—Understand

Encourage students to investigate federal government and local municipal housing programs. Some students may know the names and details of these programs, but you may want to allow them to research online and ask family members about affordable housing programs and new housing programs in their area.

VOCABULARY

A great way to help your students expand their vocabulary is to have them identify different forms of words they know. Have students explore verb-adjective patterns with words in the text; these might be *afford–affordable*, *rent–rentable*, *collapse–collapsible*, and *change–changeable*.

GRAMMAR future forms

A Read the article in READING B again. Underline sentences with *will*, *going to*, and the present progressive. Then read the sentence below and write if it refers to the present or the future.

1 My train leaves at nine o'clock tomorrow morning. future

B Complete the grammar rules with words from the box.

arrangements intentions predictions schedule

1 To make predictions about the future, we use *will* or *going to*.
2 To talk about future intentions, we use *going to*.
3 To talk about future arrangements, we use the present progressive.
4 To talk about future events that happen on a schedule, we use the simple present.

For more practice, go to page 154.

C Choose the correct option.

1 I rent / **'m going to rent** an apartment downtown next year.
2 I meet / **am meeting** my friend tomorrow at 9 a.m.
3 Do you think you **will rent** / are renting an apartment in the future?
4 What do you do / **are you going to do** this weekend?
5 My new job **starts** / will starting next month, and I need to find somewhere to live.

D IN PAIRS Ask and answer the questions.

1 What fun things are you doing this week?
2 What are you going to do this weekend?
3 When does your next vacation start? What are you going to do?

GO TO page viii for GRAMMAR step-by-step instructions.

SPEAKING

A Check (✓) the housing problems your neighborhood or city faces. Then add more ideas.

☐ Rents are high.
☐ Houses/apartments are expensive.
☐ There aren't enough places to live.
☐ The construction isn't good.
☐ Houses/apartments are too small.
☐ ______

B How do you think your neighborhood or city is going to change over the next five years? Choose if you *Agree* or *Disagree*. Add two more ideas.

1 Companies or the government are going to build many more houses or apartment buildings. Agree / Disagree
2 Young people will move to other areas to live. Agree / Disagree
3 Companies or the government will build cheaper places to live. Agree / Disagree
4 ______ Agree / Disagree
5 ______ Agree / Disagree

C IN PAIRS Discuss the questions. Use the Confident Communicator box to help you.

1 What are some problems with housing in your area?
2 How do you think housing will change in your area?

CONFIDENT COMMUNICATOR
KEEP TALKING

Use the following expressions to ask for opinions.
What do you think? *What about you?*
What's your opinion? *Do you agree?*

GO TO page xii for SPEAKING step-by-step instructions.

GRAMMAR

Tell students the best way to understand grammar is in context. This activity directs students to look for sentences in the article containing the grammar. This is a skill they should develop. When learning grammar, encourage students to find examples of usage.

CULTURE NOTE

A serious problem with housing in many countries is overdevelopment without suitable oversight. There is evidence of poor urban planning in many cities. In some cases, there are not enough roads and no public transportation to service areas with many new condos. There is a lack of infrastructure to support new growth in communities, and so they have problems with water and sewer systems.

All over the world, poor materials and neglect of safety regulations have caused major tragedies in urban housing.

LESSON 2 I Might Live Downtown

VOCABULARY living together

A Complete the sentences with words from the box.

apartment hunting	live alone	roommate	share the chores
housemate	rent a room	share the bills	studio apartment

1 I'm going to go __apartment hunting__ this afternoon. I want to find a place to live.
2 You share a house with a __housemate__, but you share a room or an apartment with a __roommate__.
3 You __live alone__ if you don't live with other people.
4 When you live in a house that you share with other people, you __rent a room__ in a house.
5 When people __share the bills__ and __share the chores__, they pay for things together, and they take turns doing the chores.
6 A __studio apartment__ is an apartment with one room and a bathroom.

MAKE IT YOURS

Do you live in an apartment, a house, or a townhouse? Search online or use a dictionary to find the right words and phrases.

B IN PAIRS Would you rather live alone or have roommates? Discuss. Explain why using the phrases from A.

GO TO page xi
for **LISTENING** step-by-step instructions.

GO TO page 145
for **AUDIO SCRIPT**.

LISTENING

A 9.02 LISTENING SKILL—Listen for attitude Listen to two people talking. Choose the word that describes each person's attitude.

1 Ashley: **a** uncertain **b** afraid **c** unhappy
2 Ethan: **a** nervous **b** excited **c** uninterested

B 9.02 Listen again and choose the correct option.

1 Ashley … living with her family.
a likes **b** doesn't like
2 Ethan's brother and his friends …
a share an apartment. **b** live near each other.
3 Ashley … to live with a friend.
a wants **b** doesn't want
4 Ethan says that … might be hard.
a finding a cheap apartment **b** traveling to work

C THINKING SKILL—Evaluate What are the advantages and disadvantages of living with a friend?

GO TO page ix
for **PRONUNCIATION** step-by-step instructions.

PRONUNCIATION /aʊ/ and /oʊ/

A 9.03 Write each word in the correct category. Then listen and repeat the words.

allow	found	know	own
sound	below	now	phone

1 /aʊ/ like *house*: __allow__ __found__ __now__ __sound__
2 /oʊ/ like *go*: __below__ __know__ __own__ __phone__

VOCABULARY

Some ideas for VOCABULARY **B** are:

- **Living alone: For:** You have peace and quiet, privacy, and independence. **Against:** You may be lonely and have to pay all the bills and rent.
- **Living with roommates: For:** Roommates often become lifelong friends. **Against:** They might be messy or nag you about being messy.

LISTENING

LISTENING SKILL—Listen for attitude

When listening for attitude, tell students to listen to the tone of voice and the speed of speech. Have students consider how they show attitude in their own language.

PRONUNCIATION

Students have to be able to hear the difference in sound before they'll be able to reproduce it well. With these sounds, the main difference is the position of the lips; they are forward and rounded with /ou/ as in *go* and back and stretched with /au/ as in *house*.

GRAMMAR future possibility and certainty

A **Read the sentences. Then choose the correct option.**

I **might** still be at home with Mom and Dad.	I **probably won't** have enough money for that.
You **could** live with a friend.	I **will definitely** miss them!
You **may** find something cheap outside the city.	

1 We use *may*, *might*, and *could* to talk about things that are sure / possible in the future.
2 We use *probably* when we are not sure / almost sure about the future.
3 We use *definitely* when we are not sure / very sure about the future.

For more practice, go to page 155.

B **Read the conversations and choose the correct option.**

1 A: Do you think you might live in your home town after you graduate?
B: Oh, yes! I ________ live there. I'm sure of that.
a probably will **b** might **c** will definitely

2 A: Do you think you'll live in another city in the future?
B: Maybe, but I ________. I'm not sure.
a might not **b** could not **c** won't

3 A: Do you think you might live in another country one day?
B: Well, I guess I ________ get a job in another country. I don't know.
a will **b** may not **c** could

4 A: What kind of place do you think you might live in after you graduate?
B: I ________ have enough money for a house, so I might rent a small apartment.
a may not **b** could not **c** might

C **IN PAIRS Talk about future possibilities. Finish the sentences and ask each other questions.**

1 This evening, I might … 2 Tomorrow, I may … 3 This weekend, I'll probably …

SPEAKING

A **Rate how likely each possibility is for you in the future: 1 (*definitely won't*), 2 (*probably won't*), 3 (*may, might, could*), 4 (*probably will*), or 5 (*definitely will*).**

live in a small town ____
live in another country ____
live in the center of a big city ____
live in a house with a yard ____
live with your parents ____
live with other family members ____
live in an apartment building ____
live with a friend ____

B **IN PAIRS Talk about where you might live in the future. Ask questions about your predictions. Use the Confident Communicator box to help you.**

A: I'll probably live in another country for a few years.
B: Why is that?
A: I might get a job and …

CONFIDENT COMMUNICATOR — KEEP TALKING

Use the following expressions to ask for reasons for opinions.
Why is that?
Why do you think that?
Why do you say that?

GRAMMAR

Might, *could*, and *may* show degrees of possibility.

In GRAMMAR **C**, let students know that the follow-up questions should arise naturally in a conversation. If they are stuck for follow-up questions, they should think about asking *Wh*–questions. For example, *Who are you going to go with? What time are you going to go?*

SPEAKING Alternative Activity

As you read out the possibilities for the future, ask students to raise their hand and show the number corresponding to their response with their fingers. They can look around the room and see who else shares their options for future possibilities.

CULTURE NOTE

Ask students their opinion about how living possibilities are different for boys and girls. Have they noticed any trends? Were there any answers that they thought were informed by gender? Remind them to be respectful of others' opinions in all group discussions.

The Future of Houses

VOCABULARY appliances

A IN PAIRS Choose the three things you think might change most in the future. Discuss how you think they might change.

1 air conditioner

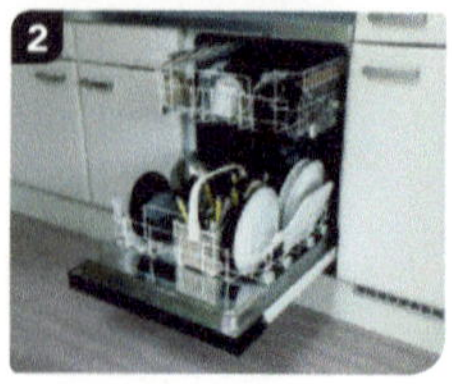

2 dishwasher

3 solar panel

4 lighting

5 kitchen stove

6 heater

7 washing machine

B IN PAIRS Discuss the question and check the meanings of the words and phrases in bold.

How can **sunlight** help us **save energy** and **save money**?

LISTENING

A You are going to listen to a talk. Look at the picture and say what you think the talk is about.

Suggested answers:
We can tell them that it costs less and they can save money. We can also tell them that it is renewable.

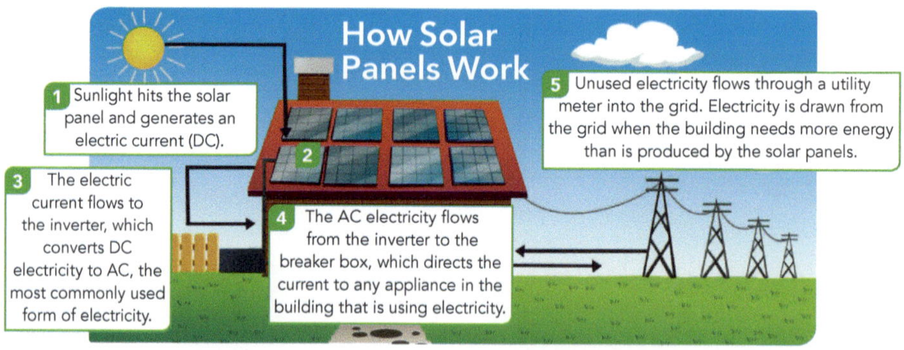

GO TO page 145 for AUDIO SCRIPT.

B 9.04 LISTENING SKILL—Take notes Listen to a talk and complete the notes.

solar panels
- receive **1** sunlight on sunny days
- create **2** electricity from special materials

inverter
- takes DC current from the **3** solar panels
- sends AC current to the **4** appliances

electricity grid
- takes electricity that the house **5** doesn't need
- provides power when there is **6** no sun

C THINKING SKILL—Evaluate How can we persuade more people to use solar power?

VOCABULARY

These are home appliances that all use electricity (the stove is gas, but the oven might be electric). Can students think of any other home appliances that use electricity? Some examples might be: *iron, electric kettle, TV, blender, coffee maker, microwave oven, refrigerator, toaster, rice cooker,* and *phone charger.*

LISTENING

Draw students' attention to the notes under the diagram, and show them that when they take notes in academic lectures, they do not have to write in full sentences. They can write phrases, words, and abbreviations. Visual organizers are useful for taking notes, too.

THINKING SKILL—Evaluate

Here are some ideas for persuading more people to use solar power: Make it cheaper. Subsidize the installation of solar panels on homes. Install solar panels on all government buildings. Make it compulsory. Have an educational campaign about the benefits of clean energy.

WRITING

A Read the article and answer the question.

Future Homes

What will the homes of tomorrow be like? I think we'll see big changes in entertainment. For example, homes will have 3D movie theaters with amazing sound. We might have virtual reality in some homes. I don't think that will be very popular because it will be expensive. There could also be big changes in the kitchen. For instance, you might choose a recipe and the stove will know how to cook it. It will tell you when your food is ready. Finally, parts of your house will change. Take windows, for example. They might go dark automatically at night to help you sleep. Or the windows might show messages to people at your door. Houses are going to change in many ways, and I can't wait!

According to the writer, what changes might we see in entertainment, in kitchens, and in windows?

B Choose the correct option.

1 The way we use energy will change. As / For example, all houses will have solar panels.
2 Rooms will change. One / For instance, houses might have a special room just for virtual reality.
3 Some rooms will change. Take / Look bathrooms, for example. We will use much less water.

C Choose three things you think are going to be different in our homes. In your notebook, write the main way you think each one is going to be different.

robots: They will clean our homes.

D Write a paragraph about how you think houses might change in the future.

E IN PAIRS Share your paragraphs from D. Comment on the way your partner uses examples.

MAKE IT DIGITAL

Search online for ideas on homes of the future. Tell the class what you find.

SPEAKING

A Check (✓) the future changes in homes that you are interested in. Add your own ideas.

- ☐ robots in the home
- ☐ virtual reality
- ☐ entertainment
- ☐ ______
- ☐ use of energy
- ☐ use of water
- ☐ security
- ☐ ______

B IN PAIRS Talk about the things that interest you about the future of homes. Give reasons for your opinions. Use the Confident Communicator box to help you.

CONFIDENT COMMUNICATOR – KEEP TALKING

Use the following expressions to give reasons for your opinions.
I think we'll have robots in the home because they can do housework for us.
The reason for that is robots will do housework for us.
That's because robots will do housework for us.

GO TO page xiv for **WRITING** step-by-step instructions.

1 We might see 3D home movie theaters with amazing sound or virtual reality in the home.
2 Your stove will know how to cook a recipe and tell you when it is ready.
3 Windows might go dark automatically or show messages.

WRITING

Point out useful phrases for students to use in WRITING **D**: *I think we'll see …, We might have …, There could also be …*

Tell students to think of the rooms in a house and how their uses may change in the future. Discuss what we do in our homes and how this may change in the future.

MAKE IT DIGITAL

Have students investigate future housing online. What can they find out about home sharing, homes made with 3D printers, prefabricated homes, communal homes, co-living buildings, or tiny homes?

They may be interested in Grant Imahara's web series called *Home of the Future* about prefabricated, mass-produced, technologically enhanced homes.

SPEAKING

In groups with others who chose the same area of interest, have students brainstorm and discuss all of their ideas related to the topic. Then form groups of students with different interests to share their views on the topic. Remind them to give reasons for their opinions and examples of possible future changes during their conversations.

GO TO page xv
for LANGUAGE AND LIFE step-by-step instructions.

Language and Life

Decision-making – Developing a Neighborhood

A 9.05 **Read the article and answer the questions below.**

Neighborhoods are changing all the time. That means someone has to make decisions about these changes. It might be urban planners or members of local government. They often have to decide between different plans for a neighborhood. They may have to think about costs, housing, and the needs of local people. How do they make their decisions?

One tool to help planners make a decision is a decision matrix. In a decision matrix, they list the important results they want for the neighborhood. For example, local people may want more houses, less traffic, or more parks. Planners develop several plans to get these results. They then score each plan against each result: –2 for a very negative effect, –1 for a negative effect, 0 for no effect, +1 for a positive effect, and +2 for a very positive effect. The plan with the highest total score is the one to choose.

People can use a decision matrix to help with all kinds of decisions, from large business decisions to personal decisions like making a budget or planning a vacation.

	Plan A	Plan B	Plan C
Result 1			
Result 2			
Result 3			
Total			

1 Who makes decisions about how neighborhoods develop? urban planners or local government

2 What is the purpose of a decision matrix? It helps you make a decision.

B **IN GROUPS Think about people in a neighborhood you know. Look at the ideas below and add your own. Which do you think are most important to them? Choose four.**

- ☐ cheaper places to live
- ☐ more public transportation
- ☐ more stores
- ☐ __________
- ☐ more job opportunities
- ☐ more green spaces
- ☐ better quality housing
- ☐ __________

OBJECTIVE

In this lesson, students learn how to use a decision matrix, which is a table that helps in identifying, evaluating, and rating facts related to a problem. It allows the user to prioritize options based on criteria in a methodical, mathematical way. This promotes objectivity when confronted with a problem to solve.

PROCESS OPTIONAL 9.05

Students first read an article about who makes the decisions for urban development, some of the decisions that have to be made, and how they do it. Then, groups choose criteria they think are most important to people living in a community. Their choices go in the decision matrix. In pairs, students read three proposals for a community. Next, they score each line of the matrix, comparing the criteria to the plans. The total score says which plan best matches with what people want. Finally, they compare their results on the decision matrix in **E** with another pair's, and discuss their results.

C Write your four choices from **B** in the first column of the decision matrix in **E**.

D **IN PAIRS** Read the plans for neighborhood development and discuss which one you prefer.

Plan A

The city is going to build a number of apartment buildings. Half the apartments will be available to buy and half will be available to rent. The apartments will be different sizes. The first floor of each apartment building will be for stores.

Plan B

The city is going to knock down some houses and build a park. They will clean up the area, and the park will have a playground and a picnic area. There will also be basketball courts and other sports facilities.

Plan C

The city is going to build a large mall. There will be a small number of apartments for rent in the mall. The mall will include large and small stores, together with restaurants and a movie theater. A new bus route will connect downtown with the mall.

E **IN PAIRS** Score each plan from **D** from −2 to +2 for each result.

What our city needs	Plan A	Plan B	Plan C
Total			

F **IN PAIRS** Add up the total score for each plan and write it in the table in **E**. Your preferred plan is the one with the highest score. Complete the list.

First choice: Plan _____
Second choice: Plan _____
Third choice: Plan _____

MAKE IT DIGITAL

Search online for "plans for development" in your city or a city near you.

G **IN GROUPS** Compare your results from **F** and explain your thinking.

H Discuss the questions.

1 How useful was the decision matrix?
2 In what other situations do you think the decision matrix would help?

ALTERNATIVE ACTIVITY

Ask students to look for a decision matrix online that they can understand. There are many very involved examples that don't make a lot of sense to the outsider, but tell them to keep looking until they find one that makes sense to them.

CULTURE NOTE

Making decisions can vary from country to country, company to company, and house to house. Have students consider who makes the decisions in their houses. Are decisions made democratically or autocratically? Does everyone get to weigh in? Does everyone get to put forward their argument? Does someone have veto power?

CAREER NOTE

Are there any careers related to housing available in your area? Find out from people you know.

GO TO page xvii
for UNIT REVIEW step-by-step instructions.

1 apartment hunting
2 washing machine
3 stove
4 air conditioner
5 solar panels
6 hall
7 balcony
8 studio apartment
9 couch
10 roommate

UNIT 9

VOCABULARY review

SCORE: / 10

A Complete the text with the words from the box.

air conditioner	balcony	hall	solar panels	studio apartment
apartment hunting	couch	roommate	stove	washing machine

This month, I have to go **1** ________ to find a new place to live. I want an apartment with built-in appliances: a **2** ________ to wash my clothes, a **3** ________ to cook on, and an **4** ________ to keep the air cool. I want 5 ________ to get energy from the sun. I'd like to have a small **6** ________ inside the front door, and a **7** ________ to sit outside. I don't need much furniture because right now I have a small **8** ________ . I have a nice **9** ________ that becomes a bed. I have a small desk and two chairs, and that's it. I'd like to get a bigger apartment, but then I'd need to find a **10** ________ to share the bills.

GRAMMAR review

SCORE: / 10

A Choose the correct option. If both answers are correct, choose both.

1 Do you think your neighborhood **is getting** / **will get** better in the future?
2 Tomorrow morning, I **am going** / **go** apartment hunting with a friend.
3 Where **do you live** / **are you going to live** when you graduate?
4 I think I **will rent** / **am renting** an apartment downtown when I get a job.
5 Our new housemate **is arriving** / **arrives** tomorrow from his hometown.

B Complete the sentences with the correct expression of future possibility or certainty.

1 I want a studio apartment, but I __might not__ have enough money for one.
2 I __may/might__ go back and live with my parents for a few months. I haven't decided.
3 If I don't find a job, I definitely __won't/will not__ be able to afford my own place.
4 I guess I __could__ live in another country one day. Who knows?
5 My friends and I are sure we __will definitely__ rent a house together.

16–20 correct: You can talk about living situations and appliances. You can talk about future possibilities and certainty.
0–15 correct: Look again at the Vocabulary and Grammar sections in the unit.

TOTAL SCORE: / 20

WHAT DO YOU KNOW NOW? Look back at page 87 and add the words you know now to the boxes.

GO TO page xviii
for STUDY SKILLS step-by-step instructions.

STUDY SKILLS PROBLEM SOLVING

A Take the quiz. Then go to **Study Skills** on page 135. Find the answers and learn more about problem solving.

1 Why is problem solving a useful skill to develop? Choose all the answers that apply.
a It can help you to improve your research skills.
b It can activate your knowledge on a subject.
c It helps you to develop your creativity.

2 Choose all the ways that a team can solve a problem.
a Brainstorm ideas to get different ways of looking at the problem.
b The leader of the project should make all the decisions so the team can work well.
c Research similar problems and solutions.

96 Unit 9 Room for Me

CLASSROOM MANAGEMENT

Do the review activities as timed activities. Give students five minutes to complete each activity. Then have them exchange books with a partner, who will give them a score as you read the answers aloud.

FURTHER DISCUSSION

Put students in groups of three and ask the following questions for them to discuss:

- If you could change your house, would you?
- How many homes have you lived in?
- How do you look after your home?
- What's your ideal home like?
- What are some alternative housing options?

UNIT 10 Wellbeing

GO TO page vi
for **UNIT OPENER** step-by-step instructions.

WHAT DO YOU ALREADY KNOW?

1 Think about words that describe your health.

2 **IN PAIRS** Share and compare your ideas. Add more words to your list.

Food

Exercise

STUDENTS MAY ALREADY KNOW:

- **Food:** fruit, vegetables, carbohydrates, protein, sugar, fresh.
- **Health:** nutrition, healthy, diet, exercise routine.

VIDEO

DISCUSS & SHARE

3 **IN GROUPS** Watch the video and answer the question.
SYM Which is more important for good health, nutrition or exercise?

GO TO page xx
for **VIDEOS IN SYM** step-by-step instructions.

In this unit, you will ...

- talk about brain power, accidents, and illnesses, and improving fitness.
- use thinking skills: brainstorm, evaluate, and understand.
- read about brain power.
- use strategies to start and keep talking by agreeing and disagreeing, asking about an illness, and making a statement stronger.
- use critical thinking skills to develop an ad campaign to improve public health.
- follow a family physician to learn about this job and the skills needed for the health care industry.

Unit 10 Wellbeing 97

WHAT DO YOU ALREADY KNOW?

If you notice students are struggling to understand what to do, you can provide one or two examples to help them get started:

- **Food:** I like to eat well. I'm on a low-carb diet.
- **Exercise:** I try to work out every day. I don't like high-energy exercises.

VIDEO

Before viewing, ask:

What does Ken do to have a good health? *eat healthy, keep junky food under control*
What does Theresa do to have a good health? *exercise because it is great for the body and important to stay healthy*

After viewing, put the continuum on the board.

nutrition —— exercise

Have students mark the continuum and explain their preferences.

DISCUSS & SHARE

Discuss how health is affected by a combination of nutrition and exercise. Ask students what the pros and cons are of keeping up with only one of these. Is it OK to only eat well or only exercise?

GO TO page x
for READING step-by-step instructions.

LESSON 1 **Power Up Your Brain!**

READING

A As a class, say if each statement is true for you. Explain why or why not.

1 I generally eat well. **2** I generally get enough sleep.

B **READING SKILL—Scan** Read the article quickly and check (✓) the ideas it mentions.

- [x] healthy food
- [x] making decisions
- [x] taking a break
- [x] learning an instrument
- [ ] doing well in school

How can you help your brain work better? Here is some advice from the experts.

• Get healthy
One way to help your **brain** is to get healthy by exercising more and eating better. In one study, people had a better **memory** after six weeks of physical training. Some studies found that if you exercise for 10 minutes before thinking about a problem, it improves your problem-solving and decision-making skills. Your **diet** is also important. Vitamins and minerals from food—like fish, vegetables, and **nuts**—help keep your brain healthy.

• Sleep better
Sleep isn't just rest for the body. It also rests your brain. During sleep, your brain organizes your **experiences**, often through dreams. When you are learning new skills, you actually get better at them while you sleep! Sleep helps you think clearly while you're awake. Most people who sleep only four to six hours in one night don't think clearly the next day.

• Keep learning
Your brain can change, something known as neuroplasticity. If you challenge your brain, it will develop more connections between its **neurons**. One thing you can do to challenge your brain is to learn a new skill, such as a new language or a musical instrument. Some people enjoy brain training—online sites and apps that use **puzzles** or other tasks to exercise your brain. Many of these sites and apps don't have much effect on the brain, and they certainly won't make you more **intelligent**. However, psychologists have created some types of puzzles that make your brain work faster. Doing these tasks makes some people feel sharper in their everyday lives.

C 10.01 Read the article in B again and answer the questions.

1 How might you improve your decision-making skills? by doing 10 minutes of exercise
2 What happens to most people after only getting four to six hours sleep? They don't think clearly.
3 Does brain training work? Most braing training doesn't work, but some types of puzzles do.

Suggested answers: travel and have new experiences, meet new people, lower the stress in your life

D **THINKING SKILL—Brainstorm** What are other ways you could develop your brain?

GO TO page vii
for VOCABULARY step-by-step instructions.

VOCABULARY

A Complete each sentence with a bold word from the text in READING B.

1 Your ___diet___ is all the things you usually eat.
2 Your ___experiences___ are the things that happen to you each day.
3 ___Puzzles___ are games or tasks where you have to think carefully to find the answer.
4 ___Neurons___ are the cells in your brain.
5 If you are ___intelligent___, you are smart and you think very clearly about things.
6 Your ___brain___ is the organ inside your head that controls your body.
7 Your ___memory___ is the part of you that remembers things.
8 ___Nuts___ are the dry fruit of some trees. They have a hard shell.

READING OPTIONAL 10.01

Students should raise their hands to respond to the statements in READING **A**. Use prompts to help them explain their responses. For example, *When don't you eat well? What happens when you don't get enough sleep?* Allow them to qualify the statements by substituting *generally* with another adverb—for example, *always, usually, sometimes,* and so on.

THINKING SKILL—Brainstorm

Brainstorming is a group discussion to produce ideas. There is sometimes a problem to be solved, but brainstorming can also be used for planning. This activity is an open question designed to generate ideas for developing the brain.

VOCABULARY Alternative Activity

Play Word Association Chain. In pairs, ask students to choose one of the vocabulary words and say it out loud. Their partner repeats the word and then says the first word they think of related to that word. Keep the chain going as long as possible.

GRAMMAR zero and first conditional

A Read the sentences. Then choose the correct answer.

Zero conditional
If someone sleeps more, his or her brain works better.
if clause — result clause

First conditional
If you start learning a new skill, your brain will work faster.
if clause — result clause

1 The zero conditional expresses general facts and scientific truths / real possibilities in the present or future.
2 The first conditional expresses general facts and scientific truths / real possibilities in the present or future.

For more practice, go to page 156.

GO TO page viii for GRAMMAR step-by-step instructions.

B Circle the verbs in each clause of the sentences in A. Then complete the grammar rules.

Zero conditional
1 In the *if* clause, use the ____________ tense.
2 In the result clause, use the ____________ tense.

First conditional
3 In the *if* clause, use the ____________ tense.
4 In the result clause, use ____________ + base form of the verb.

1 simple present
2 simple present
3 simple present
4 will

C Complete the text with the correct form of words from the box.

be get learn do grow practice

If you **1** ____________ a new skill, your brain **2** ____________. The density of white matter in your brain increases and your neurons work better. However, it has to be an active skill, such as learning the piano. You **3** ____________ better if you **4** ____________ every day. Each time you practice, you create new connections between your neurons. Play for just a short time and it makes a difference. If you **5** ____________ that for a year, you **6** ____________ amazed at your progress.

1 learn
2 will grow / grows
3 get / will/'ll get
4 practice
5 do
6 will/'ll be

D IN PAIRS Discuss if you agree or disagree with the statements. Explain your answers.

1 You can do anything if you try hard enough.
2 If you relax and stop worrying, you will succeed.

SPEAKING

GO TO page xii for SPEAKING step-by-step instructions.

A Choose the option that you agree with the most.

1 If I study ..., I learn more.
a alone **b** with friends

2 I will do better on an exam if I ... the night before.
a relax **b** study for hours

B IN PAIRS Compare your answers from A and discuss the reasons for your choices. Explain why you don't agree with the other choices. Use the Confident Communicator box to help you.

CONFIDENT COMMUNICATOR — START TALKING

Use the following expressions to say you agree or disagree with an idea.
I agree that it's a good idea to study with other people.
I disagree that it's easier to concentrate if you listen to music

GRAMMAR

Proverbs are a good way to illustrate the zero conditional because they often state general truths. One proverb that illustrates the zero conditional is *(If you) lie down with dogs, (you) wake up with fleas,* which means you should choose your friends carefully. Ask students to look for a proverb online that uses the zero conditional.

SPEAKING

Demonstrate the activities by telling students your responses to the prompts. Give more information about your statements.

CONFIDENT COMMUNICATOR

Draw student's attention to the Confident Communicator box and let them know that when you agree or disagree with a statement, you give reasons. Reasons can be personal anecdotes, personal preferences, or more information. For example, *I disagree that it's easier to concentrate if you listen to music. I need complete silence. If I listen to music, I will start selecting different songs and then I never get back to my work.*

LESSON 2 **Accidents and Illnesses**

VOCABULARY accidents and illnesses

A Complete the phrases with the words from the box.

ankle head throat arm leg

1 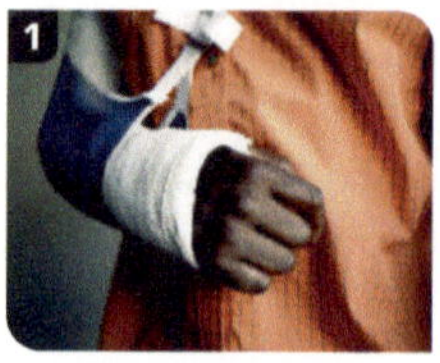
break your / have a broken arm

2 
have a head ache

3 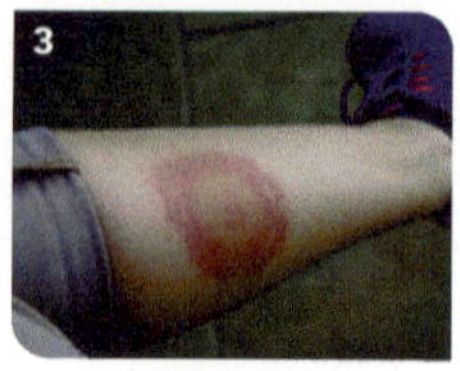
have a rash on your leg

4 
sprain your / have a sprained ankle

5 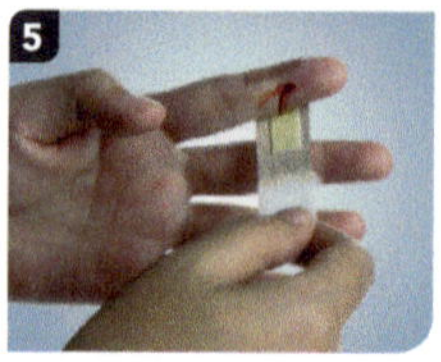
have a cut

6 
have a sore throat

7 
have a cold

8 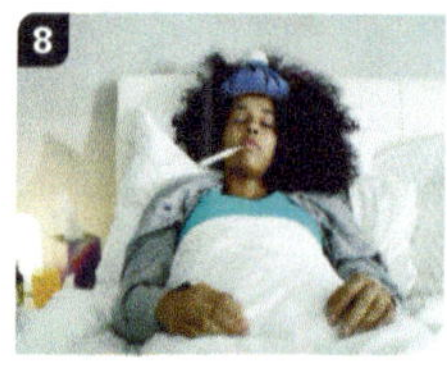
have a fever

B IN PAIRS Discuss the questions.

1 Have you ever hurt a part of your body? What happened?
2 When was the last time you felt sick?

MAKE IT YOURS

Make a list of other words you might need to talk about accidents and illnesses.

GRAMMAR second conditional

A Read the table and choose the correct option to complete the grammar rule.

Second conditional

If you broke your arm, it would / might / could be hard to drive.
if clause — result clause

1 We use the second conditional to talk about ...
a real possibilities in the present or future.
b hypothetical or impossible situations in the present or future.

For more practice, go to page 157.

B Read the sentence. Then complete the grammar rules.

If I **broke** a bone, I **would go** to the hospital.

1 In the *if* clause, use the simple past tense.
2 In the result clause, use would + base form.

MAKE IT REAL

Note that in formal English we use *if* + *I/he/she/it* + **were** instead of *was*. However, many English speakers do not use this form anymore and simply use *was*.

VOCABULARY Extra Practice

For further practice, ask students to add adjectives and adverbs to the illnesses. There are some set phrases for describing illnesses; for example, *I have a bad headache. I have a deep cut. I have a really sore throat. I have a nasty cold. I have a high fever.*

MAKE IT YOURS

These are some more words for describing illness: *(I have) asthma, a backache, a cough, diarrhea, an earache, the flu, a stomachache, a stuffy nose, a toothache. (I feel) sick, cold, unwell, clammy, hot, nauseous* (/ˈnɔːzɪəs/).

GRAMMAR

Let students know they can have more than one past tense action in the *if* clause. For example, *If you broke your arm and didn't go to the hospital, it might not heal.*

C IN PAIRS Discuss the questions.

What would you do if you …

1 lost your phone? 2 won the lottery? 3 broke your leg?

LISTENING

A 10.02 Listen to the podcast and choose *True* or *False*.

1 Madison Gray is a doctor. True / False
2 The right skills are very important. True / False
3 You should help someone up right away if he or she falls. True / False
4 You should always call an ambulance after a fall. True / False
5 With a broken arm, you should first find something long and hard. True / False

B 10.02 LISTENING SKILL—Listen for cause and effect Listen again and answer the questions.

1 If someone was injured, and you helped the person up, what could happen?
You could make the injury worse.

2 If someone breaks an arm, why do you have to stop any bleeding first?
Because the person can lose a lot of blood very quickly.

C IN GROUPS THINKING SKILL—Evaluate Should we teach first aid in schools? Why or why not? Discuss.

PRONUNCIATION intonation in conditional sentences

A 10.03 Choose the correct intonation. Then listen and check.

1 If I had a cough, I would buy some medicine. (↗ ↘)
2 If I had a cough, I would buy some medicine. (↘ ↗)

B 10.04 Practice saying the sentences with the correct intonation.

1 If I broke my leg, I would call an ambulance.
2 If I had a rash, I'd search for information online.
3 If I sprained my ankle, I'd ask a friend for help.

SPEAKING

A IN PAIRS Read the situation and discuss your answers. Use the Confident Communicator box to help you.

A friend who only speaks English is visiting you. How would you help your friend in each of the situations? What would you do if he or she …

- had a headache?
- had a cough and a sore throat?
- had a fever?
- had a sprained ankle?

B IN PAIRS Role-play the situation in A. Student A, you are the English-speaking friend. Describe your problem. Student B, try to help Student A.

CONFIDENT COMMUNICATOR
KEEP TALKING

Use the following phrases to ask for and give details about someone who is sick.

What's wrong? *What's the matter?*
Where does it hurt? *Where do you feel pain?*
I have a fever, and my head hurts.
It's not just my head. It's also my throat.

GO TO page xi for LISTENING step-by-step instructions.

GO TO page 146 for AUDIO SCRIPT.

GO TO page ix for PRONUNCIATION step-by-step instructions.

LISTENING

Have students read in silence through the statements in LISTENING **A** before they listen to the podcast. Reading the information first helps students preview what to listen for. It also helps the brain start making connections to what is already known about the subject.

PRONUNCIATION

Tell students that getting the right intonation is important when speaking another language because listeners are used to a cadence. They are attuned to certain rhythms, stresses, and rising and falling intonations in their language. If you change the natural intonation, you will not be understood easily.

SPEAKING

CONFIDENT COMMUNICATOR

Draw students' attention to the Confident Communicator box for useful phrases to use in their conversations. Tell them to use gestures and facial expressions to show pain when acting out their conversations. Remind students to use the right intonation. Each student should practice both roles.

LESSON 3 **Improve Your Fitness**

VOCABULARY collocations with *get*

A Complete the sentences (1–8) with *get* and a word from the box.

home	in shape	sick	tired	hungry	ready	started	upset

1 I joined a gym because I want to *get in shape.*
2 I usually just turn the TV on when I get home from work.
3 I don't seem to have much energy, and I get tired easily.
4 My brother is training to get ready for the marathon next month.
5 There's a lot of work to do, so let's get started!
6 Don't get upset. I'm sure everything will be okay.
7 I always get hungry by 10 a.m. because I don't eat breakfast.
8 When you are in bad shape, you often get sick and take time off work.

B IN PAIRS Discuss the questions.

1 What do you usually do when you get home from class/work?
2 What are some ways people can get in shape?
3 Do you eat only at mealtimes, or do you get hungry between meals?

LISTENING

A Mark the scale with how active you are. Compare with a partner and explain.

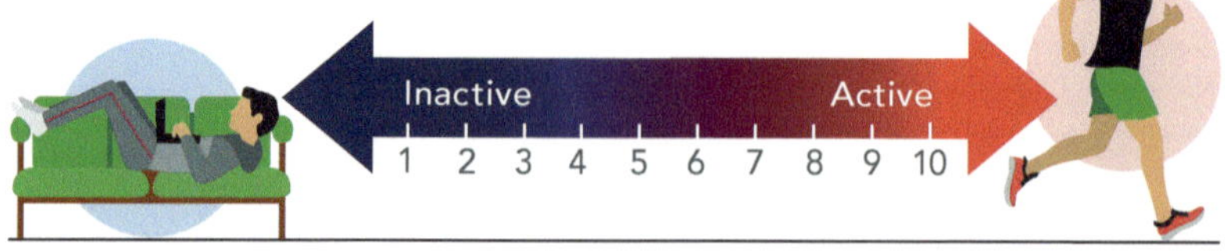

GO TO page 146 for AUDIO SCRIPT.

B 10.05 LISTENING SKILL—Listen for gist Check (✓) the ideas that are mentioned.

☐ This program is for people who run a lot.
☑ You need to eat well to get in shape.
☑ With Couch to 5K, you start slowly and then get faster.

C 10.05 Listen again and complete the sentences with a word or short phrase.

1 You might need to see ________ if you have health problems.
2 In Week 1, you run for ________.
3 You'll run for 30 minutes after ________.
4 When you eat the right things, you don't ________ when you're exercising.

1 a/your doctor
2 a/one minute
3 9/nine weeks
4 get tired

D IN PAIRS THINKING SKILL—Understand Discuss the questions.

1 Do programs like Couch to 5K work for everyone? Why or why not?
2 Is it important to be in shape? In what ways?

VOCABULARY

Get has many uses. In activity **A**, we see examples of *get* combined with nouns, as in *get home*, and *get* combined with adjectives, as in *get tired*. *Get* + place means *reach* or *arrive*, and *get* + adjective means *become*. *Get* + adjective usually shows a change in state, as in *get hungry*, *get hot*, or *get cold*.

LISTENING

You may want to ask if anyone knows what Couch to 5K is. Have them explain it to the class if they do. If no one is familiar with it, you may want to ask the class to predict what they think it is. Tell them they will find out what it is as they listen to the conversation.

THINKING SKILL—Understand

Discussion questions give students the opportunity to show they understand the concepts of health and fitness. It is important for cardiovascular health to be in shape. The Couch to 5K may not work for everyone, which is why it's important to get a health check if you have any doubts.

WRITING

A Read the comment from a website. In your own words, explain how Hugo got in shape.

A small change can make a big difference! I wanted to get in shape, but I didn't have time to go to the gym. I drove to college every day, so I didn't get much exercise. One day, I decided to park my car far away from the building I needed to go to on campus, and I walked the rest of the way. Each week, I parked a little farther away. After a month, I started to feel better. After two months, people started to ask me if I was working out! There are always ways to get more exercise into your life. Why don't you try walking a little more? Start small and you'll be amazed at what you can do!

Hugo Oliveira, Curitiba, Brazil • 1 day ago

B IN PAIRS **Choose three small life changes you would like to try. Discuss why you would like to try them.**

- ☐ eat smaller meals
- ☐ use a fitness app
- ☐ eat at the dining table
- ☐ eat a protein-rich breakfast
- ☐ use a calorie-counting app
- ☐ stop keeping snacks at home
- ☐ drink more water
- ☐ walk instead of drive
- ☐ walk during breaks from work/class

C Complete the sentences to persuade someone to make a change.

1. You should ______.
2. Why don't you ______?
3. Have you thought about ______?
4. I suggest ______.

D Imagine you made one of the small life changes in **B**. What happened? Write a comment for a fitness website about your experience.

SPEAKING

A Check (✓) the problems that keep you from getting completely in shape and healthy. Then add your own ideas.

- ☐ not enough money
- ☐ not interested
- ☐ can't cook
- ☐ no gyms near me
- ☐ don't like sports
- ☐ don't know about healthy eating

______ ______

B For each problem you checked in **A**, imagine what you would do if that problem didn't exist. Make notes in your notebook.

There are no gyms near me. If there were a gym near me, I would join and start exercising.

C IN PAIRS **Discuss the problems from A and what you would do if they didn't exist. Use the Confident Communicator box to help you.**

CONFIDENT COMMUNICATOR — START TALKING

Use *really* to make a statement stronger.
*I was **really** out of shape, so I started playing tennis.*
*It was a **really** small change, but it helped a lot.*

GO TO page xiv for WRITING step-by-step instructions.

Suggested answer: He started to park his car far away from class. Then he walked. Each week he parked farther away and walked a little farther. After two months, people said he looked like he was in shape.

Suggested answers:
1. You should use a calorie-counting app.
2. Why don't you start doing a sport?
3. Have you thought about walking instead of driving?
4. I suggest you eat smaller meals.

WRITING

Here are some more small life changes to help you get in shape:

1. Take the stairs instead of taking the elevator.
2. Sip water on your commute to work.
3. Add a vegetable to your breakfast menu—add grated carrots to your eggs.

Additional Activity

Have students visualize what may happen when they make small life changes and write an imaginary comment for a fitness website in their notebooks.

SPEAKING

These activities create a hypothetical situation so students can practice using the second conditional. It is also a kind of visualization exercise, which some say is the first step on the road to change. Once students start to visualize themselves in the hypothetical situation, they may become empowered to try it out.

Remind students that the use of *really* to make statements stronger is a good tool in conversation but not in formal writing.

GO TO page xv
for LANGUAGE AND LIFE step-by-step instructions.

Language and Life

Critical Thinking – Improving Public Health

A 10.06 **Read the article and choose the correct option.**

Many countries face serious public health problems. One example is obesity. According to the Organisation for Economic Co-operation and Development, one in two adults and nearly one in six children in its member countries are overweight or obese. That puts pressure on health services. Some countries are looking at ways of improving public health.

One way is to encourage people to eat better. Some countries, such as the United States and the United Kingdom, have five-a-day campaigns. They tell people that they should eat five portions of fruit or vegetables each day. Many countries have laws about labels on food. Producers have to show the amount of fat, protein, and carbohydrates in each food. Some countries have a "traffic light" system. Green means the food has a small amount of fat, sugar, and salt. Yellow means the food has a medium amount. Red means there's a high amount of fat, sugar, or salt. The labels help people make better choices.

Public health departments are always looking for new ideas to improve public health.

1 About ___________ of all adults are overweight or obese in OECD countries.
   a a third **b** a sixth **c** half
2 Obesity causes problems for ___________.
   a all countries **b** health services **c** mainly children
3 Some countries say you should eat ___________ each day.
   a no more than five meals **b** five types of vegetable **c** five servings of fruit and vegetables
4 In a "traffic light" system, you can eat less fat if you choose a label where the fat is in ___________.
   a green **b** yellow **c** red

B Check the brainstorming tips you have used.

- ☐ Suggest as many ideas as you can.
- ☐ Accept all ideas, useful and not useful, and write them down.
- ☐ Make sure everyone in your group offers an idea.
- ☐ Go online and quickly look at other people's ideas.
- ☐ Try to put ideas together and see what happens.
- ☐ Look at a problem from different points of view.

OBJECTIVE

In this lesson, students practice brainstorming to come up with creative ideas for improving public health. They are encouraged to think critically about the problem of obesity and poor food choices and suggest possible solutions. Students then choose the best ideas. They will discuss why some ideas will not work.

PROCESS OPTIONAL 10.06

Students first read an article about public health, obesity, and poor food choices. The article outlines some solutions being implemented, such as mandatory food labeling and government health education programs. Students will review ways to brainstorm. In groups, students brainstorm ways to improve the health of the population. The activity asks for solutions for three different target groups within the population. The groups then decide which ideas won't work and why. They choose the best ideas and explain why they will work. Finally, they present their best ideas to the class and predict what would happen if the public health department used their ideas.

C **IN GROUPS** Brainstorm ways you could help the public health department improve the health of each of the people. Make notes of all your ideas.

a child

a young adult

a senior citizen

1 Child: *ban cartoon characters from unhealthy food packaging*

2 Young adult: *create a cool fitness app*

3 Senior citizen: *provide low-cost, simple, healthy recipes*

D **IN GROUPS** Choose one age group. Look at your ideas. Cross out ideas you think wouldn't work. Explain why.

If we banned cartoon characters from unhealthy food packaging, children would still want that kind of food.

E **IN GROUPS** Choose your best ideas. Explain why those ideas would work.

Idea 1: ______

Idea 2: ______

Idea 3: ______

F **IN GROUPS** Present your ideas to the class. Predict what would happen if the public health department used your idea.

If we created a cool fitness app for young adults, they would want to get more exercise.

G Discuss the questions.

1 Why is it important to consider different points of view?
2 In what other situations do you need to think critically and creatively?

MAKE IT DIGITAL

Research ways public health officials in your country are working to solve your country's most serious health problems.

CULTURE NOTE

Many people consider a Mediterranean diet to be the healthiest in the world. In Mediterranean countries like Italy, Greece, Spain, and Turkey, people eat a lot of fruit, vegetables, whole grains, legumes, and olive oil. They also eat more fish and chicken than red meat.

MAKE IT DIGITAL

Latin American countries are being creative in combating obesity and diabetes caused by sugary carbonated drinks. Mexico introduced a tax on sugary drinks, and the consumption of these drinks decreased.

GO TO page xvii

for **UNIT REVIEW** step-by-step instructions.

UNIT 10

VOCABULARY review

SCORE: / 10

A Complete the sentences. The first letter of the missing words is given.

Ella: Oh, Frank! You have a **1** broken arm! How did you do that?
Frank: I was trying to get **2** in shape and I changed my **3** diet so that I was eating better.
Ella: Oh, yes. I remember.
Frank: Well, it wasn't working well, so I decided to try skateboarding. I'm a beginner, but I tried to do a few tricks. That wasn't very **4** intelligent. In fact, it was kind of stupid. It was going OK, but then I got **5** tired and made a mistake. I fell on my arm! I had to go to the hospital.
Ella: That's awful!
Frank: The next day, after I got **6** home from the hospital, I got **7** sick. I had a temperature of 100 degrees, and I had a **8** sore throat. I had a **9** fever!
Ella: Oh, no! I hope you didn't get **10** upset!
Frank: Nah. It was fine. But I'm looking forward to getting back on my skateboard!

GRAMMAR review

SCORE: / 10

A Match the sentence beginnings (1–5) to the sentence endings (a–e). Write the letter.

1 If you eat better, b
2 If you buy less candy, e
3 You probably exercise more a
4 It's possible to run 5K d
5 If you don't have a personal trainer, c

a if you live close to a gym.
b you will have more energy.
c you might not do the exercises correctly.
d if you run a little farther each week.
e you won't have so many problems with your teeth!

B Complete the sentences with verbs in the correct tense. Add any other words you need.

1 What ________ (you/cook) if you wanted to help your family lose weight?
2 I ________ (go) to the gym more often if I had more time.
3 If people ________ (eat) five portions of fruit and vegetables a day, there would be less obesity.
4 You'd get more exercise if you ________ (walk) to class instead of driving.
5 If I ________ (have) more money, I would probably join a gym.

1 would/could/might you cook
2 would go
3 ate
4 walked
5 had

16–20 correct: You can use collocations with *get* and talk about accidents and illnesses.
You can recognize zero, first, and second conditionals.
0–15 correct: Look again at the Vocabulary and Grammar sections in the unit.

TOTAL SCORE: / 20

WHAT DO YOU KNOW NOW? Look back at page 97 and add the words you know now to the boxes.

GO TO page xix

for **FOLLOW A PRO** step-by-step instructions.

FOLLOW A PRO HEALTH CARE

Take the quiz about the medical profession. Then go to **Follow A Pro** on page 136. Find the answers and learn more about the health care industry.

1 How many doctors are there in the US?
a about 250,000 **b** about 500,000 **c** over 1 million

2 Patients with female surgeons do better than those with male surgeons.
a True **b** False

3 Where was the first hospital in North America built?
a Toronto **b** New York **c** Mexico City

106 Unit 10 Wellbeing

VOCABULARY Alternative Activity

Play Hot Potato. In groups, students crumple a piece of paper to use as a "potato." They toss it to each other while saying an illness, injury, or accident. Set a timer for 30 seconds, and whoever is holding the potato when the timer goes off is out. Have three rounds until just one person is left. Students can't repeat a word.

FURTHER DISCUSSION

Put students in groups of three and ask the following questions for them to discuss:

- What illness or accident would you hate to have?
- Do you know someone who is on a diet?
- Do you think exercise or dieting is a more effective way of getting in shape?

UNIT 11

Use and Reuse

GO TO page vi
for **UNIT OPENER** step-by-step instructions.

WHAT DO YOU ALREADY KNOW?

1 Think of words you know about recycling and improving the environment. Write the words.

2 **IN PAIRS** Share and compare your information. Add more words to your lists.

Save the Earth

STUDENTS MAY ALREADY KNOW:

- **Recycling:** recycle, plastic, paper, metal, trash, waste.
- **Environment:** planet, earth, sea, land, pollution, air.

VIDEO

DISCUSS & SHARE

3 **IN GROUPS** Watch the video and answer the question.

SYM Which do you use, paper or plastic?

GO TO page xx
for **VIDEOS IN SYM** step-by-step instructions.

In this unit, you will ...

- talk about what things are made of, how new materials are made, and how plastic can be recycled.
- use thinking skills: brainstorm, understand, and analyze.
- read about how T-shirts are made and recycled.
- use strategies to start and keep talking by ordering steps in a process, stating who made something, and suggesting alternatives.
- use innovation skills to brainstorm ways to upcycle materials.
- learn tips about using precise language in academic writing.

WHAT DO YOU ALREADY KNOW?

If you notice students are struggling to understand what to do, you can provide one or two examples to help them get started:

- **Recycling:** organic, reuse, repurpose, manufacturing
- **Environment:** sustainable, eco-friendly, air quality, single-use plastic

VIDEO

Before viewing, ask:

What are some advantages of paper bags? *can be recycled, save trees, biodegradable*
What are some advantages of plastic bags? *onvenient, good to hold wet things, reusable*

After viewing, put the continuum on the board.

plastic bags —— paper bags

Have students mark the continuum and explain their preferences.

DISCUSS & SHARE

Do you have your own reusable bags for when you go shopping? If not, consider what types of bags you are using and the impacts they can have on the environment. Have a class discussion about using reusable bags versus paper and plastic bags.

LESSON 1 The Lifecycle of a T-shirt

GO TO page x
for **READING** step-by-step instructions.

READING

A **As a class, discuss how you think people make the following items: jeans, shoes, jewelry.**

B **11.01 Read the article and choose the correct options.**

From Seed to T-shirt

T-shirts are a basic part of almost everyone's closet. Over two billion T-shirts are sold every year around the world. So how are they made? And where do they **end up**?

The story starts with the seed of the cotton plant. The plants are grown on large farms. The cotton is collected and sent to a factory. There, it is cleaned and made into **yarn**. The yarn is made into cloth. This is used to make T-shirts.

The T-shirts are then **transported** around the world. Just take a look at the label on one of your T-shirts and see how far it came! The T-shirts go into stores and are sold to consumers. That's you. You probably have the T-shirt for a while, and it is worn, washed, and dried again and again. When you decide to **get rid of** it, you have a few options. You might throw it in the trash. But if you knew how much of the Earth's **natural resources** go into making a T-shirt, you might think again! A lot of energy and water are used in making and washing clothes. A lot of chemicals are used in this process, too.

One option is to recycle your old T-shirts. When a T-shirt is sent to a recycling center, it is made into other things, such as cleaning cloths. Another idea is to upcycle your T-shirts. Old T-shirts are sometimes made into belts, scarves, or bags.

1 Where does the story of a T-shirt start?
   a in a factory **b** on a farm
2 What information on a T-shirt label does the writer mention?
   a the country the T-shirt comes from **b** how to wash the T-shirt
3 Where in the lifecycle do we use a lot of energy and water?
   a growing the cotton plant **b** producing and cleaning the T-shirt
4 When a T-shirt is upcycled, it might become …
   a a scarf. **b** another T-shirt.

consumers: people who buy products

label: a small piece of material on an item of clothing giving information

upcycle: use something old for a different purpose

C **READING SKILL—Understand words from context** **Find the words from the box in the text in B. Read the context and explain what you think they mean.**

consumers label upcycle

D **THINKING SKILL—Brainstorm** **What other uses for old T-shirts can you think of? Make a list in your notebook.**

GO TO page vii
for **VOCABULARY** step-by-step instructions.

VOCABULARY

A **Match the bold words from the text in READING B to the definitions (1–5).**

1 very long, thin piece of cotton or wool: yarn
2 moved from one place to another by truck, train, or boat: transported
3 come to a final place or situation that is not expected: end up
4 things we use from the Earth, such as water, oil, or trees: natural resources
5 throw away: get rid of

READING OPTIONAL 11.01

Prompt students during the discussion with questions. For example, *Are jeans, shoes, and jewelry made in a factory? What things are made by hand? What's an assembly line? What machines are used in manufacturing? Is what you are wearing made domestically or internationally? What are they made of?*

THINKING SKILL—Brainstorm

Another use for repurposed T-shirts might be rags for cleaning cars. They could be sewn into shopping bags or woven into baskets. Cut the T-shirts up into strips and make headbands. Weave the rags into rugs. Make them into washable diapers.

VOCABULARY

Ask students to categorize the words into verbs and nouns. Ask them to point out the phrasal verbs (*end up, get rid of*) and then define phrasal verbs.

A *phrasal verb* is a combination of a verb and an adverb or preposition, which has a particular meaning, such as *look after* or *hurry up*.

GRAMMAR simple present passive

GO TO page viii for GRAMMAR step-by-step instructions.

A Underline examples of the passive voice in the article in READING B.

Over two billion T-shirts <u>are sold</u> every year around the world.

B Choose the correct option to complete the rules for forming and using the present passive voice.

1 Use the auxiliary **be** / have in the simple present followed by the simple past / **past participle** of the verb.
2 Use the present passive to focus on the thing that does / **receives** the action.
3 Use the present passive when we **don't know** / are interested in who or what does something.
4 Use the present passive when it's important / **obvious or unimportant** who or what does something.

For more practice, go to page 157.

C Complete the sentences with the present passive form of the verb in parentheses.

Do you know how a notebook **1** _is made_ (make)? First of all, trees **2** _are cut_ (cut) down. The wood from the trees **3** _is turned_ (turn) into paper. Color **4** _is removed_ (remove) from the paper to make it white. Lines **5** _are printed_ (print) on the paper. Glue **6** _is used_ (used) to stick the pages together. Finally, a cover **7** _is put_ (put) on the notebook.

D IN PAIRS Look at what you are wearing and what you have with you. Discuss what your things are made of.

A: I'm wearing a T-shirt. It's made of cotton. *B: I have a bag. It's made of plastic and metal.*

SPEAKING

GO TO page xii for SPEAKING step-by-step instructions.

A Use the prompts to write sentences in the simple present passive.

1 water / drink by the consumer _Water is drunk by the consumer._
2 plastic / melt to make a bottle _Plastic is melted to make a bottle._
3 oil / take from the ground _Oil is taken from the ground._
4 bottle / transport to a store _The bottle is transported to a store._
5 oil / make into plastic _Oil is made into plastic._
6 the bottle / recycle _The bottle is recycled._
7 the bottle / send to landfill _The bottle is sent to landfill._
8 the bottle / fill with water _The bottle is filled with water._

B IN PAIRS Look at the pictures and tell your partner about the lifecycle of a plastic bottle. Use the Confident Communicator box to help you.

First, oil is taken from the ground. Then, ...

CONFIDENT COMMUNICATOR
START TALKING

Use the following expressions to order steps in a process.

First, it's grown ... *Next, it's painted ...*
Then, it's transported ... *Finally, it's sold ...*
After that, it's made into ...

GRAMMAR

We use the passive voice when we don't know or don't care who performs the action. The result of the action is the focus of the sentence. Students need to remember when to use *is* and *are*. They also have to know the past participle forms of the verbs.

Have students look for a list of verbs and tell them to notice patterns in the past participle forms of irregular verbs. If necessary, tell students to review the past participle forms of irregular verbs on page 139 in their Student's Books.

SPEAKING

In the SPEAKING section, students practice the passive forms. Let them know that contractions are usually used in speech—for example, *Water's drunk* ... or *It's drunk* ... Tell students they will use the sentences from SPEAKING **A** to talk about the life cycle of a plastic bottle in **B**.

Extra Practice

For more simple present passive practice, have students research the life cycles of other things and talk about them in the passive. They could talk about a coffee bean, a cereal box, and so on.

LESSON 2 An Accidental Discovery

VOCABULARY clothing materials

A IN PAIRS Discuss the questions.

button

zipper

Velcro

fur

fake fur

nylon

1 Do you prefer buttons, zippers, or Velcro on your clothes? Why?
2 Can you tell the difference between real and fake fur?
3 What do you think of clothes made from fur? Do you think people should wear them?
4 Do you prefer clothes made from nylon or clothes made from natural materials, such as cotton or silk? Why?

B IN PAIRS Describe how your clothes and items fasten and unfasten.

GO TO page ix
for **PRONUNCIATION** step-by-step instructions.

PRONUNCIATION silent *t*

A 11.02 Listen to the words. Notice that the *t* is silent.

castle whistle wrestle fasten listen soften

B 11.03 Listen to the sentences and practice saying them.

1 Listen to the way he whistles.
2 You fasten and unfasten the jacket with a zipper.
3 Chemicals are used to soften the cloth.

GO TO page xi
for **LISTENING** step-by-step instructions.

GO TO page 147
for **AUDIO SCRIPT.**

LISTENING

A 11.04 LISTENING SKILL—Listen for key words Listen to an interview. Complete the sentences with the words or phrases you hear.

1 Angela says Velcro __was invented__ with the help of a dog.
2 Plants stuck to the __fur__ of George de Mestral's dog.
3 In the beginning, Velcro was made of __cotton__.
4 It became __popular__ when it was used by astronauts.
5 In the 1980s, Velcro was used on __children's__ sneakers.

VOCABULARY Alternative Activity

Review vocabulary for clothes with a game. Play Hot Potato in groups of four. Tell students to crumple up a piece of paper to use as a "potato." They toss it to each other while saying an item of clothing. Set a timer for 30 seconds or play some music for 30 seconds, and whoever is holding the "potato" when the timer or music goes off is out. Students shouldn't repeat the vocabulary words.

LISTENING

Before students listen to the interview, teach *burr* and *hook*. The easiest way to do this, if you have the internet connected to a screen, is to search for an image. If you don't have an internet connection, you could draw a picture or describe them. A *burr* is a part of some plants that is covered all over with prickles, and a *hook* is a curved piece of metal or plastic to hang something on.

B 11.04 **Listen again and choose *True* or *False*.**

1 George de Mestral was looking for plants while he was walking his dog. True / **False**
2 The burrs had hooks that caught onto his pants. **True** / False
3 De Mestral soon produced a commercial product. True / **False**
4 In the beginning, Velcro was used on clothes and bags. **True** / False
5 Velcro was used on sneakers in the 1970s. True / **False**

C IN PAIRS THINKING SKILL—Understand Explain why NASA used Velcro in the 1960s.

GRAMMAR simple past passive

A Read the sentences. Choose the correct option to complete the grammar rules.

De Mestral noticed that his dog **was covered** in burrs. His pants **were** also **covered** in them.

1 We form the simple past passive with the verb **be** / *have* in the simple past followed by the **past participle** / *–ing* form of the verb.
2 We use the simple past passive when we are talking about the past and …
- we want to focus on the thing that does / **receives** the action.
- we are interested in / **don't know** who or what does something.
- it's **unimportant** / essential who or what does something.

For more practice, go to page 158.

MAKE IT DIGITAL

Search online for the history of an invention (cell phone, TV, the internet, etc.). Find out how it was invented. Tell the class.

B Complete the text with the simple past passive form of the verbs in parentheses.

Superglue **1** __________ (discover) by accident. In 1942, Dr. Harry Coover was trying to make clear plastic. This **2** __________ (need) for military equipment. A number of chemicals **3** __________ (create) in the laboratory, and one of them was called cyanoacrylate. It wasn't a clear plastic, but it was a strong glue. It **4** __________ (develop) because it wasn't useful for that project. Nine years later, Coover was working on jet planes and cyanoacrylate **5** __________ (use) again. This time, Coover realized how useful it was. Superglue **6** __________ (release) as a commercial product in 1958.

1 was discovered
2 was needed
3 were created
4 wasn't developed
5 was used
6 was released

SPEAKING

A Answer the questions for you.

1 Think of something that was bought for, made for, or given to you. What was it? __________
2 When was it bought/made/given? __________
3 Who was it bought/made/given by? __________
4 How did you feel when it was bought/made/given? __________

B IN PAIRS Discuss your object from A. Ask and answer questions about it. Use the Confident Communicator box to help you.

A: I have a guitar. It was bought for me by my grandfather.
B: When was it bought for you?
A: A year ago. It was given to me for my birthday, and …

CONFIDENT COMMUNICATOR
KEEP TALKING

Use *by* to say who or what did something in the passive.
It was made by my uncle.

GRAMMAR Alternative Activity

Play a game. Practice the simple past passive with Two Truths and a Lie. Write three sentences about inventions on the board; one contains false information and two are true. Have students read them and identify the false statement. For example,

1 The light bulb was invented by Thomas Edison.
2 The first smartphone was created by Apple.
3 Peanut butter was invented by the Incas.

Number 2 is false. The first smartphone was created by IBM.

SPEAKING

Suggest students start with things they are wearing or things they have with them. For example, *This T-shirt was given to me by my friend Jay.*

Once students have discussed the object(s) from SPEAKING **A** in pairs and they have asked and answered questions, have them form groups of four or five. Extend the speaking practice by asking students to report to the group about what their partner told them.

LESSON 3 Using and Reusing Plastic

LISTENING

A You are going to listen to a lecture. Look at the picture. What do you think the lecture will be about?

B 11.05 **LISTENING SKILL—Listen for gist** Listen to the first part of the lecture and choose the correct summary.

GO TO page 147 for AUDIO SCRIPT.

1 Thato faces a number of problems. She works in a school that has no electricity. The children are tired after their trip to school. They find it hard to do their schoolwork.

2 Thato thought about the problems of schoolchildren. Getting to and from school is sometimes dangerous. They live without electricity and it is difficult for them to do their homework.

C 11.06 Listen to the rest of the lecture. Then complete the sentences with the words from the box.

GO TO page 147 for AUDIO SCRIPT.

a light | drivers | plastic bags | schoolbags

1 There is a problem with plastic bags in South Africa.
2 Thato made schoolbags out of trash.
3 Her products have a solar panel, a battery, and a light.
4 The children can be seen by drivers.

Note: An example of easily recycled plastic is plastic water bottles. Examples of plastic that can't be recycled easily are plastic bags and food wrap.

D **THINKING SKILL—Analyze** Categorize the materials from the box.

aluminum | ceramic | cotton | leather | plastic | steel | cardboard | copper | glass | nylon | rubber

1 can be recycled easily: aluminum, cardboard, copper, glass, plastic, leather, steel
2 can't be recycled easily: ceramic, nylon, cotton, rubber, plastic

VOCABULARY collocations connected to materials

A Match the phrases (1–4) to the definitions (a–d). Write the letter.

1 cause pollution d
2 harm wildlife b
3 last a long time a
4 reduce the amount we use c

a stay in the environment for years
b have a bad effect on animals
c use less
d have a bad effect on the environment

B **IN PAIRS** Discuss the questions.

1 What materials cause pollution where you live?
2 Does the pollution in your area harm wildlife?
3 What materials last a long time in the environment?
4 Do you think people should reduce the amount of plastic they use?

MAKE IT YOURS
Are there any materials around you that you don't know the English word for? Look online or in a dictionary and find out.

LISTENING

Encourage students to look up Thato Kgatlhanye and the Repurpose Schoolbags online.

Have students look up "What happens to plastic bottles when they are recycled?" online to see what they find (shopping bags, park benches, etc.). Have them choose an article, read it, and report back to the group.

THINKING SKILL—Analyze

Tell students to use their phones or a bilingual dictionary to look for the translations of the words in the box that they don't know. They should suggest an item that is commonly made of each material to help them remember the meanings of the words.

VOCABULARY

Collocations are words that are usually used together, such as *salt and pepper*. It relates to the frequency of use of certain words in a certain order. These phrases should be learned as chunks for easy retrieval. Idioms are fixed collocations because if you move or change one word, it sounds odd.

WRITING

A Read the email and answer the questions.

New Message

To: supporter@mail.co Cc Bcc

Subject: Spread the Word

Dear Supporter,
Thank you for supporting Use Less Plastic. We rely on people like you to get the message out that we need to reduce the amount we use. Plastic lasts in the environment for thousands of years and harms wildlife.
We're writing to you now to ask for your help. We want you to send an email to your local news website to explain why we need to Use Less Plastic. Explain that plastic causes pollution. And remember to tell them what we can all do to Use Less Plastic.
We need to educate people about this problem to solve it.
Sincerely,
The Use Less Plastic Team

Send

1 Who does the Use Less Plastic team want you to write to? __________
2 What three things do they want you to mention? __________

B Choose the correct option.

1 The ... for this is that we use too much plastic.
a result b reason c fact
2 This is ... we use too much plastic.
a since b result c because
3 We are responsible for this problem ... we use too much plastic.
a since b reason c why

C **IN PAIRS** Complete the notes.

1 Main causes of plastic pollution: plastic bags, __________
2 Problems it causes: trash in the streets, __________
3 How to use less plastic: reuse plastic bags, __________

D In your notebook, write an email to your local news website to explain why people need to use less plastic.

GO TO page xiv for WRITING step-by-step instructions.

1 a local news website
2 the causes of plastic pollution, the problems plastic pollution causes, what we can do to reduce the use of plastic

SPEAKING

A Think about your own use of plastic. Answer for you.

1 How many of these things do you buy or use each week?
drinks in plastic bottles: ____ drinking straws: ____
drinks in to-go cups: ____ (other) ________ : ____
items in plastic packaging: ____
2 Add up your weekly score and multiply it by 52. Write your annual total plastic items here: ________

B **IN PAIRS** Compare your scores and discuss how you could use less plastic. Use the Confident Communicator box to help you.

CONFIDENT COMMUNICATOR
START TALKING

Use *One / Another option is* + *to* infinitive to suggest alternatives.
One option is to use a refillable drinking bottle.
Another option is to take your own bags to the store.

WRITING

Before WRITING **C**, students brainstorm causes of plastic pollution, problems it causes, and how to use less plastic:

- **Causes of plastic pollution:** too many single-use plastic bags, straws, and water bottles, and too much plastic packaging
- **Problems caused by plastic waste:** pollution of oceans, lakes, and waterways, animals getting trapped in trash, and pollution of soil and land
- **Solutions:** ban all single-use plastic, use alternative materials, and use reusable shopping bags and water bottles

SPEAKING

Once students have calculated their individual yearly use of plastic, add their numbers together and calculate the whole class's yearly use of plastic. Everyone will be shocked!

Draw students' attention to the Confident Communicator box to get them started with their conversations about how to use less plastic.

Some good sites for tips on using less plastic can be found by searching on the internet for "waste reduction tips" or "reducing plastic use."

GO TO page xv
for **LANGUAGE AND LIFE** step-by-step instructions.

a greenhouse made from plastic bottles; plant containers made from coffee cans or old rubber boots; notebook covers made from rubber tires; shadow art made from trash

Language and Life

Innovation – Upcycling Projects

A 11.07 **Read the article and list the examples of upcycling that are mentioned.**

plant containers made from old rubber boots

upcycled art by Tim Noble and Sue Webster

UPCYCLING PROJECTS

We humans use a lot of materials. Take plastic, for example.

According to Statista, every year, around 350 million metric tons of plastic are produced around the world. Sadly, not much of it is recycled. In fact, about half of the plastic is used just once and is then sent to a landfill, according to Plastic Oceans International. In 2007, Charles Fishman of *Fast Company Magazine* reported that a million plastic bottles are bought every minute of every day in the US, but only around 23% are recycled. Four trillion plastic bags are produced each year, and only 1% are recycled, according to Waste Management. Our use of other plastics is not much better. Plastic use is a big problem.

Many people are looking at ways to upcycle different materials. Upcycling involves finding new uses for materials at the end of their original use. In one project, a greenhouse was created using old plastic water bottles. In others, large coffee cans or old rubber boots were turned into containers for plants, and old rubber tires became notebook covers. Artists, too, upcycle materials. Tim Noble and Sue Webster, two British artists, create what look like piles of trash. When a light shines on the trash from a certain angle, it makes an interesting shadow on the wall.

These days institutions such as colleges and companies are looking for smarter ways to use materials. This involves reducing the amount of materials they use and thinking of ways to upcycle materials so that they last a long time.

B IN GROUPS Read the situation and discuss the questions.

Your college supports a local upcycling campaign. They want to encourage people to upcycle more. They want students to suggest interesting ways to upcycle. Here are the main problems the college wants to solve:

1. Students use a lot of plastic water bottles. They create trash and many of them go to the landfill. Are there ways they could be upcycled?
2. The college receives a lot of deliveries every day, which means there are a lot of cardboard boxes. They are usually recycled, but that uses energy. Are there ways they could be upcycled?

114 Unit 11 Use and Reuse

OBJECTIVE

In this lesson, students will brainstorm and choose the best idea for upcycling plastic. They will think about the amount of plastic that becomes waste every day. Students will analyze the problem and suggest ways of reusing plastic around their homes and in their communities every day in order to reduce pollution and decrease the amount of landfill we create.

PROCESS OPTIONAL 11.07

Students first read an article about the quantities of plastic waste produced every day in the world and the small percentage that is recycled. They will read about some projects for upcycling. Next, they will consider the amount of plastic waste in their school or workplace, thus establishing a problem to be solved. Then, they will brainstorm ideas for upcycling that plastic and cardboard. Once groups have exhausted their ideas, they will choose the best two ideas and develop them further with more explanation about how they will work. Finally, they will present their ideas. The class will vote on the best ideas presented.

C **Write about plastic and cardboard waste at your school or workplace.**

1 Estimate how many plastic bottles are thrown out every day.

2 Estimate how much cardboard is thrown away each week.

D **Brainstorm ways of upcycling. Write as many ideas as you can.**

1 Ideas for plastic bottle reuse and upcycling

use plastic bottles as plant containers

2 Ideas for cardboard reuse and upcycling

use boxes to store books

E **Choose your best two ideas from D and add more detail. How will your idea work? Who will do it?**

Idea 1:

Idea 2:

F **Tell the class about your ideas from E.**

G **What are your favorite ideas? Take a class vote.**

H **Discuss the questions.**

1 Did working in a group help you imagine new ideas?
2 In what other situations do you need to innovate to solve problems?

MAKE IT DIGITAL

Search online to see if any of your ideas from **E** are available online, and find more ideas for ways to upcycle other products.

CULTURE NOTE

The country with the best recycling rate is Germany, which recycles more than 54% of its municipal waste according to the environmental consultancy firm Eunomia (2017). Eunomia found that the next best countries for recycling are Taiwan, Wales, and South Korea.

MAKE IT DIGITAL

Have students do a search to see if any of their ideas can be found online.

Alternatively, direct students to research sites that give them ideas for upcycling by typing into a search engine "ways to upcycle plastic bottles" and "ways to upcycle cardboard boxes," and ask them to choose the best project.

GO TO page xvii
for UNIT REVIEW step-by-step instructions.

UNIT 11

VOCABULARY review

SCORE: / 10

A Unscramble and write the word in parentheses.

1 Many jackets are fastened with a zipper (ppzeir).
2 We need to use fewer natural resources (oseercus).
3 I can't unfasten (snnefatu) my jacket.
4 I'm trying to reduce (deecru) the amount of plastic I use.
5 Are your socks made of nylon (lnyno)?
6 A button (otubnt) came off my shirt!
7 I need yarn (rayn) to make a sweater.
8 Plastic causes a lot of pollution (inltolpou).
9 Does waste harm wildlife (leliiwdf) in your area?
10 The label (eblla) says "Made in China."

GRAMMAR review

SCORE: / 10

A Complete the sentences with the present passive form of words in the box.

add make make take wear

Sweaters 1 are made of wool. The wool 2 is taken from sheep. It 3 is made into yarn. Color 4 is added to the yarn, and it is knitted into sweaters. Sweaters 5 are worn during cold weather.

B Rewrite the sentences in the passive.

1 My uncle bought this bag for me.
This bag was bought for me by my uncle.
2 Did the Chinese invent paper?
Was paper invented by the Chinese?
3 Someone discovered penicillin by accident.
Penicillin was discovered by accident.
4 People first used CDs for music in 1982.
CDs were first used for music in 1982.
5 They didn't use plastic 150 years ago.
Plastic wasn't used 150 years ago.

16–20 correct: You can use collocations with materials and describe clothing materials. You can use simple present passive and simple past passive.
0–15 correct: Look again at the Vocabulary and Grammar sections in the unit.

TOTAL SCORE: / 20

WHAT DO YOU KNOW NOW? Look back at page 107 and add the words you know now to the box.

GO TO page xviii
for STUDY SKILLS step-by-step instructions.

STUDY SKILLS USING PRECISE LANGUAGE IN ACADEMIC WRITING

Take the quiz. Then go to Study Skills on page 137. Find the answers and learn more about using precise language in academic writing.

1 It's natural for people to enjoy spending time outdoors. This statement is …
a a fact. b an opinion.

2 A lot of people were killed in the earthquake. This statement is …
a precise. b imprecise.

3 Eighty-five percent of people in the US go to work by car. This statement is …
a precise. b imprecise.

4 About 150,000 people are employed by this company. This statement uses …
a the active voice. b the passive voice.

116 Unit 11 Use and Reuse

CLASSROOM MANAGEMENT

Have students look over the unit and then work individually to complete the review activities. Have them check with a partner before checking the answers as a class. Ask students to identify an area they would like to review.

FURTHER DISCUSSION

Put students in groups of three and ask the following questions for them to discuss:

- Do you try to reuse plastic?
- Do you think upcycled plastic can be made into useful items?
- What will happen if we don't stop polluting with plastic?
- Do you clean up trash in public spaces?

GO TO page vi
for UNIT OPENER step-by-step instructions.

UNIT 12 I'm a Member

WHAT DO YOU ALREADY KNOW?

1 Think about your social life and the activities you like to do with other people. Write the words.

2 IN PAIRS Share and compare your ideas. Add more words to your lists.

STUDENTS MAY ALREADY KNOW:

- Social life: friends, family, hang out, hobby, sport, music, concert, movies, restaurant, weekend, interests.

Social life

DISCUSS & SHARE

VIDEO

3 IN GROUPS Watch the video and answer the question.

SYM Do you prefer to have friends who are similar to you or different from you?

GO TO page xx
for VIDEOS IN SYM step-by-step instructions.

In this unit, you will ...

- talk about types of communities, networking, and youth subcultures.
- use thinking skills: analyze and understand.
- read about the different types of social groups.
- use strategies to start and keep talking by making guesses, showing certainty, and adding a further point.
- use media literacy skills to design an ad campaign to reach a target group.
- follow an entrepreneur to learn about this job and the skills needed for the business field.

WHAT DO YOU ALREADY KNOW?

If you notice students are struggling to understand what to do, you can provide one or two examples to help them get started:

- **Social life:** go out with friends, get to know new people, go to new and interesting places, learn new things

VIDEO

Before viewing, ask:

How are Sam's friends different from him? *from different countries, speak different languages, have different majors in college*

How are Jenny's friends similar to her? *enjoy group activities, like the same movies, books, and clothing style*

After viewing, put the continuum on the board.

similar —— different

Have students mark the continuum and explain their preferences.

DISCUSS & SHARE

Have students think about their closest group of friends. Are they all similar in appearance, mannerisms, and style? Or are they unique in appearance, mannerisms, and style? Perhaps some students have a group of friends who are similar in some ways to themselves but different in other ways.

GO TO page x
for **READING** step-by-step instructions.

READING

A **Do you belong to a club or other social group? If so, what activities do you do in this group? Discuss as a class.**

B 12.01 **READING SKILL—Understand the main ideas** **Read the article. Then match the sentence halves.**

TYPES of COMMUNITY

We all **belong** to different social groups. We choose some of them ourselves, and some of them are chosen for us. The social groups we belong to often give us support. They also say a lot about who we are and how we see ourselves.

There are many different types of community. One type is community of place. The place could be a neighborhood, a region, or a country. A second is community of interest. The people might all be interested in a certain hobby or a certain type of music, for example. A third is community of **purpose**. People in this type of community **share** the same purpose, such as learning a language or running a successful company. A fourth is community of practice. This is a group of people who share the same profession.

Each type of community can offer different things to its members. A community of place might offer people to **chat** with and to support you in difficult times. A community of interest can give you friendship and a way to learn more about a subject. A community of purpose can help you learn ways of achieving your goals. Also, people working together can often **achieve** more than a person working by himself or herself. A community of practice gives you opportunities to share ideas as well as the chance to **network**.

Any particular group might be more than one type of community. For example, a local cycling club is a community of place and a community of interest. If the members decided to raise money for a local charity, they would also be a community of purpose.

Read more

1 People in a community of place __d__
2 People in a community of interest __b__
3 People in a community of purpose __a__
4 People in a community of practice __c__

a want to achieve the same thing.
b might have the same hobby.
c might do the same job.
d might live in the same area.

C **THINKING SKILL—Analyze** **List your social groups in your notebook. Then write what type of community each of your social groups belongs to.**

GO TO page vii
for **VOCABULARY** step-by-step instructions.

VOCABULARY

A **Replace the underlined words in the sentences with synonyms from the box.**

achieve	chat	purpose of	belong to	network	share

1 You need to meet people in your profession if you want to find a better job. __network__
2 You learn more if you tell other people your ideas. __share__
3 I hope to do a lot in my career. __achieve__
4 I am a member of a chess club. __belong__
5 The reason for our study group is to practice our English. __purpose of__
6 I'm very busy studying, so I don't have time to sit and talk with friends. __chat__

READING OPTIONAL 12.01

In open-class discussions, try to give equal time to a range of responders. Don't let one person speak for too long. Keep the flow of the discussion going. You may want to have students speak in pairs before opening it up to group discussion. This will give them confidence.

THINKING SKILL—Analyze

Remind students that their social groups do not have to be in real time. They may belong to groups online that are related to their field of study or a hobby. Demonstrate different communities by analyzing your social groups; these might be a tennis club (interest), school friends (place), childhood friends (place), or work friends (practice).

VOCABULARY

This is an example of understanding words through context. As students progress in their English-language learning, reading and deciphering words in context will be an important skill.

GRAMMAR reflexive pronouns

A Read the article in READING B again and complete the table.

	Subject pronouns	Reflexive pronouns
Singular	I	myself
	you	yourself
	he	**1** himself
	she	**2** herself
	it	itself
Plural	we	**3** ourselves
	you	yourselves
	they	themselves

MAKE IT REAL

Reflexive pronouns are used in many idiomatic expressions in English. Examples are *teach yourself to do something* (learn something without a teacher), *help yourself to something* (get something without the assistance of your host), and *behave yourself* (behave correctly).

B Match the functions (1–2) to the examples (a–b). Write the letter.

We use reflexive pronouns …

1 when the subject and the object of the sentence are the same. b

2 to mean "without help from another person." a

a *Did you start the fan club yourself or did you have help?*

b *I see myself as a professional person.*

For more practice, go to page 158.

C Complete the text with reflexive pronouns.

The way we see **1** ourselves may depend on the groups we belong to. For example, if you have a large social life, you probably consider **2** yourself to be friendly and confident. People who belong to a sports club may think of **3** themselves as good members of a team. This can help in their future careers. Different groups can also give you different experiences. Someone who joins a community of purpose, such as a local action group, may achieve something that he or she can't achieve by **4** himself or **5** herself. If you can't find the right group, then you might think about starting one **6** yourself. This can also be an interesting experience.

PRONUNCIATION /s/ vs. /ʃ/

A 12.02 Listen and choose the word or phrase you hear.

1 self / shelf
2 yourself / your shelf
3 herself / her shelf
4 sock / shock
5 so / show
6 sign / shine

SPEAKING

A IN PAIRS Discuss the questions. Use the Confident Communicator box to help you.

1 What different communities of interest do you belong to or did you belong to in the past?
2 What do/did you enjoy the most about each different group?

CONFIDENT COMMUNICATOR
START TALKING

To talk about something when you're not completely sure or when you're still thinking about your opinion, use *I guess*:
I guess I enjoy sharing ideas with people the most.

GO TO page viii for **GRAMMAR** step-by-step instructions.

GO TO page ix for **PRONUNCIATION** step-by-step instructions.

GO TO page xii for **SPEAKING** step-by-step instructions.

GRAMMAR

Each pronoun has its reflexive pronoun. Reflexive pronouns are used less frequently in English than in some languages. See if students can identify reflexive pronouns in their own languages.

Extra Practice

Practice reflexive pronouns with these discussion questions: *Do you see yourself as outgoing or shy? Do you consider yourself to be friendly and confident?*

PRONUNCIATION

Tell students the differences in the /s/ and /ʃ/ sounds are produced by the different positions of the tongue. In *self*, the tongue is forward, just behind the top teeth. In *shelf*, the tongue is flat and back.

SPEAKING

Some communities of interest students might belong to are: drama clubs, sports clubs, book clubs, art classes, walking groups, movie clubs, or video-gaming groups.

Students might be part of interest groups online. Encourage them to think about those.

LESSON 2 Developing Your Network

VOCABULARY networking

A Complete the sentences with words or phrases from the box.

contact	intern	job hunting	stay in touch
get to know	introduce yourself	make time for	

1 When you make friends with someone, you __get to know__ him or her.
2 When you say hello to someone for the first time, you __introduce yourself__.
3 When you fit something into your schedule, you __make time for__ it.
4 An __intern__ is someone who works for experience and usually isn't paid.
5 When you continue to communicate with an old friend, you __stay in touch__ with him or her.
6 When you are looking for work, you are __job hunting__.
7 Someone you know in a profession is a __contact__.

B IN PAIRS Discuss the questions.

1 Do you find it easy to introduce yourself to people and get to know them?
2 How can contacts help when you are job hunting or looking for a position as an intern?
3 Is it important to make time for old friends and stay in touch with them?

GO TO page xi
for **LISTENING** step-by-step instructions.

GO TO page 148
for **AUDIO SCRIPT.**

LISTENING

A Read the statement and say if you agree or disagree.

It's not what you know that's important—it's who you know.

B 12.03 LISTENING SKILL—Listen for the main ideas Listen to part of a radio show and check (✓) the advice the speaker gives.

- [x] speak to people in your office
- [x] speak to members of your family
- [x] speak to old school friends
- [x] join online groups
- [ ] research companies online
- [x] go to career fairs
- [x] write to companies

C 12.03 Listen again and complete the sentences with the words or short phrases you hear.

1 You can learn a lot from __chatting with__ people in your office.
2 When you leave a job, it's a good idea to __stay in touch__ with people.
3 Ask questions, __join discussions__, and post comments in online groups.
4 In online groups, you might be the first to hear about __job opportunities__.
5 You could ask companies about working as __an intern__.
6 In speed networking, you talk to each person for __a few minutes__.

D THINKING SKILL—Understand Explain how career fairs are useful.

Suggested answer:
Career fairs are useful because you can find a job, they help people get hired, and you can attend to job seekers conferences.

VOCABULARY

Demonstrate an informal handshake and greeting, and ask students to practice introducing themselves informally by shaking hands and saying hello in pairs.

Then demonstrate a more formal introduction. Tell students that one person usually introduces two others. In a more formal introduction, full names are given and something is said about each person. The people being introduced shake hands and greet each other with some form of *It's nice to meet you.*

LISTENING

THINKING SKILL—Understand

Career fairs are useful, but students should watch out for things that are not. They should beware of pushy salespeople who are trying to sell them courses or memberships they don't need. Tell them to research the companies and institutions participating in career fairs to see which ones are legitimate. If the person they are talking to is more interested in selling their own course rather than listening, they should move on.

GRAMMAR review of tenses

A Match the sentences (1–5) to the functions (a–e). Write the letter.

1 My contact works in the accounting department. c
2 I am looking for an internship. d
3 I was nervous about meeting people when I started working here. a
4 I was chatting to a colleague when you called me. b
5 Have you spoken to your friends about their career plans? e

a a past state or habit
b an action in progress at a past moment
c a present state or habit
d an action in progress now
e an action at an unspecific time in the past

For more practice, go to page 159.

B Choose the correct option.

1 My plane … at six, so I'll be in Washington at nine.
a leaves **b** has left **c** was leaving
2 Lola … as a waitress until she can find a job in engineering.
a works **b** has worked **c** is working
3 I … to a speed networking event next weekend.
a am going **b** have gone **c** go
4 If you … a professional association, you would make useful connections.
a join **b** joined **c** have joined
5 I … in this office for six months.
a work **b** am working **c** have worked

C Choose the correct option.

When I **1** have worked / was working at my last job, I **2** was trying / tried to speak to everyone in my office once a day. After I **3** was leaving / left that position, I **4** was staying / stayed in touch with all my colleagues. I **5** am thinking / think it's important because you never **6** know / have known when you might want someone's help. And it **7** has helped / was helping me a number of times. Right now, I **8** am looking / look for a new job, and I **9** ask / have asked my contacts about job opportunities. Fingers crossed!

SPEAKING

A IN PAIRS Discuss the questions. Use the Confident Communicator box to help you.

1 What are you thinking of doing to develop your network?
2 In what ways is networking important in your chosen profession?

B Check (✓) the things you personally are thinking of doing to develop your network. Then add details and other ideas.

☐ speak to family members
☐ speak to friends
☐ join online groups
☐ contact companies directly

______________________ ______________________

CONFIDENT COMMUNICATOR
START TALKING

To say how certain you are about a plan, use *probably* (*not*) or *definitely* (*not*):
I will definitely stay in touch with my friends.
I'll probably get a job as an intern.

GRAMMAR

Allow students to work together as they identify the tenses in GRAMMAR **A**. For further practice, have them write more examples of each form in their notebooks. Sometimes it is helpful to see different tenses juxtaposed. It gives students the chance to compare and contrast grammar at a glance.

SPEAKING

Once students have talked about possibilities for developing their networks, set the task of actually networking for homework. Then have them report back to the group about what they discovered while networking. Did they learn anything new? What surprised them? Who did they speak to? What information was useful?

CULTURE NOTE

Have students investigate salaries for different positions they are interested in. Tell them to research starting salaries and consider how they will be able to live on what they might be making. Will they make ends meet? Will they have to take on two jobs? How about an internship or an apprenticeship?

LESSON 3 **Youth Subculture**

VOCABULARY appearance

A **Look at the pictures. Write the hairstyle or clothing style you think each person wears.**

Hairstyle:	Clothing style:
beard mustache short/long hair color	dark/bright clothes jewelry earrings necklace tight/loose costume make-up

1

goth
long, dark hair, dark clothes and make-up

2

hipster
beard, mustache, short hair, tight clothes

3

otaku
long, light hair, costume, make-up

B **IN PAIRS Discuss the questions.**

1 Do you prefer to wear bright or dark colors?
2 Do you have a particular clothing style? Is it similar to your friends' clothing style?
3 Do you generally wear accessories? Which ones?

MAKE IT YOURS

Think of the clothes and accessories you own. Do you know the English word for all of them? Check in a dictionary and make a note of any you don't know. Describe your personal style to a classmate.

LISTENING

A **IN PAIRS Have you seen people who look like the pictures in VOCABULARY A, either in real life or on TV/ online? Why do you think they dress in that style? Discuss.**

GO TO page 148 for AUDIO SCRIPT.

B **12.04 LISTENING SKILL—Listen for gist Listen to a podcast and number the sentences in the correct order (1–4) to create a summary.**

2 Young people want to look different from their parents.
4 Young people want to show their personality.
1 Young people in different groups wear different clothes.
3 Young people want to feel they belong to a group.

C **12.04 Listen again and write short answers.**

1 What does the speaker say about goths?
They wear dark clothes and make-up.
2 What example of a youth subculture in the past does the speaker mention?
American teenagers in the 1940s
3 What might youth subcultures tell you about someone you've never met?
if they are like you

D **THINKING SKILL—Understand Describe the youth subcultures that exist in your country. Discuss as a class.**

VOCABULARY

Here are more words for hairstyles, clothing styles, and accessories:

- **Hairstyles:** braid, pigtail, plait, ponytail
- **Clothing style:** designer clothes, sportswear, fashionable, graceful, sophisticated, tasteful, trendy, ultra-chic, ultra-cool, ultra-hip
- **Accessories:** cape, gloves, handbag, scarf, shawl, sunglasses, umbrella, hat, belt

LISTENING

LISTENING SKILL—Listen for gist

Have students read the statements in LISTENING **B** before listening. This will help them think about what they might hear. Tell students to listen all the way through once and then answer the listen-for-gist questions. Listen again for LISTENING **C**. Allow students to confer with a partner before checking their answers.

THINKING SKILL—Understand

Once students have understood the content of the listening, they can apply their understanding to subcultures in their country. These youth subcultures, or urban tribes, might be referred to as *emos*, *skaters*, *punks*, or *nerds*. Students will be the best sources of information on the topic of youth culture in your country.

WRITING a description

A Read the description and match the sentence halves. Write the letter.

One youth tribe in my country is cosplayers. A Japanese reporter invented the term *cosplay* using the words *costume* and *play* in 1984. Cosplayers are interested in video games. They create costumes based on characters from popular video games and movies. Cosplayers wear bright colors and often wear make-up to make them look like their favorite characters. They meet to show each other their colorful costumes, and they often take selfies to show people online. They often like listening to the music from video games. Personally, I think cosplayers are brave. They aren't afraid to dress like their heroes. Cosplaying is a great way to meet people with the same interests.

1 First, __b__
2 Second, __c__
3 Third, __a__

a the writer gives his or her personal opinion.
b the writer gives background information and a little history.
c the writer describes what the people look like and what they do.

GO TO page xiv for WRITING step-by-step instructions.

B You are going to write a description of a youth subculture. Make notes to answer the questions before you write.

1 What youth subculture are you going to write about? ______
2 What kind of clothes do they wear? ______
3 What do members do together? ______
4 Do they listen to a particular kind of music? ______
5 What is your opinion of that subculture? ______

C Write your description in your notebook. Be sure to include some history, a physical description, and your opinion.

SPEAKING

A Do you think it's a good idea or a bad idea to belong to a subculture? Make notes on why.

______

______

B IN PAIRS Discuss the questions. Explain your reasons. Use the Confident Communicator box to help you.

1 Do you think it's a good or a bad idea to belong to a subculture?
2 What are the advantages and the disadvantages?

CONFIDENT COMMUNICATOR
KEEP TALKING

To add a further point, say:
Also …
In addition to that, …
Not only that, but … also …
You can express your personality in a subculture. Not only that, but you can also meet people.

WRITING

Students will use the same structure in their writing as in the description. The answers in WRITING **B** will give them an outline for their descriptions. Students will then add some history, details, and opinions about the group they chose. Once they have completed the descriptions, go through the stages of editing and redrafting.

SPEAKING

Allow students time to think on their own and make notes about what they think belonging to a subculture means. Have students talk in groups with students who hold the same opinions and reasons. Then regroup the class into groups of students with different opinions so they can hear another viewpoint.

CULTURE NOTE

Remind students to be respectful when talking about youth subcultures and alternative groups. Even if they don't agree with the way the groups dress and socialize, they should speak calmly and give reasons why they think joining them would be a good or a bad idea.

GO TO page xv
for LANGUAGE AND LIFE step-by-step instructions.

Language and Life

Media Literacy – Reaching a Target Group

A 12.05 **Read the article. Summarize how advertisers reach a particular target group. Write one sentence for each step in the process.**

REACHING A TARGET GROUP

Sometimes, a business has a product that it wants to sell to a certain group of people. For example, there is no point advertising a new car to people who don't drive. Governments, too, sometimes want to get information to a specific group. This might be information about children's health that they want to give to parents. In both cases, it would be a waste of money to inform everyone. It's better to aim your message at the people you want to reach. How do you do that?

First of all, it's important to clearly identify the group of people you want to reach. Is it parents? Is it teenagers? Is it homeowners? When you have a clear idea of your target group, then you can think about how to reach people in the group.

Second, you need to think about how to communicate with that group. Teenagers and young adults spend time on social networks. That might be the best way to reach them. It might not work so well for senior citizens or other groups.

Third, you need to express your message in the right way. With professional people, you may want to use serious language. With teenagers, you may want to use slang or informal language.

When you aim your message at a clear target group and use the right form of communication, your message is more effective.

1 First, advertisers identify their target group.
2 Second, they decide how to communicate with that group.
3 Third, they need to express their message in the right way.

B **IN PAIRS** **Read the situation and say in your own words what you need to do.**

You work in the marketing department of a restaurant chain. Sales are slow and they want to get more customers. Your boss has asked you to think about some target customers and to suggest ways of advertising to them.

OBJECTIVE

In this lesson, students choose the best ways to communicate with a target audience. They will identify different target markets, explore advertising to different ages and groups, and consider how to reach them with an advertising message. They will learn that it is important to understand market segments in advertising.

PROCESS OPTIONAL 12.05

First, students read an article about how advertisers reach a particular target group. Then, they are guided to write a summary of the article. Next, students are presented with a problem. They have to identify the types of restaurants four different groups might like. Students suggest how elements of a restaurant would change to appeal to each group, including food, furnishings, and service. Students choose a group from the previous activity and work together with others who chose the same target market to design an ad for the restaurant. Each group presents their ad and, finally, explains how it reaches their market.

C **IN GROUPS** **Suggest what each group may want from a restaurant. Consider the elements from the list. Make notes below each picture.**

- Type of food
- Type of tables and chairs
- Type of music
- Special services

1 
families with young children

____

____

2 
teenagers

____

____

3 
professional people

____

____

4 
senior citizens

____

____

D **IN GROUPS** **Choose one group from C. Answer questions to design an advertisement to reach that group.**

1 Which group is your target group? ______________________
2 What is the main thing they want from a restaurant? ______________________
3 What is the best way to communicate with your target group? ______________________
4 What kind of language will you use? ______________________

E **IN GROUPS** **Design a poster, a TV ad, or an online post to communicate with your target group.**

F **IN GROUPS** **Share your ad with the class. Explain what you plan to do to reach your target group.**

G **Discuss the questions.**

1 Whose ad do you think would reach the target group best? Why?
2 In what other situations or jobs do you need to create ads?

MAKE IT DIGITAL

Research online for creative ways to reach members of your social group or the social group of someone you know.

MAKE IT DIGITAL

Ask students to research ways to reach different social groups through marketing. For example, senior citizens may respond to direct marketing through the mail, while teens may be more open to digital marketing. Ask students to look for creative ways to reach people through advertising. Then have them report back to each other.

ALTERNATIVE ACTIVITY

Have students make a 30-second video advertising a restaurant to a particular target market. Tell them to write a script and shoot the video using any props they have on hand.

CULTURE NOTE

Ask students to share what they know about advertising in different countries. Have they seen any ads from other countries? Are there different regulations about how to advertise? Are there rules about who can be advertised to or what can be advertised? If they don't have any firsthand knowledge, have them search online.

GO TO page xvii

for **UNIT REVIEW** step-by-step instructions.

UNIT 12

VOCABULARY review

SCORE: / 10

A Circle the correct option.

1 Networking is a good way of coming / **getting** to know people in your profession.
2 I like wearing **loose** / tight clothes because they're more comfortable when it's hot.
3 It's important to do / **make** time for your family when you are busy at work.
4 Do you **belong** / join to any clubs?
5 In my company, we have meetings every morning to **share** / tell ideas.
6 My mom doesn't often wear rings, earrings, or other **jewelry** / make-up.
7 I'm job **hunting** / looking right now, so I'm writing to ask companies about vacancies.
8 Do you have any **contacts** / interns who can help me get a job in that company?
9 I like to purpose / **chat** with other students after class. It helps me make new friends.
10 My dad has a mustache, but he doesn't have a **beard** / belt.

GRAMMAR review

SCORE: / 10

A Complete the sentences with reflexive pronouns.

1 After the lecture, I introduced myself to the speaker.
2 My brother hurt himself in an accident.
3 I would rather do things myself than have help from other people.
4 In an exam, make sure you give yourself/yourselves enough time to check your answers.
5 Amy tried to tell herself not to worry when she lost her job.

B Complete the sentences with the correct form of the verbs in parentheses.

1 How long ________ Mrs. Anderson? (you/know)
2 When you called, I ________ something on Netflix. (watch)
3 If you ________ a lot of money, what would you do with it? (find)
4 I ________ Matt, but he sounds like an interesting guy. (meet)
5 Sara ________ with her parents until she finds an apartment. (live)

1 have you known
2 was watching
3 found
4 haven't met
5 is living

16–20 correct: You can talk about networking and physical appearances. You can use reflexive pronouns.
0–15 correct: Look again at the Vocabulary and Grammar sections in the unit.

TOTAL SCORE: / 20

WHAT DO YOU KNOW NOW? Look back at page 117 and add the words you know now to the box.

GO TO page xix

for **FOLLOW A PRO** step-by-step instructions.

FOLLOW A PRO BUSINESS

Take the quiz about business. Then go to Follow A Pro on page 138. Find the answers and learn more about business.

1 Which company was the first to be worth $1 trillion?
a **Apple** b Amazon c Microsoft

2 How many new businesses started up each month in the US during 2016?
a 50,000 b 250,000 c **550,000**

3 Who is most comfortable with starting their own business?
a people over 35 b 25- to 35-year-olds c **people under 25**

4 According to a recent report, what is the best country to be an entrepreneur in?
a Japan b **Germany** c the US

126 Unit 12 I'm a Member

CLASSROOM MANAGEMENT

Have students read through the entire text in both the vocabulary and grammar before completing the activities. They shouldn't worry about words or how much they understand. The aim is to skim the sentences and activate their minds. Once they have read through the material, they can go back to complete the activities.

FURTHER DISCUSSION

Put students in groups of three and ask the following questions for them to discuss:

- What different interest groups are people in your family members of?
- Do you know any professional organizations related to your major?
- Would you ask a friend to introduce you to someone in your field?

UNIT 1

STUDY SKILLS

GO TO page xviii for STUDY SKILLS step-by-step instructions.

A **Read the two texts. Which is a personal narrative? Which is a factual account?**

1 factual account
2 personal narrative

USING PERSONAL EXPERIENCE

1

Biggest Storm in 100 Years Hits the Country

Yesterday, strong winds of 100 kilometers per hour hit a popular coastal town. Businesses closed early, and buses and trains stopped running. By three p.m. yesterday afternoon, the streets were empty as people stayed inside. Hospitals, however, were very busy as over 100 people were injured by falling trees and flying debris. Luckily, no one was killed.

Sixty centimeters of rain fell in just 24 hours. Streets became rivers, and around 350 people had to leave their homes. Many buildings were damaged by the wind.

An estimated $25 million dollars will be required to repair the damage caused by this storm.

2

An Incredible Storm

I was on a camping trip with some friends. We were hiking in the state park when suddenly there was a huge storm. The sky turned black, and the wind became very strong. We started to feel really scared because we were far from the campground, and no one knew exactly where we were. We hiked back to the start of the trail, but it was really dangerous. Tree branches were breaking, and they almost hit us as they flew. When we arrived at the campground, there was no power, and there was water in the tent. Luckily, we found a hotel for the night. We were happy to be out of the storm!

B **How can you tell factual accounts from personal narratives? Write *FA* (factual accounts) or *PN* (personal narratives).**

1 PN use words that describe feelings.
2 FA often use the passive voice, e.g.: "Many homes were damaged."
3 FA often use numbers, measurements, and percentages.
4 PN usually tell stories.
5 FA are objective.

C **Match the columns to make sentences. What effect does it have when you combine fact and personal experience?**

Combining personal narrative with factual content makes writing more interesting.

1 The earthquake of 2010 left 350,000 people homeless, d
2 When the biggest music festival in the county took place, a
3 At 4,810 meters, Mont Blanc is the highest mountain in Europe; c
4 I think that Tokyo is one of the most exciting cities in the world, b

a I was there, along with 500,000 other music lovers.
b and with a population of over 37 million, it's also the biggest.
c it is also the place where I learned to ski.
d including my mom, my dad, my brother, and me.

D **In your notebook, combine the personal narrative and the factual account from A. Write a paragraph of about 100–125 words.**

Remember:
- Don't overdo it. Two to three facts should be enough for a personal narrative.
- Choose the facts you add carefully. Use them only if they add impact to your writing.

When the biggest storm in 100 years hit the coastal area, I was hiking with my friends in the state park. We ...

MAKE IT HAPPEN

Think of an exciting experience you have had. Write a paragraph about it, combining facts and personal experience.

E **THINKING SKILL—Analyze Where do you usually read personal accounts? Where do you usually read factual accounts? Which type of story is more interesting to you? Which is more truthful? Why?**

Answers to the quiz on page 16
1 b and c 2 a 3 a and b

127

STUDY SKILLS TASK

Students study the difference between factual accounts and personal narratives. In any good factual account, there should be some personal narrative, and in any good personal narrative, there should be some facts.

THINKING SKILL—Analyze

Personal narratives are found in novels and short stories, emails to friends, anecdotes, gossip, diary entries, and personal letters.

Factual accounts are found in newspaper articles, scientific papers, nature documentaries, history essays, and encyclopedias.

MAKE IT HAPPEN

Have students think about an exciting or dramatic experience they have had, such as an accident, getting lost, or their first day on campus. Remind them that a personal narrative needs a beginning, middle, and end, and that they should include sequencing words, time phrases, and a few pertinent facts. Have students write a paragraph combining a personal narrative and a factual account with the right balance.

GO TO page xix

for **FOLLOW A PRO** step-by-step instructions.

UNIT 2

FOLLOW A PRO

A **Read about a hotel manager's job. Answer the questions below.**

A HOTEL MANAGER

Albert Chaparro is the hotel manager for a large chain hotel in Lima, Peru. After graduating with a degree in business administration, he joined the chain's graduate training program. There, he learned how to apply his general business skills to the hospitality industry.

His role involves a wide range of activities. He might solve problems with the staff or check hotel supplies. He plays an important role in hiring and training staff, so he might interview applicants or train new workers. He has to manage both people and money.

His job also involves hotel services. He might arrange a large celebration for a group of business visitors. For this, he needs to work closely with the kitchen staff, in particular the head chef. They have to agree on a menu and a budget. During an important event, he monitors wait staff and makes sure everything runs according to plan.

He expects to continue in this job for a few more years. He hopes to get a higher position in hotel management, running a number of hotels in the same chain.

1 What did Albert study before training in hotel management? business administration
2 What does Albert do with members of staff? solves problems with the staff, hires and trains them
3 Who does Albert work closely with when arranging a celebration? the head chef and the kitchen staff
4 When does Albert make sure wait staff are following the plan correctly? when they have an important event
5 What does Albert expect to be doing in a few years? He expects to be working as hotel manager for a number of hotels in the same chain.

B **Discuss the questions as a class.**

1 Do you think Albert's job is interesting? Why or why not?
2 What do you think is the hardest part of Albert's job?

GO TO page xx

for **VIDEOS IN SYM** step-by-step instructions.

VIDEO

WATCH THE VIDEO AND FOLLOW AN EVENT PLANNER.

C **IN GROUPS Answer the questions.**

1 What job is the video about? an event planner
2 What does the person do every day? She works with her clients to execute their events.
3 Does the person like the job? Why or why not? Yes, her job is great because she can plan parties.
4 What's the hardest part of the person's job? when clients change their mind
5 What skills does the person need for the job? creative, good with people, and organized
6 What education or training did this person have?

6 She went to school for Recreation and Event Management and she was an intern with a professional.

D **IN GROUPS Check your answers to the quiz on page 26 and discuss the questions.**

1 Do you know people who work in hospitality?
2 What jobs in hospitality do you know?
3 How does knowing English help if you work in hospitality?
4 What personal qualities do you need to work in hospitality?
5 What opportunities to work in hospitality are there where you live?

Answers to the quiz on page 26
1 a 2 c 3 c

128

ALTERNATIVE ACTIVITY

If students are struggling with the text have them look for words that fit in the following categories. Some examples include:

- **Hotel words:** manager, chain hotel, supplies, services, kitchen staff, head chef, menu, wait staff.
- **Business words:** degree in business administration, business skills, solve problems, hiring, training, interview applicants, manage people, manage money.

FURTHER DISCUSSION

- What hotels are there in your area?
- What jobs do people have in those hotels?
- What are the lower-paid and higher-paid roles in hotels?
- How do you get promoted in the hotel industry?
- How are small hotels and big hotels different?

VIDEO

Watch with sound off. Look for: *office, tablet, lights, computer, smartphone, school bus, fish.*

While viewing, listen for: *meetings, parties, budget, creative, organized, event planning, DJ, work extra hard.*

After viewing, ask: *What is one of Valerie's favorite event?* a school dance with the theme "Under the Sea"

UNIT 3

STUDY SKILLS

GO TO page xviii for STUDY SKILLS step-by-step instructions.

A A group of students is researching how college students watch entertainment at home. Read the questionnaire they wrote. Are the questions designed well? Why or why not?

DESIGNING A QUESTIONNAIRE

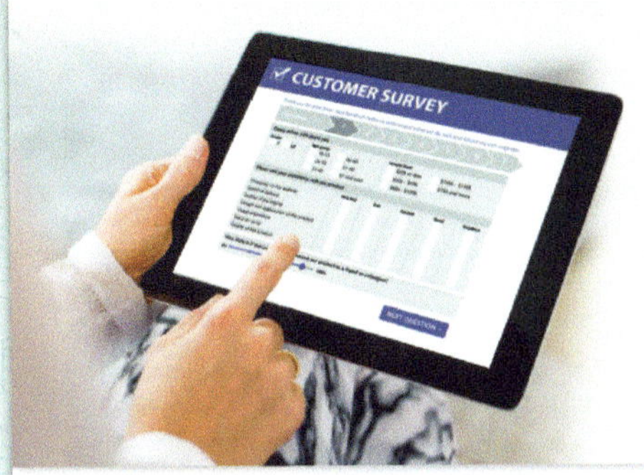

1 Which of the following best describes your job?
Full-time / Part-time

2 How many hours of TV do you watch per day?
Do you prefer series or movies on the internet?
Series / Movies

3 What do you think about reality shows?

4 I prefer to watch TV with friends.
a Strongly agree **b** Agree **c** Neither agree nor disagree
d Disagree **e** Strongly disagree

5 Do you ever lie about how much TV you watch?
Yes / No

B Read the tips for designing questionnaires. Write the question numbers from A next to all the tips that can improve them. Then underline the questions from the questionnaire in A that follow the tips.

a Use closed questions that have one answer only. You can count the answers quickly for your research. 3

b Make sure that your questions ask for just one piece of information. Don't ask two questions at the same time. 2

c Ask each question the same way. Use all questions or all statements. Write the answer choices in the same way, too. 4

d Make sure all your questions are on the topic you are researching. 1

e Make sure your questions don't embarrass or upset the people who might answer them. 5

C Rewrite the questionnaire from A in your notebook. Use the tips to help you write good research questions. Write three more well-designed research questions. Ask about the following:

Suggested answers:

1 Do you work full time or part time?
Full time / Part time

2 How many hours of TV do you watch per day?
Less than 2 / More than 2

3 Do you prefer TV series or movies on the internet?
TV series / Movies on the internet

4 Do you like reality shows?
Yes / No

5 Do you watch TV alone or with other people?
Alone / With other people

6 Do you think you watch a healthy amount of TV?
Yes / No

6 channel surfing: How often do you channel surf?
Rarely / Sometimes / Often

7 binge-watching: Do you ever binge-watch TV series?
Yes / No

8 how they feel about their TV watching habits: Do you think you watch too much TV?
Yes / No / Don't know

D Write three well-designed survey questions to find out what snacks people eat when they're watching TV.

E **THINKING SKILL—Question** When might you use a questionnaire as part of a job? What jobs depend on getting accurate, useful information from questionnaires?

MAKE IT HAPPEN

Design a questionnaire for a class, e.g., science, history, geography, or psychology. Decide on a research topic and write four to five questions to research it. Then ask your classmates to answer your questionnaire. Report the results to your class.

Answers to the quiz on page 36
1 a 2 a 3 b
(It's better to ask closed questions.)

129

STUDY SKILLS TASK

Students will learn how to design good questions for questionnaires and consider professions in which questionnaires are used. Some advantages of questionnaires are: they are easy to use and to analyze and all information is collected in a regulated way.

THINKING SKILL—Question

The ability to write good questions for questionnaires is a beneficial skill. Questionnaires are used in marketing to find out about market needs, in sales to check if a campaign reached its target, and in medicine and health sciences to find out about peoples' habits and preferences.

MAKE IT HAPPEN

Students apply what they have learned in the lesson about writing questions for questionnaires to designing a questionnaire for a class. Tell them to make it interesting and relevant. Suggest they practice answering the questionnaire themselves to see what they need to improve.

GO TO page xix
for **FOLLOW A PRO** step-by-step instructions.

UNIT 4

FOLLOW A PRO

A Read about a school psychologist's job. Answer the questions below.

A SCHOOL PSYCHOLOGIST

I'm Laura Cardoso and I work as a school psychologist. I work for the school district in a large city. I have a master's degree, and right now I'm working toward my PhD.

Children have different personalities, abilities, and needs. Most of them do fine in the educational system. However, some children need expert help. Some children find schoolwork hard, while other children are bored because their schoolwork doesn't challenge them enough. A school psychologist works with children to help them with their problems so that they can get the best education possible.

There are two main parts to my job. I work with children, parents, and teachers to plan a learning program for each child that needs help. I try to understand the personalities of the children I work with and any problems they have. I use my training to help them learn. The other part of my job involves training teachers in my city. I travel from school to school and explain common problems children have. It's very motivating to help children do their best.

1. What degree does Laura have? She has a master's degree.
2. Why do some children need a school psychologist? Children might find schoolwork hard or they might not be challenged (they might be bored).
3. Who does Laura work with when planning a learning program? She works with children, their parents, and their teachers.
4. What does Laura do besides work with children? She trains teachers.
5. What does Laura like about her job? She likes helping children do their best.

B Discuss the questions as a class.

1. Would you like to work as a school psychologist? Why or why not?
2. What skills are important for this job?

GO TO page xx
for **VIDEOS IN SYM** step-by-step instructions.

VIDEO

WATCH THE VIDEO AND FOLLOW A TEACHER.

C IN GROUPS Answer the questions.

1. What job is the video about? a school teacher
2. Where does the person work? in a very large school
3. Who does the person work with? He teaches fifth grade and has 20 students in his classroom.
4. What special education does this person have? ____
5. Is the person happy in this job? yes
6. What does the person say is the best part of the job? ____

4 He has a bachelor's in elementary education and a master's degree in literacy education.

6 being able to inspire students and help them understand the world in a better way

D IN GROUPS Check your answers to the quiz on page 46 and discuss the questions.

1. Do you know any people who work in education?
2. What other jobs in education do you know?
3. In what ways might English be useful for a psychologist in the field of education?
4. What personal qualities do you need to work in education?
5. What are the best and worst things about working in education?

Answers to the quiz on page 46
1 c 2 c 3 a

130

CAREER NOTE

Before reading "A School Psychologist," write *Jobs in Schools* on the board and ask volunteers to give examples of the jobs that people do in schools. Then ask them what they think a school psychologist does.

School psychologists are trained both in psychology and education. Their preparation includes coursework and practical experience. They can work in private schools, preschools, public schools, and juvenile centers.

FURTHER DISCUSSION

- Is there a psychologist at your school?
- What does the psychologist at your school do?
- Where do other psychologists work?
- Is anyone in your family a psychologist?
- Where in your region can you study psychology?

VIDEO

Watch with sound off. Look for: *desks, chairs, children, whiteboard, computer, schedule, classroom.*

While viewing, listen for: *eading, math, students, literacy edutacion, teachers, subjects, administrators, parents, flexible, challenge questions.*

After viewing, ask: *What else does Drew do for his classes?* plans the lessons, grades assignments, meets with the administration and co-workers, and communicates with parents

UNIT 5

STUDY SKILLS

GO TO page xviii for STUDY SKILLS step-by-step instructions.

A Look at the study notes below for one minute. Try to memorize as many words as you can. Then close your book and write what you remember. Was the task hard? Why or why not?

ORGANIZING TO HELP MEMORIZATION

Travel Vocabulary

book a flight
go sightseeing
try the local specialties
check in at the airport
go through security
airplane
chill out on the beach
plane
baggage claim
bus
check-in desk
stay at a campsite
rent a vacation home
take lots of pictures

B Read the tips about organizing your notes for better memorization. Match the memorization tips (1–4) to the examples in the notes (a–d).

1 Organize the words by category. __a__
2 Write the words in short phrases. __b__
3 Write a short sentence with some of the words. __d__
4 Write several sentences that make a story with the words. __c__

a *People in a Hotel*	*In the Room*	*Things to Ask the Receptionist*	*Verbs for Hotels*
valet	*king bed / queen bed / twin bed*	*Is breakfast included in the price?*	*book a room*
hotel receptionist	**b** *room with a balcony*	**d** *Can we get some extra towels, please?*	*check into the hotel*
housekeeping	*refrigerator*	*Could you recommend a good restaurant nearby?*	*check out of the hotel*
concierge	**c** *The room in Cancun was perfect. I got a room with a balcony so that I could look at the beach. There was a mini-fridge for snacks, but if I was very hungry, I called room service and ordered lunch.*		*call room service*

C Organize the notes in A so that the words and phrases are easy to remember. Study them for one minute. Then write as many words as you can remember.

Things to Do on Vacation

chill out on the beach

Suggested answers:
Types of Transportation
plane
airplane
bus

Flying
book a flight
baggage claim
check in at the airport
go through security

Accommodation
check-in desk
rent a vacation home
stay at a campsite

Things to Do
take lots of pictures
try the local specialties
go sightseeing
chill out on the beach

D **THINKING SKILL—Recall** How do you organize information when you need to memorize facts for your classes? Do you organize information in a similar way when you study a language?

MAKE IT HAPPEN

Choose one of the subjects you are studying now. Organize a vocabulary list for that subject so that the words are easier to memorize.

Answers to the quiz on page 56
Students' own answers

131

STUDY SKILLS TASK

Students will probably find the first activity difficult. The goal of the lesson is for them to discover that if they organize the information they have to remember, they will remember it more easily. In this lesson, students will learn ways to organize information for better memorization.

THINKING SKILL—Recall

Once students have learned some strategies for organizing information, they will discuss ways they memorize information for other classes. Encourage them to suggest techniques they use in other classes that would be good for use in the English classroom.

MAKE IT HAPPEN

Students apply what they have learned in the lesson by choosing one of the subjects they are studying now and organizing a vocabulary list. You may want to encourage them to revisit a unit of this book they have studied recently and reorganize their vocabulary list from it.

GO TO page xix
for **FOLLOW A PRO** step-by-step instructions.

UNIT 6 FOLLOW A PRO

A Read about the job of an ecological architect. Choose the option that is NOT correct.

AN ARCHITECT

Emilia Johnson is an architect in a company that specializes in ecological architecture. She completed her bachelor's degree in architecture and environmental design and then got a paid internship with the company. Four years later, she passed the Architect Registration Examination. She has worked at the company for eight years, and she plans to stay there for several more years.

Ecological architects design buildings that are a natural part of the world. They design buildings that use natural resources, such as solar energy. They also design buildings with natural materials, such as a green roof (plants growing on top of a building). Emilia works with civil engineers and interior designers to make sure that her designs have a positive impact on the environment. She explains her designs to urban planners so that her buildings can become part of a larger plan for a city.

Emilia needs good technical skills and creativity. She has to make beautiful buildings that are also water and energy-efficient. She visualizes the design of the project and then creates drawings using CAD (Computer Aided Design) software. She checks that construction workers are following her design.

Emilia loves being an ecological architect. The best part of her job is seeing her clients living and working happily in a building that fits in the world naturally.

1 For four years, Emilia worked as an intern / as a volunteer / before passing an exam / on ecological buildings.
2 Ecological architects create buildings with natural materials / solar panels / plants / plastic roofs.
3 Emilia's designs are used by engineers and designers / created on computers / made by clients / explained to urban planners.
4 Ecological architects need good marketing / communication / technical / creative skills.

B Discuss the questions as a class.

1 Do you think it is important to create ecological architecture? Why or why not?
2 How can architects help make buildings more ecological?
3 Have you been in any buildings that are "green"? How do those buildings save water or energy?

GO TO page xx
for **VIDEOS IN SYM** step-by-step instructions.

VIDEO

WATCH THE VIDEO AND FOLLOW AN URBAN PLANNER.

C IN GROUPS Answer the questions.

1 What job is the video about? an urban planner
2 What are the person's working hours? 8 a.m. to 5 p.m.
3 What are some of the good and bad things about the job? good thing: taking the architectual drawing into reality; bad thing: it can be difficult come up with a solution that will make everybody happy
4 Is the person's job hard? Why or why not? Yes, the job is complicated. He needs a degree in architecture, good people skills, and creativity.
5 What skills does the person use at this job? to be able to draw, to have good communication

D IN GROUPS Check your answers to the quiz on page 66 and discuss the questions.

1 What other jobs in architecture do you know?
2 Do you need English to be an architect?
3 What personal qualities do you need for this job?
4 Are there opportunities in the field of architecture in your country?

Answers to the quiz on page 66
1 c 2 b 3 a 4 c

ALTERNATIVE ACTIVITY

Ask students to circle words related to athlete and underline words related to psychology:

- **Athlete:** physical condition, training, athletic success, physical training routine, competitions, athletic performance
- **Psychology:** mental condition, mental training, focus, positive, calm, sports psychologists, emotions, anxiety, visualization, relaxation techniques, mindfulness, self-confident

FURTHER DISCUSSION

- Are you an athlete?
- Would you like to be a professional athlete?
- If you were a professional athlete, would you use a psychologist?
- Do you think sports psychologists help performance?
- If you were a sports psychologist, what sport would you like to specialize in?

VIDEO

Watch with sound off. Look for: *office, plans, computers, screens, drawings, buildings, street, working helmets.*

While viewing, listen for: *cities, plans, construction sight, regulations, draw, engineers, urban planning, passion, solution.*

After viewing, ask: *What is an urban planner?* Is a person who plans and creates cities.

UNIT 7

STUDY SKILLS

GO TO page xviii for **STUDY SKILLS** step-by-step instructions.

A **Look at two personal narratives. Which story is more interesting, in your opinion? Why?**

Suggested answer: The second text is more interesting, as the writer compares the college to a different planet. This gets across how strange and unfamiliar everything seemed to her on the first day, and it creates strong images in the reader's mind.

CREATIVITY

My First Day of College

I was a little nervous on my first day of college. I got lost on campus, and it took me half an hour to find my class. The professor seemed irritated that I arrived late, and I felt really stressed. I was lost and lonely because I didn't know anyone at the college. I didn't really need to worry because the other students were very nice. I'm still good friends with some of the people from my first day. The teachers here are very nice, too, and now I can find my way around the campus easily.

By Sebastian

My First Day of College

The college campus looked like a different planet. It felt light-years away from Earth and everything was unfamiliar. Finding my class on the first day was like going to the moon. It seemed like I was walking around in circles. I hunted for the classroom for half an hour before I landed there. I was a lonely alien in a crazy, crowded campus. Fortunately, the other life-forms on the planet were fun-loving and peaceful and became my new friends. After some time, everything became less strange.

By Elsa

B **Read Elsa's story again. What words does she choose to describe …**

1. the college campus? a different planet
2. how she arrived in class? landed
3. the other students? other life-forms (fun-loving and peaceful)
4. how she felt? like a lonely alien on a crazy, crowded campus

C **IN PAIRS Read the definitions of a simile and a metaphor. Then write similes or metaphors to describe the things below.**

Students' own answers

Simile: When you compare two things, saying that one is like another, e.g.: "The college campus looked like a different planet."
Metaphor: When you describe something as being something different (to show the similarities between the two things), e.g.: "I was a lonely alien."

1. falling in love ________
2. a stressful exam ________
3. a family party ________
4. a pet you love ________

D **Choose one of the ideas in C and write a paragraph. Use the simile or metaphor in your paragraph to make your writing interesting.**

My dog Laika is a hurricane. When she rushes into the room, there's noise, and nothing is safe ...

E **THINKING SKILL—Brainstorm In what ways are you creative? Do you enjoy expressing your feelings, solving problems, or inventing things? How can you use your creative gift in your life or work?**

MAKE IT HAPPEN

Keep a notebook of things you want to write about. Then choose one of the topics to write an essay about.

Answers to the quiz on page 76
1 c 2 b (It makes you more creative.) 3 b 4 b

133

STUDY SKILLS TASK

Creativity needs time and space. Advise students to relax and find a comfortable place to think when they want to be creative. Or they could go for a walk. Tell students they should let ideas flow freely in their minds.

THINKING SKILL—Brainstorm

Put on some slow music to allow students to think about the ways in which they are creative. Encourage them to look for ways they are creative in their everyday lives—ways of expressing themselves, small problems they solve every day, or ways they make other people's lives better through their creativity.

MAKE IT HAPPEN

Tell students to use Elsa's essay as a model for their essay. They can write about whatever they want to, but they should include the figurative language shown in **A**. Advise them to use similes and metaphors.

GO TO page xix
for **FOLLOW A PRO** step-by-step instructions.

UNIT 8

FOLLOW A PRO

A **Read about a resort activities coordinator's job. Choose *True* or *False* below.**

A RESORT ACTIVITIES COORDINATOR

Sergio Herrero is an activities coordinator at a large resort hotel in Costa Rica. He plans and directs sports and entertainment activities for children and adults, and he takes guests on nature walks along the beach. Sergio also coordinates the activities section on the hotel's website and helps manage the budget for his department.

Sergio is 24, and he has a degree in hotel management. He says that getting a management job right after graduation is very hard, and being an activities coordinator gives him some experience working for a large hotel. Sergio says the salary isn't great, but his expenses are low. He lives at the hotel and eats his meals there for free. Guests often tip the activities coordinators, and that's always nice!

Sergio says that an activities coordinator should have a college degree in a field like hotel management, sales and marketing, or sports management. It's important to speak English and one other language, especially at international resorts. And having the right personality is essential. Activities coordinators have to love people. They have to be friendly and enthusiastic, and they have to know how to play games and sports, and even sing or dance.

Sergio is enjoying his job and learning a lot about the hotel business. He says he especially likes meeting people from many different places around the world.

1 Entertaining guests is Sergio's only job responsibility. True / False
2 Sergio is working as an activities coordinator to get experience in hotel work. True / False
3 Being an activities coordinator has some benefits apart from the salary. True / False
4 You only have to speak one language to be an activities coordinator. True / False
5 Activities coordinators work with people of all ages. True / False
6 Sergio thinks that being an activities coordinator is a good way to enter the hotel business. True / False

(Answers highlighted: 1 False, 2 True, 3 True, 4 False, 5 True, 6 True)

B **Discuss the questions as a class.**

1 Is an activities coordinator's job important? Why or why not?
2 Have you ever seen an activities coordinator working? If so, tell the class about what you observed.
3 Would you like to be an activities coordinator? Why or why not?

GO TO page xx
for **VIDEOS IN SYM** step-by-step instructions.

VIDEO

WATCH THE VIDEO AND FOLLOW A RECREATION COORDINATOR.

C **IN GROUPS Answer the questions.**

1 What job is the video about? a recreation coordinator
2 What does the person do every day? He checks emails, chats with staff, makes sight visits, meets with people in the community.
3 What is interesting about this job? meeting different kinds of people
4 Does this person work long hours? Yes, he works from 8 a.m to 6 p.m.
5 Is the person satisfied with the job? yes
6 Is there anything the person doesn't like? He doesn't like unhappy park visitors.

D **IN GROUPS Check your answers to the quiz on page 86 and discuss the questions.**

1 Do you think you have the right qualifications to work as an activities coordinator?
2 What are some advantages and disadvantages of working as an activities coordinator?
3 What other leisure industry jobs can you think of?
4 What leisure industry jobs would be interesting to you?
5 What qualifications do you need to work in different jobs in the leisure industry?

Answers to the quiz on page 86
1 c 2 b 3 a, b, c, d, e

134

ALTERNATIVE ACTIVITY

Ask students to circle the paragraph that describes the job Sergio does and underline the paragraph that outlines the skills needed for the job. (The first paragraph describes the job and the third paragraph outlines the skills needed.)

FURTHER DISCUSSION

- How many resorts can you name?
- What are the biggest resort areas in your country?
- Do you like resort vacations?
- What kind of people are resort vacations suited to?
- What's the difference between a tourist and a traveler?

VIDEO

Watch with sound off. Look for: *park, office, pool, swings, children, trees, dancing.*

While viewing, listen for: *parks, summer camps, softball, have fun, smile, special event, community, park visitors.*

After viewing, ask: *What skills does a recreation coordinator need?* organizational skills, being flexible, and being patient

GO TO page xviii
for STUDY SKILLS step-by-step instructions.

UNIT 9

STUDY SKILLS

A Read the conversation about a group of students working on a research project. Are the students using good problem-solving skills? Why or why not?

PROBLEM SOLVING

Carla: For our group assignment, we have to offer solutions to the lack of safe, affordable, and quick transportation to the college. It says here that we need to present three ideas for transportation, outlining the advantages and disadvantages of each idea.
Bobby: Right. Well, that's easy. Let's present an idea for a college taxi service. That's all we need!
Maggie: Yeah, it's safe, affordable, and it would be quick, too! Nice job. We're done!
Carla: Hold on! We're not finished yet. We need three different ideas, not just one.
Bobby: Oh, I forgot about that. So, we've already got a taxi service. How about self-driving taxis, too?
Carla: Yeah, OK. And maybe ride sharing, too?
Maggie: Yes. And why don't we find out how most students get to college in a typical week?
Bobby: Good idea. I'll ask my friends, OK? That'll be quick. That can be my part, and you can do all the other stuff.
Carla: No, we need to do more research than that! And we probably need to write a report. What do you think?
Maggie: Is that necessary? Can't we all just say what we want in a presentation?
Bobby: Yeah, that's probably the best plan.
Carla: Hmm … I'm not sure that's enough.
Maggie: Well, if you think we need a report, you can write it.

B Choose all the correct answers about the conversation in A.

The students aren't using good problem-solving skills because …

1 They haven't divided the work equally.
2 They aren't thinking about how to effectively research the problem.
3 They haven't considered several different solutions before deciding on three.
4 They haven't decided on a good way to research their topic.
5 They aren't sure if they have to write a report or just give the presentation.

C Number the steps in the problem-solving process in the correct order (1–4).

__4__ Write down how you managed to solve the problem.
__1__ Read the task carefully and make sure you understand it.
__3__ Look at the problem in a few different ways. Think about many possible solutions.
__2__ Decide what information you need to help you solve the problem.

D In your notebook, rewrite the conversation in A using your ideas and the problem-solving tips in C. Show good problem-solving skills.

E THINKING SKILL—Evaluate Employers look for employees who can help solve problems. What qualities does a good problem-solver have? Make a list.

Listens to everyone's opinion, …

MAKE IT HAPPEN

Apply some of the problem-solving techniques you have learned to your own studies or work. Keep a journal about the process you used to solve a problem and decide what helped you reach a solution.

Answers to the quiz on page 96
1 a, b, c 2 a and c

135

STUDY SKILLS TASK

The conversation demonstrates what not to do. By analyzing the wrong way to go about working in groups to do a project, students think about some good strategies for approaching the task.

THINKING SKILL—Evaluate

Let students know that qualities a good problem solver might have are: creativity, research skills, the ability to work on a team and see many sides of a problem, emotional intelligence, and decision-making skills. Employers are not looking for people with all the answers; they are looking for people who know how to find the answers.

MAKE IT HAPPEN

Students who work through the activities for good problem-solving skills are introduced to the problem-solving process. Have students share their problem-solving plan for their own studies or work. Time management is another important problem-solving skill. Ask them how they approach time management when faced with multiple assignments and exams.

GO TO page xix
for **FOLLOW A PRO** step-by-step instructions.

UNIT 10 FOLLOW A PRO

A Read about a family physician's job. Answer the questions below.

A FAMILY PHYSICIAN

There are many different kinds of doctors. Grace Lincoln is a family physician.

"I always wanted to be a doctor from the time I was very young. I took a lot of science classes in high school and then majored in biology in college. I took anatomy, biology, and chemistry—all classes that are in a pre-med curriculum. After that, I went to medical school for four years and then had four more years of practical training before I got my present job. It's a long, hard road, but I can't imagine doing anything else.

"I use a lot of different skills every day. I need medical knowledge, of course, but I also need to be good with people. When my patients are ill or injured, they need the right treatment, but they also need to know that I understand how they feel. And I have to be ready for anything. My next patient might be an elderly person with a broken arm or a child with a fever. I love the feeling that I'm making a real difference in people's lives."

1 What kind of doctor is Grace? She's a family physician.
2 When did Grace first want to be a doctor? when she was very young
3 What was Grace's major as an undergraduate? biology
4 How many years of medical school and training did Grace complete before she got her job? eight years
5 What does Grace like about her job? She like making a difference in people's lives.

B Discuss the questions as a class.

1 Would you like to be a doctor?
2 What do you think is the best part of being a doctor?

GO TO page xx
for **VIDEOS IN SYM** step-by-step instructions.

VIDEO WATCH THE VIDEO AND FOLLOW A PHYSICAL THERAPIST.

C IN GROUPS Answer the questions.

1 What job is the video about? a physical therapist
2 What special skills or education does this person have? She needs to know how the body works, anatomy, physiology, exercise science, be a good communicator, medical knowledge.
3 Who does the person work with? a receptionist, office manager, two to three other therapists
4 What are some of the good and bad things about the job? good: help people get back to live their normal lives; bad: when people think she is a masseuse
5 Is the person's job hard? Why or why not? Yes, she needs to educate and teach people how to help themselves.
6 Does this person need multiple languages to do this job? yes

D IN GROUPS Check your answers to the quiz on page 106 and discuss the questions.

1 Do you know anybody who works in health care?
2 How does someone become a doctor in your country?
3 What skills do you think a doctor needs?
4 Do men and women do the same jobs in health care in your country?
5 What area of health care would you most like to work in?

Answers to the quiz on page 106
1 c 2 a 3 c

136

CAREER NOTE

Elicit as many different medical specialties as students can think of and the areas of medicine they work in. If necessary, explain the differences between each medical specialties. For example, a pediatrician is a doctor who deals with children and the medical treatment of their illnesses; a neurologist is a doctor who is an expert in the study of the nervous system and the diseases that affect it.

FURTHER DISCUSSION

- Do you go to the doctor often?
- Who do you turn to when you are sick?
- Do you have any doctors in your family?
- If you were a doctor, what kind of doctor would you be?
- What problem-solving skills do doctors need?

VIDEO

Watch with sound off. Look for: *seniors, exercise, knee pad, bed, desk, medical equipment, hand, leg, treadmill.*

While viewing, listen for: *injury, pain, body, stretch, schedule, knee injury, back pain, angel, help, stressful.*

After viewing, ask: *What makes Diana's job worth it?* A "thank you, I feel so much better now because of you" from a patient.

UNIT 11

STUDY SKILLS

GO TO page xviii
for STUDY SKILLS step-by-step instructions.

A **Yadira is working on an essay for her science class. Read her notes and her paragraph. Has she used all of the facts in her writing? Underline the words she should replace with precise facts.**

USING PRECISE LANGUAGE IN ACADEMIC WRITING

Research Notes

- *70% of the Earth is covered in water*
- *less than 3% of the Earth's water is fresh water*
- *17% of people don't have clean drinking water*
- *cholera and dysentery are diseases caused by unclean water*
- *in developing countries, 80% of illnesses are caused by dirty drinking water*

How can we help more people have clean drinking water?

Most of the world's surface is covered by water, but not much of it is fresh. Many people have no access to clean water and this is really terrible. Clean water is very important for our health, and it is also important for keeping everything clean. Unclean drinking water causes some serious diseases, such as cholera and dysentery. These diseases stop people from working and cause economic problems. I think it's terrible that rich countries don't do more about this.

B **Read the tips on writing academic essays. Then rewrite the sentences with more precise language.**

Sentences 1–4 are suggested answers.

- Use specific facts in your writing and be precise in your language. Look for statistics from reliable sources, such as books, journals, and trusted internet sites.
- Don't use generalizations (a lot of people say … , no one wants … , more people prefer …).
- Opinions are your personal beliefs. Don't give opinions in academic essays unless you also have facts to support your opinions.

1 Many students in my English class have studied English for more than a year.
90% of students in my English class have studied English for more than a year.

2 Some students take a class in the morning, and some take a class at night.
30% of the students take a class in the morning, and 70% take a class at night.

3 I like taking a class at night because I don't like getting up early in the morning.
The top reason students take a class at night is they don't like getting up early.

4 A face-to-face class is more fun than an online class. That's why a lot of students prefer to attend a class.
50% of students who take a face-to-face class think it is more fun than an online class.

C **In your notebook, rewrite Yadira's paragraph in A using the tips for academic writing in B.**

70% of the world's surface is covered by water, but less than 3% of it is fresh. 17% of people have no access to clean water. Clean water is very important for our health. Unclean drinking water causes 80% of serious diseases, such as cholera and dysentery. These diseases stop people from working and cause economic problems.

D **THINKING SKILL—Apply** **Why is it important to know how to be precise in your writing? How could remembering these tips help you to be a better writer?**

MAKE IT HAPPEN

Choose a topic from your work or studies. Research facts about the topic and write a paragraph in academic style. Use data and precise language to explain the topic.

Answers to the quiz on page 116
1 b 2 b 3 a 4 b

137

STUDY SKILLS TASK

Let students know that this lesson will help them write better academic essays. They will learn how to include facts and research-based information in their essays. Give students the choice to work alone or in pairs, because some students learn better studying alone and some learn better when discussing ideas with others.

THINKING SKILL—Apply

Academic writing and narrative writing are different. Academic writing is objective. In academic writing, facts support a thesis, and the argument is proven by research-based information, not just opinion.

MAKE IT HAPPEN

In this activity, students put into practice everything they have learned in the lesson and choose a topic from their own studies to practice improving by using precise language. Give them a chance to show their paragraphs to a partner and do some peer counseling.

GO TO page xix
for **FOLLOW A PRO** step-by-step instructions.

UNIT 12 FOLLOW A PRO

A Read about an entrepreneur's job. Answer the questions below.

AN ENTREPRENEUR

I'm Juana Geller. I run my own ethical jewelry business. My company designs and sells jewelry made from eco-friendly materials. I started my business when I was a teenager. I wanted to buy and wear jewelry that was different from everyone else. I made necklaces from glass beads. My friends liked my designs, so I started making necklaces and selling them to friends and family.

After high school, I learned about eco-friendly jewelry. I attended workshops on materials that could be recycled. I worked very hard and did a lot of networking. I visited many stores and talked about my ideas. A few stores decided to sell my jewelry, and the managers gave me advice on running my business. Young people liked my jewelry and talked about it on social media. The business started to grow, and I decided to get a degree in business administration to help me run it better.

Today, my company employs 50 people, and our jewelry is in stores across the country. We also sell a lot online. To be successful as an entrepreneur, you need to be able to take risks and be confident while you do it. You won't get much sleep for the first few years, but with a little luck, it'll be worth it in the end!

1 What does Juana's company produce? environmentally-friendly jewelry
2 Why did Juana start her business? She couldn't buy what she wanted.
3 How did Juana get started? She visited stores and spoke to the managers.
4 What qualifications does Juana have? a degree in business administration
5 What does Juana say about being a successful entrepreneur? You need to take risks and be confident.

B Discuss the questions as a class.

1 Is being self-employed a good idea? Why or why not?
2 Can you imagine being self-employed?

GO TO page xx
for **VIDEOS IN SYM** step-by-step instructions.

VIDEO

WATCH THE VIDEO AND FOLLOW AN ENTREPRENEUR.

C IN GROUPS Answer the questions.

1 What kind of job does this person do? an entrepreneur
2 Where does this person work? in his office or his clients' offices
3 What are the person's working hours? from 8 a.m. to 10 p.m.
4 What special skills does this person need? know web design, how to run a business, selling skills
5 How did this person learn the skills for the job? ___
6 Why do you think this person likes his job? He can be who he really is and be creative.

5 in college for web design, classes for business development, and life experience as a salesman

D IN GROUPS Check your answers to the quiz on page 126 and discuss the questions.

1 Do you know people who have started their own businesses?
2 Would you like to start your own business? Why or why not?
3 What are the risks of starting your own business?
4 In what ways would English help in starting your own business?
5 What skills does an entrepreneur need?

Answers to the quiz on page 126
1 a 2 c 3 c 4 b (Japan was second and the US was third.)

138

ALTERNATIVE ACTIVITY

Have students look in the article for words related to jewelry and words related to business and record them:

- **Jewelry:** eco-friendly materials, necklaces, glass beads, designs
- **Business:** workshops, networking, stores, ideas, managers, advice on running a business, social media, degree in business administration, employ, sell online, entrepreneur, take risks, be confident

FURTHER DISCUSSION

- Do you wear jewelry?
- What is the jewelry you wear made of?
- What does being eco-friendly mean to you?
- Can you name any sustainable materials?
- What do you think the challenges of growing a small business are?
- What kind of small, eco-friendly business would you like to start?

VIDEO

Watch with sound off. Look for: *white board, computer, office, clothes, shoes.*

While viewing, listen for: *creative, goals, websites, advertising, partner, business, creative, photoshoot.*

After viewing, ask: *What did Mark do for his client?* design her website, logo, schedule a photoshoot, advertise in social media

Student's Book Grammar Answer Key

Grammar Quiz Answer Key

A **1** What's **2** 's **3** are **4** 'm **5** 's **6** is **7** not

B **1** loves **2** checks **3** wakes **4** sends **5** uses **6** have **7** don't need **8** do, spend

C **1** are you having **2** I'm having **3** Did you buy **4** I made it **5** should **6** serves **7** want to

D **1** Are you almost ready, Julie? **2** I'm so excited about going to ~~the~~ Amsterdam! **3** What do you want to do when we're there? **4** I want to go sightseeing around the city. **5** Yeah, I'd / I would like to do that, too. **6** I'd like to, but I can't/cannot ride a bike!

E **1** the **2** Your **3** a **4** a **5** X **6** the **7** 's **8** her

Grammar Review Answer Key

A **1** g **2** d **3** f **4** b **5** e **6** c **7** a **8** h

B **1** want to **2** Would, like to **3** need to **4** has to **5** plan to **6** like to

C **1** celebrated **2** went **3** didn't have **4** was, enjoyed **5** didn't go **6** did

D **1** cheaper **2** better **3** healthier **4** friendlier **5** more popular **6** closer

E **1** She can run really fast. **2** She speaks English well. **3** Can you speak more slowly, please? **4** You need to do this very carefully. **5** He caught the ball easily. / He easily caught the ball. **6** He studied hard for his exam.

F **1** There are **2** there are **3** There is **4** there's **5** There aren't **6** Are there

G **1** is taking **2** is updating **3** is posting **4** are sending **5** is going **6** is looking **7** aren't speaking

H **1** some **2** How much **3** some **4** These **5** those **6** How much

Grammar Reference Answer Key

Unit 1

past progressive vs. simple past

A **1** were **2** was reading **3** painting **4** hit **5** gave **6** was drawing **7** saw **8** were talking

B **1** was watching **2** called **3** was writing **4** were discussing **5** asked **6** got

Unit 2

quantifiers: *some, any, too much/many, a lot of, a little, a few*

A **1** There's only a little milk in the refrigerator. **2** I think there's too much salt in this meal. **3** You need a lot of tomatoes to make tomato soup. **4** Can you please buy me a few apples when you're at the store? **5** Don't eat too much candy! It's not good for you. **6** Can I have some grapes, please? / Can I have a grape, please?

B **1** a lot of **2** Some **3** a little **4** too many **5** too much **6** a few

enough / not enough

A **1** Do we have enough food for this party? **2** I think we have enough. **3** Do we really have enough pizza? **4** We have enough pizza. **5** Are there enough chairs? **6** We don't have enough time to get more chairs!

Unit 3

indefinite pronouns: *any, some, no, every + one/body/thing/where*

A **1** something **2** no one **3** Everyone **4** something **5** anyone **6** anyone

B **1** When I first moved here, I didn't know anyone. **2** Everyone seemed to have their own friends, so it was hard to meet people. **3** I felt lonely and I needed to do something about it. **4** I looked around everywhere for clubs I could join. **5** Finally, I found something I was interested in—a video gaming club. **6** Everyone is so friendly!

used to

A 1 Did your brother use to singing in a band? **2** He used to be the lead singer of a hard rock band. **3** I didn't use to like hard rock, but now I love it. **4** Did you use to take a music class at school? **5** Yeah, I used to take one, but I stopped! **6** The last teacher used to make us work too hard!

B **1** used to **2** didn't use to **3** didn't use to **4** use to **5** used to **6** used to **7** use to

Unit 4

comparative review and *(not) as … as*

A **1** not as tall as **2** are bluer **3** as serious as **4** more sociable **5** as easygoing **6** as lazy

B **1** ~~more good than~~ better than **2** ~~expensiver than~~ more expensive than **3** ~~isn't modern as~~ isn't as modern as **4** ~~as hard like~~ as hard as **5** ~~getting badder~~ getting worse **6** ~~importanter~~ more important **7** ~~as happy than~~ as happy as

superlative adjectives

A **1** the most hardworking **2** the most easygoing **3** the laziest **4** the most creative **5** the best **6** the nicest

Unit 5

modals of intention, offer, and prediction

A **1** Can **2** I'll **3** Will **4** I'll **5** won't **6** won't

B **1** Will **2** won't **3** Can **4** 'll **5** Will **6** 'll **7** won't

modals of request and permission: *could, can/can't, may*

A **1** Can I **2** can't **3** May I **4** may **5** May **6** can't **6** can

B **1** Can I open the window? **2** May I see your ID? **3** Yes, you can use my bike. **4** Yes, you may go now. **5** Can I have your email address? **6** Could we have some more orange juice?

Unit 6

present perfect with *for* and *since*

A **1** since **2** for **3** for **4** since **5** for **6** since

B **1** I've lived **2** for a long time **3** long have you had **4** Have you been there? **5** I haven't had a vacation since **6** It's been a long time since

present perfect with *ever* and *never*

A **1** ever **2** haven't **3** tried **4** have **5** been **6** never

B **1** e **2** f **3** a **4** d **5** b **6** c

Unit 7

present perfect with *already, just,* and *yet*

A **1** I've just applied for a job with a PR firm. **2** I've just seen the perfect job for you! **3** I've already seen that job ad. **4** I haven't sent my resume yet. **5** Have you had any interviews yet? **6** I've just had an email.

B **1** yet **2** already **3** just **4** yet **5** already **6** just

present perfect and simple past

A **1** had **2** Have you ever done **3** I've worked **4** seen **5** thought

B **1** Did you have **2** have worked **3** had **4** applied **5** Have you seen

Unit 8

gerund phrases as subject and object

A **1** <u>Facing</u> a blank page is always scary, but thinking up new ideas is great for your creativity. **2** If you hate <u>brainstorming</u>, why not try doing it with a friend? Two heads are better than one! **3** <u>Doing</u> what you enjoy will help you feel more creative. Do you love <u>being</u> outdoors? Then get outside and enjoy some fresh air to help you think more clearly. **4** <u>Being</u> open to ideas is really important. If an idea doesn't work for you, then <u>try</u> another one. **5** Ask the right questions. <u>Knowing</u> what you want to do is probably the most important part of the creative process.

B **First blank:** **1** Doing **2** going **3** Joining **4** spending **5** Visiting **6** Having **7** Doing; **Second blank:** Students' own answers

verb + gerund or infinitive

A **1** to chill out **2** to waste **3** to go **4** to stay **5** stay **6** to see

Unit 9

future forms: *will, going to,* present progressive, and simple present

A **1** going to, you'll **2** won't, We'll **3** I'm moving, does **4** are thinking, We're meeting

future possibility and certainty (*may, might, could, will, won't, probably, definitely*)

A **1** might **2** probably **3** might **4** probably **5** definitely **6** may **7** might **8** probably

B **1** I'll definitely rent an apartment next year. **2** We'll probably share the bills. **3** Do you think you'll live alone next year? **4** She may study in a different country. **5** I might not go to the movies. **6** Our new apartment probably won't have a balcony. **7** They'll definitely be there tomorrow.

Unit 10

zero and first conditional

A **1** I feel dizzy **2** If you work at the computer **3** If you make bad choices **4** you'll stop getting headaches **5** I'll have more energy **6** If you make small changes

second conditional

A **1** won **2** I'd call **3** I'd **4** I'd **5** I might want **6** would go **7** buy **8** If **9** I'd

B **1** If you <u>did</u> more exercise, you'd feel better. **2** If it snowed tomorrow, <u>I'd / I would</u> go skiing. **3** If I lived near the beach, <u>I'd / I would</u> learn to surf. **4** If they asked you to work for them, <u>would</u> you say yes? **5** What would you do if <u>you missed</u> the bus? **6** If you spoke a foreign language, you <u>could</u> get a really good job. **7** If we <u>had</u> a yard, we'd have a barbecue every night in the summer.

Unit 11

simple present passive

A **1** The glass is emptied. **2** The glass bottle is taken to the recycling center. **3** The glass is sorted by color. **4** The glass is crushed and melted. **5** The glass is made into new products. **6** The new products are sold in stores. **7** The glass is emptied and is taken to the recycling center.

B **1** Our room is <u>being</u> cleaned at the moment. **2** English is <u>spoken</u> all over the world. **3** Credit cards are <u>accepted</u> here. **4** About 100,000 people are <u>employed</u> by this company. **5** His invention is now <u>sold</u> in 45 different countries. **6** Her name is <u>known</u> throughout the country.

simple past passive

A **1** was given **2** were invented **3** was given **4** was taken **5** were knitted **6** were made of

Unit 12

reflexive pronouns

A **1** a **2** f **3** e **4** d **5** c **6** b

B **1** myself **2** yourself **3** see myself **4** motivate myself **5** do it myself **6** herself **7** ourselves

tense review

A **1** Have **2** I **3** was leaving **4** I've **5** know **6** I'm playing **7** might not know

Irregular Verbs

Infinitive	Simple past	Past participle
be	was/were	been
become	became	become
begin	began	begun
break	broke	broken
bring	brought	brought
build	built	built
buy	bought	bought
catch	caught	caught
choose	chose	chosen
come	came	come
cost	cost	cost
cut	cut	cut
do	did	done
draw	drew	drawn
drink	drank	drunk
drive	drove	driven
eat	ate	eaten
fall	fell	fallen
feed	fed	fed
feel	felt	felt
find	found	found
fly	flew	flown
get	got	gotten
give	gave	given
go	went	gone
grow	grew	grown
hang	hung	hung
have	had	had
hear	heard	heard
hit	hit	hit
hold	held	held
hurt	hurt	hurt
keep	kept	kept
know	knew	known
leave	left	left
let	let	let
lose	lost	lost
make	made	made
meet	met	met
pay	paid	paid
put	put	put
read	read	read
ride	rode	ridden
ring	rang	rung
rise	rose	risen
run	ran	run
say	said	said
see	saw	seen
sell	sold	sold
send	sent	sent
set	set	set
sing	sang	sung
sit	sat	sat
speak	spoke	spoken
stand	stood	stood
stick	stuck	stuck
take	took	taken
teach	taught	taught
tell	told	told
think	thought	thought
throw	threw	thrown
understand	understood	understood
wake	woke	woken
wear	wore	worn
win	won	won
write	wrote	written

Pronunciation Symbols

Vowels

ɪ	did
ɛ	bed
æ	bad
ʌ	cup
ʊ	book
ə	banana
i	feed
ɑ	father, box
ɔ	tall
u	student, food
ɝ	shirt, birthday
eɪ	date, table
aɪ	cry, eye
ɔɪ	boy
oʊ	comb, post
aʊ	about, how

Consonants

p	park, happy
b	back, hobby
t	tea
d	die
k	came, kitchen, quarter
g	game, go
f	face, photographer
v	vegetable
θ	thing, math
ð	then, that
s	city, summer
z	please, goes
ʃ	she, shop
ʒ	leisure
h	hot, who
tʃ	chicken, watch
dʒ	jacket, orange
m	men
n	sun, know
ŋ	sung, singer
w	week, white
r	rain, writer
l	light, long
j	yes, use, music

Unit 1

Track 01

Lila Downs

My role model is Lila Downs. She was born in Oaxaca, Mexico, in 1968. She is a Mexican-American singer-songwriter and actress. At the age of eight, she started singing mariachi songs. She became a professional singer when she was at school. Her family emigrated from Mexico to the US when she was 14. While they were living there, her father died. After that, Lila and her mother moved back to Mexico.

While she was working in her mother's store, she met her future husband, the musician Paul Cohen. He had a business in the US, so Lila moved from Oaxaca to Minnesota. She went to the University of Minnesota. While she was studying there, she started a music group called La Trova Serrana. It was very successful, and Lila decided to leave school to focus on music. Lila had a small role in the movie *Frida* and worked on the music for the movie *Like Water for Chocolate*.

Here are three things you probably don't know about Lila:

- In 2010, while she was traveling the world on her Black Magic Woman Tour, she revealed that she had an adopted son named Benito Dxuladi.
- In 2014, scientists named an insect after her. The Liladownsia fraile is a very colorful grasshopper. They named it after her because Lila often wears colorful, traditional clothes.
- She sings in Spanish, English, and her native language of Mixtec.

I really look up to Lila Downs because she looks for ways to improve people's lives through music. I'd love to meet her and ask her this question: "What were you singing about in the song 'Shake Away'?"

Track 02

Host: We asked four people to tell us about memorable events. Here's what they said.

Katrin: I remember we were walking downtown to buy groceries. Suddenly, a police officer shouted, "Hide!" We hid in a café. A man said wild animals escaped from a zoo. I don't remember feeling scared. I think I was worried that they would kill the animals. Luckily, they caught the animals!

Giovanni: I was watching the game at my friend's house when the phone rang. It was my mom. She said my wife was having the baby! I raced to the hospital. We lost the game 2–1, so it was the end of our World Cup, but that wasn't important. I was so thrilled about the new baby!

Kyle: I was working for NASA on the Mars mission when it happened. My boss called me in the middle of the night while I was sleeping, so I was very confused. "The Italians found an underground lake on Mars," he shouted.

Gemma: When the plane came down, we were staying in a hotel. I turned on the TV, and what I saw was unbelievable. All the people were standing on the wings of the plane. I was so glad that everyone was OK. I decided to train to become a pilot after that.

Track 03

Suddenly a police officer shouted, "Hide!" We hid in a café.

Track 04

1	hid	hide	**3**	mad	made
2	at	ate	**4**	rid	ride

Track 05

About two years ago, my cousin was walking home when he saw a woman. He thought it was me.

A month later, my friend said, "I saw you in the library last week."

"But I was on vacation in Hawaii last week!" I said.

About a month after that, I was shopping for food when a woman came up to me. I looked at her and … well, she looked exactly like me–same hair color, same eyes, same everything!

Track 06

While I was talking to her, I thought we might be related. She said she was an only child. She was adopted when she was two and lived in San Diego until she was 18. Her parents divorced when she was eight. She is engaged to a guy from Australia.

I said I lived in Los Angeles until I was 12. I told her I was single and came from a large family. I have seven brothers and sisters. We were laughing about how we looked the same, but how we had very different lives. Anyway, we exchanged phone numbers and said goodbye. Later on, I called my mom to check if I had a twin sister! She said I didn't.

The next day, I called the woman, and we agreed to meet for coffee. We see each other all the time now. I'm so glad I met her. In the end, she became one of my best friends. It was such an amazing coincidence that we met!

Track 07

About two years ago, my cousin was walking home when he saw a woman. He thought it was me.

A month later, my friend said, "I saw you in the library last week."

"But I was on vacation in Hawaii last week!" I said.

About a month after that, I was shopping for food when a woman came up to me. I looked at her and … well, she looked exactly like me—same hair color, same eyes, same everything!

While I was talking to her, I thought we might be related. She said she was an only child. She was adopted when she was two and lived in San Diego until she was 18. Her parents divorced when she was eight. She is engaged to a guy from Australia.

I said I lived in Los Angeles until I was 12. I told her I was single and came from a large family. I have seven brothers and sisters. We were laughing about how we looked the same, but how we had very different lives. Anyway, we exchanged phone numbers and said goodbye. Later on, I called my mom to check if I had a twin sister! She said I didn't.

The next day, I called the woman, and we agreed to meet for coffee. We see each other all the time now. I'm so glad I met her. In the end, she became one of my best friends. It was such an amazing coincidence that we met!

Track 08

Victor Karlsson

Meet 20-year-old Victor Karlsson from Malmo, Sweden. When Victor was eight years old, he became blind in an accident. With help from his family and friends, Victor is now a local hero in Malmo. Victor and his guide dog Charlie are helping improve the lives of blind children and adults by raising money. In 2018, Victor raised 1,500 euros walking 111 km between Malmo and Copenhagen. In 2020, he is planning to run a half-marathon. "Everyone looks up to Victor," says his friend Katya. "He's a true role model."

Petra Gonzales

Nineteen-year-old Petra Gonzales saved her sister from a fire in their home in Mexico. Petra, a university student, woke up one night to the smell of smoke. She woke up her sister. She was carrying her sister out of their apartment when she saw the fire on the other side of the house. Amazingly, firefighters arrived in time to save both girls. Petra got an award from the local mayor. "I was really scared," said Petra, "but I was just doing what any sister would do."

Mimi Kallas

While Mimi Kallas was working in a tourist office in her home town in Greece, she noticed men and women on the streets asking for food. Mimi stopped working at her job and started a food service for homeless people. She collects extra food from stores and cooks up to 100 meals a day in the kitchen of a school. She gives out the food for free to anyone who needs it. "Without Mimi, we couldn't survive," said one man. "She is an amazing woman. I'm so glad she is here to help us."

Unit 2

Track 01

Every Day Is a Holiday!

Take a look at your calendar for the year ahead. Some dates show an official event that people celebrate somewhere in the world. For example, Americans celebrate Independence Day on July 4. On October 8, the Japanese celebrate Health and Sports Day. A lot of people get the day off work, and schools and businesses are closed. People may eat special food on these days or give and receive gifts.

Then there are unofficial holidays. These are days when people sometimes arrange a party at school or at work. Unofficial holidays celebrate unimportant and fun things like food, movies, books, and TV shows.

To show you what I mean, last week, a colleague said, "It's 'Take a Selfie Day'! Today you can take a lot of selfies." In my opinion, there's too much time spent taking selfies—you don't need a special day for it!

There are a few websites that list all these celebrations. Think of any day of the year, and there is something to celebrate. I learned there are days of the year for everything: Read in the Bathtub Day (February 9), World Yoga Day (February 22), and my favorite, Make Music Day (June 21). A lot of days celebrate food, like Caesar Salad Day on July 4 and Eat a Peach Day on August 22. There are too many dates for me to remember!

I am thinking of asking my boss if I can get the day off on the second Friday of March. It's World Sleep Day. And a little advice for you—don't think of asking me to do anything on Lazy Day (August 10)!

Track 02

Jen: Do you know what I don't like?
Will: What?
Jen: Commercialization.
Will: What do you mean?
Jen: Well, it's when businesses use celebrations to make money. For example, all the things for Valentine's Day—decorations, candy, cards—are in stores in January, when the holiday is in February!
Will: And Halloween stuff is in stores in September, when the holiday is in October.
Jen: I have enough decorations. I don't need to spend money on new ones every year. It's easy to overspend.
Will: Some people waste money on crazy costumes for Halloween. One hundred dollars for a monster costume! That's too much money!
Jen: Yeah! I found a great Halloween costume for $15 online. You can find cheaper things if you shop around.
Will: That's true. I don't like commercialization. I know a few families who borrow money to pay for gifts at Christmas. They don't have enough money but feel like they have to buy things.
Jen: That's too bad. Celebrations should be a time for rest and relaxation, not stress and buying.

Track 03

Before I start cooking, I'd like to tell you a little bit about dumplings because they're a very important part of the celebration. It's traditional for families all over China to sit down together at midnight to eat them. In fact, they say that the person who eats the most dumplings will have good luck throughout the whole year!

Track 04

There are different types of dumplings, but I'm going to show you how to make fried vegetarian dumplings with mushrooms, water chestnuts, and green onions.

So for the outside of the dumplings, you will need two packages of dumpling wrappers. You can find these in Chinese markets or get them online.

Next, you need the ingredients for the inside: one can of water chestnuts, one bag of green onions, two boxes of mushrooms, and two teaspoons of Chinese spices. You also need garlic and a small bottle of oil for frying.

Now let's start cooking. Chop the water chestnuts, green onions, garlic, and mushrooms. Fry them in a little oil. Add the Chinese spices and stir. Cook for about 10 minutes until the mushrooms are soft.

Now let's wrap the dumplings. Put the dumpling wrappers in some water for 30 seconds, until they're soft. Take a little mushroom mix and put it in the center of the wrapper. Don't add too much. Fold over the edge of the wrapper and press. There you go! You should get about 30 dumplings. Fry them for a few minutes on each side.

You can also make a delicious sauce with one jar of sweet chili sauce, sesame seeds, chopped ginger, and half a bottle of soy sauce.

There you go–my delicious Chinese New Year dumplings!

Track 05

1 shop chop **2** ships chips **3** sheep cheap

Track 06

Graduation Ceremonies Around the World

Sweden

Swedish graduates wear sailor's caps to their graduation ceremony. The ceremony usually starts with singing. Parents arrive and give their children gifts tied with ribbons, and the graduates wear the ribbons around their necks. At the end of the ceremony, there is a parade through the streets of the town, and local people come to congratulate the students.

Japan

In Japan, graduation happens in March, before the new school year. High school students wear their school uniforms for their graduation ceremony. If their school doesn't have a uniform, they wear formal clothes, such as a suit for men and a kimono for women. The principal usually gives a speech. Then the student president gives a speech.

United States

In the US, it's common for a famous person (sometimes a graduate of the university) or a politician to give a speech to congratulate the graduates. In some large American universities, the ceremony happens in a sports stadium. Students normally wear special caps and gowns in the colors of their university or department.

South Africa

Graduates from the University of Witwatersrand in Johannesburg have an interesting musical tradition. The graduation ceremony there starts with a formal procession by the teachers and workers at the university. After that, they play the song "I Got You (I Feel Good)" by James Brown for the students to dance to.

Argentina

Students in Argentina usually wear old clothes for their graduation ceremony. The reason? Family and friends throw sticky or messy food at the graduates, like flour, eggs, ketchup, and soda. It's supposed to bring them good luck!

Unit 3

Track 01

Street Entertainers From Around the World

Juan Eze is a street entertainer from Buenos Aires. "Everywhere I go, people always ask me what my trick is," he says, "but I never tell anyone the secret of my act. Nobody knows." Juan sits for up to four hours at a time without moving, but says he doesn't get bored. What's amazing is that he looks like he's floating. "Everyone thinks I'm doing nothing, but I'm actually watching everything around me."

Marcel Debard, a fire-eater and acrobat, works on the streets of Casablanca. "I started performing about 15 years ago in a circus in Paris. Then someone asked me to help with the fire-eating act and I started to learn how to do it. Is it dangerous? Well, yes, but it's more dangerous for the audience. We have to make sure nobody gets hurt. That's why we blow the fire over the heads of the people."

Huang Jun does a puppet show on the streets of Yangzhou, China. "Puppets are popular forms of entertainment in China, for adults and kids," he explains. "In most puppet shows around the world, no one sees the person controlling the puppets. In Chinese puppet shows, everybody can see everything. It's part of the entertainment—to see how we make the puppets move."

Track 02

Host: As part of our look at careers in the music industry, I'm talking to music producer Scott Fleming. Scott, how did you get into the music industry? Did you use to be in a band?

Scott: Well ... no, I didn't. Actually, I started as a sound technician. I used to check the sound at music concerts. It was hard work!

Host: I bet!

Scott: Also, I used to work as a DJ in a club, and then I went into music production.

Host: And what does a music producer do?

Scott: I help bands produce their songs. We go into the studio together–me, the lead vocalist, the backup singers, the band–and record the song.

Host: And do you write the songs?

Scott: No, that's the job of the songwriter. Bands used to write their own music, but not so much these days.

Host: And what's the most important change in the music industry?

Scott: I think it's probably the importance of music videos. Before MTV started in 1981, people used to listen to music on the radio. Bands used to only record music, but with the start of MTV, they needed to make music videos too.

Host: Why?

Scott: Because the music video was important for marketing. Look at the music video for "Thriller" by Michael Jackson. It was 13 minutes long, and it changed the way people thought about music. I was 14 at the time of "Thriller." It was awesome.

Host: It seems these days people go crazy for the dances in the videos. In 2012, "Gangnam Style," a popular music video from Korea, became world famous.

Scott: Exactly. That's the power of the internet. YouTube started around 2005. Now anybody can make a music video, post it to YouTube, and become successful. People didn't use to do that.

Host: You're right. I read that "Despacito" was the first music video to have over three billion views on YouTube. That happened in August of 2017.

Scott: Yeah, amazing.

Host: Well, thanks for taking the time to talk to us, Scott.

Scott: You're welcome. Thanks for having me.

Track 03

1 A: Did you use to work in marketing?
B: No, I used to work in information technology.

2 A: Did you use to walk to the office?
B: No, I used to take the bus.

3 A: Did your parents use to own a restaurant?
B: No, they used to own a bakery.

Track 04

Speaker 1

I used to watch TV with my mom and dad, but now we all like different shows. They really like police dramas, but I think they're boring! I like streaming shows over the internet. I watch programs from all over the world. Some are in Spanish, but I watch TV shows in English too, and that helps me learn English. I love sitting on my sofa, watching TV.

Speaker 2

I don't watch a lot of TV. I'm very busy at work, so I don't have much time. When I look for things to watch, everything I like is on late at night and I go to bed early. I really like comedy shows, so I watch them on my tablet on demand. I like watching them when I'm eating breakfast. On the weekend, I sometimes binge-watch episodes of a show I like.

Speaker 3

I never watch TV. I think there are too many commercials, and I get bored waiting for them to end. I like watching stuff on YouTube, though. Or I download shows and watch those on my smartphone. I usually watch them on the bus on the way to and from school.

Speaker 4

When I was a kid, I only used to watch TV shows on Saturday mornings. We had a black and white TV. When I was about 12 we got a color one. It was great watching in color! But there used to be only a few channels, and there wasn't that much to watch. As my children grew up,

I remember watching a lot of TV shows with them. I still watch TV with my daughter or granddaughter, but we usually watch something on cable.

Track 05

Let's Go to the Movies!

Nowadays, large movie theaters (called multiplexes) are everywhere. They have many screens showing different movies. They show 2D and 3D movies. Some show IMAX movies on giant-sized screens. Some also stream live theater shows or music concerts. In addition, some movie theaters that used to sell only popcorn and candy now have restaurants or cafés where you can enjoy a meal before or after the show. Because of competition from TV movies and home entertainment, movie theaters must find new ways to get people back into their seats.

Some movie theaters now provide an experience where the audience dresses in costumes or sings along to the music. Outdoor or rooftop movie theaters are popular in some cities in the summer. You can also go to a drive-in movie theater (where you watch the movie in your car). There are about 400 drive-in movie theaters in the US today, although they're not as popular as in the 1950s and '60s.

In the past, almost everyone went to the movies. No one had a TV, so it was an exciting form of entertainment. Many beautiful movie theaters opened in the 1920s and '30s when people of all ages went to see the latest Hollywood movie on the big screen. Some of these theaters, such as the Pathé Tuschinski movie theater in Amsterdam and the Orinda Theater in California, are still open today. However, many of the old buildings that used to be movie theaters now have other uses or are closed.

Unit 4

Track 01

What's Your Personality Type?

Are you friendly and outgoing? Or are you the quiet type? Do you like to work as part of a team or do you prefer to work alone? Psychologists try to understand people by studying their personalities. Read on to find out more about four different personality types.

Type As

Type As are often successful, professional people. They are very organized and focused, and they work hard to succeed. Sometimes, they can be impatient with co-workers who aren't as hard-working as they are. They enjoy taking risks, but get stressed easily.

Type Bs

Type Bs are usually easygoing and don't get stressed. They love to spend time with friends and have fun. Usually, they're cheerful and optimistic. Their worst characteristics are that they can be lazy and take a long time to make decisions.

Type Cs

Type Cs are interested in small details and numbers. They are very good problem solvers. They like to be alone and don't always like working as part of a team. They are often shy and find it hard to communicate. Type Cs get as stressed as Type As at work. Take time to relax, Type Cs!

Type Ds

Type Ds aren't as optimistic as Type Bs. In fact, they can be very pessimistic. They often worry, see the negative side of things, and get depressed when things are hard. They like to feel comfortable and don't like to take risks. However, they are patient and hard-working.

Remember that most people are a mix of these different types. It's unusual to find a person who is only one personality type.

Track 02

Jonah isn't as good as Frida at making friends.
I think New Orleans is as interesting as New York.

Track 03

1 I don't think swimming is as difficult as skiing.
2 I'm not as cheerful as my best friend.
3 Learning grammar isn't as easy as learning vocabulary.

Track 04

Lisa: Hello everyone. I think we're ready to begin. Good afternoon and thank you for being here. There are lots of interesting presentations about teamwork this afternoon, so we're very glad you decided to come to this one.

Chris: Yes, thank you. As you can see from the slide, I'm Dr. Chris Baxter and this is my colleague Professor Lisa Perkins. We'd like to talk about working as part of a team …

Lisa: … yes, and the types of personalities you need to make your team the most successful.

Chris: I think that working as part of a team can be one of the most interesting things we do as people.

Lisa: But it's not always easy. People have very different personalities. How do you know who will work well together?

Chris: One answer is to have different types of personalities on the same team. You don't want a team where all the members are workaholics or all the members are risk takers. That is the worst mistake you can make! A good team needs different personalities and skills.

Lisa: At the start of the project, choose the leader. He or she must be the best at solving problems, helping team members communicate, and keeping the main goals in mind. A good leader also knows when to lead and when to ask others to take the lead.

Chris: Most projects also need an expert. An expert has the greatest knowledge about a subject important to the project. The expert will explain all the most important details to the team. For example, many companies have a technology expert to help their employees with new computer technology.

Lisa: Another important member of the team is the creative thinker. The creative thinker is often not the most organized person on the team. But he or she will probably have the best imagination and think of good ideas!

Chris: Remember that these ideas apply to all kinds of areas–at work for sure, but also any area where people come together as a group. That might be a book club, a band, a sports team, or even a classroom.

Track 05

Speaker 1

I think I'm really like my dad. I'm as tall as he is, and we have the same hair and eye color. We're both really bossy. That makes my sister mad! She says I'm always telling her what to do. My sister is like Mom. She looks like her too–they both have brown hair and blue eyes. Also, they are both creative; my sister is studying art and my mom makes her own clothes.

Speaker 2
We're twins, but we're not identical—we don't look like each other at all. He's got brown hair, and I'm blond. He wears glasses, and I don't. I think he looks like our dad, but I look like our mom. Our personalities are similar, though. We're both very adventurous. But I'm not as smart as my brother. He's the smartest person I know.
Speaker 3
People say I look like my aunt. We both have brown eyes and we're both small. Maybe that's why people sometimes think I am her and she is me! She's only six years older than me, so people think we're sisters. She doesn't look like my mom, so it's funny that I look like her. I'm like her in personality, too–we're both a little selfish. I think that's because we both have lots of brothers and sisters!
Speaker 4
When I was born, everyone said I looked like my grandfather! But now that I'm older, they all say I look like my dad. He's bald, and so am I. I guess I'm the tallest in the family, although my dad's tall too. Our personalities are very different. I'm easygoing, but my dad's very strict. Maybe it's because he was a teacher.

Track 06

Lana: Thanks for coming to the meeting. I made notes on the things we need to do. I think we need to focus on this year's fundraiser and organize it.
Ben: A fundraiser? We tried that last year. You know, we spent a lot of money on T-shirts, and we didn't make any money. I think that's a bad idea.
Lana: How much money did we make? And how much did we lose? Alex?
Alex: I have that information right here. We spent $456 on T-shirts, and we made $153. We had a lot of T-shirts that didn't sell. We also spent $120 on food and drink.
Marta: I think fundraisers are fun! I had a great time at the one last year and I think people enjoyed it. OK, so we didn't sell many T-shirts, but maybe we can do something different this year, like have a raffle or a popcorn stand.
Ben: A popcorn stand? I hate popcorn.
Marta: OK, maybe not popcorn. How about we sell cookies? Everyone loves cookies! I can make some.
Alex: Maybe we should find out how much the ingredients cost and how many we need to make. I'm happy to do that.
Lana: Those are all interesting ideas, but I think we need to focus on two things. First, we need to decide on a date for the fundraiser and second, which person can do which job. I think that would be very useful. Alex, take notes, please ...

Unit 5

Track 01

Clerk: Bonjour, Hôtel Paris.
Shiro: Hello. Uh ... Do you speak English?
Clerk: Of course, sir. Good morning. How can I help you?
Shiro: Good morning. My name is Shiro Ito. My wife and I have a reservation for four nights starting tomorrow, but we have a problem. Your website says that check-in time is two o'clock, but our flight arrives at eight a.m. We'd like to check in at about eleven o'clock if possible.
Clerk: We probably won't have rooms before two, but I'll check to see if any rooms might be ready early. One moment, sir ... I'm sorry, Mr. Ito, but I can't check you in at eleven. However, I can check you in at 1:30, and I can give you a voucher for a free lunch in our restaurant. They have a very nice buffet.
Shiro: That's fine, thank you. We'll eat lunch while we wait.
Clerk: Good. We'll take care of your luggage at the front desk while you have lunch. I think you'll like our restaurant. The food is excellent, and you won't feel so tired if you have some of our good French coffee!
Shiro: I'm sure we'll enjoy the meal, but I won't have coffee because I want to sleep in the afternoon.
Clerk: I understand, sir. Have a good flight, and we'll see you tomorrow.
Shiro: Thanks for your help.
Clerk: You're welcome, Mr. Ito.

Track 02

Conversation 1
Zara: OK, let's plan the party. First, the date.
Lucas: Well, the course ends on June fifth, so how about Saturday, June ninth?
Zara: That sounds good. It's going to be a big party. Where can we have it?
Mika: What about having it in the auditorium here in the institute? I think they'll give us permission to use it.
Zara: That's a good idea, Mika. Could you talk to the director about that?
Mika: Yes. I'll talk to her tomorrow morning.
Zara: Great. Thanks, Mika. What about music, food, and drinks?
Lucas: I'll bring the music. I can make playlists, and I'll bring my big speakers.
Zara: Awesome. Now, food and drinks?
Lucas: Can I make a suggestion?
Zara: Of course.
Lucas: Why don't we ask each class to bring their own food and drinks?
Zara: Perfect. Next—invitations! Lucas, you're a designer. Can you design an invitation?
Lucas: Sure, no problem.
Mika: I'll let you know about the auditorium tomorrow.
Lucas: OK. Can you text me?
Mika: Yes, of course.
Zara: OK. That's it for now. Let's meet again next week.
Conversation 2
Ms. Jenkins: Good morning, Zara.
Zara: Good morning, Ms. Jenkins. Could I talk to you for a minute?
Ms. Jenkins: Yes, of course. Come in.
Zara: Thanks. We're planning a party for the end of the course. May we use the auditorium for it?
Ms. Jenkins: When is the party?
Zara: On Saturday, June ninth.
Ms. Jenkins: We have an event in the auditorium the morning of the ninth, but you may use it in the evening.
Zara: Oh, thank you very much, Ms. Jenkins!
Ms. Jenkins: One thing, you can't stay after 10 p.m.
Zara: That's fine, but can four or five of us stay after 10 to clean up the auditorium?
Ms. Jenkins: Yes, you can. I'll let Mr. Carter know.

Zara: Thank you, Ms. Jenkins. I think it will be a great party.
Ms. Jenkins: You're welcome, Zara. Have fun!

Track 03

1 I can make a cake.
2 May I invite my boyfriend?
3 Could you help me, please?
4 I can design an invitation.
5 I won't have coffee.
6 We can't invite friends.

Track 04

Susana: I sent an RSVP to accept Amy's wedding invitation. I'm excited about her wedding!
Jessica: Me too. It's going to be fun!
Susana: Can you tell me about weddings here? I mean, what should I wear?
Jessica: Well, the wedding is in the afternoon, and it's outside, so it isn't very formal, but people usually dress up for weddings.
Susana: OK. I'll wear my new blue dress.
Jessica: Oh, yeah, that dress will be perfect.
Susana: And can you give me some ideas for a wedding gift?
Jessica: Go to the gift registry online and buy one of the gifts on the list. They'll send it to Amy's house.
Susana: Oh, that's easy. Um, am I also invited to the wedding reception?
Jessica: Of course. They're getting married at the Green River Events Center, so the reception is at the same place, right after the wedding ceremony.
Susana: Um, could I go to the wedding with you? I don't have a car.
Jessica: Sure. Rick and I will give you a ride.
Susana: Great. Thanks, Jessica.

Track 05

Social Customs in the US

When you travel to another country, it is important to understand the customs of the country. Here are some useful tips for visitors to the US.

Greetings

- When Americans meet someone for the first time, especially in business situations, they usually shake hands. Young people do not usually shake hands in informal situations. Kissing on the cheek is not a common form of greeting.
- At small social events, Americans sometimes greet each person, but normally people say hello to the group in general.
- Use a person's title (Mr., Ms., Dr.) and last name in business situations or when the other person is much older than you. Never use a title with a first name.

Social Events

- Do not accept an invitation to an event if you don't plan to go. Simply say something like, "I'm sorry, but I have plans that evening. Thanks for the invitation."
- For a dinner party, arrive on time or no more than 5 or 10 minutes late. For an informal party, you can arrive and leave at any time.
- It is typical to take a small gift like flowers or chocolate to a dinner party but not to more informal events.

Food and Restaurants

- In restaurants, Americans often divide the bill so that everyone pays an equal part. If someone says, "My treat," or "I'll get it," that person will pay the bill. Don't argue. Just thank the person.
- If you invite someone to go out to eat, ask if there are foods that they can't eat or don't like before you choose a restaurant.
- Americans often have potluck dinners. This means that everyone brings a large dish to share.

Tipping

- In the US, the normal amount to tip in a restaurant is about 15%, but 20% is common in a very good restaurant. You don't have to tip in fast-food or self-service restaurants. For groups of six people or more, restaurants sometimes add the tip to the bill.
- It is common to tip taxi drivers about 15%.
- In hotels, tip car valets and bellhops $2.00 to $3.00.

Unit 6

Track 01

The Status Quo Bias—Why People Don't Like Change!

If you prefer the status quo, you don't like change. You prefer things to stay the same. Psychologists call this the status quo bias. Many people have a status quo bias, but some people really like change.

Joe and Elena are both 35 years old, but they have very different attitudes about change. Joe has lived in the same city in the same apartment since 2005. He has been with the same company for 12 years. He hasn't bought a new phone for five years, and he has had his car since 2010. Elena has moved three times in the past two years, and she has had four different jobs since 2012. She has worked in her current job for two years, but she thinks she'll probably look for a new job next year.

There are some advantages to the status quo. Life is less stressful in your comfort zone. You feel that you are in control because everything is familiar. There are no risks!

However, it can be a good idea to leave your comfort zone and take some risks. This can help you in your professional and personal life. How long have you had the same job? Are there other jobs that pay better or are more interesting? Do you sometimes feel bored with your living situation or your social life? How many times have you eaten at the same restaurant, listened to the same music, gone to the same places on the weekend? If the answer is "a lot," try making a few small changes. Go ahead, order something different the next time you go to that restaurant!

Track 02

1 I've studied English for several years.
2 You've been here since four o'clock.
3 She's lived here since November.
4 It's been very hot outside for two weeks.
5 We've been in class for 45 minutes.
6 They've worked here for a long time.

Track 03

Craig: Good morning, and welcome to *Consider This*. I'm your host, Craig Smith. Today my guests and I are talking about our bucket lists. A bucket list is a list of things that you want to do before a certain age or during your life. For example, I've never flown in a helicopter, and I would like to do that. Jake and Laura, have you ever flown in a helicopter?
Jake: No, I haven't, but I've flown in a small plane. It's pretty cool.

Laura: I have. It's really fun because you have a great view of everything.
Craig: What are some of the things on your bucket lists?
Jake: Well, I've never really thought about a bucket list, but you know, I really like singing, and I'm a pretty good singer. I think I'd like to sing at an open-mic session. And … I've never been to Washington, D.C. It's the capital of my country, so I'd like to do that.
Laura: I really like cars, and I've never driven a sports car. I would love to drive something like a Porsche or a Maserati.
Craig: Wow, that's interesting! OK, after a commercial break, I'm going to talk about how to make a bucket list.

Track 04

I have a couple of tips for making a bucket list. First, try to be realistic. Your list should include things that you think are possible. For example, traveling into space is probably not possible, so traveling to Europe is probably a better option. Next, don't include too many things on your list. You probably won't have time to do all the things on a very long list. One idea is to have one or two big things, like traveling around the world, and several smaller things, like buying a car or moving to another city. Thanks for listening, and good luck with your bucket list!

Track 05

Host: Good afternoon. For today's episode of *Changing Cities*, I'm in Pittsburgh, Pennsylvania. Thanks for inviting me to visit your hometown, Amy. It's beautiful here!
Amy: Yes, it's beautiful now, but it has changed a lot.
Host: Really? How has it changed?
Amy: Pittsburgh was a very industrial city in the past, and it was really polluted. They've really cleaned it up.
Host: Oh, wow. How long has it been this way?
Amy: Since the 1980s, I think. That's when the factories closed and the city started to change.
Host: So what kinds of changes have happened?
Amy: Oh, lots of things. They've created a lot of green spaces with walking trails and playgrounds. They've also put in pedestrian areas and created bike lanes, so now people walk and bike a lot more.
Host: That's really cool. Hey, what are all those people doing around that truck?
Amy: Oh, that's a food truck. Do you have those in your city?
Host: No, we don't.
Amy: Food trucks have become very popular in the US. They have lots of different kinds of food, and it's fast and not very expensive.
Host: That's a great idea!
Amy: That truck has Chinese food. Do you want some?
Host: Yeah, I'm hungry!

Track 06

Guest Opinion: Tourist in Your Own Town

By Lynn Williams

I have decided to become a tourist in my own town and the areas near my town. I read an article that said that many people do not know their own towns, and I thought, "That's me!" I've lived here for 15 years, but I always do the same things and go to the same places. I did some research about activities and places in and near my town, and I've made a list of things that I've never done, or that I haven't done in a long time:

- I've never gone to a high school sports event.
- I've been to the history museum only once, several years ago.
- I've never seen the sunset from Pine Mountain.
- There are about 20 restaurants that I've never tried.
- I've never shopped in the farmer's market.
- I haven't taken a walk on the trail next to the river in five years.

Those are only a few of the things on my list. I imagine that it's the same for almost everyone. We all have our routines, and we never do or see a lot of the fun, interesting things near us. So start a sentence with "I've never …" and see how many ways you can complete it. Do some research to find out what there is to do and see in your area. Then go out and become a tourist in your own town!

Unit 7

Track 01

How Career-Ready Are You?

Have you started your career yet? If you have just started working, you are probably very happy and are learning a lot about your job. However, if you have already worked for a while, you are probably thinking about how to improve your career options. If you haven't started working yet, you are probably thinking about what kind of career you want. It is always a good idea to think about the next step in your working life.

First, it is important to understand that being career-ready refers to more than training and knowledge about a job or a career. It refers to a combination of knowledge, skills, and personal characteristics.

Knowledge includes the academic or technical information that you need for a career area or a specific job, but it also includes other types of knowledge. For example, you may need general math skills or a good level of English.

Skills include specific technical skills, but they also include skills like using your time well, the ability to communicate, and working in a team. One of the most important skills today is the ability to solve problems.

Finally, you need to understand what personal characteristics and personality types are ideal for different jobs and careers. Some people with excellent academic qualifications are unhappy in their careers because their jobs don't really match their personalities.

It doesn't matter if you have just graduated from high school or college, haven't graduated yet, or already have a job; you should take some time to think about your future. How career-ready are you?

Track 02

yard, year, yellow, yes, yesterday, yet, you, young; jacket, jet, job, John, juice, Julie, jump, just

Track 03

1 Julie bought a yellow jacket yesterday.
2 Yes, you can have some juice.
3 Have you met John yet?
4 James has just started a new job in New York.

Track 04

Host: Welcome to *Our Community*. I'm interviewing Carmen Vega, a very successful entrepreneur in our community. Carmen is the owner of That's Cool!, the most popular ice cream shop in town. Carmen, how long has the shop been in business?

Carmen: I've been in business for five years now. When I started, I hired one employee. I made the ice cream and she served the customers.

Host: That's Cool! is now the number one ice cream shop in the community. Why have you been so successful?

Carmen: That's simple. We have great ice cream!

Host: The ice cream is fantastic, but for a business to succeed, it also needs good management. Do you have a degree in business?

Carmen: No, I don't. I started college, majoring in architecture, but I didn't graduate.

Host: What happened?

Carmen: Well, one summer I was bored, so I took a class to learn how to make ice cream. I loved it! I made about twenty kinds of ice cream that summer.

Host: Is that when you started the business?

Carmen: No. I went back to college in the fall, but I really wasn't very interested in it. Then my sister said, "Why don't you try to sell your ice cream?" I thought it was an excellent idea, so when school was out in the spring, I opened the ice cream shop. I never went back to college.

Host: Do you like owning your own business?

Carmen: I love it! I didn't have to apply for a job, try to get a raise or a promotion, or climb the corporate ladder.

Host: Well, you've had an interesting career path. How many ice cream flavors have you invented so far?

Carmen: I'm not sure, but more than twenty, I think. I've just created a new flavor called Orange Chill. It has green chilies and oranges.

Host: Oh, wow! Have you started selling it yet?

Carmen: Yes, we have. We started selling it last week, and we've already sold out!

Host: Carmen, thanks for talking to me, and congratulations on your success.

Carmen: Thank you.

Track 05

Nick: Good morning. I'm your host, Nick Walker, and the topic of our talk today is getting a job in the 21st century. Please welcome Barbara Nelson, from Job Search Consultants. Barbara, can you explain what 21st century employability skills are?

Barbara: Yes, of course. In the past, employers usually looked at two things, college degrees and work experience, but that has changed. Now employers want to hire people who also have other skills, and sometimes those skills are more important.

Nick: That's interesting. Is it possible that someone who is, for example, very organized, creative, and motivated could get a better job than someone with a degree from a good university?

Barbara: Definitely. Let me give you an example. I had two good candidates for a job as finance manager for a big company. I'll call them Joe and James. Joe had a master's degree in finance from a very good university. James didn't have a master's, and he went to an average university.

Nick: Let me guess. James got the job.

Barbara: Yes, he did. Joe had good technical knowledge, but a manager has to work with people, and James had better interpersonal skills. He showed that he was flexible and enjoyed working in a team. He was also curious, and he asked a lot of interesting questions about the bank and its employees. Finally, he seemed more motivated to learn new things and try creative ways to solve problems.

Nick: So if you're flexible, motivated, curious, and creative, you can sometimes stand out more than someone with only excellent academic qualifications or a lot of work experience.

Barbara: That's right. Of course, it's best to have excellent skills and great qualifications.

Nick: Sure. Barbara, thank you for this important information.

Barbara: You're welcome, Nick.

Track 06

Turn Skills into Sales

Have you ever thought about starting your own business? These days, more and more young people are doing just that. There are many types of businesses that are not very expensive to start. Often you just need a computer, but you also need to be motivated and patient because starting a business takes a lot of time and hard work.

There are several areas that offer good business opportunities for young people.

- If you are creative, make handmade items: clothes, jewelry, soap, hand-painted T-shirts, origami designs, or greeting cards.
- Are you good at photography? Take pictures and sell them to online stock photo companies. Take photos or make videos of weddings, family reunions, or community events. Start a pet portrait business.
- Can you cook? Make cookies or cupcakes to sell to friends, at community events, or online.
- Do you love animals? Think about dog walking or pet sitting. You can also make different flavors of dog treats.
- If you have good computer skills, there are many possibilities for making money. Start a device setup service to help people get started with new computers, tablets, phones, or any other device. Become a tech tutor to teach children or older people how to use computers.
- Do you like public speaking, writing, or performing? If you have interesting things to say, you can start a blog or a vlog and get money from advertisers. Maybe you can become a video personality, or create videos to teach people how to do things.
- Finally, one of the easiest ways to make money is to sell things online. Sell items that your family doesn't use anymore, and buy things online or at garage sales and resell them.

Unit 8

Track 01

Kids + Adults = Kidults

Adults like having toys—no, not boats, sports equipment, or expensive audio equipment, but actual children's toys. They are making things with building blocks, coloring in coloring books, making art with 3D pens, and doing difficult puzzles; they are bouncing inside enormous plastic balls and flying kites. There is a new term for adults who love playing like children: *kidults*.

Why is this happening? Experts think that in part it is because people, especially millennials, want an escape from the complications of the modern world. Acting like a child is a way to return to a simpler time, but there is another reason for this trend. Doing kids' activities is fun! Why shouldn't adults enjoy doing things like flying kites or coloring?

People over 50 also spend time doing children's activities. Many grandparents are very healthy and active, and they love playing with their grandchildren. Seniors are playing board games, doing arts and crafts, and participating in other activities that kids love.

Being an adult doesn't mean that you have to be serious all the time or pay a lot of money for entertainment. Are you creative? Try building a model or making a sculpture with clay. Maybe you love being active, but you can't stand playing competitive sports. Try jumping rope or flying a kite. Find your inner child and enjoy being a kidult!

Track 02

Marta: Yay, today's Friday!
Ken: Yeah! What do you guys want to do this weekend? Kate?
Kate: I want to do something different. We always do the same stuff – go to a movie or hang out at somebody's house. Doing the same things all the time is boring!
Stefan: Kate's right. Why don't we actually make a plan for the whole weekend?
Marta: Great idea! OK, what do we all like doing? I love going out to hear live music. I'd like to do that Saturday night.
Ken: Sure. Live music is a good idea.
Stefan: Cool. I'll find out who's playing at the clubs. What about during the day?
Kate: I'd like to do something creative. There are one-day classes in arts and crafts at the community center. You can learn how to make something, like candles or simple jewelry.
Ken: I don't know. I'd rather do a physical activity. I don't really like doing arts and crafts.
Marta: I know! Let's go paddle boarding on the river.
Ken: Paddle boarding is an awesome idea! Stefan and Kate? What do you guys think?
Stefan: Sure. Let's go for it. I prefer doing physical activities, too.
Kate: Fine with me. So Saturday is paddle boarding and then live music in the evening. What about Sunday?
Stefan: Why don't we have a picnic? We can go for a drive and look for a nice place to spend the morning.
Ken: OK, but I would prefer to do it later in the day. I hate getting up early on Sunday!
Kate: That sounds good. I'd prefer to go later, too.
Stefan: So do we have a plan, or would you rather think of some other options?
Marta: I'm fine with this plan.
Ken: Me, too.
Kate: That sounds good. It will be fun and different.

Track 03

Omar: Would you like to go to the new museum tomorrow?
Jamal: That sounds great. We should go early, when there are fewer people.
Omar: Actually, I would rather go in the afternoon. Is that OK?
Jamal: That's fine. Could you pick me up?
Omar: Sure.

Track 04

Professor: Good morning. I have a question for you. How often do you do nothing, and how do you feel when you are doing nothing?
Noah: I get bored. I would rather be busy all the time.
Tasha: Yeah, I agree. If I sit around and do nothing, I feel guilty. I prefer to finish everything I have to do.
Paul: Wow, I totally disagree. I think doing nothing helps you relax, so when you start working or studying, you feel rested. I often take a break to sit in the park or just lie on the sofa.
Magda: I agree about relaxing, but I'd rather watch a movie or read a book. To me, that's doing nothing. It makes me nervous to do absolutely nothing.
Professor: OK, how many think that things like reading or checking your social media are doing nothing? OK, about half the class. How many think that doing nothing is bad? More than half.
Paul: So, Professor Nelson, is it bad to do nothing?
Professor: Not necessarily. In fact, a lot of psychologists say that doing nothing is healthy. Being busy all the time is stressful, and it's hard to work or study well when you're stressed. Also, doing nothing helps you be more creative, and that helps you solve problems.
Magda: So, Professor Nelson, can our homework be to do nothing?
Professor: Yes, it can! Actually, your homework for next class is to take some time to do nothing, at least one hour, and I mean absolutely nothing. No social media, TV, reading, or whatever. Just do nothing. After one hour, write down what you were thinking and feeling while you were doing nothing. Was it a positive or a negative experience?

Track 05

Mindfulness for Mental Relaxation

Study, work, family, friends, pets, social media … We feel tired and stressed because we can't do everything. The effects of this are that we are less efficient, less creative, and less happy. We all try to do leisure activities like playing sports or watching movies, but what about leisure time for the mind?

In recent years, many people have started to practice *mindfulness*. Being mindful means that you are paying attention to what you are doing at the moment, to your feelings, and to the things that are happening around you. You are not thinking about things that have already happened or worrying about what is going to happen. For example, if you notice how the sun feels on your face, or how your clean clothes smell, you are being mindful.

There are some simple things that you can do to practice mindfulness. Do you like walking? Go for a walk, but don't think about walking fast or going a certain distance. Walk slowly. Think about how your body feels. Stop and look at trees or flowers. Stop and close your eyes. What do you hear, feel, or smell? Would you rather do something creative? Paint something or do a craft. Don't worry if it isn't good. Think about the process. How does the paintbrush feel in your hand? What does each color make you think of? Giving your brain time to relax can help you feel less stressed and more rested. The result is more creativity and better problem solving.

Unit 9

Track 01

Housing Solutions

In many areas, people can't afford to buy or rent a place to live. It's a problem that will become worse in the future. Some cities have found interesting solutions.

One example is half-houses in Chile. An earthquake hit the town of Constitución in 2010 and destroyed about 80% of the buildings. The local government hired an architecture firm to provide low-cost houses. They built houses that are only half-finished. The owners finish the house when they have the money. It means that each family can decide what they need: a garage, another bedroom, a hall, a balcony. One resident says: "We're going to build another bedroom and bathroom in two years. We can add our personal style."

Another solution is micro-units, like those at Carmel Place in New York City. These are very small apartments, around 28 square meters. They are too small for a family, but perfect for single young professionals. Each one-room apartment has the usual appliances—a stove, a refrigerator, and a microwave—and there's a room in another part of the building for washing clothes. The smart use of special furniture means the room can become a bedroom, kitchen, office, or living room. The desk becomes a dining table and the couch becomes a bed. The coffee table folds down and goes under the bed at night. A young resident says: "I'm having a friend over for dinner tonight. I just turn the bed into a couch, the desk into a table, and we're good to go!"

Track 02

Ethan: We graduate this summer, Ashley. I'm going to start apartment hunting. Where do you think you might live next year?

Ashley: Oh, I don't know. I want a job in finance, so maybe I'll live in an apartment near the financial district. If I don't find a job, I won't be able to afford it. And I might still be at home with my mom and dad. And that's fine. I like living with them.

Ethan: You could live with a friend. My brother and a couple of friends rent an apartment together. They have their own bedrooms and they share a living room, kitchen, and bathroom. They share the bills and the chores.

Ashley: I'd like to have roommates, but renting is so expensive. I probably won't be able to afford that.

Ethan: You may find something cheap outside the city. But then you have the problem of traveling into the city every day for work.

Ashley: What about you?

Ethan: I can't wait to have my own place. If I find a good job, I might rent a studio apartment downtown. I'd like to be downtown because I'd be close to all the restaurants and places to go.

Ashley: That sounds great, but you might get lonely living alone. You should think about renting a room in a house. And won't you miss living with your family?

Ethan: I will definitely miss them! But they could come and see me. I think I might ask my brother what it's like. Maybe I could live with him!

Ashley: Good idea!

Track 03

1	/aʊ/ like *house*:	allow	found	now	sound
2	/oʊ/ like *go*:	below	know	own	phone

Track 04

Hello, everyone. Today, I want to talk about the future of our homes. We're going to see many changes in our homes, but I'd like to focus on energy. The appliances in our houses, such as air conditioners and heaters, use a lot of energy. In the future, more and more people are going to be using renewable energy such as wind power, wave power, and solar power.

Here's a diagram explaining how solar power works. On the roof of the house, we have solar panels. These receive sunlight on sunny days. The light falls on special materials, which create electricity. This electricity is direct current, or DC. That goes to the inverter from the solar panels. The inverter changes the DC into AC, or alternating current. It then sends the electricity to the appliances in the house. Things like your kitchen stove, dishwasher, and washing machine need AC to work.

Sometimes, the system creates a lot of energy. In that case, the electrical grid takes the power that the house doesn't need. That way, other houses can use the electricity. And on days when there is no sun, the grid provides the house with power.

In the future, we might see solar windows on buildings. We could also see solar clothes or solar sunglasses. You wear them and they work like solar panels, creating energy to power your devices.

Track 05

Neighborhood Development

Neighborhoods are changing all the time. That means someone has to make decisions about these changes. It might be urban planners or members of local government. They often have to decide between different plans for a neighborhood. They may have to think about costs, housing, and the needs of local people. How do they make their decisions?

One tool to help planners make a decision is a decision matrix. In a decision matrix, they list the important results they want for the neighborhood. For example, local people may want more houses, less traffic, or more parks. Planners develop several plans to get these results. They then score each plan against each result: –2 for a very negative effect, –1 for a negative effect, 0 for no effect, +1 for a positive effect, and +2 for a very positive effect. The plan with the highest total score is the one to choose.

People can use a decision matrix to help with all kinds of decisions, from large business decisions to personal decisions like making a budget or planning a vacation.

Unit 10

Track 01

3 Ways to Power Up Your Brain!

How can you help your brain to work better? Here is some advice from the experts.

- Get healthy

One way to help your brain is to get healthy by exercising more and eating better. In one study, people had a better memory after six weeks of physical training. Some studies found that if you exercise for 10 minutes before thinking about a problem, it improves your problem-solving and decision-making skills. Your diet is also important. Vitamins and minerals from food—like fish, vegetables, and nuts—help keep your brain healthy.

- Sleep better

Sleep isn't just rest for the body. It also rests your brain. During sleep, your brain organizes your experiences, often through dreams. When you are learning new skills, you actually get better at them while you sleep! Sleep helps you think clearly while you're awake. Most people who sleep only four to six hours in one night don't think clearly the next day.

- Keep learning

Your brain can change, something known as neuroplasticity. If you challenge your brain, it will develop more connections between its neurons. One thing you can do to challenge your brain is to learn a new skill, such as a new language or a musical instrument. Some people enjoy brain training—online sites and apps that use puzzles or other tasks to exercise your brain. Many of these sites and apps don't have much effect on the brain, and they certainly won't make you more intelligent. However, psychologists have created some types of puzzles that make your brain work faster. Doing these tasks makes some people feel sharper in their everyday lives.

Track 02

Dan: Hello, I'm Dan Foster. This week, our guest is Madison Gray. Madison is a nurse, and she's going to be talking to me about being ready for accidents. Madison, what's the first thing we should know about accidents?

Madison: The most important thing is to have some basic training in first aid for common accidents. If you saw someone trip and fall while walking on the sidewalk, what would you do?

Dan: I guess I would help the person up.

Madison: That's not a good idea. If the person was injured, you could make the injury worse. First, I would see if he or she was awake. If the answer was yes, I would ask the person how he or she felt. I would check for injuries like a broken wrist or a sprained ankle. Then I might help the person sit up, and if that was OK, I'd help the person stand.

Dan: And what if the person wasn't awake?

Madison: Then I would see if he or she was breathing. If not, I'd do CPR and call an ambulance. If the person was breathing, I would try to make him or her comfortable. Then I would call an ambulance.

Dan: OK. What about something like a broken arm?

Madison: First, I would check for any cuts. It's important to stop any bleeding first because you can lose a lot of blood very quickly. If there were any cuts, I would press on them with a clean cloth. Then I would find a way to keep the arm from moving. If I could, I would put ice on the arm for the pain. Finally, I would call an ambulance.

Dan: We'll be back with more from Madison after these messages.

Track 03

If I had a cough, I would buy some medicine.

Track 04

1 If I broke my leg, I would call an ambulance.
2 If I had a rash, I'd search for information online.
3 If I sprained my ankle, I'd ask a friend for help.

Track 05

Aiden: Hi, Emily!

Emily: Hi, Aiden. Hey, you look like you're going to go running. I didn't know you were a fitness fanatic!

Aiden: I wasn't a fitness fanatic. I used to just sit in front of the TV when I got home from work, but I really needed to change that.

Emily: So you're running now?

Aiden: Well, yeah. There's a new program, called Couch to 5K. It's for people who want to get fit but don't know where to start. They take you from lying on the couch to running five kilometers in just nine weeks.

Emily: Sounds interesting! What did you have to do to get ready to run that much?

Aiden: Before I got started, I went to my doctor for a check-up. He said I was good to go and could get started any time.

Emily: So you just started running?

Aiden: Not exactly. In the first week of the program, I did three runs. On each run, I ran for one minute and then walked for a minute and a half. And each week, the program says to run just a little longer, and then walk. I'm only on Week 5, but after nine weeks, I'll run for 30 minutes and do five kilometers.

Emily: That sounds like a good way to get fit. I think even I could do that! What else do you have to do?

Aiden: You can get apps to help you improve your diet. You enter what food you eat and it tells you about the calories, the protein, that kind of thing. If you eat the right things, it means you won't get tired when you're exercising.

Emily: I might try it. Enjoy your run, and I'll call you later. You can tell me more about it.

Aiden: OK. See you later.

Track 06

Public Health

Many countries face serious public health problems. One example is obesity. According to the Organisation for Economic Co-operation and Development, one in two adults and nearly one in six children in its member countries are overweight or obese. That puts pressure on health services. Some countries are looking at ways of improving public health.

One way is to encourage people to eat better. Some countries, such as the United States and the United Kingdom, have five-a-day campaigns. They tell people that they should eat five portions of fruit or vegetables each day. Many countries have laws about labels on food. Producers have to show the amount of fat, protein, and carbohydrates in each food. Some countries have a "traffic light" system. Green means the food has a small amount of fat, sugar, and salt. Yellow means the food has a medium amount. Red means there's a high amount of fat, sugar, or salt. The labels help people make better choices.

Public health departments are always looking for new ideas to improve public health.

Unit 11

Track 01

From Seed to T-shirt

T-shirts are a basic part of almost everyone's closet. Over two billion T-shirts are sold every year around the world. So how are they made? And where do they end up?

The story starts with the seed of the cotton plant. The plants are grown on large farms. The cotton is collected and sent to a factory. There, it is cleaned and made into yarn. The yarn is made into cloth. This is used to make T-shirts.

The T-shirts are then transported around the world. Just take a look at the label on one of your T-shirts and see how far it came! The T-shirts go into stores and are sold to consumers. That's you. You probably have the T-shirt for a while, and it is worn, washed, and dried again and again. When you decide to get rid of it, you have a few options. You might throw it in the trash. But if you knew how much of the Earth's natural resources go into making a T-shirt, you might think again! A lot of energy and water are used in making and washing clothes. A lot of chemicals are used in this process, too.

One option is to recycle your old T-shirts. When a T-shirt is sent to a recycling center, it is made into other things, such as cleaning cloths. Another idea is to upcycle your T-shirts. Old T-shirts are sometimes made into belts, scarves, or bags.

Track 02

castle whistle wrestle fasten listen soften

Track 03

1 Listen to the way he whistles.
2 You fasten and unfasten the jacket with a zipper.
3 Chemicals are used to soften the cloth.

Track 04

Ryan: My next guest is Angela Miller, and she's here today to talk to us about lucky discoveries. Welcome, Angela. What lucky discovery are you going to tell us about?
Angela: I'm here today to tell you about this material, Ryan.
Ryan: I know that sound. It's Velcro.
Angela: That's right. And did you know that Velcro was invented by a dog?
Ryan: By a dog?!
Angela: Well, almost. Swiss engineer George de Mestral was out with his dog in 1941, and he noticed that some plants stuck to his dog's fur like glue.
Ryan: I know the kind of plant you mean. They're round and sticky.
Angela: Yes. They're called burrs. De Mestral noticed that his dog was covered in burrs. His pants were also covered in them. When he got home, he looked at the plants under a microscope and saw that they had tiny hooks. The fur, and the material of his pants, had small loops. His dog's fur and his pants were caught by the hooks.
Ryan: How was Velcro created from that idea?
Angela: At the time, clothes were made with buttons and zippers. De Mestral wanted to create a new material so people wouldn't need buttons and zippers. It wasn't easy, and it took some time to develop a commercial product, but, after ten years, Velcro was finally created. In the early days, Velcro was made of cotton, but nylon worked better.
Ryan: What was it used for in those days?
Angela: It was used on clothes and bags. It became popular after it was used in space by NASA in the 1960s. It was used by astronauts to hold things in place.
Ryan: Now you can see sneakers that fasten with Velcro. When did it appear on sneakers?
Angela: It was first used on children's sneakers in the 1980s. It's great for children and disabled people because it's very easy to fasten and unfasten.
Ryan: I guess the lesson is to always keep your eyes open because you never know what you might discover. Angela, thank you for joining us today.

Track 05

In today's lecture, I want to tell you about Thato Kgatlhanye. Thato is a young businesswoman from South Africa. She noticed that many poor schoolchildren in South Africa face some problems. First of all, school is often a long way from home. Each morning and evening, these children have to walk many kilometers to school and back again. It is dangerous because there are a lot of cars and trucks on the roads. Second, their homes often don't have electricity. When they get home, they find it difficult to study in the dark.

Track 06

Thato also realized that South Africa has a problem with plastic bags. A lot of plastic bags are thrown away and end up as trash in the streets. In fact, children often carry their books to school in simple plastic bags. Thato thought that she could solve both of these problems. She decided to create schoolbags from recycled plastic bags. They are called Repurpose Schoolbags.

Repurpose Schoolbags were designed to help schoolchildren. They have a solar panel, a battery, and a light. The battery is charged during the day and it powers the light at night. That means that children can do their homework after the sun goes down. They no longer have to hurry home. The bags are also reflective. That means drivers can see the children as they walk along the busy roads. The children are safer. Thato is just one of the many young inventors trying to make life better in Africa.

Track 07

Upcycling Projects

We humans use a lot of materials. Take plastic, for example.

According to Statista, every year, around 350 million metric tons of plastic are produced around the world. Sadly, not much of it is recycled. In fact, about half of the plastic is used just once and is then sent to a landfill, according to Plastic Oceans International. In 2007, Charles Fishman of *Fast Company Magazine* reported that a million plastic bottles are bought every minute of every day in the US, but only around 23% are recycled. Four trillion plastic bags are produced each year, and only 1% are recycled, according to Waste Management. Our use of other plastics is not much better. Plastic use is a big problem.

Many people are looking at ways to upcycle different materials. Upcycling involves finding new uses for materials at the end of their original use. In one project, a greenhouse was created using old plastic water bottles. In others, large coffee cans or old rubber boots were turned into containers for plants, and old rubber tires became notebook covers. Artists, too, upcycle materials. Tim Noble and Sue Webster, two British artists, create what look like piles of trash. When a light shines on the trash from a certain angle, it makes an interesting shadow on the wall.

These days institutions such as colleges and companies are looking for smarter ways to use materials. This involves reducing the amount of materials they use and thinking of ways to upcycle materials so that they last a long time.

Unit 12

Track 01

Types of Community

We all belong to different social groups. We choose some of them ourselves, and some of them are chosen for us. The social groups we belong to often give us support. They also say a lot about who we are and how we see ourselves.

There are many different types of community. One type is community of place. The place could be a neighborhood, a region, or a country. A second is community of interest. The people might all be interested in a certain hobby or a certain type of music, for example. A third is community of purpose. People in this type of community share the same purpose, such as learning a language or running a successful company. A fourth is community of practice. This is a group of people who share the same profession.

Each type of community can offer different things to its members. A community of place might offer people to chat with and to support you in difficult times. A community of interest can give you friendship and a way to learn more about a subject. A community of purpose can help you learn ways of achieving your goals. Also, people working together can often achieve more than a person working by himself or herself. A community of practice gives you opportunities to share ideas as well as the chance to network.

Any particular group might be more than one type of community. For example, a local cycling club is a community of place and a community of interest. If the members decided to raise money for a local charity, they would also be a community of purpose.

Track 02

1 self **3** herself **5** show
2 your shelf **4** sock **6** shine

Track 03

Host: Welcome to the show. Today I'm talking to Sean Johnson. Sean's the head of an employment agency and he's going to talk to us about networking. Sean, what is networking?

Sean: Networking is speaking to people in your profession. This gives you a community of practice.

Host: Tell us where we can network and how.

Sean: If you're working, you can start with your office. Try to make time to speak to everyone. If there's someone you haven't met, introduce yourself. Get to know each person. Ask about his or her job. You'll be surprised how much you can learn just from chatting with people.

Host: What if you don't have a job yet?

Sean: You can start to find contacts in your chosen profession. Start with friends and family. Maybe you already know someone who works in an area you are interested in. Think about people you knew in college. What are they doing now? Maybe they can help you when you are job hunting. That's a good example of why you should always stay in touch with people from high school when you go to college, or with old colleagues when you start a new job.

Host: What about online groups?

Sean: They can be a great way of sharing ideas. Find a group connected to the profession you want. Ask questions, join discussions, and comment on posts. You'll learn about your profession and get to know people. You might even hear about job opportunities before other people do.

Host: Does all networking happen online?

Sean: Not at all. Your college might organize a career fair when companies come to campus. That's a good chance to speak to people in your future profession. You can also contact companies directly and ask about opportunities to work as an intern. You don't always get paid, but you get a lot of experience. Another interesting option is speed networking. Some colleges and companies organize these events. You have a few minutes to talk to one person, then everyone changes partners. That way, you can make a lot of useful connections in a very short time.

Host: Thanks, Sean. So what do you think about networking? Call us now and tell us.

Track 04

Hello and welcome to today's podcast. I want to talk to you today about different social groups. You might see people who wear dark clothes, dark make-up, and call themselves *goths*. Others, such as *otakus*, might dress as characters from comics or video games. We call these youth subcultures, or youth tribes. They often have one thing in common. You can see who is a part of the group by looking at them. They dress differently from other young people. There are three reasons for this.

First, many young people want to look different from their parents to show that they are a new generation. This has been true for decades. American teenagers in the 1940s started to wear jeans and T-shirts when their parents often wore shirts and ties. It was a way of saying: "We're here, and we're different."

At the same time, young people want to feel like part of a group. They want to spend time with other young people who share their opinions and beliefs. When you are part of a youth tribe, you can see who is like you and who is different, even if you've never met them before. If they are in the same youth tribe, they probably have the same interests as you.

Finally, young people want to express their personality. They choose a sub-culture that shows who they are. And, of course, that can change. Today's goth might be tomorrow's hipster. So, what do you think of youth subcultures? Contact me and I'll read some of your comments on the next podcast.

Track 05

Reaching a Target Group

Sometimes, a business has a product that it wants to sell to a certain group of people. For example, there is no point advertising a new car to people who don't drive. Governments, too, sometimes want to get information to a specific group. This might be information about children's health that they want to give to parents. In both cases, it would be a waste of money to inform everyone. It's better to aim your message at the people you want to reach. How do you do that?

First of all, it's important to clearly identify the group of people you want to reach. Is it parents? Is it teenagers? Is it homeowners? When you have a clear idea of your target group, then you can think about how to reach people in the group.

Second, you need to think about how to communicate with that group. Teenagers and young adults spend time on social networks. That might be the best way to reach them. It might not work so well for senior citizens or other groups.

Third, you need to express your message in the right way. With professional people, you may want to use serious language. With teenagers, you may want to use slang or informal language.

When you aim your message at a clear target group and use the right form of communication, your message is more effective.

Workbook Answer Key

Unit 1

Lesson 1

READING A 1 True 2 False 3 True 4 True 5 False 6 False

READING B 1 role model 2 October 7, 1955 3 seven 4 Harvard University 5 German and anthropology 6 14 Grammy awards 7 Petunia 8 (very large) insects 9 sign

VOCABULARY A 1 insect 2 emigrated 3 focus on 4 improve 5 revealed 6 successful 7 look up to 8 role

GRAMMAR A 1 was 2 were 3 was 4 wasn't 5 weren't 6 wasn't 7 Was 8 Were 9 Was

GRAMMAR B 1 was 2 were 3 wasn't 4 Were 5 living

GRAMMAR C 1 was listening 2 were performing 3 weren't starring 4 Were … practicing 5 wasn't reading 6 were studying

GRAMMAR D 1 doing 2 watching 3 studying 4 walking 5 looking 6 thinking

Lesson 2

VOCABULARY A 1 thrilled 2 disappointed 3 scared 4 confused 5 glad 6 worried

VOCABULARY B 1 glad, thrilled 2 confused, disappointed, scared, worried

LISTENING A 1 c 2 b 3 a

LISTENING B 1 essay 2 200 (two hundred) 3 disappointed 4 fifth 5 Mars 6 4 (four) 7 3 (three)

GRAMMAR A 1 past progressive 2 simple past 3 when 4 while 5 beginning 6 end

GRAMMAR B 1 was performing, began 2 walked, wasn't working 3 were packing, stopped 4 stole, was looking 5 were enjoying, made 6 drove, were eating

GRAMMAR C 1 was preparing 2 rang 3 were waiting 4 wrote 5 was searching 6 realized 7 were asking 8 didn't come

GRAMMAR D 1 was becoming, became 2 was jumping, jumped 3 house they, house, they 4 while, when 5 didn't watch, weren't watching 6 read, was reading

Lesson 3

VOCABULARY A 1 an only child 2 engaged 3 divorced 4 a large family 5 twins 6 adopted 7 is a single parent 8 single

VOCABULARY B 1 twins, an only child, adopted 2 engaged, single parent, divorced, single 3 large family

LISTENING A b

WRITING A 1, 3, 4, 5, 6, 8

WRITING B 1 b 2 f 3 c 4 a 5 e 6 d 7 g

Unit 2

Lesson 1

READING A 2

READING B 1 b 2 c 3 a 4 b 5 b

VOCABULARY A 1 celebrate 2 receive 3 calendar 4 get the day off 5 official 6 arrange 7 colleague

GRAMMAR A 1 a 2 a 3 b 4 b 5 b 6 a 7 b

GRAMMAR B 1 True 2 False 3 False 4 True 5 True

GRAMMAR C 1 any 2 a little 3 too many 4 a lot of 5 a few

Lesson 2

LISTENING A 1 a exactly b I know c yeah d you're right e that's true 2 a not sure b I disagree

LISTENING B 1 b 2 a 3 b 4 b 5 b 6 a

VOCABULARY A 1 c 2 b 3 b 4 c 5 a 6 a 7 c

GRAMMAR A 1 the right amount 2 not the right amount 3 both countable and uncountable nouns

GRAMMAR B 1 enough 2 not enough 3 not enough 4 not enough 5 enough 6 enough

GRAMMAR C He thinks that there ~~are~~ **is** not enough to buy everything we need. He's worried that there ~~is~~ **isn't** enough time to get everything ready. Well, do you have ~~not~~ enough time to have a meeting with him about it this afternoon? I was thinking that there ~~is~~ **are** enough people here to make the preparations quickly. David is so busy—he always says that there ~~is~~ **isn't** enough time to do everything, so let's get ~~not~~ enough people to help and then it won't be a problem!

Lesson 3

VOCABULARY A 1 b 2 c 3 c 4 a 5 b 6 c 7 a 8 c

VOCABULARY B 1 box of 2 package of 3 jug of / bottle of 4 bag of 5 carton of 6 bottle of / can of 7 can of 8 jar of

LISTENING A 1 a birthday 2 both sweet and healthy food

LISTENING B 1 False 2 False 3 True 4 False 5 True

WRITING A 1 celebrate 2 official 3 a lot of 4 so 5 waste money 6 because 7 enough 8 some 9 box of

Unit 3

Lesson 1

READING A 1 b 2 b 3 a

READING B 1 True 2 True 3 False 4 False 5 True 6 False

VOCABULARY A 1 floating 2 trick 3 blow out 4 dangerous 5 fire 6 puppet

VOCABULARY B 1 perform 2 puppet 3 trick 4 control 5 blow 6 dangerous

GRAMMAR A 1 some 2 every 3 any 4 no 5 some 6 any 7 no 8 every 9 any 10 no 11 some 12 every

GRAMMAR B 1 everywhere 2 no one/nobody 3 somewhere 4 everything

GRAMMAR C **1** anywhere **2** someone **3** everything **4** no one **5** something **6** everywhere

Lesson 2

LISTENING A **1** 19th (nineteenth) **2** 4 (four) **3** 1960s

LISTENING B **1** b **2** c **3** b **4** a **5** b **6** c

VOCABULARY A **1** songwriter **2** sound technician **3** stylist **4** manager **5** director **6** the lead vocalist **7** producer **8** backup singer

VOCABULARY B **1** backup singer **2** lead vocalist **3** producer **4** songwriter **5** director **6** manager **7** sound technician **8** stylist

GRAMMAR A **1** aren't happening now **2** base **3** didn't use to **4** did (you) use to

GRAMMAR B **1** used to perform **2** didn't used to write **3** did you use to be **4** used to take **5** did they use to spend **6** didn't use to sing

GRAMMAR C Most people watch music videos on YouTube these days, but everyone ~~use~~ **used** to watch them on either MTV or VH1. Nowadays, these TV stations play reality TV shows and rockumentaries, although they didn't ~~used~~ **use** to have this kind of programming. They used to ~~showing~~ **show** music videos—and only music videos—all day long. People used to ~~to~~ see them on some TV stations in the 1970s occasionally. Before television became popular, cafés all over the world in the 1950s used **to** present music videos on something called a "video jukebox." The very first music video ever made was in 1894, when filmmakers ~~use~~ **used to** make movies with simple lanterns and slides. They made a video to sell their songs, and they sold 2 million copies. How ~~used people~~ **did people use** to view movies back then, or even a music video? Simple … they used ~~going~~ **to go** to theaters, where they would see them on the big screen.

GRAMMAR D **1** My sister and I would watch **2** We wouldn't listen **3** Katy Perry wouldn't sing **4** Would they perform **5** Would you play **6** I would write

Lesson 3

VOCABULARY A **1** channel surf **2** on demand **3** episode **4** stream **5** TV series **6** binge-watch **7** commercial

VOCABULARY B **1** stream **2** commercials **3** TV series **4** episodes **5** binge-watch **6** on demand **7** channel-surf

LISTENING A **1** movie screen **2** cell phone **3** laptop **4** smart TV

LISTENING B **1** True **2** True **3** False **4** False **5** False **6** True

WRITING A **1** I used to watch videos on my laptop, but now I have a smart TV. **2** Lisa doesn't like commercials, although there is one (that) she loves. **3** YouTube is a great site, though most videos are not worth watching. **4** She enjoys TV shows, but she didn't use to watch them when she was a student. **5** Kids can watch things online, though many things are not safe to view. **6** I don't go to sporting events, although I might watch a game on TV.

WRITING B **1** Now, in the past **2** In the past, now **3** now, in the past **4** in the past, now **5** In the past, now **6** now, in the past

Unit 4

Lesson 1

READING A **1** True **2** False **3** True **4** False **5** True

VOCABULARY A **1** lazy **2** optimistic **3** impatient **4** depressed **5** easygoing **6** shy

VOCABULARY B **1** impatient **2** shy **3** easygoing **4** lazy **5** depressed **6** optimistic

GRAMMAR A **1** equally **2** are **3** more **4** than **5** not **6** aren't

GRAMMAR B **1** a **2** b **3** a **4** b **5** b

GRAMMAR C **1** isn't as funny as **2** isn't as good as **3** isn't as organized as **4** as easygoing as **5** are as impatient as **6** isn't as optimistic as

Lesson 2

VOCABULARY A **1** a **2** b **3** b **4** b **5** a **6** a

VOCABULARY B **1** workaholic **2** a risk taker **3** loners **4** an expert **5** leader **6** creative thinker

LISTENING A **1** positive

LISTENING B **1** a leader **2** an expert **3** a creative thinker **4** a risk taker

GRAMMAR A **1** False **2** False **3** True **4** True **5** True

GRAMMAR B **1** the most **2** the best **3** the funniest **4** the tallest **5** the cheapest **6** the worst

GRAMMAR C **1** a **2** a **3** b **4** a **5** a **6** b

GRAMMAR D **1** the most interesting **2** The best **3** the most productive **4** the worst **5** the busiest **6** the greatest

Lesson 3

VOCABULARY A **1** rude **2** selfish **3** generous **4** adventurous **5** bossy **6** smart **7** honest

VOCABULARY B **1** bossy **2** generous **3** adventurous **4** rude **5** selfish **6** honest **7** smart

LISTENING A **1** their families **2** similar to

LISTENING B **1** b **2** c **3** b **4** a **5** a

WRITING A **1** c **2** e **3** a **4** d **5** b

WRITING B **1** c **2** a **3** d **4** e **5** b

Unit 5

Lesson 1

READING A 1 b 2 b 3 a
READING B 1 Atlanta 2 May 3 $1,000 (a thousand dollars) 4 5-star restaurant 5 email 6 6 (six)
VOCABULARY A 1 a 2 b 3 a 4 b 5 b 6 b
VOCABULARY B 1 flight 2 reservation 3 arrive 4 voucher 5 check in 6 luggage
GRAMMAR A 1 guess the future 2 will and won't 3 we plan to do 4 will and won't 5 help 6 can
GRAMMAR B 1 I can help 2 I'll have 3 you'll enjoy 4 I'll have 5 you can have 6 I can bring
GRAMMAR C 1 We can find 2 I think I'll 3 I think you'll 4 I can give 5 I won't

Lesson 2

LISTENING A 1 birthday 2 a lot
LISTENING B 1 c 2 b 3 c 4 c 5 a 6 a
VOCABULARY A 1 about 2 make 3 don't 4 Let's 5 about 6 let
VOCABULARY B 1 Why don't 2 let me know 3 How about 4 Let's 5 what about 6 make a suggestion
GRAMMAR A 1 can 2 could 3 can 4 may and could 5 can't
GRAMMAR B 1 Can 2 Could 3 can't 4 could/may 5 Can 6 can't
GRAMMAR C 1 Can 2 can't 3 Can 4 May 5 can't 6 could
GRAMMAR D 1 Can you put up posters in the school? 2 Could you help me with this invitation? 3 You can't have the party in the library. 4 May/Could we use the classroom for a party? 5 Can we have the party outdoors? 6 Could you bring all of the food?

Lesson 3

LISTENING A 1 b
LISTENING B 1 False 2 False 3 True 4 True 5 False
VOCABULARY A 1 accept 2 gift 3 up 4 up 5 wedding 6 send 7 up
VOCABULARY B 1 reception 2 pick 3 wedding 4 dress 5 RSVP 6 invitation 7 show 8 registry
WRITING A 2, 3, 5
WRITING B 1 First 2 However 3 Next 4 but 5 that 6 such as 7 if 8 Finally 9 all

Unit 6

Lesson 1

READING A 1 False 2 False 3 True 4 False
VOCABULARY A 1 b 2 b 3 a 4 a 5 c 6 c
VOCABULARY B 1 comfort zone 2 risk 3 attitude 4 in control 5 advantage 6 status quo
GRAMMAR A 1 actions or situations 2 Since 3 For 4 How long 5 have/has
GRAMMAR B 1 has 2 for 3 How long 4 since 5 Since
GRAMMAR C 1 wrote written 2 had have 3 since for 4 Has Have 5 for since 6 has have

Lesson 2

LISTENING A 1 doesn't have 2 Both Rowan and Janet want 3 doesn't like 4 can't 5 Only Rowan wants
LISTENING B 1 b 2 c 3 a 4 a 5 c 6 b
VOCABULARY A 1 been 2 eaten 3 ridden 4 sung 5 done 6 heard 7 gone 8 won 9 met 10 run
VOCABULARY B 1 won 2 eaten 3 been 4 gone 5 sung 6 heard 7 ridden 8 met 9 done 10 run
GRAMMAR A 1 an unspecific time 2 questions 3 an affirmative verb 4 have or has
GRAMMAR B 1 never 2 ever 3 haven't 4 ever 5 hasn't 6 never
GRAMMAR C 1 ever never 2 Has Have 3 went been 4 Have Has 5 fly flown 6 have has
GRAMMAR D 1 never done 2 ever gone/been 3 haven't 4 ever won 5 has 6 never been 7 never been 8 never eaten

Lesson 3

VOCABULARY A 1 a 2 c 3 a 4 b 5 c 6 b 7 a 8 c
LISTENING A 1 changing cities in general 2 is
LISTENING B 1 True 2 False 3 True 4 True 5 False
WRITING A **Good changes:** food trucks and playground **Bad changes:** shopping mall, bike lanes, walking trail
WRITING B I really prefer the ~~risk~~ **status quo**. But I now have a very positive ~~advantage~~ **attitude** to it, and I think I have never ~~live~~ **lived** in such a nice place. I think one of the best changes is the new pedestrian **area**. We've had the bike lanes ~~since~~ **for** two years, and they have made a big difference to safety. It's very good, because we ~~has~~ **have** never had somewhere to play sports before. They are much cheaper than a restaurant, and I have never ~~ate~~ **eaten** such delicious food before.

Unit 7

Lesson 1

READING A 1 b 2 c 3 a 4 a
READING B 1 b 2 b 3 a 4 b
VOCABULARY A 1 career 2 training 3 knowledge 4 degree 5 skill 6 qualifications
GRAMMAR A 1 just 2 already 3 yet 4 already
GRAMMAR B 1 yet, just/already 2 yet, already 3 already, yet
GRAMMAR C 1 Have you started yet 2 haven't yet finished 3 I've already done 4 you've already learned 5 I've just completed 6 you're already found

GRAMMAR D **1** I haven't / have not started my training program yet. **2** Have you finished your English paper already? / Have you already finished your English paper? **3** He's / He has just graduated from high school. **4** She's / She has already found a well-paid job. / She's / She has found a well-paid job already. **5** They haven't / have not decided on their careers yet. **6** Jessica's / Jessica has just started working for an engineering firm.

Lesson 2

LISTENING A **1** False **2** True **3** False **4** True

LISTENING B **1** b **2** a **3** b **4** a **5** c

VOCABULARY A **1** get **2** hire **3** get **4** corporate **5** benefits **6** apply **7** path **8** get

VOCABULARY B **1** apply **2** degree **3** benefits **4** promotion **5** raise **6** hire **7** corporate **8** career

GRAMMAR A **1** a **2** b **3** a **4** b **5** a **6** a **7** b **8** b

GRAMMAR B **1** finished **2** opened **3** has been **4** helped **5** took **6** haven't decided

GRAMMAR C **1** Have you hired a new employee yet? **2** She already ate her ice cream. / She ate her ice cream already. **3** How many items have you sold so far? **4** Did you apply for the job yet? **5** They just bought the whole company! **6** Martin has already finished his degree. / Martin has finished his degree already.

Lesson 3

VOCABULARY A **1** independent **2** organized **3** motivated **4** flexible **5** honest **6** creative **7** curious

VOCABULARY B **1** interpersonal **2** intrapersonal **3** cognitive **4** cognitive **5** interpersonal **6** cognitive **7** intrapersonal

LISTENING A **1** advertising, commercials **2** accounting, spreadsheets **3** photography, magazines

LISTENING B **1** creative, curious, university degree **2** organized, intelligent, thinking skills **3** independent, motivated, flexible, good contacts

WRITING A **1** e **2** a **3** b **4** d **5** c

Unit 8

Lesson 1

VOCABULARY A **1** flying a kite **2** jumping rope **3** Making things with clay **4** make things with building blocks **5** building a model **6** coloring

READING A **1** False **2** False **3** True **4** True **5** False **6** False

GRAMMAR A **1** True **2** False **3** False **4** True

GRAMMAR B **1** object **2** object **3** subject **4** subject **5** subject **6** object

GRAMMAR C **1** b **2** a **3** c **4** c

GRAMMAR D **1** hate playing **2** being **3** Building **4** enjoy doing **5** prefer playing

Lesson 2

VOCABULARY A **1** b **2** b **3** c **4** a **5** c **6** a **7** b **8** c **9** a **10** b

LISTENING A **1** a **2** b **3** b

LISTENING B **1** False **2** True **3** False **4** True **5** True **6** False

GRAMMAR A **1** True **2** False **3** True **4** False

GRAMMAR B The thing is, I'd really like to ~~having~~ **have** some more fun! Maybe, but I'd rather ~~to~~ do something more energetic. My sister loves ~~go~~ **to go / going** paddle boarding.

GRAMMAR C **1** to spend **2** to feel / feeling **3** to work / working **4** to play **5** watch **6** to be / being

Lesson 3

LISTENING A **1** bad **2** more **3** disagree

LISTENING B **Mr. Lodge:** 1, 3, 4
Ms. Ramirez: 5, 6, 7

VOCABULARY A **1** stressed **2** rested **3** guilty **4** nervous **5** bored

WRITING A **1** First **2** Second **3** Finally **4** However

WRITING B **1** I love **2** stressed **3** relaxing **4** rested **5** playing video games **6** I'd rather **7** I'd like **8** flying a kite **9** yoga **10** bored

Unit 9

Lesson 1

READING A **1** b **2** b **3** b

READING B **1** terrible **2** never own his own home **3** three **4** is **5** he built it **6** cook dinner for his friends

VOCABULARY A **1** balcony **2** rent **3** low-cost **4** hall **5** afford **6** couch

VOCABULARY B **1** afford **2** hall **3** low-cost **4** rent **5** balcony **6** couch

GRAMMAR A **1** make predictions **2** intentions **3** arrangements **4** future events that happen on a schedule

GRAMMAR B **1** are meeting / are going to meet **2** are going to buy **3** moves / is moving / is going to move **4** is not going to / won't enjoy

GRAMMAR C **1** are going to like, prediction **2** move, schedule **3** are meeting, arrangement **4** am going to ask, intention **5** will be, prediction **6** am not going to buy, intention

GRAMMAR D **1** Maria's / Maria is going to buy a new couch later today. **2** He's going to / He will live in a nice house someday. **3** We're looking at a new house tomorrow morning. **4** Are you going to change the space in your house? **5** I move / I am moving into my new apartment on October 1st. **6** They're not going to / They won't rent a place forever.

Lesson 2

VOCABULARY A **1** share **2** live **3** apartment **4** studio **5** share **6** a roommate **7** rent **8** housemates

VOCABULARY B **1** bills **2** studio **3** rent **4** chores **5** housemates **6** hunting **7** roommate **8** alone

LISTENING A **1** unhappy **2** annoyed **3** worried

LISTENING B **1** True **2** True **3** True **4** False **5** False **6** True

LISTENING C **1** may not **2** could **3** might not **4** definitely **5** will

GRAMMAR A **1** definitely **2** probably **3** could/may/might

GRAMMAR B **1** might **2** will definitely **3** could **4** probably **5** may

GRAMMAR C **1** will probably **2** will definitely **3** might **4** could **5** probably won't **6** definitely won't

GRAMMAR D **1** I will probably live with my parents. **2** We definitely won't share all the bills. **3** Tonya may not find a roommate. **4** They will definitely get a studio apartment. **5** We probably won't go apartment hunting today. **6** Could you live with your parents after graduation?

Lesson 3

VOCABULARY A **1** solar panels **2** lighting **3** washing machine **4** heater **5** kitchen stove **6** dishwasher **7** air conditioner

LISTENING A 2, 3, 4, 5

LISTENING B **1** b **2** a **3** c **4** a **5** b **6** b

WRITING A Take doing the dishes, for example. A robot could also take care of the laundry. Last, robots may be able to help us save on our bills.

WRITING B **1** a **2** b **3** a **4** c

Unit 10

Lesson 1

READING A **1** month **2** self-confident **3** times **4** surprised **5** Toronto **6** important

READING B **1** many **2** likes **3** motivation

VOCABULARY A **1** b **2** a **3** a **4** b

GRAMMAR A **1** True **2** False **3** True **4** False **5** True **6** True

GRAMMAR B **1** eats **2** won't be **3** get **4** feel

GRAMMAR C **1** c **2** b **3** b **4** b **5** a **6** a

Lesson 2

LISTENING A **1** did **2** don't always **3** two kinds

LISTENING B **1** False **2** False **3** True **4** True **5** False **6** False

VOCABULARY A **1** b **2** c **3** a **4** a **5** c **6** c **7** a **8** c

VOCABULARY B **1** fever **2** broken arm **3** sprained ankle **4** headache **5** rash **6** cold **7** sore throat **8** cut

GRAMMAR A **1** hypothetical **2** future **3** past simple **4** would/might/could **5** base form

GRAMMAR B **1** would **2** happened **3** be **4** broke **5** have **6** would

GRAMMAR C **1** ~~win~~ won **2** ~~has~~ had **3** ~~to go~~ go **4** ~~will be~~ was / were **5** ~~won't~~ wouldn't **6** ~~can~~ could

GRAMMAR D **1** would not do / wouldn't do **2** sprained **3** would not be / wouldn't be **4** did **5** changed **6** would give

Lesson 3

VOCABULARY A **1** started **2** sick **3** hungry **4** upset **5** home **6** in shape **7** ready **8** tired

VOCABULARY B **1** sick **2** hungry **3** tired **4** upset **5** home **6** ready **7** in shape **8** started

LISTENING A **1** True **2** False **3** False **4** True

LISTENING B **1** positive **2** praises **3** not happy **4** difficult

WRITING A **1** c **2** f **3** e **4** b **5** a **6** d

WRITING B **1** diet **2** get **3** upset **4** joined **5** throat **6** ankle **7** memory **8** will **9** in shape **10** home

Unit 11

Lesson 1

READING A **1** False **2** False **3** True **4** False **5** True

READING B **1** a **2** b **3** b **4** a **5** b **6** a **7** b

VOCABULARY A **1** yarn **2** get rid of **3** transport **4** natural resources **5** end up

VOCABULARY B **1** end up **2** natural resources **3** transported **4** get rid of **5** yarn

GRAMMAR A **1** a **2** b **3** c **4** a

GRAMMAR B **1** are designed **2** is made **3** Is all trash transported **4** Are **5** aren't made **6** wasn't grown

GRAMMAR C **1** isn't grown **2** are found **3** is made **4** aren't repaired **5** Are … filled **6** is … sold

GRAMMAR D **1** That scarf is made in Chile. **2** Are those T-shirts produced in a factory? **3** The instructions are not / aren't written on the label. **4** Is that clothing worn in your country? **5** Those bottles are recycled at a recycling center. **6** Water is not used to make yarn.

Lesson 2

LISTENING A **1** True **2** False **3** True **4** False **5** True

LISTENING B **1** developed **2** fish teeth **3** an engineer **4** tire **5** boots **6** old-fashioned

VOCABULARY A **1** button, Velcro, zipper **2** fake fur, fur, nylon

VOCABULARY B **1** nylon **2** Velcro **3** fake fur **4** buttons **5** zipper **6** fur

GRAMMAR A **1** simple past of be + past participle **2** We want to focus on the thing that receives the action. We don't know who or what does something. It's unimportant who or what does something.

GRAMMAR B **1** c **2** c **3** b **4** b **5** c **6** a

GRAMMAR C **1** were introduced **2** was used **3** wasn't considered **4** weren't harmed **5** was replaced **6** were made

GRAMMAR D **1** isn't wasn't **2** use used **3** is was **4** making made **5** weren't wasn't **6** were was

Lesson 3

LISTENING A 1, 3, 5

LISTENING B **1** a **2** c **3** c **4** a

VOCABULARY A **1** cause **2** harm **3** last **4** reduce

VOCABULARY B **1** amount **2** wildlife **3** pollution **4** long time

WRITING A **1** False **2** True **3** True **4** True **5** False

WRITING B **1** reason **2** why **3** so

Unit 12

Lesson 1

READING A **1** All people **2** place of work **3** is **4** difficult **5** Some

VOCABULARY A **1** b **2** a **3** b **4** a **5** b **6** b

GRAMMAR A **1** the same **2** the help **3** myself **4** yourself **5** himself **6** herself **7** itself **8** ourselves **9** yourselves **10** themselves

GRAMMAR B **1** myself **2** yourselves **3** itself **4** yourself **5** themselves **6** herself **7** ourselves **8** himself

GRAMMAR C **1** myself **2** ourselves **3** themselves **4** yourselves **5** himself **6** herself **7** yourself

Lesson 2

LISTENING A **1** talking to new people **2** Anyone **3** Listening **4** one person **5** contact the people you met

LISTENING B **1** False **2** False **3** True **4** False **5** True **6** False

VOCABULARY A **1** make time for **2** intern **3** a contact **4** job hunting **5** stay in touch **6** get to know **7** introduce yourself

VOCABULARY B **1** job hunting **2** contact **3** make time for **4** introduce yourself **5** intern **6** get to know **7** stay in touch

GRAMMAR A **1** False **2** True **3** True **4** True **5** True

GRAMMAR B **1** stayed **2** has gotten to know **3** introduced **4** Are you traveling **5** is

GRAMMAR C **1** looks is looking **2** have seen saw **3** am having have **4** work working **5** went been

GRAMMAR D **1** am **2** were looking **3** did you find **4** told **5** works **6** is working **7** do you want **8** have not had / haven't had **9** am working **10** Have you eaten

Lesson 3

VOCABULARY A **1** A **2** A **3** C **4** B **5** B **6** C

VOCABULARY B **1** bright, loose, short hair **2** costume, tight **3** long, necklace **4** earrings, jewelry **5** dark, makeup **6** beard, mustache / mustache, beard

LISTENING A **1** happy **2** doesn't wear **3** are practical **4** doesn't always wear

LISTENING B **1** Speaker B **2** Speaker A **3** Speaker B **4** Speaker D **5** Speaker C **6** Speaker D

WRITING A **1** is called **2** was invented **3** dark and tight **4** based on **5** old and modern **6** way of life

WRITING B **1** b **2** c **3** b **4** b **5** c **6** a

Exam Training

Reading

MATCHING A **1** c **2** b **3** c **4** c **5** a **6** b **7** a

MULTIPLE-CHOICE GAP FILL A **1** b **2** c **3** a **4** b **5** a **6** c

READING OPEN GAP FILL A **1** are **2** the **3** to **4** were **5** out **6** going

Listening

SEPARATE TEXTS WITH MULTIPLE-CHOICE QUESTIONS A **1** c **2** c **3** b **4** b **5** a

MATCHING A **1** g **2** a **3** f **4** h **5** c

ONE LONGER TEXT, MULTIPLE-CHOICE QUESTIONS A **1** c **2** b **3** a **4** c **5** c

Writing

WRITING A STORY BASED ON PICTURES A second

WRITING A STORY BASED ON PICTURES B gone went, her herself, choose chose, some any/ enough, on in, him her

WRITING A STORY BASED ON PICTURES C 4, 2, 7, 5, 1, 3, 6

Unit 1

Track 1

Speaker 1: I was listening to a program about Barack Obama. I really enjoyed it!

Speaker 2: I love that band, the Heartbreakers. They were performing their best songs all night!

Speaker 3: You told me you had the lead role in that movie, but you weren't even starring in it!

Speaker 4: I heard the twins in their violin lessons. Were they practicing all afternoon?

Speaker 5: I wasn't reading a book when you called. I was already asleep.

Speaker 6: School has been so busy lately. We didn't even go to the concert because we were studying for a test.

Track 2

Mila: Danny, you look really happy. What happened?

Danny: I just got some really good news. I won a trip to the Kennedy Space Center in Florida! I can't believe I won. There were thousands of people in the contest, so I got really lucky.

Mila: That is good news, Danny! I'm happy for you. Science is your thing, isn't it?

Danny: It's what I study in college. I'm getting a degree in astronomy, so this is a dream come true for me. I've always wanted to visit the Kennedy Space Center, ever since I was a kid. I love to watch space launches on television. To be honest, I wouldn't mind traveling into space one day, but I'm not sure I'd make a good astronaut.

Track 3

Mila: So, what did you have to do to enter the contest?

Danny: I had to complete an essay about why I love space. It wasn't easy, though. I had so much to say, but the essay had to be less than 200 words.

Mila: Hmm, well that's not too bad.

Danny: After my first try, I read it and I was disappointed, so I wrote it again, and again … and again! It got better each time, but still, I wanted to write something amazing to win.

Mila: Of course. Often when we write something, it doesn't turn out so well the first time around.

Danny: True. Well, I was writing about how I feel about space. While I was writing my fifth attempt, I suddenly had a better idea. I decided to write about why we should spend money on exploring space, you know, for space missions to Mars. That was the winning essay!

Mila: Wow, great job! What did you win exactly?

Danny: I won a four-day trip to Cape Canaveral, Florida, where the space center is. Everything is paid for, including my hotel stay and all of my meals. The best thing is, I can take three people along with me.

Mila: Oh, that's very nice. Who are you taking?

Danny: Well, I want to take my mom and dad. They were helpful with my writing. Would you like to join me, too? I'd love it if you came.

Mila: Really? Oh, thanks! I would love to come!

Track 4

Host: Tell us about your amazing story, Rick.

Rick: Well, it all started at my job about four years ago. I started work at a construction site, and about a month after that, I became friends with a coworker, Samuel. We were friends for years after that. We had a lot in common. We both like construction. We even worked together at different places after we left that first job. We even looked a lot like each other. At least that's what many of our other friends said.

Track 5

Host: And you noticed something strange over the years.

Rick: Yes, like I said, we worked together at different jobs. Our other coworkers often said we looked like each other. But Samuel and I didn't think we looked alike at all, I guess because of the age difference. I just didn't see it. But the thing is, I was adopted. At some point, I told Samuel about that. Immediately, Samuel told me that his mom gave up her first child for adoption. We looked into it, and a few days later, we learned that Samuel and I had the same mother! She had me when she was very young, and she couldn't raise me. So, in the end, Samuel and I found out we were half-brothers. How great is that? All those years, and we never knew!

Host: That's an amazing coincidence!

Unit 2

Track 1

Karen: Hey, Ceci, what do you think we should do for Labor Day? I think we should have a barbecue party like last year. It was great!

Ceci: That's a good idea, Karen, but there were too many people at the barbeque last year! We didn't have enough hamburgers for everybody! This year we should do something quiet. What about having a picnic in the park?

Karen: Yes, that's true. But everyone loves a barbecue! Let's have a smaller barbecue party this year with only a few people.

Ceci: Well, OK, but remember that last year was so expensive, too! We don't want to spend too much money on food this time. We bought all that food and we spent so much money.

Karen: OK, yes. Well, then, I think we should ask everyone to bring some food. That way, we don't need to buy it all. We can share the food and there will be enough for everyone.

Ceci: Yes, good idea, and we can ask them to bring some drinks as well, maybe just some juice and water. We don't want to have too much like we did last year.

Karen: Yeah, do you remember we had like 15 bottles of soda after the party! And there wasn't any juice or water—only soda! It was very unhealthy.

Ceci: Yes! So, let's tell people to bring some food, some juice, and some water … and we don't want any soda this time!

Karen: Great, and like I said, we won't invite a lot of people and so there won't be too much food or too many drinks. Oh, and I know you want to go to the park, so we can have the barbecue there!

Ceci: Perfect!

Track 2

Katy: It's a big day for Bianca next week. She joined the company ten years ago, so we should get her a gift. Abril, you're good with money. What should we get her? It's an important day, but we don't want to spend too much money!

Abril: Well, Katy, I never like wasting money on gifts, so we should make something. That's also more personal. What do you think, Mike?
Mike: I think it's a good idea to spend money on something nice for a special day. It means you took time to think about what they like, and it's not so bad if you look for something cheap.
Katy: You know, I disagree with that. When you make something for someone, it shows you thought about something just for them.
Abril: Think about holidays like Valentine's Day—they are just all about money now, and everyone just buys flowers!
Katy: Yes, exactly, Abril. A card would be much more personal.
Abril: You know, last Valentine's Day my brother had to borrow money from our parents to take his wife away for the weekend!
Mike: Yes, I know, everything is so expensive these days. You know, Americans spend over 220 dollars each on Valentine's Day!
Abril: Wow! Well look, I think we should make her a card and get everyone at the office to sign it. That's very personal.
Katy: Hey, yeah! That's a great idea!
Mike: OK, you're right, Abril. She's going to really like that.
Abril: We can make her a cake, too! She loves cake!
Katy: Well, that's true. OK, let's do it. Does anyone have any paper to make the card?

Track 3

I'm Tyler from New Jersey, and this afternoon, we're having a party for my girlfriend! I am going to buy all the food and my friends are going to get the drinks, so I'm going to make a list of what I need from the store. First, I'll get a can of nuts and a jar of olives so that everyone can have something to eat when they arrive. Then, I'll probably cook pizzas for everyone with cheese and tomato. Everyone loves pizza! Now, my friends are going to bring some cartons of juice and I'm also going to make a jug of lemonade. We need to have enough to drink. It's a hot day today, so maybe I should get some bottles of water, too. After the pizza, we're going to want dessert, of course. I think I should get a bag of apples and oranges so that I can make a fruit salad. That's a nice and healthy dessert, but I think most people are going to prefer something very sweet. Maybe I will also pick up a package of cookies from the store as well! Oh, I nearly forgot! We're going to celebrate my girlfriend's birthday, so I need to get her a chocolate cake! She loves chocolate.

Unit 3

Track 1

Speaker 1: I just want to walk around, and I don't care where we go.
Speaker 2: I would like to see that street entertainer that performs with fire.
Speaker 3: For my performance, I'm bringing a box to stand on and three small red balls. That's all I need!
Speaker 4: There are so many people here, and I don't know any of them!
Speaker 5: I didn't like a lot of the performances, but I liked the one at the very end.
Speaker 6: We call that street entertainer "Mr. Silver," and he performs all over town.

Track 2

Host: We're here in the studio talking to music manager Rob Star. Thanks for joining us.
Rob: Hey, thanks for having me!
Host: I wanted to ask you what you think about boy bands. There have been so many of them over the years. Why are they so popular?
Rob: Good question! I do know my history on boy bands. They've been around for a long, long time. Would you believe the first boy bands ever appeared in the 19th century! They were usually a group of four men, and they sang in barber shops.
Host: Yes, they were called barbershop quartets.
Rob: Exactly. They weren't really called boy bands back then, but they were popular for a long time, and their music style didn't change much. Then came the Beatles in the 1960s, and everything changed.

Track 3

Host: Do you think the Beatles were the original boy band?
Rob: Yes, I do. They had all the looks of a boy band: good-looking, stylish, talented musicians, and loved by girls all over the world! They've sold over 800 million records and won seven Grammy Awards! They've also had 20 number-one hits on the Hot 100 chart, which is a record. The lead vocalist, Paul McCartney, is a rock legend and still really famous today.
Host: How many boy bands can you think of?
Rob: Oh, I can think of a few, about four or five of them. I remember the most famous ones, of course, like the Jackson 5, New Kids on the Block, the Backstreet Boys, NSYNC, and One Direction.
Host: Most boy bands don't last very long. They might last about five years, and even the best ones only last about ten. Then, they disappear.
Rob: It all depends on their talent. For many boy bands in recent memory, the musicians, or "boys," don't do much. They just sing and look good. Oh, and they can dance! Looking good is very important. Directors make cool videos for them. Managers make sure they act a certain way in public. Stylists often make each member look a certain way. Every boy band member is a certain type: the cool one, the shy one, the bad boy, and so on. They have to be a type that many girls will fall in love with. I mean, you never see the funny one or the silly one, right? Not that a girl can't love a funny, silly guy.
Host: I know what you mean. Image is very important for boy bands today. They need to look trendy, but they still have to be good singers and songwriters.
Rob: Well, I'm not so sure! A sound technician can make an ordinary singer sound great, and there are often other people writing their songs. The Backstreet Boys and NSYNC didn't write much of their own music. That used to be fine, but in recent years, it's necessary for each boy band member to be talented in many ways. One Direction is an example of that. Their band members have written many of their songs. Really, it's only the most talented boy bands that live on in our memory, so sometimes dancing, singing, and looking cool just isn't enough.

Host: Well, thanks so much for your time, Rob.
Rob: You're welcome!

Track 4

Speaker 1

A lot of people watch movies on mobile devices, like iPhones, tablets and laptops. I think that's fine, but I don't like small screens. It hurts my eyes to look at a computer that long. Besides, it isn't the same as seeing a movie in the movie theater. The image is so big and powerful, and it sounds great, too. That's how I like to enjoy movies.

Speaker 2

I don't have much time to watch TV programs or movies. I'm really busy with work, and when I get home, I have a family to take care of. I like to watch things on my phone while I'm traveling to work in the morning and home in the afternoon. There didn't use to be Wi-Fi in the subway, but now there is, so it makes it quite easy to stream things. I'm glad we have that now!

Speaker 3

I work outside of the office very often, and I've always got my computer with me. When I need to take a break from work and I'm near a Wi-Fi hotspot, I'll stream an episode of my favorite program and watch that. I don't even have a TV at home, so that's the only way I can watch things anyway. That's fine, really. I was never crazy about watching TV.

Speaker 4

I have the best ways to watch movies and TV shows in my house. It's actually on our living room wall and it has a wide screen with great sound. We can download or stream anything we like. We just sit on our comfortable sofa and choose our favorite TV series or a new movie. I think if you're going to watch a program, there's no place better to watch it than the comfort of your own home.

Unit 4

Track 1

Freddy: OK, come on, everyone. Let's focus! We have to decide how we're going to organize the next concert. Lianne, what do you think?
Lianne: We need to think about which songs we do first. It's important to start the concert with exactly the right song. That immediately tells the audience what the concert is going to be like.
Mike: Shouldn't we decide where we are going to play first? I think we should play somewhere totally different this time.
Josh: Really? Is that a good idea?
Mike: Yes, Josh! We always play at the same places like parties. We should play at a restaurant, so people can listen to us when they are having dinner! We could play at the Italian restaurant downtown, what do you think, Freddy?
Freddy: Yes, Mike, great idea. I'll contact the manager and ask. And Josh, how are the songs going?
Josh: Great! I wrote some new ones that we could try. I changed our style a bit to make it sound like jazz. It was a lot of work, but I did it!
Lianne: Let's see, Josh. Hey, I like these! Do you think you can play this, Mike?
Mike: Yeah, sure, but I have an idea. I think we should play completely different instruments this time. I think Josh should play bass guitar and I should play the drums! Maybe it won't work, but we should try it! What do you think, Freddy?
Freddy: Well, sure, let's do it! Josh, what do you say?
Josh: Sounds good to me! And I'll start thinking about the design for the posters. Let's hope the restaurant says we can play.
Lianne: Oh, and Freddy, we need to think about the lights, too. Sometimes the lights in restaurants aren't very good. But I bought some new ones last week.
Freddy: Well done everyone! I think we have a plan!

Track 2

Travis: Wow Chris, is that your older brother or your cousin in that picture? He looks exactly like you!
Chris: Actually, Travis, it's my dad! He looks very young. We look similar but we have very different personalities. We're both very short and we have blue eyes. But I have blond hair and he has dark brown hair. And my dad's the most adventurous person I know, but I'm not adventurous. He is a movie director, and he travels around the world a lot. I prefer to stay at home!
Travis: So who are you like in your family?
Chris: Well, I'm like my mom. She's a bit bossy because she has her own restaurant! I am quite bossy, too. I think it's because I organize events at the sports club, so I need to tell people what to do. What about you, Travis? Who are you like?
Travis: Err … well, I think I'm a lot like my brother. We're not twins, but we're both tall and we have brown hair. We're both pretty smart, too. We always got the best grades at school. But he's very generous with money. I'm not at all! It's not because I'm selfish. I'm a student and I don't have a lot of money.
Chris: I know what you mean!
Travis: Well, it's true. My brother is now a computer programmer, and he gets great money for his job. And who's that? Is that your sister? You look identical!
Chris: Yes, it is! She is short like me, and she has blonde hair and blue eyes. So does our aunt. Our mother looks very different, though. My sister's probably the smartest person in the family, too. Also, some people think that she's a bit rude sometimes. For me, she's just honest! Anyway, it's only because sheis stressed because of her studies. She is finishing medical school this year and she has a lot of exams.
Travis: Oh, I see.

Unit 5

Track 1

Waiter: Are you ready to order?
Alma: Everything on your menu looks so good! Can you recommend anything?
Waiter: Certainly, I can help you with that. The chicken with roasted potatoes is my favorite.
Alma: Oh, good. I'll have the chicken with potatoes, then.
Waiter: I'm sure you'll enjoy your meal, ma'am. And for you, sir?
Yair: I'm on a diet, so I guess I'll have the fish. That seems light. I just hope I'm not hungry later.
Alma: If you're hungry after you finish, you can have some of my potatoes.

Yair: Thank you, dear.
Waiter: If you like, I can bring some bread to the table.
Yair: That would be wonderful, thank you!

Track 2

Andrea: Let's have a party for Annabelle next Saturday. I think she would really like that.
Miguel: That's a great idea. How about we have it at her favorite restaurant?
Andrea: Can we do that? We probably need to ask them for permission.
Miguel: I know they have an area in the back for parties. We just need to make a reservation, and check they have the space for a lot of people.
Andrea: Why don't you give them a call? Maybe they can also make a cake for her.
Miguel: Well, you can't put out candles on a plate of spaghetti! I'll call them tomorrow and let you know what they say …

Track 3

Andrea: Did you talk to the people at the restaurant?
Miguel: Yes, I did. I didn't make a reservation though, because I wanted to talk to you first. The manager says there are two rooms available. One of them seats up to fourteen guests, and the other seats twenty-five.
Andrea: I see. And what about the cost?
Miguel: Well, they are both the same price, 20 dollars per person. That doesn't include any food or drinks, of course.
Andrea: That would be nice if meals were included! Well, I think that sounds really good. I think it's affordable.
Miguel: Yes, and the manager says the rooms are available on both Saturday and Sunday, so we can choose either date.
Andrea: OK. And what about the cake? Do they make any special arrangements?
Miguel: They can provide a cake, but we have to bring the candles.
Andrea: Sure, that's easy. Well, I think we should get the room that seats twenty-five people. I'm not sure if we'll have that many, but there will be more than fourteen. And how about having it on Saturday?
Miguel: It might be better to have it on Sunday. There's a big game at the college stadium on Saturday, and everyone wants to go to that.

Track 4

Host: Most people get married in a church, but my guests today got married 16,000 feet in the air! Meet Oscar and Beth, a wedding couple who decided to have a very unusual wedding ceremony. This lovely couple, along with a minister, the best man and the maid of honor, all jumped out of a plane and had their ceremony in the sky! Oscar, Beth, thank you for joining us.
Oscar: Thanks, it's good to be here.
Beth: Thank you!

Track 5

Host: What made you decide to have a wedding in the clouds?
Beth: Well, it's funny. Oscar and I met while we were with a skydiving group. We started dating and later fell in love. One day at a friend's party, Oscar joked that we should get married while skydiving. I said yes! He wasn't actually asking me to marry him, but he really liked my answer, so we decided to do it.
Host: That's great! Did you invite people to join you?
Oscar: We sent fifty invitations, and everyone sent an RSVP! Of course, they weren't jumping with us. They waited down below outdoors, where we had our wedding reception.
Host: But you weren't the only ones to jump, right?
Beth: Yes, well, we needed a minister to marry us, and we needed to have a best man and a maid of honor. Every wedding ceremony needs that!
Host: That sounds difficult to arrange.
Oscar: It was very hard to find a minister to agree to jump. The best man, who is my best friend Ricardo, and the maid of honor, Beth's best friend Leia, have jumped many times. That was easy. The minister only agreed if a professional skydiver would go with him. So, there were six of us.
Beth: It was also difficult to organize because of the weather. Luckily it was OK on the day of the jump, but a bit cold. Weather can make any wedding a disaster, but especially a skydiving wedding!
Host: I'm sure! Well, thanks for sharing your story. What a great way to have a wedding!

Unit 6

Track 1

Janet: So Rowan, what's on your bucket list?
Rowan: My what, Janet?
Janet: Your bucket list. You know, the things that you've always wanted to do. Like, I've never sung in front of people before and I've never met anyone famous. I have a whole list.
Rowan: I met someone famous once. Anyway, how long have you had this bucket list for? I don't have anything like that.
Janet: A long time! I'd love to ride an elephant for example. I've never done that. What about you?
Rowan: Well, I'd never want to sing in front of people, and I've never ridden an elephant either, but I don't really want to. I'd love to do some more traveling. I've never been to Paris. They say that it's beautiful.
Janet: Well, that doesn't interest me so much, but talking about traveling, what about seeing the Northern Lights or the pyramids or Machu Picchu on the Inca Trail in Peru?
Rowan: I'm not really interested in the Northern Lights, but the pyramids or Machu Picchu sound great! But you have to do too much physical effort to do the Inca Trail!
Janet: Yeah, but I'm sure it's amazing! Imagine looking over that landscape with the sun coming up first thing in the morning.
Rowan: Yes, that would be great. We should do something like that. So what else?
Janet: I've done a half marathon, but I've never run a full marathon before. That would be an incredible thing to do.
Rowan: You like to get lots of exercise! I like being more relaxed and doing things like watching all the Star Wars movies, one after the other.
Janet: Rowan, you've seen the Star Wars movies a million times! What about learning to dance

salsa? Imagine how great that would be. Your friends would be amazed.

Rowan: Yeah, they would. And so would I! I am not good at dancing at all. I tried tango last year, and the waltz. I was really bad.

Janet: I'm not very good at it either, but it'd be good to learn. What do you want to do instead, then?

Rowan: I'd like to just take it easy and stay at an ice hotel. I think they have one in Russia or Sweden. Or Alaska.

Janet: I think it's in Sweden but that isn't my kind of thing at all. We don't have very similar ideas for our bucket lists, do we?

Rowan: Well, we agree on Machu Picchu!

Track 2

Welcome to the podcast. Now, has your city changed in the last few years? And why does a city government decide to make changes in a city? For example, some cities change because more and more people live there, so they are not as small as they were in the past. But there are many things for the city government to consider before they change a city. They try to think about quality of life and what the changes can offer. For example, is the city just full of high-rise buildings, or are there green spaces, too? Not all cities have them. Also, are there many families in the city? We all know that kids are full of energy. Because of this, some city governments may build a playground or create a walking trail so that they can have fun and explore. Also, what about shopping facilities? OK, not everyone enjoys shopping malls, but governments should make sure there is somewhere practical to go shopping. Ideally, this might be a pedestrian area with cafés as well. Another thing to consider is transportation. A city should have good transportation connections like buses or trains, so that it is easy to travel. Transportation can be a big issue in any city, and a lot of cities, especially the large ones, can have thousands of cars. But many city governments create bike lanes to help with this problem, not just more roads. This way, families can move around more safely. And hopefully, when people get hungry, there might be some great food trucks, too, for a snack! Many food trucks sell burgers and hot dogs, but some of them sell more healthy food. So, when city governments are making decisions on how to change cities, they hopefully think about all of these things and more. By doing this, they can make sure that the city you live in today is definitely better than the one you used to live in.

Unit 7

Track 1

Gina: Carlos, congratulations on the new job! Have you started yet?

Carlos: No, I haven't yet finished my training. I've already done three weeks of it.

Gina: Wow, that's a lot! I imagine you've already learned many new skills.

Carlos: Yes. In fact, I've just completed a test on customer communication. I think I did well!

Gina: That's great! I'm glad you've already found a good job right after graduating.

Track 2

Host: With us today is young entrepreneur Vera Rodriguez. Vera is only 28 years old, but she's already started her own business. Vera, can you tell us about it?

Vera: Of course. Thanks for having me on the show. Well, my business is a flower shop. I sell flowers to the public, and I also make flower arrangements for events like weddings and awards ceremonies.

Host: Interesting. Was it your dream to open a flower shop?

Vera: Not exactly. I've always wanted to own my own business, but I didn't think it would be a flower shop. I studied business in college, and I got a degree in finance. Immediately after college, I applied for a job at a large bank and worked there for quite some time. So really, my best skills are at math.

Host: Hmm, so you haven't studied plants, at least not formally.

Vera: No, but I really love flowers and I've taught myself a lot of things about them. I've also taken training programs on how to make flower arrangements and how to take care of plants.

Track 3

Host: So I imagine you were bored working for a big company. A 9-to-5 job can be a little boring sometimes, and it's not easy to have the same routine every day.

Vera: No, I wasn't bored at all. In fact, I loved the company I worked for and I think big companies are a fantastic place to get experience. I got a raise after a year, and I even got a promotion not long after that. Big companies are a great place to start because they often have many jobs available. So, anyone who wants to follow a career path in a big business and climb the corporate ladder has a chance of being successful. But of course, we have to do what we want to do the most, so I took a risk and changed my path.

Host: When you say you took a risk, what do you mean exactly?

Vera: Well, opening your own business is frightening! You don't know if it's going to work. When I decided to leave my job, I was really concerned about whether I did the right thing. But my friends and family supported me.

Host: That's very good. It's good to have family members by your side. Some parents don't support their children when they take risks.

Vera: Yes, that's true. When I told my mom and dad, they asked me if that was what I truly wanted to do. When they understood that it was, they told me they were very happy for me and they said they would do anything to help me. That was incredible!

Host: My final question is: how has your college education helped you with your business? You have a flower shop, but you studied business and finance?

Vera: My qualifications in business help me with money matters a lot. I have to know how much to sell things for, and how much to pay for expenses like the rent on my store and the supplies I buy for it. I'm not sure I would be able to run a flower shop with just a degree in botany or floral design, to be honest. But I think this kind of degree is very interesting anyway.

Host: Well, thanks so much for your time. Good luck with your business!

Vera: Thank you!

Track 4

Miranda

I work in an advertising company, and my job is to create interesting commercials. The idea is to create a commercial that will impress the person watching, so you have to be very creative to make interesting ones. I spend a lot of time looking at other commercials. When I hear about an interesting commercial that someone has done, even in another country, I am curious to find out about it. When I applied for the position, my boss was very interested in my qualifications, so having a university degree is very important.

Yosef

My job is in an accounting firm, so I spend a lot of time looking at large spreadsheets full of numbers. I work with a lot of different forms for many different companies. So, to be successful in the firm, you must be very organized. Because we work with difficult problems at my firm, you have to be quite intelligent, and it's necessary to have excellent thinking skills for those hard-to-solve problems.

Serena

I'm a photographer, and I take photos for a number of different magazines. I don't work in an office. I visit different locations where I can take great photos, so I have to be very independent, which I am! Also, I don't have anyone telling me to start my work or to be on time somewhere, so I have to be motivated to get my work done on my own. In addition to that, I have to go to many different places for my work, and I often don't know where I'm going from one day to the next, so I have to be flexible. It can be hard to get work sometimes, which is why you must have good contacts to do well in this kind of work.

Unit 8

Track 1

Amanda: Hey, Matias! What are you up to?

Matias: Hi, Amanda. I'm really tired and I've had so much to do this week in class. I love the idea of us having some fun this weekend! I was thinking about going to an amusement park.

Amanda: Yes, my week wasn't easy either. I had no time to rest! An amusement park is an interesting idea! You're such a kidult! Which one were you thinking of going to?

Matias: Well, I've never been to Six Flags. There are so many fun things to do there and it's right here in New Jersey. We don't have to go to New York.

Amanda: Well, going there sounds OK. I mean, I've lived in New Jersey all my life and I've never been there. But you know, I think I prefer to do something a little bit less energetic.

Matias: I know what you mean. I have no energy right now! Well, how do you feel about going to the Adventure Aquarium? It's really close to us.

Amanda: Matias, no way! Fish are boring and I hate seeing sharks—they scare me. Anyway, I like the idea of doing something artistic.

Matias: OK. What do you think of seeing the sculptures at that place, what's it called, Grounds for Sculpture? They have a lot of art there.

Amanda: Looking at some art does sound good, but I need some exercise as well. Maybe we could go do some yoga afterwards?

Matias: Doing some yoga sounds like a great idea. Let's do that. I can't stand not being active for a whole weekend. Let's go to South Mountain Yoga. I've heard that's supposed to be a great place to go.

Amanda: OK, perfect! So, where is the sculpture place?

Matias: It's on Sculptor's Way, obviously! So getting there will be easy. We'll just take the bus from downtown.

Amanda: Great!

Track 2

Host: Hello, everyone, and welcome back to *Life and Work*. In the studio with us now we have two experts in psychology, David Lodge and Celia Ramirez, who are going to be talking about the pros and cons of doing nothing. David, first of all, some people say that doing nothing can be useful in your work day. What's your opinion?

David: Well, I really think that doing nothing is a waste of time. Everyone has work to do. Can you imagine everyone deciding to do nothing in the office? It makes people unproductive.

Celia: I have a different opinion about that. Many people have work that takes a long time and they can get very bored. Spending some time having a cup of coffee or talking to a colleague means you can go back to your work feeling rested.

David: I think people feel guilty when they do nothing. I understand that people get tired with their jobs, but doing nothing isn't the answer. Doing nothing would make you stressed because you are not doing your work. Imagine you have a big presentation coming up. Sitting and looking out the window for twenty minutes may seem relaxing, but it can make some people more nervous. Doing nothing at all is not the way to progress in your job.

Celia: You may have a point, although I must say that taking time out to just look at the world and think your own thoughts can make people more creative. That's good for problem solving, too. And I think that doing nothing can help us get back our attention and helps us relax. People don't do enough "nothing."

Host: We'll be back with more on this subject after these words from our sponsors.

Unit 9

Track 1

Antonio: This is the house I wanted to show you. I think you are going to like it here.

Veronica: I hope so. I move in exactly one month. I need to find a place soon. It looks very big. I can't wait to go inside.

Antonio: The owner should be here soon. We are meeting him at 10 a.m., and it's 9:50 right now.

Veronica: I made a list of questions for the owner. I am going to ask him about many things.

Antonio: That's a very good idea. I'm sure he will be happy to answer them.

Veronica: I hope so, or I am not going to buy it!

Track 2

Ivy: How is your living situation, Eli?

Eli: It's a little bit better, but it's still not very good. I'm getting along with my roommates, but we don't spend much time together. But that's OK. They're just roommates, not friends. They're fine about sharing chores, but they are not very good at sharing the bills. They don't pay on time. It's pretty irritating!

Ivy: Oh, that's terrible. What are you going to do about that?

Eli: Well, I can't look for another place to live. I'm too busy with school. Also, I really don't like the idea of moving. It gives me stress and makes me feel worried.

Ivy: You could talk to your roommates about sharing the bills.

Eli: Yes, well, I have done that already. So they know they should pay.

Track 3

Ivy: Oh no, Eli. I think you have to move. I know you have a lot of schoolwork right now, but it's terrible to live with roommates who aren't responsible. You know, there's a studio apartment near my work. I think you might like it. The apartment may not be close to your school, though, but the neighborhood is quite nice.

Eli: Really, Ivy? That sounds interesting. I think I could afford a studio apartment. Maybe my parents can give me some money to help with rent, and I can probably get a part-time job to pay for the rest. The thought of more work worries me, but you're right. I can't live like this!

Ivy: That's a good idea. I can help you move if you like. I guess moving might not take very long. It depends on how much stuff you have. Do you have a lot of stuff?

Eli: Not really. I have my bed, and I also have a couch. My roommates definitely use it more than I do!

Ivy: Well, I think they will have to find a new couch soon!

Eli: Thanks a lot for your help, Ivy. I'm starting to feel better already.

Track 4

Today I want to share with you some tips on keeping your house cool in the summer and warm in the winter.

First, I'll start with keeping it cool. Being hot in the summer is the worst! Most people use air conditioners to keep cool. Not everyone can afford that though. The electricity to use an air conditioner can be expensive so I tell people to keep them off if possible. It's better to use something that can move the air around your house, such as a fan, because that uses less electricity. It might also be a good idea to open some windows, so the hot air can get out. Finally, it's important to turn lights off if you don't need them. Lights create heat, and that makes things hotter.

What's the best way to stay warm in the winter? You will probably have to use a heater, especially if it gets very cold where you live. Of course, you will definitely have your windows closed, but air may still be getting into your home. That's true around the doors, also. You want to make sure no cold air is coming inside. If you put your hand around your windows and doors, you might be able to feel air, especially if it's windy outside. If that happens, you could ask someone to come look at it and fix the problem. Then, your heater will work better, and you may not have to use it as often.

What ideas do you have for staying cool in the summer and warm in the winter? Get in touch and let us know what you think.

Unit 10

Track 1

Agus: Hey, Amy, you have one of those brain-training apps. Have you seen this research on brain training? I heard about it on the radio and on TV, too, but I got all the details in a magazine and it's really fascinating.

Amy: No, I haven't, Agus. I've had this app for a long time and I'm not sure it's improving my math skills or creativity. But I think my memory's better.

Agus: Well, that's what it says here. They did this research on a group of people using a brain-training app. They discovered that they improved at the activities in the app, but that was only because of practice. If you practice anything every day, you get better at it. It's simple science.

Amy: Really? Oh. Well, will the training from the apps help you if you do other things? If you use a puzzle app, will it help you get better at problem-solving? I heard it helps you with things like making decisions and understanding things.

Agus: Well, apparently, yes, it will. But it's not necessarily the app. It's just the constant practice with the puzzles.

Amy: Ah, I see. So does the article say what we can do if we want to exercise our brains?

Agus: Yes, it does. But I think you'll be surprised! It says that the best way to improve your brain is not by using apps or brain-training games but just to do most of the things we do every day.

Amy: Wait. So, will I be more intelligent if I just watch TV and chat with my friends online?

Agus: Yes and no! First, any kind of brain training won't make you more intelligent, but it will improve your attention. And apparently, socializing is one of the best ways of doing this—but in person, not over the internet or on the phone.

Amy: That's easy. What else?

Agus: Apparently you exercise your brain if you exercise your body! Plus, you need to sleep more and eat more nuts and vegetables.

Amy: That sounds great! So I don't really have to change my life completely! Well, apart from the exercise, maybe …

Track 2

Host: Hi, everyone. This week, we're continuing our series *Doing My Job*, and today we're at the clinic of Dr. Mark Li. Dr. Li, you've had many years of training to do your job, but do you think it's possible for people who aren't doctors to help people?

Dr. Li: Well, I think it's important for people to have some basic medical knowledge. There are times when you need to help someone immediately. You can if you have some basic training.

Host: Do you mean helping someone if they break their arm?

Dr. Li: Well, if someone breaks their arm, they need specific medical attention. It's not something you should try to deal with without a doctor, but if someone has a cold or a cut, it is a good idea to be able to take care of them.

Host: So what can you do to help if someone has a cut?

Dr. Li: For a small cut, the first thing you need to do is wash your hands. If you wash your hands, you will reduce the chances of infection. Then, you need to wash the cut with soap and water and then dry it. Finally, you should put a clean bandage on the cut.

Host: OK, perfect. And what about when people have a fever? I've heard that it's a good idea to make sure that people don't eat anything if they have a fever.

Dr. Li: Actually, that's not true. If someone has a fever, they should eat. Of course, not lots of pizza and hamburgers, but they should eat healthy foods so they get all the nutrients they need to get better. Also, some people think that it's a good idea to have a cold bath if you have a fever. In fact, this is a very bad idea! If you have a cold bath, the fever will probably get worse.

Host: So what should we do if someone has a fever?

Dr. Li: If someone has a fever, they need to drink lots of liquids, like water or tea. If not, they will dehydrate. Also, they should stay in bed and rest, and they should try to stay cool. If they wear too many clothes or blankets, it could make the fever worse.

Host: And what if someone had a very high fever?

Dr. Li: Well, if it's a very high fever, and if it lasts for over three days, it would be better to take them to the doctor. But in general, it's important not to worry too much about fevers. A fever shows you that the body is fighting the illness, and that's a good thing!

Track 3

Speaker 1

After years of doing no training at all, I've finally made the decision to get in shape and join a gym. It wasn't easy to get started at first, but I have to say that I'm feeling much better now. I have more energy and I get a lot less tired than I used to. And my trainer says that if I continue like this, I'll be able to run a five-mile race by the end of the year. It's great!

Speaker 2

After I get home from work, I usually have dinner and watch a movie or something. I get tired just thinking of going for a run. I don't know how people do it! Last week, my sister took part in a basketball tournament and she had to train every evening after work for months. That's really amazing, and it'd be so good if I could do that! But if I did that much exercise, I think I'd get sick!

Speaker 3

My friends and I are not very active at all. We love staying at home and eating pizza on a Friday night. Recently I've noticed that I get tired very easily. To be honest, I get upset about it because I'd love to have more energy. So we've decided to join an aerobics class at the local gym. We're getting ready for our first lesson right now, and I know it'll be good for me, but I'm a little nervous!

Speaker 4

I've played many different types of sports since I was at school and I'm used to training for sports events. So it was very strange when I started getting hungry during my marathon training recently. That never happened to me before. I spoke to a friend about it and she told me that it's very normal when you're training for a long race and that I should take some food with me on a run. It's not very easy to carry it with me, though!

Unit 11

Track 1

Speaker 1: This cotton isn't grown here. It comes from Texas.

Speaker 2: We don't have many natural resources here. Most are found in Alberta province.

Speaker 3: This T-shirt is made by the clothing company I work for.

Speaker 4: They fix belts and shoes, but rings and necklaces aren't repaired here.

Speaker 5: Are these bottles filled with water from a natural source?

Speaker 6: Do they have the new Marc Jacobs bag, or is it sold somewhere else?

Track 2

Host: With us today is fashion designer Leon Fernandez. Leon designs jackets, pants, belts, and other types of clothing. His latest collection includes leather jackets with many zippers on them. Thanks for joining us today.

Leon: You're welcome.

Host: You must really like zippers. I think I counted 12 of them.

Leon: I like to try out new things. Last year it was Velcro, this year it's zippers. Maybe next year, I'll do buttons. Zippers, though, are very interesting. They're like small machines, with so many metal parts.

Host: Yes, I never thought of that.

Track 3

Leon: I was doing some research on zippers, and I found out that they were first developed in the 1850s, but they were not successful. One fancy type of zipper was shown at the Chicago World's Fair in 1893, but still, no one was interested in it. It didn't look much like a zipper. It looked more like fish teeth on long pieces of very thin metal.

Host: Perhaps the designs weren't very useful.

Leon: I'm guessing that they were hard to use, or they got stuck easily. The kind of zipper we see today was designed in 1913 by Gideon Sundback, a Swedish-American engineer.

Host: I guess that's why they look like machines.

Leon: Exactly! You know, the name of "zipper" wasn't given by Sundback himself. His device was bought by a tire company that used it in a special pair of boots that they produced for workers. They called it a zipper, and the name stuck.

Host: Interesting.

Leon: The first zippers were mostly used in boots. Designers didn't use them in clothing until the 1930s or so. Back then, buttons were used on pants to pull them together. Eventually, the buttons were replaced by zippers.

Host: You mentioned buttons earlier. Perhaps you will use buttons in your next designs.

Leon: Maybe, although I don't really like buttons. They're so old-fashioned. I prefer zippers, because they are like little machines for our clothes. Well, who knows what I will do next year …

Track 4

I live in an area where there is not a lot of recycling. This is because our government hasn't done much to make it easy for people to recycle. Recycling centers aren't set up nearby, and a lot of glass, paper, and plastic bottles end up in the landfill. The result is that our landfills are full, and there is very little room for the regular trash. Then, the regular trash isn't collected, and our trash bins are always too full.

Track 5

My neighbors talk about how the neighborhood is becoming a trash pile, which makes me sad. Well, I plan to do something about this problem.

The first thing I'm going to do is send an email to the government and ask them to set up a recycling center. If the trash keeps getting worse, I believe the situation will become dangerous, and people will start to get sick. So, the government has to do something about this before it becomes a health problem.
Also, I believe a recycling center can help the government, because the government can sell glass, plastic, and paper to companies that can use it to make things. Then, they can make money from the sales. Isn't that a smart idea? I'm sure I will be able to convince them of this plan.
If they don't take me seriously, I will organize a group of neighbors to visit government offices and speak to officials in person. I hope that will get their attention!
I believe, with some hard work, we can make our neighborhood a clean and healthy place to live.

Unit 12

Track 1

I'm no good at telling jokes at all, but one of my favorites is about networking. "What did you like most about the conference?" said a manager to her employee. "The coffee break," he said. Not very funny, I know, but maybe the employee wasn't joking anyway. Why not? Well, I don't think it's a joke about conferences being boring. *I* think that the employee really did love the coffee break. You see, according to business leaders, the coffee break can be more important than any event at a conference in order to get to know new contacts and develop your network. If you think of yourself as a sociable person, the coffee break is the best time to walk up to people and introduce yourself. But if you're not a sociable person, here are some tips to help you make the most of it. First, you have to promise yourself that you will meet at least three new people during the coffee break. The easiest way to do this is to walk over to people who are alone. They will always remember you as the person who talked to them. But what do you say to someone? Well, people love talking about themselves! There are not enough good listeners in the world! So, ask them something about how long they have been in town, or what they like doing when they're not working. Then, when you have your first contact, you can go around the room with that person, so there are two of you. Then, it'll be much easier to get into conversation with groups, because you'll be the one introducing the new person. So, after all that, you should be fine! Just remember to get email addresses from your new contacts so that you don't lose the new connections. And make sure you contact them! In this way, you'll start to see what that employee in the joke meant, and that the coffee break really is the best part of a conference, for all the right reasons!

Track 2

Speaker A

I'm a computer programmer and I work from home, so I usually wear loose clothes because I feel more relaxed like that. I don't really wear much jewelry, but I sometimes wear a ring that one of my friends gave me. I also have a beard and a mustache and so do a lot of my friends. I can get hot sometimes, especially in the summer! Everyone at work calls me a hipster, and I have no problem with that! I think it's cool!

Speaker B

I really like comics, movies, and superhero characters, and I go to a lot of conventions. I love wearing costumes to look just like the characters from the comics. I used to wear a lot of dark clothes when I was younger, but now I prefer bright clothes, because they make me feel happier. I don't wear jewelry, but I wear a lot of makeup when I dress up like a superhero. I have very long hair, and so does my character!

Speaker C

In the summer, I work at a sports center on the coast. I wear tight clothes, because they are the best for exercising. I also like to wear bright clothes in the summer, because they are cooler than dark clothes. I used to wear a necklace, but I broke it when I was working in the gym last month, so I don't wear one now! I also have long hair. That's not very useful in my job, I guess! I should cut it one day.

Speaker D

I'm a professional skateboarder, and I skate at competitions all over the world. I've been to three competitions already this month. I used to have long hair, but it wasn't very practical, so now I have very short hair. I always wear the same type of loose, dark clothes for training. I wear loose clothes for competitions, and I like to wear jewelry, too. Not a lot, just a pair of earrings and a necklace. I wear them because they bring me good luck!

Exam Training

Track 1

1

Emma: How was the baseball game?
Ivan: It was raining a lot during the game, so I was disappointed with the weather. I also really wanted to meet Alex Rodriguez, because he's my role model. I love baseball, and he's a great player. I was worried that I wouldn't get to meet him.
Emma: So, what happened?
Ivan: I followed him after the game, and I asked for an autograph. He was a great guy! I was really thrilled to meet him.

2

Riley: So, what should we get Ricardo for his birthday?
Leah: What about a nice pair of shoes? I don't know what size he wears, but we could find out.
Riley: I'm not sure about that. I don't want to spend that much money. How about we give him some money and he can buy what he wants? People always like to get money as a gift.
Leah: I disagree. I think money shows that you don't care enough to get someone something special.
Riley: You're right. Let's go shopping at the mall tomorrow and see if we can find a gift he would really like.
Leah: That sounds great!

3

Ethan: How was your weekend, Ana?
Ana: It was amazing! I got to fly in a helicopter for the first time.
Ethan: Oh really? I've never done that before. I've gone bungee jumping. That's the scariest thing I've ever done.
Ana: Well, flying in the helicopter wasn't scary for me. Have you ever gone skiing?
Ethan: No, I haven't.
Ana: Well, I have, and that was more frightening than the helicopter.

4

Lily: Tell me about your new house, Paolo.

Paolo: It's really cool. The rooms are quite big, which I really like. Our new house has solar panels, also. That's very nice. I've never lived in a house like that.

Lily: Yes, it will help save electricity.

Paolo: My wife and I want to buy a new kitchen stove, though, because our old one uses too much power. We did buy a new washing machine, and it uses a lot less water.

5

Ryan: What's the best way to find a job these days, in your opinion?

Luke: Well, there are so many ways to do it, and you should explore every option. I've gone to career fairs quite a lot over the years. I think those are great for meeting people and building your network. I also think joining an online group is a great way to network. That's how I found my first job.

Ryan: I see. And what about after that?

Luke: Well, it's funny, but an old school friend of mine emailed me and told me his company was hiring. I applied for a job and got it right away.

Ryan: I suppose it's very important to keep in touch with people!

Track 2

Rick: I'd really like to take up a new leisure activity. What do you think I should do?

Eva: Well, do you like to exercise? I do aerobics two or three times a week. I really enjoy it.

Rick: Hmm, I'm not so sure about that. I was thinking about what my other friends do. My friend Diego goes kayaking on weekends, but I can't swim. I'm not so crazy about that anyway.

Eva: I see. What about yoga? My brother Sam does that pretty often.

Rick: Now that I think about it, I don't want to do anything that's related to exercise. For me, that's not a leisure activity. I used to skate with my friend Maria every once in a while, but we stopped. She does paddle boarding now.

Eva: I see. My friend Jessica likes to make furniture. She used to do pottery, but she decided that she needed a change.

Rick: That sounds really interesting. My friend Annabelle makes jewelry, although I'm not so crazy about that. I think I'll give making furniture a try.

Eva: I'll introduce you to Jessica. She can tell you all about it!

Track 3

Darius: Sofia, are you interested in joining the neighborhood recycling program?

Sofia: Yes, I am. I was watching the news the other day, and a reporter said people in our town don't recycle enough. I mentioned it in my class, and they agreed. We need to do more about recycling.

Darius: Yes, well, my neighbor Tomas told me about the program, so I decided to help.

Sofia: That's great. What does the program involve?

Darius: Well, there are different things to do. Some people will go around the neighborhood collecting things to recycle that are just lying around, such as paper and plastic. I've decided to help people recycle larger items, like computers and TVs. Many people have old ones in their homes that they don't use, and they don't know how to get rid of them properly. I think that's a really big problem, which is why I want to help with that. Another thing to do is to hand out flyers to people or put them in their mailboxes.

Sofia: Oh, that's a very good idea. Well, I can help you with your plan. I know a lot of people in the area. My cousin's family lives very close by, so we can go there first. Then, we can visit my friend Amanda's house one block over. I know she has some things to recycle. Next door to Amanda's is the Gomez family. I watch their little girl sometimes when they want to go out, so I know them well.

Darius: Great. We can also visit people we don't know, and then, we can get to know them better.

Sofia: Yes, I was thinking that as well. We can also visit stores and businesses, local cafés and restaurants, and schools. My brother works in an office a few blocks away. There may be a lot of things to recycle that we can help with.

Darius: I like that idea a lot. One thing I haven't figured out yet … how will we get all of these things to the recycling plant? I don't have a car, but I was planning to ask my cousin Guillermo if we could borrow his. I hope that works out OK. We should have some kind of transportation. I don't want to carry these things by hand.

Sofia: Oh, that's no problem. We can use my car to carry things to the recycling plant. I have plenty of space in the back.

Darius: Terrific! Thanks for offering that. Well, let's plan to get started this Saturday, shall we?

Sofia: Great, looking forward to it!